Beethoven at 250:
Man and Music Under Siege

by
Stefan Romanó

Title: Beethoven at 250: Man and Music Under Siege
Author: Stefan Romanó
Editors: Stefan Romanó and Ruxandra Vidu

ISBN 978-1-936629-56-5

Copyright 2021 © Stefan Romanó

www.BeethovenOurContemporary.com

Reflection Books, P.O. Box 1413
Citrus Heights, California 95611-1413
E-mail: info@reflectionbooks.com
www.reflectionbooks.com

Contents

Foreword		4
PART I. BEETHOVEN ON THE SHRINKS' COUCH		7
1	*A look under the couch*	10
2	*Beethoven on the Sterba couch*	16
3	*Beethoven on Maynard Solomon's couch*	55
4	*Beethoven's second session on Solomon's couch*	74
PART II. BEETHOVEN'S MENTAL HEALTH FILE		101
5	*The Case for Beethoven's alcoholism*	103
6	*The Case for Beethoven's psychopathy*	123
PART III. BEETHOVEN POLITICS		149
7	*Enrolling Beethoven in the cause of the Twentieth Century musical Avant-Garde*	152
8	*Tia DeNora's Beethoven as a socio-political construct*	168
9	*Beethoven's alleged plagiarisms*	195
PART IV. LATTER-DAY FEMINISM *vs.* BEETHOVEN		202
10	*Susan McClary's Jihad against Beethoven and Classical Music*	204
11	*Lawrence Kramer's second leg in Beethoven's violent masculinity relay*	234
12	*Sanna Pederson's third leg of Beethoven's "Masculinity" relay*	262
13	*When DeNora meets McClary: Gendering Beethoven*	273
14	*Hollywood Beethoven*	284
15	*Skimming the Pandemic*	291
15½	*Feminist Beethoven*	296
2020 Epilogue		298
Selected Bibliography		302
Notes		314

Foreword

Beethoven's 250th anniversary hides a paradox. Classical music lovers celebrate him as one of the most enlightening beacons not only of the Western world that produced him, but of the whole human species. Two hundred years after his death, he is our contemporary. More than any other musician, he voices for us and in our name the essential emotions of humanity in the universal language of music. On the other hand, Beethoven's anniversary falls at the end of a long period in which he has been under constant, relentless attacks by modern-day scholarship. Postmodernism seems to have made it its mission to question and demolish important historical and cultural figures of the Western world, and Beethoven is arguably the most virulently attacked among the major creative geniuses. Scholars have promoted their careers, sometimes along with a political agenda, speculating wildly along the lines of the modern "-isms" and spreading falsehoods rather than pursuing new truths about Beethoven. Devotees of psychoanalysis such as Maynard Solomon put him on their coach to convince him (that is, us) that he was a delusional psychopath. Some physicians claim to diagnose him with psychopathic behaviors, invoking modern psychiatric criteria that they twist beyond recognition. Sociologists interested in music and/or musicologists interested in sociology alike make him into an incredible epicenter of both musical and non-musical politics. Even his music, once hailed as the beacon of humanity, has not been able to defend itself against the attacks of modern-day feminism united around Susan McClary, portraying it—Beethoven's music—as the epitome of "toxic masculinity."

These "novel" visions of Beethoven have never been subjected to in-depth scrutiny but have nevertheless become part of mainstream scholarship. Granted, a late twentieth or early twenty-first century biographer or musicologist is in an unenviable position: since today's classical music is virtually of no import to the general public, scholars can stir interest only by saying something new about dead personalities like Beethoven, even though at times everything seems to have already been said. Finding such novelty is not easy, perhaps, but there have been opportunities for it. Scientific and technological advances have offered new insights in certain areas of his life, but only extra-musical professions have benefitted from them. Spectrographic analysis of a lock of his hair performed at the request of the *Beethoven Center* at the San Jose University revealed very high levels of lead, resulting in a serious professional debate. DNA sequencing, if adequate samples could be obtained, might someday solve conclusively the great mystery of the identity of Beethoven's "Immortal Beloved."

Other scholars—such as George Marek, Sieghard Brandenburg and a trio of women dedicated to the Immortal Beloved mystery, Marie-Elisabeth Tellenbach, Rita Steblin and Dagmar Skwara (this list is certainly not exhaustive)—did what good researchers have always done: search for material proof, and present new biographical evidence. However, the exceptions to these praiseworthy endeavors have carried the day—more exactly, the most recent, postmodern half-century.

It may seem strange, but no professional authority has yet analyzed and diagnosed these "novel" theories as what they are: scholarly frauds. Edward Rothstein, the cultural critic-at-large of the *New York Times,* actually found some justification for these frauds in the November 26, 1995 issue of the influent newspaper. In a column chick-in-the-tongue, titled with a paraphrase of the legendary song of Chuck Berry, "Musicologists Roll Over Beethoven," he explained that these "Younger scholars [he nominated Susan McClary and Lawrence Kramer, whom we will meet later] have raised the stakes. They are grappling with a fear that classical music is becoming increasingly irrelevant. The concert hall repertory has been all but frozen, the financing for classical music is uncertain, the public is often indifferent. And pop culture has pushed classical music to the margins of contemporary life." As if it were Beethoven's fault if his twentieth-century progenies have lost touch with their public!

A few years later, the respected Beethoven scholar Robin Williams, an authorized critical voice, played the appeaser. He wrote, in the introduction "Beethoven's Critics" to the second volume of *The Critical Reception of Beethoven's Compositions by his German Contemporaries*, "Beethoven's present-day detractors have little to say about him that was not already said long ago, while the composer was still alive." Sorry to say, this is not true: what we have witnessed during the last fifty or sixty-odd years is an unprecedentedly violent and coordinated attack on Beethoven's status, both the man and his music. Another authoritative voice, that of Jan Swafford, noticed in the Introduction to his 2014 *Beethoven* that "by the postmodern end of the twentieth century, the word *genius* had evolved again, the concept becoming a sociopolitical outrage to be pulled from its pedestal and smashed," but did not put this approach to the test. In the absence of any real critical assessments of this post-modernist movement and by way of an old cynical adage—a long-time repeated lie ends up by being accepted as truth—these fabrications have become mainstream scholarship.

Putting to rest some such demonstrably fallacious speculations that have sullied Beethoven's image and his music for half a century would be a most appropriate way to honor him on his 250th anniversary, and to revive our unity around his music. Make no mistake, however: this book is not a collection of its author's opinions about Beethoven and/or about various theories about him and his music. This is a book of facts, a repertoire of facts that invalidate such fraudulent theories. It is a fact that Maynard Solomon builds a scenario describing Beethoven's alleged "delusion" based on the word "[I] know" in one of the composer's letters—which is the wrong translation of the original German with a completely different meaning. It is also a fact that Susan McClary founds her theory of the "sexist sonata form" on a particular "demonstration" ... a demonstration that never was. Such facts clearly invalidate those respective theories. Unfortunately, even the scholars that took a stand against these postmodernist theories failed the relevant and invalidating facts and their critique missed the real target. German-speaking scholars criticized Solomon's theories and signaled some flaws therein, but never noticed that the phrase "Ich könnte" does not mean "I know" in their language, as Solomon claimed. English-speaking scholars objected to McClary's theory of the sexist sonata form, but were never curious to confirm the "demonstration" of a feminist colleague of hers on which she founded her thesis. These two examples constitute only the tip of a postmodernist iceberg that this book explores to a far deeper level than has been done before, giving the reader the facts to make their own judgments.

PART I
BEETHOVEN ON THE SHRINKS' COUCH

Beethoven's behavior, quite often described as "eccentric," "uncouth" or "psychopathic," would have qualified him for a good post-mortem case study, but the father of psychoanalysis restrained from putting him on his couch posthumously. Even though the discipline Freud founded was mainstreamed and generated a flurry in Hollywood flurry (as well as a big business) before WWII, it missed Beethoven as a target for a long time. Ernest Newman's 1927 book *The Unconscious Beethoven* contained some insightful analyses, but was a far cry from a truly Freudian approach, as were a few other similar examples. The gap was filled by Editha and Richard Sterba, an Austrian scholarly couple educated at the Vienna Psychoanalytic Institute by Freud himself, who fled Nazi persecution and settled in the U.S., where they published in 1954, in English, *Beethoven and His Nephew: A Psychoanalytical Study*. Their book was well received by their psychoanalyst colleagues, was translated into French and German, and re-printed over thirty times—but found little traction in Beethoven scholarship until Maynard Solomon took the relay and advanced his own Freudian view on the composer in his 1977 *Beethoven* biography of the composer. This book, offering an entirely new picture of Beethoven, was hailed by many a respected music scholars as "a landmark in scholarship and interpretation [...] the most heartfelt and brilliant full-length study of Beethoven in more than a hundred years [...] the most compelling and interesting Beethoven biography [...] the authoritative one," to quote from the back cover of the second edition the opinions of Lewis Lockwood, Charles Rosen and others.

Some negative criticism also aimed at Freudian approaches to Beethoven. Noted German musicologist Harry Goldschmidt (1910-1986) was the first to reject the Sterba couple's approach, in a 1980 book dedicated to the "Immortal Beloved issue".[*] Since he was living in communist East Germany, where psychoanalysis was banned as bourgeois pseudo-science, Goldschmidt could not go into an in-depth analysis, although he pointed out a number of errors and inconsistencies as well as the authors' tendency to ignore or misconstrue known facts. However, he did not really tackle Solomon's similar approach to Beethoven, because he actually considered the latter's solution to the mystery of the Immortal Beloved very plausible. Another German scholar well-known for her Immortal Beloved studies, Marie-Elisabeth Tellenbach, took over the criticism of Solomon's approach in an article in the 1990s, exposing some weaknesses of argumentation and several scholarly misrepresentations.[†] Later, Gail Altman, in her 1996 published book *Beethoven, a Man of His Word*, revealed additional scholarly flaws and even frauds in his book. In spite of such

---

[*] Harry Goldschmidt, *Um die Unsterbliche Geliebte. Eine Bestandaufnahme* (Munich, 1980).

[†] Marie-Elisabeth Tellenbach, "Psychoanalysis and Historio-critical Method: On Maynard Solomon's Image of Beethoven, Part 1" (*The Beethoven Newsletter,* 1993-1994, Vol. 8, pp. 84-92).

criticism, the psychoanalytical approach became the mainstream in Beethoven scholarship. The enthusiasm incited by novelty—which characterizes any generational change—spawned more such approaches, elaborating further on Solomon's diagnosis and frequently supporting their arguments with phrases like "as Solomon has shown," or even better, "as Solomon has convincingly demonstrated." Even scholars who did not particularly endorse Freudian thought, like Peter Davies and François Mai, adopted uncritically some of Solomon's theses in their works (more about it in my essays about Beethoven's Mental Health File).

Now, after several printings of Solomon's book have been published (including a "second, revised" edition), and he has expanded his views in more works (equally well received by his academic audience) on the life and work of the musician (Beethoven Essays, Late Beethoven and various articles), I think the time is ripe for re-assessing the validity of the Freudian approach to understanding the musician's complex personality. My analysis will be, as the tone of this introduction may have suggested, a "negative" review, but it is entirely different from the above mentioned critical opinions. On the one hand, previous criticism of the Sterbas' and Solomon's psychoanalytic approach had its own flaws: it discarded the symptoms of the patient together with the psychoanalytic diagnosis; so did Barry Cooper in his biography of Beethoven.[*] And these symptoms are established facts, behaviors and attitudes in the composer's life, which are puzzling—even worrying—to any classical music lover. On the other hand, we benefit now from the latest findings of modern neuroscience, which in the last decades of the twentieth century was only beginning to investigate the human brain, but has since accumulated proof that the basic tenets of the Freudian model that lies under the shrink's couch are utterly false.

---

[*] Barry Cooper, *Beethoven* (Oxford University Press, 2000), pp. 255, 273-4.

1
A look under the couch

Freudian delusion under the magnifying glass of modern science

A thorough review of psychoanalysis as a scientific investigative method, including for biographical purposes, is far beyond the scope of the present research, but a conclusion is still reachable. In its broadest sense, psychoanalysis is the self-proclaimed science of the human brain. Its best-known constituent is the famous Œdipus complex, in which the boy is, unconsciously, the sexual competitor of his father, wants to kill him, and have sex with his mother; the girls are a kind of subservient complement to boys, as they are dominated by their "penis envy." The theory is of course much more complex than that, because it aspired to cover all areas of human behavior, but its basic axiom is that humans are defined by their sexuality, from the moment they are born: "infant sexuality" may be considered the cornerstone of his theory: all human feelings are sexual in nature and all the neuroses (symptomatic of the malfunctioning of the brain) are the result of the repression of sexuality.[1] Lying on the psychoanalyst's couch and guided by the psychoanalyst, the neurotic discovers the hidden roots of such a repression, traveling back in time until his/her childhood, where they normally reside.

At the time when psychoanalysis was founded, the only way to investigate the functioning of the brain was the observation of people who had suffered brain damage in accidents, which helped the science of neurology to be born but did not open any real door into the subconscious. Therefore, psychoanalysis was highly speculative, could not be probed by the scientific methods, and was never accepted into the newly-born science of psychiatry. Nevertheless, its apparent consistency and broad scope—as well as, I must add, its appeal in a world that had known a gradual emancipation of sexuality—yielded to the development of a whole branch of what we may call a "health industry," symbolized by "the shrink's couch." It also became a pervasive investigative tool used by academics of various humanities disciplines, such as the Sterbas and Solomon.

There has been abundant (negative) criticism of psychoanalysis throughout the twentieth century, of which Fuller Torrey's book *Freudian Fraud*[2] presents an almost exhaustive review, but the other side has not thrown in the towel. Psychoanalysis was described as both "the most stupendous confidence trick of the twentieth century [...] a vast structure of radically unsound design and with no posterity" and as "the most important body of thought committed to paper in the twentieth century."[3] We have today scientific proof that Freud's theory is false, at least in its fundamental concepts and inferences. During the last thirty-odd years, new technological tools (micro-electrodes, functional MRI techniques, psychoactive drugs, etc.) has helped the science of the brain make great leaps forward and evaluate some basic tenets of psychoanalysis. Neuroscience has begun probing one central part of the doctrine, Freud's theory of dreams, which he deemed to be his most important scientific contribution, and has proven its mechanism to be false. A summing-up of the situation by Allan Hobson, one of the leaders of neuroscience and a founder of modern dream theory: "[...] brain science has grown in parallel with objectives approaches to sleep and dreaming. The current merger of these fields yields a theory of dreaming with surprising different features from those that Freud imagined."[4] Hobson, who was educated as a psychoanalyst, was quickly led by Hobson's findings to abandon Freud's interpretation of dreams.[5] Even Mark Solms, a devoted Freudian who changed fields to neuroscience in order to find proof that his magister was right, had to concede that Freud "may have been wrong" in his theory and the bizarreness of dreams is not the result of their disguised (sexual) symbolism but of the reduced functioning, during sleep, of the pre-frontal cortex responsible for logical thinking.[6] Not that Freud was entirely wrong: as Robert Stickgold, another prominent neuroscience scholar, put it epigrammatically, "Freud was fifty percent right and one hundred percent wrong." The fifty percent is comprised of two of his basic assumptions: that dreams are emotionally charged and that their exploration is a way of deciphering the mysteries of the subconscious. (Note, these assumptions were not Freud's invention, but shared awareness of his scholarly generation.) The wrong one hundred percent refer to his dream interpretation theory. Table 1 sums up the dramatic differences between Freudian theory of dreams and what neuroscience has found so far.

Table 1. Freudian interpretation of dreams and the findings of modern neuroscience

Freud's theory (Sulloway, pp. 320-339)	What neuroscience has discovered
During the sleep, the mind is or, at least, tries to be at rest by extinguishing all external stimuli.	The mind is not at all at rest during the sleep. Only one important cerebral center "sleeps," the one performing logical thinking. External stimuli are not inhibited.
The brain (the subconscious) receives internal stimuli: emotions (especially the negative ones), fears, dissatisfaction, desires, previous day's activity, etc. In order to prevent them from disturbing the sleep (and awaken the sleeper), the brain builds dreams that process these stimuli to make them non-disturbing.	There is plenty of "internal" stimulation of the brain during sleep. The frontal lobe of the cortex is also responsible for dreams, stimulated by some specific chemicals (acetylcholine, serotonin, melatonin, etc.). However, it is obvious that just a few chemicals could not trigger the huge variety of dreams.

Table 1 continuation

Dreams are a mechanism of subconscious wish fulfillment, especially those of sexual origin that are suppressed while awake, and which are more often than not rooted in infantile sexuality.	People dream a lot every night, irrespective of fulfilled or unfulfilled wishes that they had during the day. This happens in several periods of the sleep, mostly associated with REM (rapid eye movement).
During the dream, the 'internal stimuli' generated by the dissatisfaction transform the suppressed wish into a visual fantasy in which the wish is satisfied.	Most dreams are indeed visual fantasies. As only a few chemicals cannot explain the large variety of dreams, one must accept that they may only favor the generation of the dreams' visual fantasies.
A dream has two faces: the manifest and the latent content. The manifest content is what the dreamer remembers, but is only an unrecognizable transformation of the latent content, which holds the true meaning of the dream.	No reason has been discovered for this double-faced aspect of the dreams; there is no need of a latent content. Dreams are what they are, usually expressions of our apprehensions.
The manifest content is rarely sexual, while the latent content is almost always sexual.	There is no evidence of latent content of dreams. Sexual dreams are very rare (less than 5%).
The latent content is transformed by "dream work," a convoluted "censuring" mechanism of the brain (first "pre-conscious" and later conscious), which disguises the disturbing reality of a sexual fantasy into the manifest content that has apparently no sexual connotation. In rare cases the manifest and latent content can be indistinguishable ("infantile dreams"), but Freud does not advance any criteria for identifying such dreams.	No "censuring" mechanism has been acknowledged. In fact, the brain center of logical thinking, the only one that could consciously "censure" the fantasies by contrasting them with reality, is at rest during the sleep. Even David Solms, who tried to fit modern neuro-science into the Freudian approach, acknowledged that he could see no need for a "censuring" mechanism.
The "disguising" mechanism works according to a certain *symbolism*. Elongated objects stand for the male organ or an erection; all hollow objects represent the female genitalia. In fact, almost anything may symbolize one of the two the genitalia.	No "disguising" mechanism could be identified. Dream objects are what they are, not sexual symbols. Their irrational appearance is explained by the sleep of the logical thinking brain center and, probably, by the changes in the brain chemistry during sleep.

Science has similarly dismantled the best-known construct of Freud's theory, the "Œdipus complex," which seems so deeply imbedded in the psyche that it would be impervious to direct scientific investigation. The American psychiatrist Stanley Hall had already in 1904, in his book on *Adolescence*, identified the conscious behavior—conflict with and hatred of parents—corresponding to symptoms of the alleged Oedipal unconscious in what he termed the "storm and stress" of teenage years, when sexuality kicks in with specific hormones. Hall's theory was controversial for a long time before being revitalized and updated following the exploration of the teenage brain with modern techniques (MRI a.o.), initiated by Jay Giedd shortly before 2000 and further enhanced by other researchers. The research showed that the yet "incomplete" brain of the teenager undergoes a tremendous but uneven and conflicting growth: the amygdala nucleus, the siege of the emotions, develops far faster than the prefrontal cortex, the center of critical thinking.[7] The teenager's ascent to self-image and self-confidence, a product of the fully functional amygdala conflicting with the lagging-behind prefrontal cortex that holds the key to the evaluation of the consequences of one's acts,[8] a conflict that creates personality turmoil, leading to rebellion against parental authority and exacerbating family crises. The relationship between brain and sex hormones—which is the initiator and which the receptor?—is not yet fully understood, but it is clear that a strong feedback accelerates the process exponentially.[9]

Anthropology and ethnology have weighed additional arguments against Freud's "Œdipal." In Freud's theory, this "complex" is both a central trait of the nuclear family headed by a father, and an ancestral trait of maleness as old as the human species.[10] The two requirements are incompatible: according to modern anthropology, *Homo sapiens* is about 300,000 years old, while the family—as a functional social unit still very different from its modern "nuclear" version—is far more recent in the history of the Mediterranean world that will later become the Western culture, probably not much earlier than the time of Homer's contemporary Hesiod (about 700 BC), who attested to it in his *Works and Days* poem. Freud was actually aware of the incongruity and tried to solve it, his typical way, through speculation: in his book *Totem and Taboo*, he assumed that the Œdipal complex dated from the first promiscuous human families with a strong male leader (the modern "alpha"), whose sons killed him before making him into a religious totemic symbol;[11] this Œdipal behavior would have, in time, become an innate attribute of maleness by way of so-called "Lamarckian selection,"—a (then) century-old theory claiming that acquired traits can be inherited. Modern anthropology and genetics have in the meantime fully discredited the Lamarckian selection theory, but, as one can see, that discovery has not diminished the zeal of Freudian adherents.[12]

A visit to the incipient times of the human species may actually help understand why the Œdipal complex is a misconception and also how patriarchal societies developed and embedded within unambiguous forms of oppression of women. Humans are an animal species designed by nature. Nature has no moral but only natural laws; and the fundamental natural law applying to any form of life requires it to perpetuate its kind. That law defined humankind* during its "beginnings," which lasted much longer than the so-called "historical times," which cover only a few thousand years. Surviving and perpetuating during those "beginnings" was a matter of practicality, as for every other species. Very little is known about those times, because writing was far away in the future of the newly born species, and the archaeological findings testify nothing beyond the food that humans were gathering by "foraging" around. However, anthropologists have discovered modern day tribal societies that can serve as analogs of these ancestral times, such as those living in the Amazonian lowlands, that share the practice of "multiple fathers;"[13] and historians/sociologists like Harari understandably assumed that this was happening in those "beginnings" of the *sapiens* species.[14] The very concept of "father" was very fluid, if not entirely absent, which was certainly not conducive to an Œdipus complex.

Other areas of the Freudian theory that are hard (perhaps impossible, for now) to directly probe by scientific experiments can nevertheless be checked indirectly, by evaluating their medical efficiency. For instance, how can one believe any longer in the idea that all neuroses stem from sexual repression, when a daily dose of Prozac can dispatch a disease that almost a hundred years of shrink couching based on the Freudian paradigm could only make worse? It is no surprise that the clinicians/psychiatrists who tried to build a more general theory of sexuality, taking advantage of the new technologies, were equally led to discard Freud's theory. "When we sought to make use of the Freudian model and its numerous offshoots," they state, "[...] we saw that the old models provide diagrams to a territory that cannot be found anywhere within a real person. Our patients never behaved as predicted."[15]

Neuroscience advances did not, however, convince devoted Freudians to abandon their master. After an initial recoil in the face of shocking neuroscientific findings, they complained that neuroscience cannot replace psychoanalysis.[16] This, at least, is true enough: neuroscience had never pretended to replace psychoanalysis. If I am allowed to use an analogy that is as imperfect as most analogies but still illustrative, the relationship is like that of the cathedral and the brick: cathedrals are made of bricks, but the brick does not explain the cathedral. Psychoanalysis is, or claims to be, the cathedral of the soul and neuroscience findings have revealed that the brick psychoanalysis is built from is loose sand. The psychoanalysis community next followed the old adage that "offensive is the best defense" and actually tried to confiscate the findings of neuroscience for the benefit of their own theory, now re-baptized "neuropsychoanalysis." This was easy because, as I said, those findings are only a few individual "bricks" from which this extremely complex cathedral, the brain, is built, with an internal structure that is still very much unknown. This way, one can easily claim that neuroscience has *located* the nebulous Freudian concepts of *ego* and *id*: "the upper brainstem (and associated limbic structures) performs the functions that Freud attributed to the id, while the cortex (and

---

* The Bible also sanctioned this natural law: "Be fruitful and multiply, and fill the earth" (Genesis, 1:28).

associated forebrain structures) performs the functions he attributed to the ego. This means that the id is the fount of consciousness and the ego is unconscious in itself."[17] Or, that dreams "are meaningful, wish-fulfilling manifestations of the loss of frontal executive control of mesocortical and mesolimbic "seeking systems"[18]—in plain English, the "sleep" of the frontal cortex (see Table 1) allows the brainstem, the previously identified location of the "unconscious," to express frustrations resulting from unfulfilled wishes as dreams. Re-baptizing cerebral centers and systems of centers with Freudian names does not make psychoanalysis into a scientifically validated theory.

Admittedly, the discoveries of modern neuroscience only began to accumulate after 1980, so they were unknown to earlier adepts of psychoanalysis like the Sterbas and Maynard Solomon. Nowadays, when psychoanalysis has basically lost any persuasive power, we are in a better position to assess the theory's contribution to Beethoven scholarship. This task is not as simple as it may seem, because all of the ingredients that Freud incorporated in his theoretical construct were not wild speculations, but part of the common (scientific *and* popular) wisdom that modern science has fully confirmed. The most prominent of these elements is the essential part played by childhood in the development of the human personality, in which the mother is the main player. While the mechanisms that Freud ascribes to this determination are typically wildly speculative, the parent-child relationship itself is undeniable; modern science has even found that it is far subtler than anyone would have thought a few decades ago. For instance, psychiatric research has shown that the newly-born "synchronizes" his bodily functions (such as his heart beat) with those of the parent holding him in their arms—the so-called limbic regulation.[19] As I'll show later, the psychoanalytic thesis on which the Sterba study fundamentally lies, the "identification," is very similar to the widely accepted modern concept of the "role model." Therefore, discriminating between true and false in the works of the Sterba couple and Solomon is not a simple endeavor. One cannot reject them simply because psychoanalysis as a whole is a wild fantasy without a scientific basis. Their main flaw is, as I will show, their investigative tactics—the willingness to ignore or distort evidence that does not support (or clearly rejects) their theses, as well as wild speculations about incomplete or inaccurate evidence. One could sum up their approach with one "Murphy's" famous "Laws": if the facts don't fit your theory, change the facts.

2
Beethoven on the Sterba couch

The Sterbas' book *Beethoven and His Nephew* deals with the last period of Beethoven's life, when he was his nephew's guardian, after his younger brother Carl Caspar died of consumption in November 1815. The composer's relationship with both of his brothers had been marred by disagreements and conflicts, because while Beethoven was very willing to help, he also desired strict control, which they did not want to accept, preferring to make their own mistakes. He was especially angry at their choice of wives, whom he considered no better than what he described in a 1796 letter to his brother Johann as "the whole tribe of bad women."[1] During Carl Caspar's final illness, Beethoven assured him that he would take good care of his brother's son Karl, on the condition that he had sole guardianship of the boy; his brother worded his will accordingly. However, giving in to his wife Johanna's pleading and, probably, his remorse, he added a codicil the same day, appointing her also as a guardian and, because he knew that their relationship was far from cordial, expressing his hope that the two would work in harmony for the well-being of his son.[2]

Thus began the last and the bleakest chapter of the composer's life: some twelve turbulent years leading to—and greatly *contributing* to—his death. He loved his nephew and wanted the best for him, but he was mentally and behaviorally very ill-equipped for providing this "best." He practically stole his nephew from his mother, because he deemed her a morally corrupt, "poisonous" agent of evil. Although there were moments when the thought dawned on him – even stating in public—that "even a bad mother is still a mother,"[3] and that depriving a child of his mother was morally reprehensible, he pursued his goal and, after years-long battles in the courts in which he pushed his self-righteousness to apparently inhuman heights/depths, he eventually secured the exclusive guardianship of his nephew. Not realizing or not willing to realize that his nephew was only of mediocre nature, Beethoven heaped unreasonable demands on the boy and reacted angrily when the latter disappointed him. His love for Karl was made up of exacerbated extremes: when the boy dissatisfied him—especially when he had surreptitiously met his mother—Beethoven would display fits of anger that he would later regret and attempt to compensate with over-indulging acts of love. In this way, he created a vast, prolonged amount of suffering for all parties involved—child, mother and himself—leading to a final catastrophe, young Karl's suicide attempt, which aged Beethoven overnight and likely shortened his life. It seems a miracle that he was able to also create a large body of musical masterpieces during this time, almost equaling the productivity level during his so-called "heroic period."

Beethoven's behavior had puzzled the scholars for a long time. Even Thayer, who carefully documented the events, sounded not stress-free about the issue when he cautiously stated that "there can be no doubt that [… Johanna] was wicked and vicious and that his [Beethoven's] detestation of her was as well founded as his wish to save his nephew from evil communications and influences."[4] Later, some scholars began to adopt a different angle: Newman in 1927 maintained that "Beethoven set out with a hatred and distrust of his sister-in-law that can only be regarded as an obsession bordering on the insane."[5] The Sterba couple later expanded this last euphemism, describing the composer's behavior as of a psychopathic nature, creating a "new school" that included scholars like Maynard Solomon (who displayed, however, a more nuanced Beethoven) or Alan Tyson. In 2000, however, Barry Cooper's biography of Beethoven reverted to the previous view, exonerating the composer of most charges, including those of cruelty towards his sister-in-law; Lewis Lockwood's biography basically followed suit a few years later. The controversy is still with us.

The Sterba couple tried to explain Beethoven's behavior by filtering it through the Freudian lens, which, in their opinion, "has supplied the key to an understanding of innumerable psychological forms of expression and modes of behavior which until then had been completely inexplicable" (17). [NB. Throughout this chapter, page numbers refer to Sterba (1971) unless specified otherwise.] We know now that Freud's "key" is wide of the mark, so the Sterbas' endeavor is inevitably flawed, but some aspects are still worth considering. First is the vast amount of evidence that they collected from existing literature and its direct implications. However, since other evidence pointed in the opposite direction, the Sterbas blamed almost all previous scholars for crafting a "conspiracy" that highly idealized Beethoven, belittled his nephew, and criminalized his sister-in-law without justification. Schindler, who had been for long proven to commit biographical and bibliographical forgeries, is the main villain, but Thayer is not spared either (6-7). He is accused of having indiscriminately accepted the evidence advanced by Beethoven's entourage during his last decade, which consisted in "slaves" (92) or "toadies" who, because of their admiration for the musician, were ready to tell or write him only what he wanted to hear (94). The Sterbas set themselves to clean the record, based on original documents (mostly letters and conversation-book entries), and rehabilitate mother and son. And it is true that their work has some merit in disclosing some new evidence, but, as we will see, their case for the conspiracy story holds little water and, in their turn, they committed their own share of scholarly transgressions that invalidate their theses. It is true that some of the essential facts were not known at the time when they first wrote their book, but it is also true that they refused to alter their point of view in later editions of their work, after new important facts had been revealed. They also deliberately ignored reliable testimonies, while promoting unreliable ones that supported their theories. In my analysis, I will not insist on the "drama" itself, but on the Sterbas' psychoanalytical and psychological insight of its *dramatis personae*.

The Sterbas' Beethoven

"Identification" with mother and "Motherly love". The Sterbas see two pathological—and essentially related—components in Beethoven's behavior: 1) an excessive, possessive love of his nephew, which, in their opinion is not a "fatherly" but a "motherly" love that resulted ultimately in horrible extremes of distrust and jealousy; and 2) an obsessive and delusional hate for his sister-in-law Johanna. The phrase "motherly love" peppers their book. Beethoven had allegedly shown earlier propensities of being a "mother" in his relationship with his brother Carl (28 and 43);[6] even Beethoven's "Heilegenstadt Testament" letter is alleged to have been born out of his disappointment with Carl, which would have aggravated the depression caused by the gradual loss of hearing (32). An entire chapter of their book is then dedicated to "Motherhood," in which the authors claim that the composer intended to provide his nephew a substitute for his lost mother, whom Beethoven had barred from seeing her son. A testimony of a stranger stating that "the most tender father can take no more interest in his son's development than did Beethoven in the progress of his nephew," is quoted to conclude that "the happiness of a mother finds voice in these reports" (63). Beethoven wrote to his friend Wegeler that he is a father, too, "but without a wife"; this read as "an outburst of triumph over the fact that he had acquired a child without the participation of a woman" (69). Also, the two scholars argue, "almost always when he [Beethoven] calls himself the boy's 'father,' we must substitute 'mother,' for it was such that he experienced his possession of the boy" (56). When Beethoven grew older, the Sterbas argue, love turned more and more into the feeling of possession because "it is well known [to psychoanalysts] that persons who have reached the age at which their sexual interest slackens exhibit the above-described attitude towards [attachment to] property to a far greater degree than formerly" (121). However, when dealing with Beethoven's last years, they fall back to the "neutral" claim that "he loved Karl as his own child with all the strength of which a mother's heart is capable" (159). They do not attempt to clear the incongruence between the two statements.

One finds several such inner discrepancies in the couple's analysis. According to the Sterbas, Beethoven's "motherly love" for his nephew stemmed from his "identification" with his own mother during his childhood and teenage years. At the same time, this identification was marred by the child's "not [entirely] positive" or "ambivalent" feelings for his mother (80), a claim that challenged the unanimous scholarly opinion that the mother-child relationship was healthy and fully affectionate. This "ambivalence" would have had four roots:

1) When his mother died, in the composer's seventeenth year, Beethoven began to fear that he might fall ill with consumption, the disease that killed his mother; in the very letter in which he announced her recent death to a friend, he wrote "...I have been plagued with asthma; and I am inclined to fear that this malady may even turn to consumption.."[7]

2) With regards to Beethoven's mother's personality, the Sterbas invoke the testimonies of the members of the Fischer family who had been neighbors of the Beethoven household in Bonn. They recalled the mother as a person who never laughed or smiled, who used to advise women against marriage, because it was "a little joy, but after that a chain of griefs"—an opinion that strongly resembles Beethoven's own views on marriage, as recorded in Fanny Giannatasio's diary (80-81). As I will show later, this is a misleading statement.

18

3) His mother did not seem to have "protected the boy [Beethoven] from mistreatment by his father, [...] often left the children to the care of maidservants [... and did not] bring up her children to be neat" (81).

4) His mother's death "forced him [Beethoven] into the maternal role for which his infantile experiences had presumably predetermined him," a circumstantial argument added later in the book (183).

All this would "show that his [Beethoven's] love of his mother, which is so stressed by his biographers, had a large admixture of hostility and negativism" (81). His "identification" with his mother—coupled with his "ambivalent" feelings for her—would account for all the psychopathic traits that he displayed in full strength in his relationship with his nephew. He wanted to "supplant the boy's real mother" (141) and became a "substitute-figure for his own mother," including both the loving, positive side, and the bad, "poisonous" one (183-184). His negative feelings for his mother transferred into distrust of any woman, of which his hate of his sister-in-law Johanna was only the most transparent example: for instance, his letters and entries in his later conversation books display plenty of examples of his negative feelings about "the bad Viennese women." The Sterbas even conjecture that "towns are personified by women. Ludwig's frequent outbursts against Vienna may very well have been expressions of his unconscious hatred of his mother" (35). The distrust and hate of women would have also been the root—or, possibly the effect—of Beethoven's "unconscious homosexuality," an issue that I will visit later.

The Sterbas never explained what "motherly love" is and why it would be psychopathic but, judging by the frequent occurrences of the words, we can infer that they mean love marred by "jealousy" and "possessiveness," two attributes that have traditionally derailed the relationship between mother and daughter-in-law. Throughout their book, whatever Beethoven does about his nephew, according to the Sterbas, is proof that he was jealous and possessive. He was constantly afraid that he would lose possession of Karl. The boy's mother was the main object of his jealousy; it does not seem to matter that he consistently claimed that he was only trying to protect the boy from a pernicious influence: to the authors it is just a matter of jealousy and possessiveness. They also see the composer jealous of any women who Karl might have met. When the boy approaches twenty, Beethoven is afraid that he "was taking too great an interest in Therese," the wife of his brother Johann (291), another woman that he held—without any reason, according to the Sterba couple—in very low esteem. In fact, the composer was very likely trying to protect the youth from the dangerous *physical* contact with the world of "the bad Viennese women," who were a known and feared source of the STDs of the time, primarily of deadly syphilis.

Identification with the mother has other weird offshoots in the Sterba analysis, for instance their assertion that Beethoven made a paranoid woman/poison connection. Because he suspected that Johanna had poisoned his brother and insisted that his doctor Bertolini perform an autopsy (which yielded a negative result),[8] the authors claim that Beethoven frequently "harbored" the idea of poisoning (50), but they could not offer any substantial evidence of that. It is hard to see an "idea of poisoning" informing Beethoven's complaint in court about Johanna's stuffing her son with "food and strong drink" that made the boy very sick, as the Sterbas claim (182-3). They also mention "Ludwig's intensifying distrust and fear of being poisoned" in 1824 (245); in fact, Beethoven was complaining in a letter to Karl that his cook had fed him rotten food and summoned him to go with her to supervise her purchases, because he did not want "to run the risk of being poisoned."[9] Obviously, he had food poisoning in mind, which is different from poisoning. Food poisoning happened a lot at the time, when hygiene was a term and a science not yet invented, and there were no known methods of preserving food except using salt and spices. Beethoven's frequent digestive ailments must have been a result of frequent food poisoning.

The authors' "identification" enthusiasm takes a weird turn when they make Beethoven identify with his very enemy, his sister-in-law Johanna: "[…] he attempted to replace Carl's mother for him, at the same time identifying himself with her" (275). Here his own mother and his enemy are combined into one motherly figure that would have dominated his behavior from the beginning to the end of his relationship with his nephew:

> In this identification, it was at first more the positive and loving side of the mother whose image Ludwig carried with him which found expression, even though mingled with the negative traits of possessiveness, jealousy, and distrust. Gradually, however, and hand in hand with the mental regression and breakdown which took place in Ludwig [Beethoven], the negative traits of the mother-image acquired the upper hand. Thus he became more and more the evil, poisoning mother. As such, he was inwardly compelled to poison his nephew's life. He did it so systematically, with increasing intensity and persistence, until the victim [the nephew] was stricken down (275).

When deconstructing Sterbas' argument, one can easily accept the "identification" as a reasonable idea, because Beethoven's mother would have been a far better "role model" than his father. However, the shrinks' arguments for his alleged "ambivalence" toward her are very feeble:

1) Beethoven was afraid that he had inherited his mother's illness. This is the only "proof" that can claim some support in the quoted letter voicing fear, but must it have generated "negative feelings" towards his mother? Beethoven wrote in another letter, "I have an idea that some day I shall have a stroke, like my very worthy grandfather, whom I somewhat resemble," [10] but the Sterbas never claim that the composer had any "ambivalent feelings" about this ancestor.

2) Beethoven shared his sullen mother's views on marriage as "a chain of sorrows." Even if this statement was true—and will show that it is not—it could not explain Beethoven's "ambivalent feelings" for his mother. Actually, Beethoven's opinion about marriage (recorded in Fanny Giannatasio's diary) is completely different from that of his mother. Fanny was the elder daughter of Kajetan Giannatasio, the owner of the boarding school where Beethoven took his nephew in February 1816; this young woman left a diary[11] that provides invaluable—albeit somewhat lacking in detail—evidence about Beethoven and

his nephew in the years 1816-17 and even beyond: in 1820, Beethoven visited the Giannatasios' school quite often (almost daily) to meet his nephew and had long conversations with the parents and their two daughters. Fanny recorded in her own words the composer's opinion: "he does not like the idea of any indissoluble bond being *forced* between people in their personal relations to each other,"[12] the qualification indicating a very different opinion than his mother's more universal view of marriage as a "chain of sorrows." It actually reflects his own love-life experiences, in which he fell for some married women, which could logically have caused him to resent such permanent bonds. (This issue is beyond the scope of the present topic and I deal with it in the more appropriate context of the Immortal Beloved story.)

3) He had an un-protective, neglectful mother. If she was so uncaring, the parental home must have been a mess and the young Beethoven would have grown accustomed to untidiness, which, as the evidence show, indeed became his habit. It is, therefore, hard to see any reason for the alleged negative feelings towards his mother for such a reason.

4) Mother's death "forced him [Beethoven] into the maternal role." We can understand if a boy not yet seventeen (and he thought he was fifteen!) felt overwhelmed by his new responsibilities, but Beethoven's most likely reaction was a rebellion against "fate"—the usual culprit at a time when death was a frequent companion of life. (Beethoven himself had seen three siblings die.) It is very unrealistic—not to say disgusting—to think that Beethoven would have had grudges against his mother because she died. Besides that, his father's alcoholism had made him unable to be the head of the household; his mother's death effectively forced him into the paternal role as well, in a context more likely to provoke resentment of a father who *could*, in theory, have stepped up— yet the Sterbas promote the idea of *maternal* resentment.

All in all, there is no reason to doubt Thayer's statement that "long years after [mother's death] in Vienna Beethoven was wont, when among his intimate friends, to speak of his 'excellent' (*vortreffliche*) mother."[13] Fanny Giannatasio reported the same description, accurate even to the word 'excellent', in her conversations with the musician.[14] Sterbas' thesis of "identification" with mother is only marginally interesting; one has to reject all the inferences stemming from Beethoven's alleged "ambivalence" towards her, which leaves rather little to support their theories.

"Unconscious" homosexuality. If Beethoven's identification with his mother is only marginally interesting, his "unconscious homosexuality" is a significant misrepresentation by the Sterbas. If he acted like a mother towards his brother Carl, in their view, "in his [Beethoven's] relationship to his brother Johann the homosexual trend is unmistakable" (219). They also offer as supporting evidence of "unconscious" homosexuality the friendliness that the composer showed to several good-looking young men whom he met: Amenda (a cherished friend from his young adulthood), the Frenchman Trémont (who visited him in 1809 and to which the book dedicates two pages of irrelevant quotes), and the musician Karl Maria von Weber (219-221). Such friendly behaviors towards men were, to the Sterbas, proof that Beethoven was not interested in women. It is true that Beethoven's love letters to Josephine von Brunsvik-Deym, the strongest known display of his heterosexuality, were not yet known when the Sterbas wrote their book in the early fifties, but there were plenty of testimonies from his most intimate friends, like Wegeler and Ferdinand Ries, attesting his definite interest in women. The Sterbas discarded all this reliable evidence, invoked a testimony that "one never knew when he [Beethoven] was in love"[15]—which does not say anything more than that the composer was very careful to keep his love life very private—and finally quote Friedrich Wähner "who knew Ludwig equally well [as Wegeler]" and who "asserts that love appears never to have any power over him" (97). In fact, Wähner was no friend of Beethoven and hardly knew him. In Thayer's biography of the composer, he shows only once, in the list of year 1820 compositions, amongst which a canon on the words "*Wähner es ist kein Wahn*" (a pun on words: Wähner is no illusion).[16] This vague acquaintance took advantage of his few visits to Beethoven in 1820 to publish some six pages of "reminiscences" (*Zur Errinerung*) in four successive issues of the magazine *Wiener Zeitschrift für Kunst, Literatur, Theater and Mode* in 1837. They are a mixture of utterances heard in Beethoven's circle (the most authentic of which is the composer's metaphoric description of Bach as "no brook but sea") with platitudes in the florid romanticist jargon of the time, including the claim invoked by the Sterbas.[17] Obviously, Währing's statement reflects the little he could witness in 1820 and should not supersede the combined testimony of the composer's longtime intimate friends, which attests Beethoven's very "conscious" attraction to the other sex.

Other arguments offered by the Sterba couple that Beethoven was a misogynist are equally obvious misrepresentations. In September 1812, Beethoven met Amalie Sebald, a young Berlin singer whom he had encountered at the Teplitz spa, the year before. Beethoven was ill and she came several times to his lodgings, always accompanied, and cared for him and brought him fresh homemade food. He wrote her seven short notes in which he complains repeatedly about his illness, but from which we can easily read that he was very much interested in her person—he even insisted that she continued visiting him, even alone, which was a "no go" at the time—and protested in his last note, "What on earth are you dreaming of when saying that you cannot be anything to me? When we meet again, dear A, we must discuss this point."[18] Several scholars have described this episode as Amalie administering "sisterly ministrations" to a sick child,* but the Sterbas read them as Beethoven's avoiding her under the pretext of being ill (106)—a would-be proof of his "ambiguous" feelings about women.

A similar example invoked by the Sterbas is the composer's reference to "fortresses" in several of his letters to his friend Zmeskal. They maintain that "the 'fortresses' symbolize women," therefore the composer's warning his friend to avoid any commerce with "fortresses" would be another indication of his

---

* I deal with the episode in its 1812 context in my *Immortal Beloved Controversy* book (on www.BeethovenOurContemporary.com).

repulsion of the other sex (110). The Sterbas are the exception to the near-universal scholarly opinion that the term designates only a certain category of women—those of very low sexual morality or even prostitutes (according to Solomon). After more wild speculations about Beethoven's condemnation of licentious opera librettos like those of Mozart's *Marriage of Figaro* and *Don Giovanni*, or about his own *Fidelio*, in which the female heroine acting in male outfits would supposedly be more proof of his misogyny, they conclude with a strange inference with a fully Freudian flavor: "The positive element in his extremely ambivalent relationship to the female sex was absorbed into his identification with woman [his mother]. His masculine love of woman was transformed into maternal love of his nephew" (111). Such inferences are too far-fetched to be considered further. Quite characteristically, when the Sterbas published their 1954 book in German translation in 1964, significantly *after* Beethoven's love letters to Josephine were brought to light and published (1957), they did not budge one iota in their study—they simply ignored the new facts that refuted this tenet of their theory, the composer's "unconscious homosexuality."[19] Murphy's Law in action, again.

"Sadistic Führer-like" personality. According to the Sterba couple, a few other traits of Beethoven were very significant in his relationship with his nephew and sister-in-law. Chief amongst them was his tyrannical, "*Führer* personality." They dedicate a whole chapter, "Rebel and Tyrant" (77-96), to explore the issue and explain how the same person can rebel against any form of authority—be it a social hierarchy or musical norms—and be, at the same time, a domineering figure that tries to transform everybody around him into "slaves" to be used to satisfy his egotistic needs—from his daily bread to his need for unconditional love. They present many episodes in the composer's life that illustrate mostly his "rebel" side. They may be right to look for the roots of such a dual personality in Beethoven's childhood, for example in the severity of his father (82-83), but they again waste pages on their "motherly identification" theory and Beethoven's alleged hypochondria (79-82), which are at best tangential to the rebel and/or tyrant issue. They are probably right to show that the rebel was already present, in some childish forms, in his teenage years (84-85)—we know now that this age is also very important in the development of personality.[20] The "tyrant" side of the argumentation is, however, weaker.

The main feature that the Sterbas see as "tyrannical" is Beethoven's "strength," which they illustrate with several quotes from his notes (92-93), but these quotes are about *inner* strength, not coercive power over the others. Beethoven may indeed have had some "grandiose narcissism [...] typical of the great genius" (93), but if so, it is tempered by acute self-criticism. Just when he was working on his *Eroica* symphony, he reportedly said, "I am but little satisfied with my works thus far"; and a year later, "God knows why it is that my pianoforte music always makes the worst impression on me [...]."[21] Of course, like any creator, he had to believe in his genius, and that sort of self-confidence could easily go beyond the frontiers of his musical craftiness and explain his stubbornness and arrogance in his social interactions. However, such common sense is foreign to Sterbasian psychanalytic train of thought. It keeps pushing hard towards the extremes, reaching the term "*Führer*-personality" (92, 95) "sadism" (91, resumed on 269), based on anecdotes like this one: "[…] asked to play at a gathering, he said that he would comply only if the well-known composer Wranitzky, who was also present, would crawl under the table on all fours—which the latter actually did" (91). The story is far too absurd to miss the unmistakable touch of humor when one knows the whole context.

Beethoven was well known for his reluctance to play at social gatherings. He had done it when he arrived in Vienna to establish himself as the city's foremost virtuoso, and he dazzled his audiences with his improvisations. However, he wearied of it soon, as his close friend Wegeler, who lived in Vienna between 1794 and 1796, testified in his remembrances.[22] This is at least in part because he was not just a virtuoso like many others; his improvisations were actually compositional exercises, in which he invented and developed themes and procedures and, as he explained his teenage friend Leonore von Breuning in a letter, he had often noticed that "after I had been improvising of an evening, someone somewhere in Vienna would write down many of my own ideas the next day and go about boasting they were his."[23] His unwillingness to play at social occasions was, therefore, not a matter of arrogance or vanity, but an astute strategy of "career survival" in a competitive professional environment. Nevertheless, he continued to play in the houses and the company of those who were dear to him, like the two countesses—Brunsvik-Deym and Erdödy. In the case invoked by the Sterbas, he conditioned his playing on such an absurd demand just to make sure that it would be rejected. The audience, however, was too eager to hear him play and poor Wranitzky got their message and forced Beethoven to comply and, at the same time, feel humiliated himself, because he had not wanted to humiliate another.

The allegation that Beethoven regarded his friends as "slaves" and that they accepted this humiliation because they were exhilarated to bask in the glory of his genius is another gross exaggeration. The Sterbas needed it to justify the rejection of those friends' testimonies as untrustworthy: if true, these friends would have been desperate to please him and, therefore, would have told him only what he wanted to hear. Even Solomon, who has good things to say about the Sterbas' contribution, objects to such descriptions of Beethoven's personality as "so fundamentally flawed that it cannot serve as a reliable basis for interpretation,"[24] and quotes the very apt description of the poet Grillparzer, who met the composer during his last ten years: "[…] for all his odd ways, which … often bordered on being offensive, there was something so inexpressibly touching and noble in him that one could not but esteem him and feel drawn to him."[25] His friends may have been similarly drawn, but they would not have accepted "tyranny" unconditionally and would always draw a line: some withdrew and stayed afar for many years, like his teenage buddy Stephen von Breuning, from 1815 to 1825. His friends were indeed biased, but only insofar as they were interested much more in the well-being of the genius whom they wanted to live a long healthy life for the benefit of humanity than in that of his nephew, who was just another child to them. But they soon realized that Beethoven's possessive dedication to this child was damaging him morally, psychically and physically. As we will see, they even tried to somehow separate the pair physically, encouraging Beethoven to enroll his nephew in boarding schools and later to let him move into his own lodgings when entering the Vienna University. Such patterns seem to reflect true friendship rather than slavery.

"Pathological" distrust. Distrust of others is another of Beethoven's personality traits that the Sterbas consider essential in understanding his relationships with his nephew and sister-in-law. They claim that "his distrust was a pathological phenomenon, not a reaction to outward causes, but arising from an inner need [...]" (232). In my essay *Beethoven's Raptus*, about Beethoven's alleged psychopathy, I showed that this latter statement is a gross exaggeration, too. His tendency to distrust developed primarily after realizing that he was losing his hearing and, if it later reached the paranoid level of persecution mania, it still had almost always a real "seed" at its root. He would not refuse to trust, but he would overreact at the first, slightest—and oftentimes wrong—impression that his trust has been purposefully and maliciously betrayed. I will illustrate this pattern with several episodes from Beethoven's life, mentioned by the Sterbas but always with a twist to turn them against him.

The first episode is the well-known "restaurant scene" which took place the day following the triumphant first performance of his *Ninth Symphony* in May 1824. When Beethoven found out that the success yielded only a meager profit for him, he got angry, invited his friends that had been in charge with the receipts at the restaurant and, in an irrational fit of anger, accused Schindler of having swindled him. The outrageous accusation made not only Schindler, but all the other guests leave. The Sterbas relate only part of the story (246) and not the whole context. Beethoven had been reluctant to give that concert, at a time when Vienna was in the midst of a Rossini frenzy, and was concerned about a possible monetary loss (he had to pay for everything—copyists, soloists, orchestra, and renting an opera hall), but changed his mind when his friends assured him that the concert would be a great success and also yield good money—Schindler advanced a figure of 2000 florins, plus 3000 for a second concert in a detailed report about the financial dealing.[26] And Beethoven obviously trusted his assurances. When the profit turned to be of less than 400 florins, Beethoven was understandably angered—where were his promised 2000 florins? His outrage was also fueled by what he claimed to be a "credible" source confirming the charge that Beethoven was being swindled. The source has never been identified, but was probably his brother Johann, who "was jealous of Schidler's participation in the composer's business affairs."[27] The outburst is indeed startling, but in their attempt to blacken Beethoven, the Sterbas fail to mention this mitigating circumstance.

Another episode narrated by the Sterbas (140) is even more illustrative of my contentions, because it involves his nephew. In November 1818, Beethoven found out that "Karl had talked abusively to the servants and had kept back money from them to buy sweets." This finding was to have momentous consequences that I will deal with later, but what interests us at this point is a revelatory detail that the two scholars ignored: for Karl, at the time only twelve years old, to be able to "keep back" the servants' pay, he must have had control of that money. Beethoven had trusted—not distrusted—his nephew to manage at least some of the household money. Obviously, the boy's behavior may have contributed to Beethoven's later distrust, but it was not significant enough to prevent him from later delegating to teenaged Karl some dealings with his music publishers—more proof that distrust was not a pathological "an inner need."

In fact, Beethoven was ready to sometimes trust even his arch-enemy, his sister-in-law Johanna. In 1817, forgetting that he considered her "malicious," he shared with her some negative comments about Giannatasio's school (where he had placed his nephew). The Sterbas themselves bring in this episode (130), but with an entirely different goal in mind—to prove the composer's evilness. When Johanna, reported that to Giannatasio, who reproached it to Beethoven, the latter retaliated and did not allow her to see her son for several months. Obviously, this cruel "punishment" was far too excessive and I do not intend to excuse Beethoven, but it emphasize that Beethoven's excesses were at times an aggravated response to a real event.

Love for his nephew. Sterbas' take of Beethoven's relationship with his nephew is based essentially on the "motherly love" diagnosis, which they specifically designed to this purpose, although they also applied it on a broader scale: for example, in Beethoven's attachment to his brothers. "Motherly love" for Karl would have made the composer insanely jealous and scared of losing the object of his love. Distrust would have been an adjuvant, noticeable in the composer's wild reprimands of Karl for many—in the scholars' view—imagined encroaches. We examined both of these alleged traits of Beethoven earlier, showing that the Sterbas distorted them arbitrarily.

After Beethoven's brother Carl set himself "free" from his elder brother's control and married, their rapport cooled, possibly because Beethoven did not particularly like his sister-in-law from the very beginning. The two brothers seem to have seen each other very rarely, so Beethoven was not a regular part of Carl's family life. During periods when he wanted a "surrogate family," he searched for it in those of the women he loved, Countess Brunsvik-Daym (1804-1807) and Countess Erdödy (1808-1809), or the families of friends like the Brentanos (1811-1812). There is no evidence of him developing any special feelings for his nephew before 1815, but the Sterbas' assume that he transferred his "motherly love" for his brother to the nephew during the time when he was close again to Carl during his final months (47). In fact, this remains the couple's only insight into the relationship of Beethoven and his nephew, but they are so fascinated with it that it never occurs to them that a feeling of "duty" might also have been involved in Beethoven's desire to assume the guardianship of his nephew. At a time when death was a frequent occurrence in every family, extended family ties were much stronger than they are now; uncles or older brothers behaved like fathers towards their orphaned nephews and nieces (aunts were less important in that regard, because women were not the bread-winners). The practice extended among in-laws and it was customary that the young treat their old in-laws as mother and father. We have an example of this pattern common in Beethoven's world in his *Fidelio*: the prison ward Rocco treats the heroine Leonore disguised as a man as a future daughter-in-law and calls her "sonny" in Act 1 *Terzetto*; in turn, she calls him "father" in Act 2 *Monodram*.[*] When Beethoven signed his letter to Karl as "your father," he was not usurping a title, but acting in accordance with the ethical standards of his time.[28] And conversely, Karl would not have felt constrained, nor thought it morally wrong to call his uncle "father," as he did in several of his letters. It was therefore natural that Beethoven assumed fatherly responsibilities towards his nephew. The fact that he did not want to share these responsibilities with the child's mother, however, is a different issue.

Of course, a feeling of duty did not preclude, but may supplement love, particularly love of one's kin. One can see that best in a letter that Beethoven sent a friend ten years later, in September 1826, when he had understood that he had lost his nephew's love and he was going to lose his presence too: "All my hopes have vanished, all my hopes of having near me someone who would resemble me at least in my better qualities!"[29] He had wanted to shape and see grow the last of the Beethovens, the one thin thread that was to carry his name into the future. Granted, his love was uneven, stretching between "almost cruel severity to almost limitless indulgence,"[30] but this was the general pattern of his affection, well known to all those dear to him. "Don't come to me any more!" he wrote to a friend in 1799, "you are a false dog, and may the hangman do away with all false dogs." And the next day, "Dear little Ignaz of my heart, you are an honest fellow and I now realize that you were right. So come to me this afternoon. [...] Kisses from your Beethoven [...]"[31] His brothers were not spared his mood swings, either: in an October letter to Hasslinger, Beethoven described Johann as "my Cain brother"—a really strong accusation—but wrote a letter his "dear brother" two months later.[32] And because Karl was by far more important to Beethoven than any other human being, he got a much larger share than anyone of both the ups and downs in their relationship. He was a huge disappointment to his uncle, who saw him satisfied with a mediocre future, sinking lower and lower from an artist to a scholar, to a tradesman, to a soldier. This disappointment acted like a huge amplifier of any other minor flaws or behavioral blunders from Karl, or of any imagined trespasses.

The nobility pretense. Although Beethoven was not a noble, he brought his first trial to exclude Karl's mother Johanna from the boy's guardianship in front of the judicial authority for the aristocratic class (the *Landrechte*), which accepted the case without questioning the composer's nobility. Beethoven's unusual act, involving an obvious misrepresentation, became known as "the nobility pretense" in his biography. The Sterbas do not make much of it themselves, but it will become very important in Solomon's analysis; therefore, I will deal with it only briefly before the next chapter. The Sterbas suggest only that Beethoven claimed nobility status because it was easier for him to corrupt this court through his "influential friends belonging to the highest aristocracy" (55), a claim that had little to do with psychoanalysis, so perhaps was of less interest to them. As I will show later, some "influencing" of the judges must

---

[*] Rocco: "Gut, Söhnchen, gut! Hab immer Mut." (Good, sonny, good, be always brave); Leonore: "Nein, Vater, nein, ich zittre nicht" (No, father, no, I'm not shivering).

have happened—albeit not only from Beethoven. In fact, the Beethoven family "nobility pretense" was initiated by his sister-in-law Johanna immediately after her husband's death. She instructed her attorney to deliver Carl's will and controversial codicil to the nobility court,[33] which did not check her late husband's nobility status, probably assuming that the *van* particle in his name demonstrated it. As the court appointed Johanna and Beethoven as co-guardians of Karl, it was natural that the composer would take his case to the same court to have Johanna excluded; again, the court took his nobility status at face value. When Johanna took the composer to the same court yet again in December 1818 (and again their nobility status was not checked) Beethoven unwittingly let slip the truth: when presenting his plans for his nephew's education, he said, "were he noble..." The judge did not miss this slip and questioned both sides, exposing the multiple misrepresentations. Beethoven had to admit that the *van* particle in his name was no proof of nobility and he possessed no documentary proof of it.[34]

The Sterbas found a way to insert psychoanalysis into this last episode, with what came to be known as "Beethoven's losing his nobility pretense": they invoked another well-known pattern, "Freudian" language slips. His "were he [Karl] noble ..." slip is interpreted by the Sterba couple as follows (144):

> Such a glaring error in such an important matter is produced by unconscious motives. We shall not go wrong if we assume that one of the causes of Beethoven's revealing slip was his unconscious feeling of guilt. He had repeatedly told untruths in his examinations, as the record shows. His slip is obviously a self-punishment for the lies he had told in court in his struggle for the boy and against Johanna.

This is hardly credible, even by psychoanalytic standards: the composer was very unlikely to feel guilty for lying in court about his sister-in-law, simply because he was convinced that he was telling the truth — and in fact, he was. This slip fits the Freudian explanation, but not as the shrink-scholars claim: Beethoven might have had some apprehensive feelings about his pretense to get his case ruled in the nobility court, therefore the term "noble" was on his mind and so the slip occurred.

Equally improbable is another similar claim of the Sterbas. Quoting from one of his letters 1816, "the talk of that evil woman [Johanna] has so unstrung me that today I can not answer anything," they conclude that his confusion "is doubtless also to be interpreted as a guilt reaction" (76). Anger is "doubtless" a far more likely explanation. With this, we have practically come to the end of the Sterba couple's psychoanalytical interpretations of the subject of their book. What they have to offer about other characters involved in the drama are either variations of these themes or simple, commonsense psychology insights—something they also practice and which in part saves their contribution. We must, however, know these characters better if we want to understand the drama.

A different 1816 portrait of Beethoven. It is interesting to note that the black portrait of Beethoven drawn by the two psychoanalysts is utterly different from the one that Fanny Giannatasio draws in 1816. Fanny was so impressed by "the modesty and heartiness of his disposition" (53[*]), his "goodness of heart which is his special characteristic" (55), that in March she was ready to fall in love with him and soon confided her feelings to her diary, although she felt that hers was an impossible dream (66-7). I will tell the sad story of this remarkable young lady elsewhere — it suffices here to say that she did not paint this glowing portrait of Beethoven because she was in love but, inversely, fell in love because of what she saw in him. She never dared to open up to him and he treated her only as a young friend; he was, in fact, attracted to Fanny's younger and spectacularly beautiful sister, who was engaged and soon to be married. Fanny would come to know Beethoven's dark side, too—one of his paranoid attacks of distrust was directed at her, in a murky episode that was clearly related to his obsession with his nephew and, possibly, with the boy's mother (171-3).

Fanny's diary shows that, although somewhat naïve and romantic, she had plenty of common sense and, whether in love or feeling rejected and hurt, she always kept an even balance and her testimony has always the ring of truth. She did not always agree with Beethoven. When Karl read her a letter that his uncle had sent him, she described it as "a charming letter, so full of kind and good things […]," but her next comment is the negative view of an observant pedagogue: "I do not, however, think it is quite right of him to disturb the child's present state of ingenuous ignorance, by placing a confidence in him which he is not old enough to appreciate, and which may have the effect of making him ponder over things he cannot understand" (69). Although we have this quote, the complete letter is no longer extant: we cannot know what inspired her comment, but it may be related to her remarkable intuition in foreseeing the whole future drama. When, at the end of July 1816, Beethoven decided to withdraw his nephew from Giannatasio's school, claiming that he could better educate him at home with the help of some tutors, Fanny wrote in her diary: "I can't help wishing for the boy's sake that he could remain with us; it would be better for him than living with his uncle, as the latter will find out, perhaps, when it is too late" (88). She does not substantiate this statement either, but it seems obvious that she had a poor opinion of Beethoven's pedagogical skills. Overall, Fanny's portrait of Beethoven displays the real man, with both light and shadows—the one that the Sterba couple seem never to have met.

Who was Beethoven's sister-in-law?

One of the main accusations that the Sterbas (as well as Solomon later) threw at Beethoven is his inhuman treatment of his sister-in-law Johanna, whom they portray an honest woman who had made a slight and easily forgivable mistake, and whom Beethoven vilified in the most ignominious way – even suspecting her, on the very day his brother died, of having poisoned her husband (50). Further, he deprived her of her essential right to motherhood, by allegedly corrupting the Austrian justice system into entrusting her son to him and barring her from even seeing her child. From this perspective and judged by modern criteria, we may feel entitled to condemn Beethoven as the Sterbas did—without

---

[*] All references in this paragraph refer to pages in Nohl's 1876 book.

examining the existing evidence. At the time when the Sterbas undertook their research, little was known about Beethoven's sister-in-law Johanna beyond some letters of his and entries in his conversation books, which were clearly deprecatory; the Sterbas therefore rejected them as unjustifiably biased.

Let us examine this evidence. Beethoven brought his younger brothers to Vienna in 1795-96, after he had established himself as the city's foremost virtuoso, and helped them to settle down. He even housed Carl and employed him as his private secretary, and procured for him music pupils. Following his temperament and the habit he had developed when, as a teenager, he was the head of the family, he tried to control his brothers' lives—especially their sentimental lives, advising them to beware "the bad Viennese women": a piece of advice that may have come from his own experience. Naturally, his brothers rebelled and set themselves free. Carl moved out and married Johanna Reiss, the daughter of a "prosperous upholsterer" in 1806, after an affair in which she became pregnant. Their child, Karl, was born five months after the marriage. This was not a rare occurrence in Vienna, but it was not common in either the middle or upper classes: the high illegitimacy rate (about two in every five births) around 1810 was mostly due to the tremendous growth of the working population flocking into the suburbs.[35] The Sterbas paint (27ff) a sparse but seemingly truthful picture of the family life of Beethoven's brother, about which there are very few testimonies: like "our" Beethoven, Carl had a choleric temperament and there were episodes that we would describe nowadays as "domestic violence," but that did not necessarily preclude mutual affection.

The little that was known about Johanna included an offense that took her to the Vienna Court in 1811: the nature of that offense was unknown because Thayer had made an unusual oversight and had not transcribed all the documents available at the time of his research; the court documents of that year were destroyed in a fire in 1927. With the original records missing, Beethoven scholarship could rely only on the references contained in the Beethoven literature, in which Johanna's crime was described either as "charge of infidelity" in the English Thayer-Forbes or as "embezzlement against her own husband" in the accurate German edition of Thayer-Deiters-Riemann.[36] The Sterbas correctly adopted the latter, with the additional detail that "she was condemned to a month of 'house arrest'" for it (53).* Such a crime seems so petty and indeed ridiculous (what could she have done?—stolen the family grocery money?), that Beethoven's description of it in his memoranda addressed to the court as a "horrible crime" seemed a gross misrepresentation. The Sterba couple also emphatically dismissed the repeated statements in the known evidence about Johanna's frivolity and her cheating on her husband, claiming that the sources, Beethoven's friends, were merely his toadies telling lies to please him (167, 197 and 201). The truth was revealed only in 1988 by Sieghard Brandenburg in an

---

* The Sterbas also speculate about the event, assuming that Carl had denounced his wife, which is totally incongruent to the facts now known; Carl had persistently applied to have her sentence reduced. This simple example illustrates well the mentioned danger of speculating beyond facts, to which both the Sterbas and Solomon are addicted.

article following an in-depth investigation of the partially recovered police investigation reports and Court evidence,[37] which by and large confirm the picture of Johanna as presented in the nineteenth century Beethoven literature. In a nutshell: Johanna liked to live beyond her family income (which was not unsubstantial); because her husband "kept her short," she ran a sort of consignment business of her own, which was, however, registered under her husband's name, as the law then required.

In 1811, when she had an expensive pearl necklace entrusted to her for sale, she designed a scheme to sell it directly for herself: she faked a burglary and accused her former maid of the theft. But she was stupid enough to be wearing a necklace made from half of the pearls when the police arrived, and eventually had to confess her crime—but not without claiming that she had intended to pay back the owner of the necklace. She was tried and convicted of a double felony: embezzlement against her husband (she tried to steal from the consignment business recorded as his) and calumny (because she accused her maid of the crime), and was sentenced to "one year severe imprisonment." This was reduced to two months, because of mitigating circumstances. This was not Johanna's first rub with law: she had been caught at a similar theft and framing attempt in her parent's home during her teenage years, after which she escaped with only "domestic correction," because she was underage and her parents did not press charges.[38] After her 1811 conviction, Johanna seems to have served only a few days of light police detention, because her husband persistently appealed to ever-higher levels, lastly to the Emperor, successfully having the sentence successively reduced. And it is likely that Beethoven did not lie when he claimed in his 1820 "Memorandum" to the court that it was "only thanks to the greatest efforts on the part of her husband and of my friends that, though she was not unpunished, she was exempted from the most infamous form of punishment and again discharged."[39] He must have felt bad putting his honesty on the line when pulling some aristocratic strings to get her a lighter sentence (equivalent to modern probation).

The initial Austrian court sentencing may seem to have been very harsh for such a "minor offence." How much did Johanna's try to steal? The pearl necklace was actually a pricey luxury item, evaluated at about 20,000 florins,[40] five times the yearly allowance that Beethoven received from the Viennese nobility.[41] An even better estimate is given by the deal made in 1813 by Johanna and her husband: they put 5000 gulden down payment to buy, for some 11,175 florins, a house in Vienna containing several apartments for renting,[42] which would have been a reliable safety net for their old age.

It is obvious that Johanna's "embezzlement" was more than a minor offence, but a "felony," for which contemporary Austrian Law prescribed a punishment of one to five years "severe imprisonment." The court showed considerable leniency to Johanna, either because she was a woman or because, as Brandenburg suggests, the law itself had begun to be considered too harsh.[43] Admittedly, the Sterbas were not aware of all these facts, but they quote Karl's recollection: "she [Johanna] often told me that every time she needed money her father said: 'I won't give you any, but if you can *take* money without my knowledge, it belongs to you!" (54), which should have suggested to a psychoanalyst—who is supposed to locate the key to personality in childhood—that Johanna might have been a less than perfect person. They could have also discovered her bent to shifting the blame to somebody else: when she appealed the court decision that gave Beethoven Karl's guardianship, she blamed her dead husband for her felony: her lawyer, Hotschevar, claimed, obviously at her request, that her 1811 theft "was to be ascribed rather to her husband than to Frau v. Beethoven" (316). The Sterbas also rejected as a Beethoven lie the earlier similar act by Johanna mentioned above. The court judging Johanna in 1811 located the police report confirming Beethoven's statement.[44]

The 1811 offence was Johanna's last known appearance in court, but she left a long trail of shady deals in the business documents tracked by Brandenburg,[45] because despite certain changes in circumstances, she never changed her lifestyle. After her husband's death she had a steady income—half of his pension (the other half belonged to her son) and the renting revenues from the house bought in 1813—but she always wanted more and was constantly in debt, taking new loans to pay old ones, always lying about her guarantee assets and being cheated by better liars. In 1817, she had to sell the renting property at a loss to pay some of her debts; she was practically penniless the next year and again when getting sick after 1820, when Beethoven helped her financially (he let her have her son's pension among others). She was officially bankrupt in 1829. Beethoven also blamed Johanna for being a frivolous, adulterous woman. In 1816 he wrote a friend that "the *Queen of Night* [i.e., Johanna] was at the Artists' Ball until three a.m., exposing not only her mental but also *her bodily nakedness*—it was whispered that she—was willing to hire herself—for 20 gulden!"[46] In his circle, she was described as "*canaille*" (French for "dishonest") and "notorious whore" (quoted by Sterba, 201 and 203). All these assertions were emphatically dismissed by the two scholars as fabrications inspired by Beethoven's hatred, with a promise that "material will be produced in due course which clearly testifies against any assumption that Johanna could be bought for money, and which makes it extremely improbable that she was a 'bad woman'" (61). The promised proof is the 1819 decision of the commoners' Court, the *Magistrat*, to entrust Karl's guardianship to his mother. Here is the Sterba argument in its entirety (155):

> The Magistracy, in its decision, exhibited a wholly reasonable appraisal of the situation and remained uninfluenced by Ludwig's feelings, particularly by his aggressions against Johanna. In any case, it did not agree with Ludwig's condemnations of her. We must bear in mind too that the Magistracy was on the whole composed of petty bourgeois, who were much more ready to condemn a "bad" woman than a body of noblemen would have been. The Magistracy's refusal to condemn Johanna is a strong positive datum in any estimate of Karl's mother.

This reasoning might be correct when applied to a provincial town, in which any trespass on Christian morality would have been punished by public opinion that would probably influence a Court decision. But as I mentioned, Vienna was a different environment: a city of extremely lax sexual morality, in which debauches were a matter of gossip and entertainment and not public opprobrium. The cynical chronicles of Johann Pezzl about the Viennese mores towards the end of the eighteenth century[47] are mirrored in the incensed picture drawn by John Russell, an English memorialist who visited the city thirty years later and wrote, "there cannot be a more dissolute city," in which promiscuity and adultery, both male and female, were not only allowed and condoned, but encouraged.[48] The Magistracy ruling in Beethoven's case would have savored the piquancy in Johanna's alleged behavior but likely would have discarded it in their decision, because it was not confirmed by a court document. And, perhaps, they tasted some of the piquancy too—but let us not anticipate.

In fact, Brandenburg's article provides evidence supporting Beethoven's opinion of his sister-in-law's sexual morals. The maid whom she tried to frame in 1811 stated not only that Johanna "has substantial debts, unbeknownst to her husband and her mother, spends money like water," but also that she "is having an affair with the lodger, a petty dealer, [named] Markbreit." The maid might have been taking revenge on a mistress who had tried to frame her, but the judge believed her and described Johanna as "known as an improvident, frivolous woman, given to idleness and luxury."[49] Indeed, she enjoyed "a certain reputation" in Vienna, at the moment, as confirmed by entirely independent evidence found by George Marek in the diary of Joseph Carl Rosenbaum. This employee of the Esterhazy family, otherwise unknown in the Beethoven literature and a city reveler, wrote in 1810, "Ten o'clock at the Redoute [masked ball] ... we remained until 4 A.M. Several pretty masks ... *the Beethoven woman* ... So I had a fairly good time" (original italics).[50] The appellation "the Beethoven woman" shows that Johanna had acquired already a specific reputation; Beethoven must have been aware of such goings-on for years, since he wrote later, in an 1820 "Memorandum" to the Court that his sister-in-law had already in 1811 "partly lost her good name."[51] Shouldn't we understand his anger at "the Beethoven woman," who dragged his name through the mud of Vienna *Chronique Scandaleuse*?[*] It is obvious that, contrary to the Sterbas' claim (61), there is no reason to doubt Beethoven's truthfulness when reporting similar news from the 1816 "Artists' Ball." He was also likely right when claiming that "immediately after the death of my brother, she was in secret commerce with a lover [...] was to be found on all dance-floors and at merrymakings..."[52] "It would be understandable if she had adopted desperate measures to increase her income," Brandenburg wrote,[53] stopping short of repeating what Beethoven claimed, that she was running her "money rising" campaign. Johanna's dissolute wife is, ultimately, a good illustration of the Viennese sexual morality of the time: a woman would have achieved her "sexual liberation" in her mid-thirties, when her fertility had declined with the risk of

---

[*] The original German is more compact and telling: ... "die Beethoven." The *die* feminine article is the usual way of the language to refer a woman by her family name. *Die Beethoven* points more to the composer than does its English translation.

getting pregnant. In fact, Johanna, born in 1786, was already "liberated" around 1810, in her mid-twenties; she must have been a special fertility case, because she bore only one child in almost ten years of marriage. This can be explained only in three ways: 1) the couple had a fertility problem—very unlikely, as Karl was conceived through pre-marital sex; 2) the couple stopped having sex after their first child in 1806—also hardly likely; 3) Johanna developed a special condition during or after the childbirth and would not get pregnant again with her husband. The third proposition is the only satisfactory one and would explain her loosening the moral reins and becoming promiscuous.

Eventually, in 1820, fifteen years after she had her first child, her ways caught up with her and she was in the family way again ... but without a family.[54] This child unknowingly provides us with the definitive proof that Beethoven was right (and that the Sterbas, as well as Solomon, for that matter, were wrong) about Johanna's character. We owe it to Tellenbach to have discovered this proof: a statement by Jacob Hotschevar, Johanna's in-law (married to her step-mother) and also her attorney in her final trials about Karl's custody. In 1830, she asked Hotschevar to be the co-guardian of her illegitimate daughter and he declined, explaining in a Vienna court document that "her little praiseworthy lifestyle is not of a nature that could make it acceptable to me to come into closer contact with her as a guardian of her illegitimate child."[55] Ironically, Hotschevar acted just like Beethoven—whom he blasted in Court—and for the same reason: he did not want to share guardianship with a dissolute woman.

In full fairness, we must also add some favorable traits to this portrait of Johanna. Obviously, she loved her son and wanted to have him close to her and would stop at nothing barring murder to succeed. Her love probably pushed her to pamper him and spoil him too, but it is hard to hold that against her. Although we have no pictorial representation of her, we can assume that she was an attractive woman in 1815-16 when, at thirty, she was at the peak of her femininity. Beethoven himself described her as a "charming woman" in the same "memorial" to the Austrian court, in which he calls her "frivolous, of easy virtue, stubborn, malicious [...] depraved."[56] One must also add to her portrait a later but revelatory testimony of Karl's wife, who described her mother-in-law as a person able to move "heaven and earth" to get what she wanted in her letters to authorities, in which "she knew how to present her poverty and despair in burning colors and with dramatic effect."[57] As we will see further, Johanna put this "drama queen" disposition of hers to work in the trial that she initiated in 1818 to regain the guardianship of her son, during which she succeeded into bringing the court under her "spell."

A litigious will and a hard to take decision

The complicated story of Carl's wills reflects the equally complex relationship of the composer with his brother, which had, like all his associations, evolved through marked ups and downs. Beethoven was willing to assume the responsibility to raise his nephew in case his brother Carl's would die, but he did not want to share these responsibilities with the child's mother because, as he explained later, he "did not wish to be bound up in this with such a bad woman in a matter of such importance as the education of the child."[58] Brother Carl was aware of this disposition and, two years before, when he had had the first bad bout of consumption and was afraid that he was going to die, he had given Beethoven a "declaration" – in fact a holographic will, not notarized, but dated and signed by him and three witnesses – in which he appointed his brother as sole guardian, disregarding the mother, with whom he must have been at odds at the time. He probably had a sound and recent motive for what Thayer calls "his well-founded distrust of the virtue and prudence" of Johanna,[59] for example the one that Beethoven reported later: "Some time before his [Carl's] death she drew without his knowledge a considerable sum of money. This made him want to divorce her."[60] In 1815, however, he had reconciled with his wife and decided to designate her as a co-guardian of his child, but had to overcome Beethoven's deep distrust of her. He first tried to force the latter's hand, presenting him a regular will designing him as co-guardian together with Johanna (it ran, "Along with my wife I appoint my brother Ludwig van Beethoven co-guardian"); then he quickly agreed to cross his wife's name out at his brother's request; finally, after the latter left, he re-instated her as guardian in a codicil.[61] This way, on November 17, one day after Carl's death, Beethoven and Johanna were legally co-guardians of her son, and her attorney delivered the will and the codicil, under seal, to the Court—not just any court, but the Vienna nobility court, the so-called *Landrechte*,[62] a detail that would have consequences later.[*]

Angry with the change in his brother's will and apparently without making any attempt to negotiate the issue, Beethoven asked the same nobility court to have his sister-in-law excluded from guardianship. His decision was doubtlessly cruel and harmful to everyone involved... including himself. However, let us consider commonsensically the alternatives he had, by asking a question that neither the Sterbas nor any other scholar, to my knowledge, has asked: how would a joint custody have worked? That is, with whom was the child going to live on a daily basis?

The Austrian law of the time considered the mother "the natural guardian," so Karl would have stayed with his mother, while his uncle would have taken care of the financial matters and of his education—a male privileged responsibility in a patriarchal society. Beethoven believed not only that Johanna was a "bad woman," but also that she had begun an affair ("intimate relations with a lover") immediately after her husband's death and her previous behavior suggests that he was very likely right. Many children nowadays live with a succession of boy-friends of their mothers, but that was not the norm at the time, not even in a city of very lax sexual morality like Vienna. And Beethoven, who had sown his own wild oats in his youth,[†] had become a much more puritanical

---

[*] She was actually claiming the nobility status, based on the *van* Beethoven name that she was bearing.
[†] I present this side of Beethoven's life in my book *Immortal Beloved Controversy* (see my *BeethovenOurContemporary* website).

person of late. Of course, the child could have been put in a boarding school (he actually was), but that would not insulate him from the sway of his mother, whose "casual" morality extended, as we know, well beyond sexual matters: she would have been his role model and would have taught him to cheat, to steal, to lie, and to be cynical. "She laughs at him when he speaks the truth," Beethoven complained later to the Court[63]—and the rarity of this utterance among his diatribes against his sister-in-law bears the ring of truth. It seemed to him inacceptable "to entrust our precious treasure [Karl] even for one moment"[64] to Johanna. He wrote a letter to the court expressing his hope that the judgement "will entrust me alone and exclusively with the guardianship, *or will do so by including my brother's widow* but with the latter eventuality they will protect me by means of those measures which […] *I shall consider* to be to my nephew's advantage […]"[65] That proof of flexibility probably influenced the court to rule in his favor and to exclude Johanna from guardianship (more about this later), but also granted her what we would today call "visitation rights."

Beethoven seemed satisfied with this decision and set his nephew up as an intern in the school run by Giannatasio del Rio, warning him in a February 1 letter that "… in no circumstances to allow his mother to influence him. How or when she is to see him, all this I will arrange with you tomorrow in greater detail."[66] It seems that Johanna showed up at the school before Beethoven found time to make those "arrangements" and wanted to take Karl to her home. This must have been the impetus for Beethoven to write to the court complaining that his sister-in-law's "thoughtless and unlawful desire to see her boy every day and to take him to her home whenever she likes is threatening to disturb the course of instruction [at school]" and asking full powers to decide how and when she could see Karl.[67] He also wrote Giannatasio, again instructing him, "under no pretext whatsoever may Karl be fetched from the boarding school without his guardian permission; *and the mother is never to visit him there*—if she desires to see him, she must apply to the guardian who will make the necessary arrangement."[68] The court obliged and Beethoven implemented harsh visitation restrictions on Johanna for almost a year. After that, Beethoven's attitude toward his sister-in-law, albeit generally adverse, shows some ups and downs, as recorded also by the Sterbas. If he does not seem to have felt guilt for stripping her of her son's guardianship, the new step—barring her from even seeing her son—haunted him afterwards. He left evidence of that in his *Tagebuch* (diary), which documents his most intimate emotions; quite characteristically, he addresses God in 1817, as if asking for forgiveness:

> God help me, Thou seest me forsaken by all Mankind, because I do not want to commit an injustice; hear my plea to be together with my Karl.

He later became more tolerant and allowed Johanna to see her son at his lodgings in Heiligenstadt in the summer (127); he even took Karl to see her at her place and planned to do this once each month in the future (128). He revoked his goodwill after the above mentioned incident, when he found Johanna peddling on his behalf (26 of this essay) and he did not allow her to see Karl for several months (130). Still later, remorse again crops up in the *Tagebuch* in 1818, when he asks forgiveness from God for what he thinks was an inescapable decision to choose the lesser evil:

> It would have been impossible without hurting the widow's feelings but it was not to be. And Thou, almighty God, seest into my heart, know that I have disregarded my own welfare for my dear Karl's sake, bless my work, bless the widow, why cannot I entirely follow my heart and henceforth—the widow—
>
> God, God, my refuge, my rock, O my all, Thou seest my innermost heart and knowest how it pains me to have to make somebody suffer through my good works for my dear Karl!!!"[69]

He even left a public track of his regret when agonizing over the issue, writing to a friend, "a bad mother is still a mother."[70] The Sterbas quote these notes (75-76) only to claim that such feelings of guilt served Beethoven to (frequently) justify "intensified aggression, particularly against the person toward whom he felt guilty." Actually, the tenses in the notes clearly indicate an agonizing past decision not a future one. And, as we see, he could show even compassion to his sister-in-law, and would later help her financially.

One can easily argue that Beethoven's attitude towards his sister-in-law was morally reprehensible and pragmatically wrong and that Karl would have become a better person growing with his mother. However, one cannot know what would have happened on the road not taken. We can make a reasonable guess in this case based on what we know about the daughter to whom Johanna gave birth in 1820 and raised as a single mother; years later, Karl's widow wrote Thayer that "in her old age Frau van Beethoven lived in Baden with her illegitimate daughter, who was also a dissolute woman."[71]

Scheming, lying and "influencing" in Court battles

The analysis of the court battles over Carl's guardianship involved little psychoanalytic insight in Sterba couple's book (they resort to it only in the "nobility pretense" episode presented already on page 28), but it is necessary to follow their whole argument in order to understand the topic.

The Sterbas maintain that Beethoven won the first trial and last trials only through gross manipulation, involving lies (about Johanna's character), distortions of facts (her 1811 conviction) and corrupting the Court through his "influential friends belonging to the highest aristocracy" (55), while Johanna rightfully won her case in the appeal trial. Judged by modern standards, a court decision that strips a woman of her natural right, the bond with her child, is indeed morally—and should, therefore, also be lawfully—wrong; today, Johanna would most certainly keep her custody, because she had "paid her duty to society" by her jail time. However, Austrian Law and the moral standards of the time were different from ours. The law was on Beethoven's side: the *German Civil Code of the Hereditary Lands of the Austrian Monarchy* provided an exclusionary clause: "persons unfit to be guardians [of a child] included those 'who have been found guilty of a felony.'"[72] Johanna had been sentenced in 1811 for "embezzlement," because of a much worse act than the one stipulated by the Sterbas. Therefore, Beethoven should easily have won his case—and he did in the first 1815-16 trial. That it was harder for him to win when Johanna appealed in 1818 was partly because some courts had started deeming the exclusionary clause obsolete and unfair in some cases, like those of a mother's guardianship.[73] Taking advantage of this trend, Johanna's lawyer claimed that her 1811 felony must have "lapsed" by 1816 (316) and the court agreed, deciding in 1819 that it had been "a transgression for which she had atoned years before, which had been pardoned by the injured husband himself who petitioned for leniency [...],"[74] therefore the conviction was no longer an impediment.[75] However, the letter of the Law was clear that the supposed "lapse" did not apply, as Brandenburg found in the documents of the Vienna Appellate Court, specifying the grounds on which it ruled in favor of Beethoven and again excluded Johanna from guardianship in 1820.[76]

The Sterbas also claimed that Beethoven constantly lied in court about Johanna's character, supporting their argument with the 1819 court decision that dismissed Beethoven's statements as "unproved chatter."[77] As Johanna had not been convicted of adultery during her marriage and the living proof of her promiscuity—her visible pregnancy while not married—was still months ahead, the court's decision is understandable, but it does not prove that Beethoven was lying. We now know, from Brandenburg's article and other testimonies, that Johanna was indeed a morally corrupt person—a thief, a liar, a conniving, frivolous, and very likely adulterous woman. Granted, the Sterbas could not know Brandenburg's 1988 published article and we may forgive them for discarding the testimonies gathered by Thayer, which lacked specifics. But even so, we must reevaluate the situation based on the evidence that now exists. One can therefore acquit Beethoven of the Sterbas' accusation of having consciously lied in Court. Yes, he did write some lies in his letter to the courts—for instance when claiming in 1818 that "everybody who is closely acquainted with me knows only too well that all verbal communications between me and my nephew and other people as well are carried on with the greatest ease and are by no means impeded by my indifferent hearing."[78] But he did not lie about his sister-in-law.

In fact, it was Johanna who lied in court during the suit she initiated in 1818. When, after Beethoven's previously described "language slip" revealed to the judge the false nobility both sides, the judge questioned them; we have their answers in the form registered by the court. Johanna said that "the brothers" had told her they were noble and that Beethoven "was said" to have the documentary proof. Interestingly, she added: "At the legal hearing on the death of her husband, proof of nobility had been demanded"[79] — an obvious lie meant to cover her. Beethoven did not lie; he explained that "*van* was a Dutch predicate which was not exclusively applied to the nobility" and that "he had neither a diploma nor any other proof of his nobility."[80] The judge sent the case to the lower court for commoner (the *Magistrat*), which Beethoven painfully resented, complaining repeatedly to his friends that, although he was not noble, he did not "belong to this plebeian m[ass]."[81]

Beethoven may not have lied, but still had to "influence" the Court in a different issue: the Law was both on his side and against him. The aforementioned exclusionary clause of the guardianship law also included people "suffering from mental or physical infirmity"[82] and his deafness could possibly have qualified as such. One may wonder, then, why two courts *did* grant guardianship to Beethoven. Which of the two, "the friends' influence" or his celebrity status, helped the judges ruling on the 1816 case to close their eyes to this fact is a matter of speculation: at the time, they may have determined that his deafness had not yet reached a critical point and he could still communicate orally (conversation books came into use only in 1818-19). Three years later, however, the situation was entirely different. Beethoven's complete deafness was by then well-known to every Viennese, so the court should have disqualified him.[*] And the Sterbas are probably right to point (190) to an entry in a conversation book saying "Schmerling helped a great deal" and to emphasize that this Schmerling, an in-law of Beethoven's friends the Giannatasios, "was at this time a judge at the Appellate Court and had sufficient influence to obtain a decision in Ludwig's favor"—that is, persuading the court to ignore Beethoven's deafness. Excluding Johanna from guardianship was a completely different issue: her 1811 condemnation disqualified her, as emphasized by the Appellate Court document detailing the grounds on which the court based its 1820 decision.

However, Beethoven was not the only one to "influence" the courts. Generally speaking, corruption was not a common issue in the Habsburg courts, but "influencing" was possible, because of a particular feature of the Austrian judicial system: it allowed the litigants to write to and to meet the judges in private to present their arguments.[83] Both Beethoven and his sister-in-law made use of this loophole and it is obvious that a young and attractive woman, who knew how to use her charm—an old trump card of "frivolous women"—was much better-suited to this context than a cantankerous, deaf old man. Beethoven may have used his influential friends to get a final, irrevocable, and favorable decision in 1816, but Johanna was apparently more adept at "influence" during her appeal trial. She had also strong arguments: she had consistently and verifiably been barred from seeing her son, who lived with an old deaf man known as being unable to maintain a home in a sanitary condition. And, as we know, "she knew how to present her despair in burning colors and with dramatic effect." She must have succeeded in "influencing." Otherwise, one cannot explain how this court came to the conclusion that her 1811 felony was only a minor "transgression," even though they must have had access to the full records of the police investigation, which showed the much wider scope of her offence. Beethoven complained repeatedly in his "Memorandum" to the Court that Johanna exerted "influence" on the court magistrates[84] and he was not the only one to notice that. So did Matthias von Tuscher, a member of the same court, who was appointed Karl's co-guardian by the court in March, when Beethoven—now deprived of any authority over his nephew, who was living with his

---

[*] Albrecht recently argued, based on inferences from Beethoven's conversation books, that even after starting using them in 1818, the composer was not stone deaf and could, on occasion, communicate orally (Theodore Albrecht, "The Hearing Beethoven: Demythifying the Composer's Deafness" *The Beethoven Journal*, Winter 2019, Vol. 34, Number 2, pp. 44-56).

mother—resigned guardianship. Tuscher resigned a few months later, when he "was compelled to recognize that his colleagues were wholly under the influence of Frau v B and [her lawyer] Hotschevar."[85] Note that Tuscher was not one of Beethoven "toadies" who have been described as lying to please him; his co-guardianship is his only significant appearance in the composer's life, after which he vanishes.

An angel of a child

Sterbas' take of Beethoven's relationship with his nephew is based essentially on their "motherly love" diagnosis, which they specifically designed to this purpose (though they also applied it on a larger scale, for example, in Beethoven's attachment to his brothers). "Motherly love" for Karl, in their model, would have made the composer insanely jealous and scared of losing the object of his love. Distrust (a trait we examined earlier, page 25-26) would have been an adjuvant, detectable in the composer's wild reprimands of Karl for many but (in the scholar's view) largely imagined trespasses.

As for the other half of the couple, Karl, the Sterbas make no factual attempts to define his personality or his feelings for Beethoven in a way that would explain his behavior; indeed, they include just a few scattered phrases like the young boy's "disturbed state" (73) or "a lively, pleasantly intelligent youth" (218) that cannot qualify as showing psychoanalytical or psychological insight. Basically, the Sterbas present Karl merely as an angel slandered by the "evidence conspiracy" even more than his mother; they set it as their first task to expose as biased all testimonies pointing to some very human flaws of his. The only evidence that they accept, but only so long as it fits their case against Beethoven, is what can be found in Fanny Giannatasio's diary. "Her judgement of the relationship between uncle and nephew can be trusted," they admit, but hasten to add, "to be sure, her judgment of Karl varies with Ludwig's feelings toward him" (64), because Fanny gradually fell in love with Beethoven and therefore could not afterwards be held as an impartial witness.

To the contrary, I believe that her accounts are trustworthy about both uncle and nephew without reservation. Acting as her father's right hand in running the boarding school, she had experience as an educator and was in close and frequent contact with both sides. So, let us see what she thought of Karl.

Fanny saw Beethoven's nephew as a gifted child ("one can't help being astonished at his great forwardness for his age"), unfortunately "not naturally truthful, [which] may lead him to indulge in falsehood"; she mentioned later "several misdemeanors of his,"[86] but she described in details only one incident that happened in November 1818. At the time, Karl was no longer with Giannatasio's school and lived with his uncle, but Fanny got news about him, from time to time, from the housekeeper whom the family had recommended to Beethoven. It is from her that Fanny found that Karl "had talked abusively to the servants and had kept back money from them to buy sweets" (as mentioned above on page 25). The Sterbas twisted this account to find fault with Beethoven: "the boy's actions, though reprehensible, are easy to understand. In abusing the servants, he was only imitating the example which the uncle all too

40

frequently set him, and Ludwig's parsimony probably made it impossible for the boy to satisfy his childish appetite for sweets" (140). Beethoven was certainly not a good role model—and he knew it, as he warned Karl quite often, "not to act like his uncle," as Fanny recorded[87]—but stealing? As we know, the boy had had a much stronger example of such behavior in his mother.

Why would Karl have been "not naturally truthful?" Modern pediatrics has confirmed the Freudian principle (albeit with a different foundation) that childhood plays an important part in the development of personality. It is obvious that Karl's bent for lying originated in his early childhood, when his mother had passed to him the lesson that her father taught her: how to steal (see page 31-32). She certainly modeled his character in other directions: she liked to "splurge" and she spoiled him, for instance by stuffing him with sweets and even "strong drinks"—one of Beethoven's complaints when the boy ran to his mother.[88] It is also likely that Beethoven was speaking the truth when later writing to the court that she made Karl "help her deceive his own father."[89] This side of the story is missing in the Sterba book, although they do quote (54) Karl's entry about his mother teaching him repeatedly her lesson in stealing when he was a child.

Let us now attempt to assess what feelings the young boy developed for his uncle, in response to the latter's behavior towards him. Certainly, like everybody around him, Karl was entranced by Beethoven's music. A story, quoted by the Sterbas (63), shows the boy sleeping in his uncle's lap amidst a company listening to music and waking up when the familiar tones sounded, saying, "this is the music of my uncle." The boy must also have been impressed by the veneration that important grown-ups, including counts and princesses, showered upon his uncle. He must have understood that his uncle loved him—albeit in an uneven manner—and that he cared for him, and paid for him to get a good foundation in life. However, he must also have understood that the uncle hated his mother and tried to prevent her from meeting him. He, Karl, loved his mother and knew that she loved him—and also that liked to show her love by pampering him, which his uncle, an adept of austere, Spartan-like manners, would not do. This conflict must have induced more than simply a "disturbed state" (Sterba, page 73) in very young Karl. He could not love a man who claimed to love him as a father but forbade him to see his beloved mother. To use a Sterba favorite, Karl had very ambiguous feelings towards his uncle. Being "naturally untruthful" (Fanny's description) he developed duplicitous tactics, which emulated his mother's propensities for lying and deception. And Beethoven, a very poor pedagogue, did not understand that he was actually co-operating with his sister-in-law by aggravating his nephew's (natural or acquired) deceitful demeanors.

For the period after 1818, when Beethoven had withdrawn his nephew from the Giannatasio school, we have to rely primarily on the evidence left by Beethoven's friends: the ones that the Sterba couple emphatically rejects as member of the mentioned "evidence conspiracy." The only clear evidence that they could advance for their conspiracy theory comes from the German Thayer-Deiters-Riemann version of Thayer's *Life of Beethoven*, mentioning "Karl's inclination for pleasure, for neglecting his duties, for associating with unsuitable companions did not decrease" (Sterba, 269), which was not included in the 1966 English version by Forbes (probably because it must have originated with Schindler—who had been exposed long ago as an inveterate biographical forger). When we examine closer their evidence, we discover that the conspiracy theory does not hold much water. Beethoven's "slaves" and "toadies" unanimously described his sister-in-law Johanna as a morally shameful woman—and, as we saw, with good reason—but they were far more nuanced about his nephew. It is true that some of Thayer-collected testimonies of "unpardonable behavior" or Karl being "naturally inclined to indolence and self-indulgence"[90] are not supported by any source, but he duly recorded both the good and the bad opinions: "[Karl] was at heart not a bad child but had been harmed by bad examples [...] has little spirit despite the knowledge for which he is prized [...] is behaving himself the way you would expect from a reasonable person." A similar suspicion entered in a conversation book that, when Karl reached twenty, "he was heavily in debt" is voided by another one saying, "[...] everything is paid for [...]."[91] Therefore this evidence is reliable and it sometimes confirms even the swindling Schindler.

This November 1818 incident was crucial because of its outcome, which only confirmed Fanny's dark predictions about the future of Beethoven's relationship with his nephew. The composer had remonstrated Karl so toughly— he had grabbed him by the neck and shaken him—that the boy fled to his mother, who took Beethoven to Court in a two-year long, humiliating and painful process that I presented succinctly before and in which he first lost and finally won. The nephew's statements in court were not particularly damaging to Beethoven: generally speaking, the boy "would have liked to live at his uncle's if he had but a companion, as his uncle was hard of hearing and he could not talk to him." It is true that his uncle "punished him often, but only when he deserved it; he had been maltreated only once [...];"[92] Of course, not satisfied with this deposition, the Sterbas warn us that the nephew was lying in order not to offend his uncle (143). The alleged "Beethoven toadies" have only good things to write about Karl's behavior in their conversations books during the long trial. Peters, as newly appointed co-guardian, praises his "gentle, expressive physiognomy and excellent attitude," and assures Beethoven that "he studies Greek assiduously." Blöchlinger, in whose boarding school Karl ended up after Giannatasio refused to have him back and another school proved unsatisfactory, reassures the composer that his nephew "works better in math" and "he has no mistakes in his essays and the oral examinations have always been very good."[93] Beethoven's own discontent, expressed in some letters—the worst of which is displayed in the July 1819 letter to Karl Bernard, in which he claims, "my patience is at an end, I have cast him out of my heart"[94]—stems from the boy's mother's struggle to get Beethoven out of Karl's life. When Beethoven finally won back guardianship of Karl in Court, the boy was thirteen years old—a teenager. For a very long time, the biographers paid little attention to this fact. Thayer briefly mentioned the "spirit of rebellion which grew with his [Karl's] advance towards manhood"[95] but this is an understatement. The Sterbas refer briefly to "this period of self-discovery and of rebellion" in Karl's life, but describe the rebellion as directed "against the stigmata of childhood" (218); they do not explain what "stigmata" means, but we can assume that it was the suffering from being separated from his mother, for which Beethoven was to be blamed. Even when they accept that Karl would do bad things such as lying and neglecting his school work, they blame Beethoven for it. Sometimes he would set a bad example: when Karl expressed arrogant airs of superiority in several Conversations books entries—a typical teen behavior—he would have been only adopting his uncle's own attitude toward people (his professors, brother Johann, aristocracy, all women) summing up, "the uncle is speaking through the nephew" (217). In a more sophisticated, psychoanalytic interpretation, Beethoven was guilty of pushing Karl to be bad: the boy's "love for his mother expressed itself in the form of identification [and] since his uncle represented his mother to be so bad, he became 'bad' himself" (199). Overall, the Sterbas describe teenage Karl as (218) "a lively, pleasantly intelligent youth in the bloom of adolescence, with the increased self-esteem and typical arrogance of this particular age." We suspect, however, that this lovely picture must be wrong. As popular wisdom has known for ages, a teenager can hardly be described in Sterbas' terms.

Stefan Wolf is, the my knowledge, the first to present the relationship between Beethoven and his nephew as part of a "puberty conflict" in his 1995 book *Beethovens Neffenkonflikt* (i.e., Beethoven's conflict with his nephew).[96] Barry Cooper also refers to Wolf's book for details when describing succinctly the events as "adolescent conflict" in his biography of Beethoven.[97] As I showed earlier, after year 2000, psychiatry and neuro-science have discovered why the "teenage years" (a pattern which may even extend in the early twenties)[98] is a very peculiar and important period in the development of personality, marked by inward and outward conflicts that usually lead, especially with boys, to weird and violent acts, more often than not directed at parental authority. Human nature was certainly the same two hundred years ago, as illustrated—again—in the life of Beethoven's beloved Josephine, whose son Fritz Deym displayed plenty of "adolescent boorishness" that horrified the family enough to leave traces in their memoirs.[99] It is true that teenagers were, at the time, subject to different societal rules that curbed their encroaches: most of the young would start to work physically before entering their teens, and work may induce discipline as well as responsibility, curb rebelliousness and accelerate maturing. At fourteen, Beethoven had been the main bread-winner of his parents' family and the de facto head of household by seventeen. Karl's development was different, as his uncle only asked of him to learn in order to become a "true Beethoven," which is not dissimilar to what today's parents ask of their children. Like Fritz Deym, he was very much a modern "spoiled brat" who must have at times driven his uncle crazy.

Judging from this perspective, the evidence recorded by Thayer sounds much more plausible than the portrait of an angelic victim advocated by the Sterbas. Admittedly, Beethoven showed no psychological or pedagogical depth in his dealings with his nephew's new personality and Holz's later statement that the composer "was rigorous to excess in his treatment and would not allow the slightest extravagance,"[100] is a far better description of the situation than the

Sterbas'. We do not possess many details about the goings on in this particular case, but we have a few hints pointing to the typical teenage ordeal familiar to many parents. At the time, it was not known that teenagers sleep longer hours not for being lazy, but because, as neuro-science has discovered, their development requires more sleep.[101] It is very likely that Karl did the same, as Blöchlinger, the director of the school where the latter was boarded, reported in an 1820 conversation book entry.[102] Karl wrote himself therein, "tomorrow I shall go to no professor, for I will get up only after 10 hours sleep" (217).[103] It is no surprise that Beethoven was exasperated by his nephew's "laziness" and urged him repeatedly, "get up early in the morning" and "give less time to sleep" in letters[104] and probably oftener in real life. This must have certainly irritated the youngster and embittered the relationship. Like Fritz Deym, Karl wanted to become a soldier,[105] while Beethoven hoped that he would be "an artist or scholar in order to live a high life."[106] His choice of friends was another source of conflict: an 1824 conversation book passage containing also Beethoven's entry shows his dissatisfaction with Karl's close relationship with a certain Niemetz, a boarding school mate.[107] It is likely that the friends were also responsible for what may have been a peak of the clash, an incident of drunkenness in 1823, in which Karl's defiance turned physical. The Sterbas, whom we must credit for objectively relating the event (238), quote the conversation book entry in which a contrite Karl asks his uncle forgiveness and promises never to drink again:

> Dearest father, you can be convinced that the hurt I caused you distresses me more than it does you. Anxiety has restored my reason to me, and I see what I have done. If I had to think that you believe that I purposely acted in this way, I should be inconsolable. It just happened in drunkenness. If you can forgive me, I promise you that I will surely drink not another drop, so that I shall never get into such a condition again [...] Forgive me only this once! I will surely drink no more wine, it was all because of it that I could no longer contain myself and did not know where I was. Again I beg you, forgive me!

The atonement sounds sincere and the Sterbas conclude, "it appears that this was a wholly isolated occurrence." However, the apology may have been just one of the mentioned duplicitous stratagems used by Karl. In fact, violence—whether or not accompanied by drunkenness is not known—seems to have occurred again, as suggested by an 1826 entry by Holz ("I came in just as he took you by the breast").[108] This incident was perhaps the beginning of the last act of Karl's "martyrdom."

We should not be deceived by the just-quoted "dearest father," a formula repeated several time in Karl's letters. His true feelings for his uncle are revealed in a note scribbled to a friend and found among the composer's papers, naming him "the old fool."[109] And yet we should not hold this against Karl either: it was perhaps inevitable that his already "ambiguous" feelings for his uncle did not change into filial love, but rather take a turn for the worse following clashes during his teenage years. The duplicitous tactics that he developed as a child grew into more elaborate strategies as part of his survival skills. Schindler reportedly heard him saying, "My uncle! I can do with him what I want, some flattery and a friendly gestures make things all right again right away." Of course, the reporter has been discredited and the Sterbas refuted him as a witness, but this account was confirmed by Holz.[110] We must also receive skeptically assurances that Beethoven's other sister-in-law, Therese, presented to him when he and Karl lived at his brother Johann's property in the fall of 1826, "It is you that he [Karl] loves, to the point of veneration."[111] If the youth had not put on a very good act, fooling Therese, she was just trying to comfort Beethoven.

To sum up: the relationship between Beethoven and his nephew during the latter's teenage year was a clash between two irreconcilable powers: one that tried to control everything and impose some (not always sensible) reason, the other one that rejected any control and "mature" reason. And, as I showed, the exchange of was totally skewed. Conflicts were bound to escalate and yield what the Sterbas named "Karl's martyrdom," culminating in his suicide attempt and followed by Beethoven's final sickness and death.

Before the escalation, however, a different form of misunderstanding between the two developed when Johanna, a single woman, became pregnant, which became noticeable by June 1820.[112] Karl, now a fourteen-year old boy, must have been affected by the event, but the account that the Sterbas give of his reaction is strange. First, they claim that "we do not know how Karl reacted to his mother's bearing a second child," but revert one line further: "[a]t first he seems to have been angry with his mother. We can conclude this from the fact that for a time he shared Ludwig's hostility to Johanna" (203). The youth's negative attitude toward his mother grew even worse a few years later, when Beethoven, learning that Johanna was sick and in dire straits after the birth of her daughter, helped her financially. His goodwill is evidenced in several letters to Bernard, who was acting as his counselor, in which he wrote that he had decided to let his sister-in-law have all the pension left by her dead husband (she was obliged to contribute half of it to her son's welfare) and was "prepared to help in any way." Although he did not "want to have anything to do with her personally," he also wrote her on January 8 to let her know his decision and did not forget to "wish you all possible happiness,"[113] which may have sounded rather callous after all the suffering he had forced on her. Karl entered his opposition to his uncle's resolution in strong words in the conversation books: "Although she is my mother, I must admit that I think you should first inquire fully into her circumstances. For it could easily be that such a contribution would enable her even more to continue evil life [...]" (231).[114] This is his earliest known statement acknowledging his mother's low morality, but the Sterbas see it as expressing only sibling jealousy (231). The explanation is hardly credible in the case of a fourteen-years-old. The more plausible explanation is shame. The Sterbas' statement that "illegitimate children were by no means unusual in this period ... an illegitimate child was by no means such a disgrace as, in itself, to brand Johanna as a whore" (203), is only a half truth. As I have shown, illegitimacy was rare among the middle class (page 30 of this essay) and Karl must have been ashamed when asked by his boarding school mates, "Is it true that your mother is pregnant?" He must have also been ashamed when repeating, in an entry in a conversation book, gossip heard from his other uncle, Beethoven's brother Johann: "the child [...] is by Raicz, a Hungarian who was studying medicine here, and was a roomer with us even in my father's lifetime; but Hofbauer [the alleged father] does not know this and believes it is his" (231).[115] Gossip may be frequently untrue, yet it can still hurt. Karl must have seen in all these reports a confirmation—and not a simple repetition, as the Sterbas claim (231)—of old "accusations" thrown at her mother.

Beethoven's suddenly compassionate attitude towards his sister-in-law when she was sick and in financial difficulties was in too stark a contrast to the black portrait painted by the Sterba couple, forcing them to search for an explanation. They devised a rather convoluted one: Beethoven had rekindled his relationship with his brother Johann, who came to live in Vienna for a number of years, which occasioned the renewal of the composer's clashes with his other sister-in-law, Therese, whom he also deemed as a "bad woman."[*] This would, according to the Sterbas, explain his change of heart toward Johanna: "it is as if at this time Therese had drawn all his hatred of women upon herself. Then, too, his child was with him and he enjoyed complete possession of his 'precious treasure'" (243). It is true that Beethoven might have considered Johanna less of a threat now that she had a baby to take care of, which would leave her much less time to spend with Karl. The two psychoanalysts fail to notice that one of their favorite psychological diagnosis was also very likely—feelings of guilt. And I think that Beethoven's compassion and help were most likely directed at Johanna's baby.

Karl's "martyrdom" and his suicide attempt

According to the Sterba couple, 1825 was the beginning of the end—of Beethoven's relationship with his nephew and of his own life. By that time, he had alienated all his friends, chased Schindler away and made his nephew into his personal secretary (to replace Schindler), overwhelming him with tasks at the worst time, as Karl should have been studying assiduously for admission to the Viennese Polytechnic Institute. As usual, the two scholars reject all testimonies about the nephew's flaws and faults, claiming that they come from biased sources (Beethoven's "slaves" or "toadies") and they retain only those of the Karl's tutors, who were satisfied with his academic progress (269, 271), and some of his entries in the conversation books that exhibit more maturity and calm than his uncle (247, 251). Also, Beethoven's love would have become so possessive and controlling, that he started "poisoning" and "martyrizing" the poor youth to the point that Karl broke down and tried to kill himself (279).

Their main evidence about the "martyrdom" comes from the thirty-five letters that the musician wrote Karl during the summer of 1825, some of which literally cascaded (five between May 17 and 19). The summer of 1825 was a

---

[*] This is not without reason. Her own husband, after siding with her for many years, against Beethoven's opinion, had to accept the evidence and, since divorce was not possible in a Catholic country, initiated a de facto separation from her (Thayer-Forbes 1006, quoting a letter of Johann to Beethoven).

perfect period for the Sterbas to illustrate their indictment because Beethoven and his nephew were not living together (hence the avalanche of letters). In the spring of 1825, Karl left Beethoven's house and entered the Polytechnic Institute, moving into the lodgings of Schlemmer, a government official who took it upon himself (at the composer's request) to supervise his nephew's activities.[116] At the same time, Dr. Franz Reisser, the vice-director of the Polytechnic Institute, was appointed Karl's co-guardian—a "political" move arranged by Beethoven's friend Stephen von Breuning, a man with a larger network of relationships. Neither man was part of Beethoven's close circle and, although their names appear quite often in the conversation books, they never met him before Karl's suicide attempt. Like every year, the composer moved to Baden in late spring to evade the oppressive Viennese heat wave and remained there alone for almost six months, while his nephew stayed in the city to study. In the thirty-five letters Beethoven sent, accusations (the old ones) alternate with wholehearted tenderness (Come to my arms!), demands (send me chocolate, bell-pull) with complaints (Ah, the servants! Ah, I'm alone!), veiled threats (to end guardianship) with exhortations to come and visit (256-259). The shrink/prosecutors, overcome by the delight at their diagnosis of Beethoven's psychopathy, never look at the man beyond these letters. They proffer one kind sentence, "Ludwig too was the victim of terrible mental torments" and immediately add, "caused by his jealousy, his distrust, the disappointment of his demand to possess the object of his love, and his growing fear of losing Karl" (244).

But Beethoven is at a very critical moment of his life. He knows that he is approaching old age. Isn't it normal that he cling desperately to his own kin, the only Beethoven that he knows in the whole world who can carry his name along as a "notable" like himself, as an artist or a scholar?[106] This summer is an ordeal for him. Certainly, he is working at his last quartets, but his daily routine, that Schindler duly recorded,[117] leaves him plenty of time to feel alone in the afternoons and evenings, and he does not know what his beloved "son" does, whether he studies diligently to become at least a scholar if not an artist. In fact he had reason to be concerned, since Karl had mentioned his desire to become a "soldier" the previous year and, although he had promised "I will not do anything without your consent and will, if you wish, continue to study,"[118] one could never tell. The avalanche of letters, both loving or resentful, becomes, if not forgivable, at least understandable.

We have less such evidence beginning the late fall of 1825, when Beethoven moved back to Vienna and was closer to his nephew and, consequently, wrote far fewer (only six) short letters to him, of which only one (in June 1826) hints at some misunderstanding.[119] His name occurs frequently in the testimonies of Beethoven's friends—especially Holz, who had replaced Schindler as his unpaid secretary—and they do not sound damaging to Karl's reputation. There are not many entries from Karl himself, which show that he did not visit often (a reason for some remonstrations) but only the ones toward the beginning of summer foresee trouble. Although what caused Beethoven's reprimands is unknown, some grounds are easy to guess and other ones can be reasonably linked to the uncle's "jealousy" or the nephew's alleged or real "frivolity" or "spirit of insolence," to use Thayer's description.

The drama unfolds in the full summer of 1826. On July 29, Karl leaves Schlemmer's house, telling Schlemmer's wife—or at least letting her guess—that he is going to kill himself.[120] She alerts her husband, who searches his house and finds and seizes two pistols, then warns Holz. Holz runs to tell Beethoven and a frantic search for the young man begins that leads nowhere, because after Karl bought other two pistols, he traveled to Baden where he spent the night. The next morning, Karl walks in the Hellenenthal valley—his uncle's favorite saunter—puts both pistols to his left temple and fires. One bullet misses completely and the other one wounds him superficially, remaining under his skin without penetrating the thin temple bone. He is found wounded but conscious and able to ask to be taken to his mother, who gives the news to Beethoven.

The Sterba couple's explanation of Karl's act appears reasonable (277):

> [A]n immense quantity of aggression against his tormentor, for which he could have no outlet, must have piled up in him" that he could not discharge "upon the powerful man to whom he was delivered over body and soul. Whose fame and greatness overwhelmed him, yet to whom he could not but feel bound to be grateful [...] There remained only one possible way for him to vent his monstrously increasing hatred. He must turn it upon himself.

However, I think there is far more to it. There is clear evidence of the "teenage brain" in Karl's suicide attempt. The conflict between the teenager and the adult world may reach a breaking point. Indeed, modern statistics have shown that suicidal thoughts are relatively frequent during teenagers—up to thirty percent of high school students consider it as an option[121]—even though a much lower fraction resorts to it. I think it is reasonable to assume that, since human nature has not changed fundamentally in millennia, the same pattern observed today would apply two hundred years ago. After this attempt, Karl made an interesting confession when he was arrested and interrogated (attempted suicide being a crime at the time): "I grew worse because my uncle wanted me to be better."[122] Doesn't this sounds like a *déjà-vu*, more exactly a *déjà-entendu* [heard]? I would call it a typical teenager statement, even though he was twenty-years-old at the time. It also shows that he knew he had been less than good and had even become worse, a description that hardly fits the one presented by the Sterba couple; it comes as no surprise that they omit this confession in their book. Barry Cooper also describes Karl's suicide attempt as "a classic adolescent crisis, in which suicide seemed the only way of escape [...]" The scholar goes even further, writing:

> As in many suicide attempts, Karl did not really want to die. Otherwise he would surely not have aimed so carelessly—twice—nor would he have revealed his intentions the previous week. In two minds, he played a kind of Russian roulette, aiming the pistol near enough his head to risk death and leaving himself in the hand of fate, which decreed he should live."[123]

Cooper is, to my knowledge, the first Beethoven scholar to suggest that Karl's attempt was a sham.[*] But two of the people who were close to the event had thought this at the time, and Franz Reisser and Matthias Schlemmer were not biased Beethoven "slaves" or "toadies." The former was a pro-forma "co-guardian" who barely appears in the record; the latter lodged Karl in his house and supervised him during his university years. Following Karl's act, once the commotion has subsided, Holz wrote in the conversation book that, hearing of Karl's suicide attempt, Reisser exclaimed "Spoiled brat—a comedy character!" As for Schlemmer, he entered in the same book a few days later, "if he had planned to kill himself, he certainly wouldn't have told it to anyone, let alone to a woman known for prattling."[124] The Sterbas ignored these entries, although they are on the same pages of the conversation books from which they amply quoted.

One would expect that Karl's long "martyrdom" and his suicide attempt would have left him with some psychological problems for life, but there is no evidence of that. Even the Sterbas are surprised (301) that his "traumatic experiences [...] had no perceptible ill effect on the development of his personality." After a short and unremarkable military career, Karl married and had five children, and lived quite comfortably, first from Beethoven's inheritance, to which an even more considerable one was added from his other uncle, Johann, who died childless.[125] It seems that the "martyrdom" was less so than the Sterbas claim.

Karl's suicide attempt failed, but succeeded beyond his expectations in changing his relationship with Beethoven. As the Sterbas put it, "through the act he had psychologically 'liquidated' his uncle" (282). Beethoven was grief-stricken to learn that his nephew accused him of being at the root of his desperate act. Indeed, Holz did not spare him and reported Karl's statements in Court: "He [Karl] said that he wanted to put an end to these recriminations [...] [he said] if only he did not bear your name! [...] he said that he will tear off his bandages again if you're name came up [...] you reprimanded him too much, you caused his act."[126] Beethoven also suffered to discover that many other people placed part of the blame upon him.[127] He would still put on a few more recriminating scenes in the future, but he gave in on every important issue and agreed to his nephew's plan of joining the army—an idea that he loathed, not only because it killed his dream of making his Karl into a "true Beethoven," but also because he was going to lose his presence.

"Liquidating" Beethoven

The Sterbas' term "liquidated" is almost literally right. Karl's act was an emotional or, better said, physiological blow that aged Beethoven overnight, as noted by all those that were closest to him. "The once sturdy, vigorous body now stood before us like an old man of nearly seventy, broken in will [...]"—in one

---

[*] Marek (p. 521 footnote) summed up the scholarly opinion that there is "no corroboration" for the idea of a simulated suicide attempt.

of Schindler's uncontested testimony.[128] It was in fact the beginning of Beethoven's end. He would succumb to the first sickness that struck him a few months later, probably because his suffering weakened very much his immune system that had helped him cope with many such occurrences before. And Karl might have been even directly responsible for Beethoven's untimely death.

Beethoven tried to delay the fateful parting with his beloved "son," in spite of his friends' persistent advice to let his nephew become a "Soldier at once," as Holz put it.[129] Under the pretext to give time for Karl's wounds to heal and be covered by hair (so they would not be visible when he joined the army), Beethoven accepted his brother's invitation to stay, together with his nephew, for a few months at his brother's residence near Linz, a city in Western Austria, far from Vienna. The sojourn proved disastrous. Karl, eager to leave and get away from his uncle whose presence he had come to loathe, was sullen and taciturn; Beethoven, with his usual lack of perception, restarted his incriminations, evidenced in the conversation books.[130] His relationship with his brother and sister-in-law, which had never been amiable, turned worse and his health began to deteriorate. When the crisis reached the high point at the beginning of winter in November, he decided to leave overnight, took the two-days-long journey back to Vienna in an open carriage, spent a night at an inn in an unheated room, and arrived in Vienna sick and feverish on December 2, a Saturday.[131] He was not seen by a physician until December 5, why which time he was already very sick.

Why were two days lost? The evidence about these days is thinner than usual. Some pages in the conversation books are missing, presumably removed by Schindler—but why? Schindler, who hated Karl, later accused him of having gone to play pool instead of looking for a physician.[132] Thayer's findings in the conversation books exonerated the nephew, but the question still persists: what happened in those two days? According to Beethoven's brother Johann, the musician wrote his personal physician, Braunhofer, who refused to come, pretexting that the distance was too great; a second physician, Staudenheim, promised to come and did not![133] Such dishonorable behavior of two members of a highly respected profession is hard to credit. One wonders from whom Johann, who arrived in Vienna later,[134] got this information—it could have been only from the composer or from Karl. A third doctor, Ignatz Wawruch, came immediately, although he did not know Beethoven personally—but this happened only on the 5th of December, when Holz came and took the matter in his hands. Why did Holz show up that late? He received Beethoven's letter saying, "I wrote to you immediately after my arrival [...] but the letter was mislaid. Then I fell ill and so ill that I think it is wiser to stay in bed."[135] Of course, an unfortunate accident might have resulted in Holz's delayed arrival, but what did Karl do during those two days when he could see his uncle falling very sick? A loving son would have looked for a physician, an easy task in a city that was no more than 3.5 kilometers (2 mi) in diameter—who would have refused to answer the call of one of the most famous living men in Europe? I do not mean that Karl deliberately let his uncle without medical care for two days to get rid of him; he simply did not care enough. He was not a loving son, although he was brazen enough to sign so a later letter to his dying uncle.[136]

It is almost one hundred percent certain that his nephew also hastened Beethoven's death considerably. Dr. Wawruch, who attended the musician, left a poignant testimony to that. His treatment seemed to have set his patient on the path to recovery, but, the physician's testimony says,

> On the eight day I was really shocked. At my morning visit I found him distraught with his body jaundiced all over; a terrible diarrhea with vomiting had threatened to kill him during the previous night. A violent rage, a deep woe about suffering ingratitude and undeserved insults caused the mighty explosion. Trembling and shivering, he was convulsed with pain that raged in the liver and intestines. His feet, which had only been moderately bloated, were now massively swollen. From this moment on dropsy developed.[137]

Beethoven never uttered the name of the one that had caused his collapse; neither did his friends who assisted him during his final months and who must have guessed who the culprit was. Even the Sterbas acknowledge matter-of-factly (294) that "it is probable that a last conflict with his nephew disastrously checked the recovery which had begun." Ironically, they also claim on the next page that "Karl cared for him [Beethoven] almost as an experienced, solicitous mother cares for her unreasonable sick child." Was that the result of his feeling of guilt—one of the favorite psychological devices invoked by the nephew's two apologists, the Sterbas?

De-Sterbasing Beethoven

In final analysis, we can dismiss the Sterba couple's tightly connected claims that Beethoven was a "subconscious homosexual" and that he "identified" with his mother in his relationship with his nephew, synthetized as a pathological "motherly love." What can we put in their place to explain his behavior?

Psychoanalysis is certainly right to stress the importance of childhood in the development of human personality. Modern psychiatry has indeed shown that adults tend to reproduce the family model they grow in by adopting parental "role model," a concept similar to that of "identification," a classical term in psychoanalysis. For instance, a child raised in a dysfunctional family is very likely to have, in his adult stage, a dysfunctional family and an unbalanced report with the other sex.[138] We know little about the family that Beethoven grew in, but the testimonies are unanimous in presenting his father as a harsh parent, who tormented his child by forcing him to exercise excessively, with a hope to make him a child prodigy like Mozart.[139] The mother was the "loving" parent, whom Beethoven himself described as "my best friend."[140] Undoubtedly, in his relationship with his nephew, Beethoven tried to compensate parental harshness with parental love, and only his mother (perhaps, also, Helene von Breuning, in whose family he was practically adopted as a teenager) could be his role model. However, like in the typical family of the age, the father must have been young Beethoven's expected "role model" and there is no reason to think that his mother replaced the father in that role. As a child, he certainly suffered from his father's severity, but he appears to have forgiven it later in life. Ries offers a remarkable testimony about Beethoven's attitude towards the memory of his father: "He did not like talking about his father, who was mainly at fault for the family misfortunes, but any harsh word about him let fall by a third person made Beethoven angry."[141] In fact, he emulated his father in his harsh treatment of his nephew, whom he required to study assiduously both music and academic disciplines in order to become a "true Beethoven." In this respect at least, he behaved as if he had "identified" with his father.

To the Sterbas, Beethoven's rise to the role of head of the family after his mother's death, when he was only sixteen, was just another reason for his "ambivalent" feelings towards her. I could not find, in the existing evidence, any trace of this ambivalence in his personality, but it is clear that becoming head of household at such a young age contributed greatly to make him into a domineering person, who wanted to control his siblings and, later, his nephew's life in every aspect. This added to what may have been a suspicion-minded inclination, a flaw that further circumstances, primarily his life tragedy—the loss of his hearing—aggravated to a point when it bore a psychopathic whiff, a topic I deal with in chapter 6.

This being said, I still think, like the Sterba couple and others scholars, that Beethoven's behavior in his association with his nephew and his mother was borderline psychopathic. I would describe it as the "Sarastro Syndrome." Sarastro is, obviously, the character in Mozart's opera *The Magic Flute*, which, incidentally, Beethoven highly valued. The opera is essentially a rescue story,* opposing two characters: Sarastro, the high priest of a prodigious brotherhood—supposedly modeled after the Masonic order, to which Mozart himself belonged—which is the promoter of light and of its progenitor, the Sun; and his antagonist the Queen of Night, obviously typifying the darkness with its allies—ignorance, obscurantism, fanaticism, sin and crime. The soul to be rescued is the Queen's daughter, an exceptional child—in an opera, two evil people, the queen and her husband, dead in the confrontation with Sarastro, can easily breed a paragon of virtue. In his wisdom and goodness, Sarastro abducted the queen's daughter in order to rescue her from an evil mother who would have ruined her character and her great future. Beethoven not only appreciated *The Magic Flute* above all other Mozart operas, but he modeled his relationship with his nephew and the latter's mother after this opera. He was Sarastro, the high priest of light and goodness; Johanna incarnated the Queen of Night, the epitome of evil; and her son Karl was the exceptional child (he was a Beethoven!) to be rescued from the evildoing mother. Beethoven pushed the parallel to repeatedly calling Johanna "The Queen of Night" in letters[142] and conversation books; he also once compared himself to Sarastro,[143] which clearly shows that he was perfectly conscious of the "libretto" that he was enacting. He practically abducted Karl from his mother, resorting to all kinds of chicaneries to prevent her from even seeing her son, a right fully recognized by the courts.

---

* The Sterbas also describe Beethoven's action like a "rescue" operation (page 56), but they never pursue the issue.

One wonders how Beethoven could not see beyond the schematic story in a libretto. As we have seen, Johanna had enough human flaws (dishonesty, frivolity) that could have spoiled her son's character—and they probably did to a certain extent when she raised the boy with her husband. Yet Beethoven did not seem to realize that forbidding mother and child to meet actually aggravated those flaws in both of them: the mother used bribery to see her son, and the latter justified said bribery because he desperately wanted her, too. Moreover, in spite of her flaws, Johanna was not murderous like her operatic counterpart. Did Beethoven continue to believe that she had poisoned her husband, even after the autopsy had proven his suspicion unfounded? As I have shown, the Sterbas' claim that he actually did continue believing it is not credible.

He must have thought that a mother was not indispensable to a child's development, even though the mother's essential role was plentifully acknowledged by the pedagogues of his time (including the still-famous Pestalozzi). One wonders also how he could have thought so, even though he had called his mother his "best friend." I can think of several possible reasons why. His classical readings had acquainted him with the bad mother figure (like Agrippina) who was despised and rejected by her son. He knew the nobility life style, where children were not raised by mothers but by wet nurses. The very Austrian law that excluded a mother from the guardianship of her fatherless child if she had a felony conviction was good proof, in his eyes, that the child may do well without a mother. In a "Memorandum" to the Courts, he even claimed that "[…] *our laws in general exclude the mother from the guardianship*" (his italics),[144] even though this was not true. He was not the only man who thought so. The story of Josephine Deym-Stackelberg, the most passionate love of Beethoven, illustrates another such occurrence: in 1814, long after his involvement with her, some members of her own family were concerned about "the physical and moral education of the children" with a "morally unfit" mother like her; this is documented in a letter discovered by Goldschmidt, in which the Police President Hager explained to Josephine's great-uncle the legitimate worries of the co-guardian of her children.[145] In fact Josephine lived through an ordeal similar to the one that Beethoven imposed on his sister-in-law. Eventually, her second husband obtained in court the custody of his own children with her.

Knowing that he was not doing anything illegal would have assuaged Beethoven's feeling that he had at times: that he was morally wrong. Such doubts as well as the help he later extended to Johanna render him more human, but do not absolve him. Even with these "mitigating circumstances," I too think that it takes a real whiff of psychopathy to reason as he most likely did, in spite of his own misgivings.

I do not intend to add the "Sarastro Syndrome" as another psychopathy to the long enough list of "personality disorders" in the psychiatric manuals. It is a specific form of "self-righteousness" that includes in Beethoven's case both typical and atypical elements of several such diseases, like narcissistic personality disorder, paranoia and obsessive-compulsive disorder. I say "both typical and atypical" because, as I argue in chapter 6, which deals with *Beethoven's Raptus*, there is plenty of evidence that Beethoven's psychological problems are as complex as his whole personality and are mostly the result of his personal drama—losing his hearing.

3
Beethoven on Maynard Solomon's couch

Maynard Solomon subscribes to the Sterba couple's psychoanalytical approach to Beethoven's life, but he expands it considerably, adding an entirely novel Freudian line of thought: the "family romance." He introduced this in his biography of Beethoven, published in 1977 and re-issued in a revised form in 1998, which benefitted from further elaborations in his book *Beethoven Essays* (1988). Unless specified otherwise, citations and page numbers in this chapter refer to the 1998 revised version.[1] I will touch on the other innovations in his work later.

The Sterba inheritance

Foreseeably, Solomon accepts many of the basic assessments of his older psychoanalytical peers in his biography of Beethoven. One finds "negative feelings towards mother" with their many repercussions in the composer's life, and the now-familiar "homosexual implications," all on the same page (29). He also shares many of the Sterbas' views on Beethoven's relationship with his nephew. However, he does not subscribe to the "identification with mother" theory and contends (commonsensically) that "there is abundant evidence that Beethoven's strivings were of a paternal nature" (327). He also sounds very much in accord with the statistical findings of modern psychology when writing, "[...] symptoms such as those manifested by Beethoven [in the relationship with his nephew] are most often a continuation of, and are modeled on, archaic conflicts dating from infancy and childhood." Indeed, as I have shown, the composer also emulated his father's severity in his dealings with his nephew. Unfortunately, the shrink cannot refrain from lapsing into pure Freudianism next: "on another level, Beethoven's actions can be understood as a series of violent alternations between incestuous and matricidal drives" (326) which later escalate: "[Karl] may be also have been a revenant of the first born [brother of the composer] Ludwig Maria, subject, therefore, to the vicissitudes of Beethoven's fratricidal and fraternal impulses" (328)—fortunately, Solomon does not transmute the last *may* into an *is/does* this time.

Solomon also maintains that Johanna was denigrated by "the prejudiced writings of Beethoven, his associates, and early biographers" (301). Although he quotes Brandenburg's work about Johanna's 1811 crime, he persists in calling her theft attempt a "minor offence" (300) and he qualifies Beethoven's statements about her low morality as "persecutory and sexual fantasies" (304). He lists Marek's biography of the composer among his "Selected Bibliography" (498), but he does not seem to have read the non-partisan testimony quoted therein about Johanna's reputation in Vienna. Quite strangely, he quotes a very truncated and inexact form of Hotschevar's written refusal to act as co-guardian of Johanna's daughter in 1830, presented as "an unspecific report of 1830 that her mode of life was 'less than praiseworthy'" (301). He does not forget to mention the year 1830, as if she would have waited to be forty-five to start her "less than praiseworthy" life-style. To him, Johanna's 1820 pregnancy was the result of her eagerness "to build a new life" (321), even though the presumed father of the child was only one of her (concurrent) affairs. Just as the Sterba couple, Solomon acts in observance of the already quoted Murphy law—when facts do not fit your theory, change the facts.

Notwithstanding his adherence to many of the Sterbas' theories, Solomon tries to soften their description of Beethoven as a psychopathic character with various nuances—dictator, sadist, Führer-like, etc. He documents evidence showing that the musician was torn between his moral principles forbidding him to do harm and what he considered his duty to raise his nephew the right way, which made the boy's mother suffer (325-326). Solomon refuses to be "forced to believe that the masterpieces of Beethoven's last years were composed by a cruel and unethical human being" (324), but I will show later that even when he is right, it is for the wrong reasons.

The alleged Family Romance delusion

On the very first page of his biography of Beethoven, Solomon introduces the term *delusion*, which sets the tone of the whole work, announcing its essential leitmotiv (3, preceded only by the title page of the first part). He means Beethoven's mistaken belief that he was two years younger than he really was, which he stubbornly held for almost his whole life. However, Solomon does not spend much time on the issue here and rather sends the reader to his take of it in his *Beethoven Essays* book, in which the alleged "delusion" plays a new and important role, which I will deal with in the next chapter. In his biographical work, the issue serves only to introduce the other "delusion" that Solomon attributes to Beethoven, making it into his crucial personality treat: "Family Romance."

The concept of "Family Romance" is another of Freud's made-up mechanisms that purports to explain the development of a child within his family—and it is specifically "his" family because it applies primarily to boys. According to Freud, the gradual liberation of the child from the authority of his parents—especially of his father's—has to go through several stages, reaching the one in which the child comes to fantasize himself as being the offspring of a different father, one with a much higher social standing: a prince, a king or another celebrity. Freud presented this new component of his theory in a 1909 article,[2] claiming that almost all children, especially boys, must pass through this conscious fantasy, which is "one of the essential characteristics of the neurotics and also of a comparatively highly gifted people, [... and] is seldom remembered consciously [later] but can almost always be revealed by psycho-analysis," obviously by applying his (Freud's) recipes for the retrieval of "repressed memories."[3] In fact, Freud did not elaborate in depth his new concept—he did not offer any supporting example for it... not even one clinical case! It was taken over by Otto Rank (1884 –1939), his younger colleague and disciple, who expanded it, but it was never a major component of the theory. (Sulloway does not even mention it in his massive *Freud* monograph).

A detail of Beethoven's life that barely appears in Thayer's biography (and that most readers discard with a laugh) gave Solomon the opportunity to bring his very original contribution to Beethoven literature, by introduction the previously unheard-of "Family Romance" delusion as the essential psychological trait of the composer's personality. In 1810, the very amateurish French *Dictionnaire des musiciens* reported that Beethoven was "said to be" the illegitimate son of the King of Prussia Friederich Wilhelm II[4]; the allegation was taken over by the more serious German *Brockhaus Konversations-Lexicon* published in 1814.* Beethoven was aware of the allegation, but seems to have simply ignored it for a long time. After 1819, some friends—and also his nephew—asked him several times, in his conversation books, to officially refute this misrepresentation, but he seems to have always dismissed such requests with a shrug that is hard to interpret because, naturally, the conversation books did not include Beethoven's replies. However, we can plausibly reconstruct such conversations: [5]

[Beethoven (to Peters): What did you say?]
Peters: I asked Bernard if one had not yet corrected in the *Conversations Lexicon* that you are the natural son of the late King of Prussia.
[Beethoven: What?!]
Peters: That you would be a natural son of the late King of Prussia.
[Beethoven: The story is ridiculous.]
Peters: Such things must be, however, corrected, because you don't need to borrow the luster from a king—it is actually the other way around.

The issue is left open-ended, but one can imagine that Beethoven closed it with a quote from Schiller, a poet he revered, saying "Against stupidity the gods themselves cannot fight"[†]; or he may have given the explanation he would give later to his old-time friend Wegeler, who also asked him in a letter, to rebut the rumor. Beethoven wrote him, "that has also been said to me before, a long time ago. I have, however, made it a principle never to write anything about myself nor to answer anything that is written about me. I therefore gladly leave it to you to make known to the world the integrity of my parents, and of my mother in particular."[6]

Solomon does not pay any attention to Beethoven's explanation of his attitude and sees in his silence only the composer's decision "to deny his father and to dishonor his mother's memory" (6), which can be explained with a diagnosis of a "Family Romance" delusion. More explicitly, "the denial that Johann van Beethoven was his real father is the central 'fact' in Beethoven's Family Romance" (29). Solomon then puts Beethoven on his couch (7-31),

---

* King Friedrich Wilhelm II of Prussia (1744-97) was an accomplished cellist and a patron of the arts, especially music. He was, however, mostly known at the time for his many extramarital affairs (including morganatic marriages) and bastards; he was nicknamed *Der Vielgeliebte* (the much loved one), which added some credentials to the rumor that he would have sired Beethoven.
† From act 3 of his tragedy *The Maid of Orleans*.

conscientiously following Freud's prescriptions, according to which childhood is the essential factor that defines personality, by means of the "fantasies" that the child builds to answer the questions he arrives at, because of his particular position in his family, between his parents and siblings (if any). This approach itself is legitimate—Freud was neither the first nor the last one to embrace it—but the manner Solomon applies it is not. He carefully documents the history of the marriage of Beethoven's parents and quotes known evidence of those who had witnessed the composer's Bonn years, emphasizing the father's "often cruel" treatment of the child, whom he forced to practice his clavier for long hours in order to make him into a second Mozart. He may be right that the child Beethoven had "found sustenance in inwardness, in fantasy," and that the center of his "fantasy life was his music" (27), but that does not justify his diagnosis—Beethoven's inner conviction that he had been fathered by a much more exalted individual than his father, a conviction that would have been "fed by, and perhaps had its origin" in his age delusion (30) and "may be the expression, denial and symbolic transcendence of the feeling that he was unloved and unwanted" (31). To Solomon, "perhaps" and "may" are merely steps toward the "is" and "do" when he further elaborates his diagnosis. He peppers his further elaborations with quotes from Freud and his disciple Rank and brings in "patricidal implications" combined with a "matrix of negative feelings towards his mother" (29), although he had already quoted Beethoven description of her after she died as "a good, kind mother to me and indeed my best friend" (25).

According to Freud, most boys develop such fantasies of illegitimate lineage in their teens and lose the memory of them in young adulthood, but in Solomon's view Beethoven would have kept his fantasy alive - "it apparently gained in strength and tenacity as he grew to maturity" (28). And he pursues by "identifying" it in various moments in the composer's life, beginning with his twelfth year, when he wrote his first song, "To an Infant" (WoO 108). Quoting the lyrics of the song,

> You still don't know whose child you are,
> Who wraps you in swaddles,
> Who watches over you and who she is
> That keeps you warm and breastfeeds you.
>
> Enjoy it with clean, pious mind,
> Enjoy it! In a few more years,
> Your nurse will reveal herself
> In your mother.[7]

Solomon triumphantly claims that "From here it was but a short step to the Family Romance fantasy" (31), intimating that the first line would have been Beethoven's rendition of his supposed feelings—he did not know his real father. As one can easily see, the short poem has nothing to do with the "uncertain father," but is a glorification of the mother. The "you" in the first line is not even the generic pronoun, let alone "I": it has a very clear addressee—a baby that has no awareness of the world around it, but who will recognize the mother as its "nurse" when it starts to discover the world. This was the stratagem of the poet (the obscure Johann v. Döhring) to render his point more strikingly.

Solomon goes further to apply his Family Romance diagnosis to almost any feature of Beethoven and major event in his life: not only to the age delusion, but also to nobility pretense (120, 315-16), his strained relations with his brothers (98), his relationship with nephew (328, 330, 372, 373), the dedications of his work (358, 376), and the last years of his life (359-62, 373, 376), when the alleged delusion would finally succumb under the attack of "importunities of reality and to the harbinger of mortality" (377). (He also expands it in his other major book, the *Beethoven Essays*, where he adds another delusion, to which I will get in the next chapter.) In every case, Solomon wraps his thesis in a flurry of Freudian and non-Freudian elaborations that seem to have been intended to overwhelm the reader and distract him from testing the author's theory against the known facts of Beethoven's life—facts that would invalidate it.

I will not go into a lengthy, step-by-step rebuttal of Solomon's theory of Beethoven's Family Romance simply because it is totally nullified by one known fact. It is strange that none of the critics of Solomon's view that are known to me[*] has really touched the irrational core of the alleged Family Romance delusion. Tellenbach came close but narrowly missed it in her *Beethoven Journal* article about Solomon's image of Beethoven, because of an odd misapprehension: she did not grasp the full meaning of Solomon's theory, which claims that Beethoven lived with the delusion of being the son of nobility or royalty instead of his father; she assumed that Solomon viewed it as a simple daydream based on a protracted childhood fantasy, and retained and dealt with only one alleged symptom—the musician's lack of affection for his father and his siblings, concluding:

> Beethoven's supposed aloofness toward his father and his family does not fit at all with his well-known veneration for his paternal grandfather, [...] esteemed music director at the court of Bonn, whose picture hung in his apartment. [8]

This sentence mentions the essential argument which abolishes Solomon's Family Romance theory, unfortunately without making the connection: Beethoven's reverence for his grandfather, attested to by various testimonies,[9] clearly indicates that the composer was convinced that he had inherited his musical genius from his grandfather. Could he have been so intellectually delusional as to believe that his grandfather could pass along musical genius by short-circuiting his own son?[†]

Solomon seems to have foreseen this irrefutable objection to his theory and tried to contain it with the following argument:

> It was only natural that Beethoven should have strived to emulate the Kapellmeister [his grandfather...]. It is worth noting, however, that a strong psychological identification with a

---

[*] The German scholars Harry Goldschmidt and Marie-Elisabeth Tellenbach, and the American ones Virginia Beahrs and Gail Altman, to name only the most consistent ones.

[†] Beethoven also believed that he had some bad inheritance from his grandfather. He wrote his attorney J. B. Bach, "I have an idea that some day I shall have a stroke, like my very worthy grandfather whom I somewhat resemble." (Anderson 1302)

grandfather *may* well go hand in hand with a repudiation of the father; a boy *may* try to come to terms with an unsatisfactory image of his father in idealizing a male grandparent (22, my italics).

This statement is not incorrect but, in order to support Solomon's thesis, it must distort the meaning of the term "repudiation" beyond any acceptance. Psychologically and emotionally—and also legally— repudiation is the complete refusal to participate in a relationship with a parent, but it does not include the irrational belief that it also breaks the biological link with that parent. Beethoven could not believe that he had inherited his paternal grandfather's musical talent but had been sired by a man other than the son of his grandfather.

Solomon's last quoted statement again illustrates his already mentioned rhetorical tactic—transforming a *may* into an *is/does*: a boy *may* try to ... but Beethoven *does* it. Here is another example (29): "At some point he [Beethoven] *may* have come to feel that another man was (or *should* have been) his father, ultimately leading to Johann's *being supplanted* as the father in Beethoven's inner world. For the denial that Johann van Beethoven *was* his real father *is* the central 'fact' in Beethoven's Family Romance" (my italics).

Actually, even the idea that Beethoven "repudiated" his father is, at best, a gross exaggeration. It is true that he left few traces of his feelings for his father, but we have at least three. When he was about nine years old, at the time when he must have felt his father's harshness at its highest, he jotted down on a music score this phrase: "written by my dear father."[10] From a much later time, after 1800, we have the already quoted testimony of Ries that "any harsh word about him [his father] let fall by a third person made Beethoven angry"[11]; we have also the testimony of Fanny Giannatasio, who noted in her journal that Beethoven told them "a great deal about his parents [a term including his father], and also about his grandfather."[12] It seems that, maturing, Beethoven began to appreciate his father's severity that had contributed to his fraught childhood; he probably recognized it as the whip that marched him to excellence in piano playing and, as I have shown earlier, he demanded the same from his nephew. We can recognize here Beethoven's "late identification" with his father. I think, therefore, that the term "repudiation" is a misrepresentation. All in all, with or without "repudiation," Beethoven's "Family Romance" theory remains a wild speculation.

There is further proof of the fallacy of Solomon's theory—evidence that Beethoven held no illusion about his nobility. Tellenbach made this claim long ago, but her argument was not fully persuasive. She quoted Beethoven's statement to a witness, "It is easy to get along with the nobility but one needs something with which to impress them,"[13] which implies that he did not consider himself one of them. Unfortunately, this is not proof. We have, fortunately, a clear-cut proclamation by Beethoven himself in his November 1801 letter to Wegeler in which he tells his friend that he has met "a dear enchanting girl who loves me and whom I love," adding, "unfortunately, she is not of my class."[14] Since the literature is unanimous that this un-named "enchanting girl" was Countess Julie Guicciardi, the inference is direct: at least in 1801, Beethoven knew he was not of the nobility; it is not credible that this was a new awareness or that he lost it later.

If Beethoven did not live with any such "delusion," how can one explain the circumstantial evidence that Solomon advances in support of his theory? First of all, why did the composer refuse to publicly refute the ridiculous yet publicly spread rumor, when his friends insisted he do so, as witnessed in the conversation books? His answers to their requests are not entered therein, but it is reasonable to assume that he claimed, as in his letter to Wegeler, "I have made it a principle never to write anything about myself nor to answer anything that is written about me." While this explanation may seem strange, it is obvious that Beethoven stuck to this principle throughout his life: his legacy contains very few notes about his life, family and friends—which may explain the many wild speculations made by his biographers. Actually, he seems to have given the issue some thought during his last year, after his friend Wegeler also insisted, and he made some inquiries, as evidenced in his October 1826 letter to Adolph Martin Schlesinger, the editor of the *Berliner Allgemeine musikalische Zeitung*: "If I am not mistaken, you spoke to me about placing something about me in the *Zeitung*. This could not be in vain, in that it would put an end to a great deal of untrue gossip." The gossip to which he referred was certainly his alleged noble descent. For whatever reason, Schlesinger's answer eluded the issue[15] and Beethoven was probably happy to stick to his principle. He may have also thought that a public refutation, something like, "Herr Ludwig van Beethoven, the famous composer, want by this to refute the rumors spread by well-known yet irresponsible musical publications that he would be the son of the late King Friedrich Wilhelm II of Prussia," would have been as ridiculous as the rumor itself and uselessly offensive to royalty.

It is also easy to commonsensically explain the several "trails" of Beethoven's musings spread over many years, which Solomon gleaned as support of his theory. He quotes (30) an underscored passage in Beethoven's copy of the German translation of the *Odyssey* reading, "few sons are like/their fathers; most are worse, a very few/excel their fathers," as proof that the composer doubted his paternal lineage. The verse clearly articulates a mystery still unsolved in three millennia, although DNA analysis has become a commercial business today: children can little resemble their parents in certain aspects. That it caught Beethoven's eye proves that he knew very well how family lineages develop, with ups and downs—and it actually points *against* the Family Romance theory: his father was one of the "most are worse" than his own father; and Beethoven was one of the "very few [who] excel their fathers." Another underscored *Odyssey* quote (28) seems more apt to support Solomon's theory: "My mother says that he is my father / For myself I know it not, / For no man knoweth who has begotten him." This old conundrum, which was only recently overturned by the DNA breakthrough, does not prove that Beethoven doubted his lineage; he most likely had in mind his nephew, because he thought that the latter's mother was an adulteress.

Beethoven and his sister-in law

Solomon's main contribution to the nephew and sister-in-law topics is a new Freudian theory that would explain Beethoven's claim that Johanna was prostituting herself: the composer, he suggests, would have been attracted to her; therefore he "remained in contact with her" during the first stages of their battle for Karl's guardianship in 1816 and "degraded" her to a prostitute later because he could, in this way, have sex with her in his fantasies (305-307). Indeed Solomon's Beethoven did not know how to interact with decent women, but only with prostitutes.* Even the composer's desire that his nephew call him "father" is read as the expression of the "mystifying way" in which Beethoven "may have been participating in an illusory marriage to the 'Queen of Night' [Johanna] herself" (304). The scholar-shrink supports this new theory with a Freudian quote about "mixed feelings" (of love and hate) but, since theories must be backed by facts but there is no supporting evidence, he claims that Beethoven kept these ongoing meetings with his sister-in-law "well hidden from most of his associates and especially from Karl's headmaster, Cajetan Giannatasio" (306-307). But this is not true. As I showed earlier (see page 36 above), in a letter that he wrote Giannatasio on February 21, 1816—a few days after he brought his nephew in the latter's school—Beethoven let him know that Johanna had to contact him personally to arrange every meeting with her son; therefore, the Giannatasios knew that the composer was meeting his sister-in-law quite often. In fact, as we already know from Fanny's diary, he used to speak to the family about his "sorrows with the mother."[16] The evidence already presented also shows that he was already treating Johanna as a "bad woman" before his brother's death and that he was reporting about her "selling herself" at the Artists Ball in early 1816, long before he allegedly started fantasizing that she was a prostitute.

Later on, Solomon brings in an "extraordinary rumor" spread by Johanna herself in the very Court that ruled during their 1818-20 trial: she claimed that Beethoven was in love with her! The rumor seems extraordinary indeed and it is surprising that most biographers—including Thayer in Forbes' English version—have ignored it, although it left a clear trail in the evidence. Its first mark is an entry of Beethoven's friend Bernard in a November 1819 conversation book: "I saw too that the *Magistrat* believes everything that it hears, for example that she said that you were in love with her."[17] We do not know how the composer reacted to this announcement on the spot, but in a February 1820 letter to Bernard he described "the statements that I was supposed to be in love with Frau B" as "tittle-tattle" unworthy for a court to consider.[18] Nevertheless, it seems to have looked bad enough for him to complain, in a draft of a *Memorandum* to the Court of Appeals, that the court "referent" (named Piuk) "again retailed the *well-known complaints of Fr B about me*, even adding '*that I was supposed to be in love with her, etc.*' and more rubbish of that kind" (Beethoven's emphasis).[19] The preserved Vienna Court documents (reproduced in Anderson Appendix C,

---

* For a documented rebuttal, see chapter 2 of my *Immortal Beloved Controversy* book (on www.BeethovenOurContemporary.com).

pp. 1360-1399) do not mention the rumor, but the court was aware of it, most likely from Johanna herself, who took advantage of the judicial practices of the time that allowed litigants to write and meet the judges in private, as Beethoven was also advised by his counsel, "to present arguments in his behalf." [20] This must have been the path that Johanna followed, but that does not answer the essential questions: why would she have spread that rumor? And was it true or just a lie?

Solomon never suspects that Johanna would have lied and maintains that her claim "presumably constituted her own understanding of Beethoven's attitude towards her, her explanation of his uncontrolled and passionate behavior" (318). However, he leaves the issue dangling, without pressing this argument in support of his thesis. To me, the presumption is insufficient. Johanna was certainly no *avant-la lettre* psychoanalyst, so I think we can "presume" that she would not have reached such a conclusion if Beethoven had not sent her some—clear or even disguised—signals of affection. Could he have done that? I can imagine a reasonable scenario in which he did. Let us recall first that in an 1820 letter to the court he stated that "If the mother could have repressed her wicked tendencies and allowed my plans to develop peacefully, then an entirely favorable result would have been the outcome of the arrangements I have so far adopted."[21] In a face-to-face meeting in which she confronted him viciously, he could have told her, "Woman, don't you realize that, could you have repressed your wicked tendencies, we two, you and me, might have been able to raise your child as a real family?" This Hollywood-like scenario is not utterly absurd, but the probability is still higher than Johanna was simply inventing this love—perhaps at the suggestion of her lawyer—to wrong-foot Beethoven.

About the same time when she spread the rumor that Beethoven was in love with her, Johanna was involved in an affair—or two, as rumors maintained (see page 46 above)—and became pregnant. Solomon presents the event as follows: "Grief-stricken and weary from her long struggle, eager to build a new life, and perhaps to replace her stolen child, Johanna became pregnant [...] by Johann Hofbauer, a 'noted, very well-to-do person' who later freely acknowledged his responsibility" (321). In fact, after claiming to have spent an incredibly large sum of money for Johanna's health during her ensuing sickness (again reported in a conversation book quoted by Sterba),[22] Hofbauer seems to have disappeared from her life—maybe after hearing the rumors about two lovers. Johanna baptized her daughter Ludovica, the female form of Ludwig. Solomon might be right to see in her act "an uncanny testimony of the strength of the bond between the antagonists in this drama [...]" (321-322),[*] but this could express only Johanna's feelings; there is no evidence that Beethoven showed any interest in her or her daughter later.

We know (see page 45 above) that after he had secured sole guardianship of

---

[*] Solomon does not indicate the source of his information; it must be the same from which he extracts the truncated "less than praiseworthy lifestyle" note discussed at pp. 24 and 43 of this book. Tellenbach claims the same (1993-4, note 53), without indicating a source.

Karl in 1820, Beethoven began to show leniency toward his sister-in-law and helped her financially. Solomon sees this change of heart as proof that "ultimately, Johanna's heroic and passionate struggle for her son and for the preservation of her motherhood may have prevented Beethoven from losing contact altogether with the inner core of his own humanity" (330). The scholar needed this "humanization" of the musician because he refused to be "forced to believe that the masterpieces of Beethoven's last years were composed by a cruel and unethical human being" (324). The argumentation is, unfortunately, not credible. The "de-humanized" Beethoven who had tortured Johanna before 1820 had also been able to create or design masterpieces like the *Hammerklavier Piano Sonata* (1818), *Missa Solemnis* (begun in 1819, nearly completed by the fall of next year) and the *Ninth Symphony* (work begun in 1818). Moreover, Beethoven began some "conciliatory moves" towards his sister-in-law (363) only in mid-1822; in the meantime, the not-yet-humanized Beethoven had advanced well into his mass and symphony and finished his last piano sonatas. Besides that, according to Solomon's own analysis, the newly "humanized" Beethoven also pushed his nephew to a suicide attempt later. It is obvious that Beethoven's "humanity"—or the lack of it—did not change in or around 1820. As I argued in a previous chapter (p. 51ff), all these years he was confident that he was doing the right thing, which, unfortunately but necessarily, inflicted pain on his sister-in-law. In fact, his prolonged war with his nephew's mother coincided with his way out of a long creative crisis.

Beethoven's nobility pretense as his way of "living out" the Family Romance

We have already encountered this issue in the previous chapter: although Beethoven was not a noble, in 1815 he initiated his trial to exclude Karl's mother Johanna from the boy's guardianship under the judicial authority of the aristocratic class (the *Landrechte*), which accepted the case without questioning the composer's nobility. In the second trial, introduced by Johanna at the same court in 1818 to remove Beethoven from guardianship, he committed a slip of the tongue—"were he noble ..." he said about his nephew—that revealed his own non-nobility and the court sent the case to the commoners' court, which greatly upset Beethoven. In chapter 2 we saw that the Sterbas were not particularly interested in this so-called "exposure of nobility pretense," but Solomon weaves it into the larger tapestry of his theory that makes the Family Romance delusion Beethoven's essential personality trait. And because the alleged Family Romance was Beethoven's *life-long* delusion according to his theory, so must have been his nobility "imposture."

Beethoven's (almost) life-long "imposture" Solomon is, to my knowledge, the first and only scholar to maintain that Beethoven's nobility pretense was not an episode during his 1815-1818 court battle for the custody of his nephew, but an "imposture" that he launched and expanded from the very beginning in Vienna, "when he permitted the assumption that he was an

aristocrat, which flowed from the *van* in his name, to pass unchallenged" (117).*
Solomon brings in an apparently irrefutable circumstantial piece of factual evidence: many of Beethoven's contemporaries—including the newspapers advertising or reviewing his concerts, the great German poet Goethe, and the secret police—took the *van* particle in his name as proof of nobility and even replaced it with the German *von* equivalent beginning with his first years in Vienna (117). And, while there is no evidence that Beethoven initiated this misrepresentation, there is also none that he tried to correct it—obviously, this is a case when lack of evidence could constitute evidence. It may seem strange that the Austrian nobility accepted the "imposture," apparently with ease, but the facts seem to explain it. If the Nobility Court, whose duty was to check such facts, took the *van* nobility for granted and did not request Beethoven to produce proof during three different lawsuits, we should not be surprised for the Viennese aristocracy and society at large to do the same. This argumentation seems logical, but there are other well-known pieces of evidence that raise serious doubts, and Solomon ignores them. Schindler has passed to us an unequivocal testimony that has never, to my knowledge, been denounced as one of his fabrications:

> Another characteristic [of Beethoven] that was equally important to his artistic life was his scorn of wealth and position. He regarded them as mere conventions, accidents of fate and not worthy of special consideration. He respected first of all the human qualities of a man [...] When he did show respect for a highly placed or a wealthy individual, it was because of that person's humanitarian benevolence.[23]

And later, Schindler reproduces, acquiescingly, the testimony of the wife of the French composer Cherubini, who spent nine months in Vienna and met Beethoven in society and wrote later in her *Memoires*, "He simply ridiculed their high and mighty prejudices, and showed no more deference to a princess than to a bourgeoise."[24] A certain Frau von Bernhard, a familiar of the salons in the late 1790s, left a similar testimony: "his [Beethoven's] entire deportment showed no sign of exterior polish; on the contrary, he was unmannerly both in demeanor and behavior." She remembered a scene in Prince Lichnowsky's salon, with Beethoven and his two teachers, Haydn and Salieri, "both most carefully dressed in the old-fashioned style with big-wig, shoes and silk stockings, while Beethoven used to appear even here in the freer ultra-Rhenish garb, almost carelessly dressed."[25] If Beethoven would have wanted to pass as an aristocrat, he would have not shown so much disdain for their way of living.

Solomon fails to ask a very simple question: how did the aristocracy (or those segments of it that accepted Beethoven as one of them) interact with him, supposedly a noble, too? Of course, his alleged nobility would have been of a lower rank that did not carry a brand label like "count" or "baron," so their respect for him would have had to been shown in other ways. There is very little

---

* This new thesis fits Solomon's allegation of Beethoven's nobility pretense as "living out" his Family Romance, which would have marked his whole adult life, but Solomon does not make this connection.

evidence of these kinds of interaction, but the little that we have does not fit Solomon's thesis. In the well-known episode of his quarrel with his patron and alleged friend Prince Lichnowsky in 1806, the latter treated Beethoven as a servant and even (jokingly?) threatened to have him arrested, which led to a long-time estrangement.[26] The evidence, originating from several sources, is not fully consistent. In October 1806, Beethoven was the guest of Prince Lichnowsky at his residence in Silesia (now around the tri-country border of Czechia, Poland and Germany). Lichnowsky had also some French officers visiting him and they were eager to hear Beethoven play, but the latter refused. When the Prince tried to coerce him (one account says that the Prince even threatened to have the composer arrested), Beethoven protested furiously, left abruptly and broke up with the Prince. At the time, France was at war with the "Fourth Coalition" of European powers. The Habsburg Empire did not join the coalition, but had been part of the previous one and had been defeated and dismembered, reduced to Austria (with the Emperor Franz II demoted to King Franz I). Prince Lichnowsky invited the French officers, who were passing through Silesia on their way to join the army, out of an old tradition of military "esprit de corps." For Beethoven, the French were the enemy.

We also know, from Ries's testimony, that another aristocrat treated Beethoven as a servant, long before 1815. He played at a musical soirée given by an unnamed "old countess" in honor of visiting Prince Louis-Ferdinand [of Prussia]. When he found out that there was no cover set for him at the high nobility supper table that followed, he left angrily, with "a few blunt remarks."[27] It is very unlikely that this countess was the only Viennese aristocrat who knew that Beethoven was not a noble.

In fact, it is very likely that all the Viennese aristocracy knew that he was not one of them, but did not care about it either, for a very simple reason: they would have been aware that the "von Beethoven" and "v. Beethoven" simply reflected the Viennese "craze" for titles. This craze is documented by Johann Peztzl, the chronicler of the city's social life at the end of the eighteenth century, in his book "Sketch of Vienna (1786-1890)."[28] It presents a structured social hierarchy that included a nobility of the first rank, comprised by princes, counts and old-time baron; and a nobility of the second rank, containing "honorationes"—newly created barons that were "the cogs of the machine [of state]," including councilors, commissioners, doctors, and bankers and business people.[29] Lower down the social scale, by a kind of tacit agreement the hierarchy goes:

> Men of the lower bourgeoisie are called "Herren." The salesman in the shop, valet, etc., the middling professional men and the barons are addressed as "Herr von." This title is very widely employed, and the one which is in the most common use in Vienna [...and] has exactly the same significance as the English "gentleman."[30]

Prominent musicians belonged to the "Herr von" category; Salieri was a "Herr von," as we learn from a note that young Beethoven, who was Salieri's pupil for a few years, wrote him.[31] Beethoven must have been acknowledged as "Herr von" soon after he took the aristocratic salons by storm with his improvisations, and his status is reflected in some public references to him. His *van* particle, albeit possibly a supporting argument, seems not to have been essential in establishing his new status, because it was not supplanted by the "von." The "van" was by far the predominantly used form of his name after he settled in Vienna: reviewing the occurrences of the two forms in all the German publications (digitized and available online at http://anno.onb.ac.at/anno-suche) between 1792 and 1828, I found the "von" in only 11% of cases (18 out of 162, 13 of them in Vienna).* His "von" status is best illustrated in the "official" documents, which were especially careful to observe the hierarchy, such as the income tax assessment letters that the Lower Austrian "Landesregierung" (State government) sent, in 1824 and 1825, to "Ludwig v. Beethoven,"[32] with the typical German "v." shortening of "von." One can also find a confirmation of his Vienna status in a quasi-official letter from a sponsoring organization, the "Geselschaft der Musikfreunde" (Society of the friends of music): in 1824, the society solicited the "Well-born Herr Ludwig van Beethoven" to write an oratorio for them.[33] *Well-born* (in German "Wohlgeboren") was originally a respect formula applied to low-rank nobility ("Freiherr" and Baron) but was gradually extended to designate non-noble (bourgeois) dignitaries in the nineteenth century.[34]

More of Solomon's faulty elaborations. As his thesis of Beethoven's life-long imposture is wrong, all of Solomon's further elaborations of it become irrelevant, but it is nevertheless interesting to examine them because they illustrate the weakness of his scholarly approach. For example, trying to explain Beethoven's motivations for recurring to the alleged "imposture," Solomon claims that the composer drew no economic advantage from passing as a noble (118), but he wanted "to partake of aristocratic power" (119). He does not offer any evidence for these two assertions, and I could not find any either. When evidence is missing, a legitimate speculation can rely only on educated guesses and mine go against Solomon's thesis. Noble status would have allowed young Beethoven to move more freely in the world of aristocracy, where he could find young female pupils, historically his first important means of making a living. As for Beethoven's alleged desire to "partake of aristocratic power," it hardly fits his republican political stance, which materialized in his "constant opposition to Austrian politics, the government, and the imperial court," as Schindler testified.[35] Solomon is sometimes right, but fails to follow up on his own logic when it would undermine his theses. He points out (117) that people who had known Beethoven in Bonn could not have been duped by the *van* strategy, but he fails to apply this assumption to Count Waldstein, Beethoven's first important patron, who also introduced him to the Viennese society, as Solomon acknowledges.[36] Waldstein had known Beethoven quite well in Bonn, so he

---

* It may seem odd, but (probably by way of simple repetition of the sources) "von Beethoven" survived for well over a century in the media, without ever touching the issue of nobility. It persisted for some fifty years (76 of 548 cases, 14 %, for the period 1828-1870) and subsided only slowly (7% between 1870 and 1927; 2% between 1928 and 1944), dying out only after WW2.

must have been aware of his humble social status. Although the count's estate was in Bohemia and he was away from Vienna on military assignments for many years, he had also a house in Baden, near the city, and was connected to the local aristocracy. [37] In the normal course of events, he should have dispelled Beethoven's "imposture"—or was he part of the latter's conspiracy?

The Family Romance connection. Solomon claims that "the pretense *may* well have been a medium by which Beethoven 'lived out' his Family Romance" (120). The italicized *may* (my emphasis) illustrates again a scholarly favorite stratagem—introduce a thesis under the precautionary note of "may" and elevate it to "is" or "does" later. This time, however, Solomon does not clear the uncertainty underneath the term "may," so we do not know how he would interpret Beethoven's nobility pretense if it were not his way of "living out" his Family Romance delusion. This incongruity, however, is not essential because, as I have just shown, the Family Romance theory is a scholarly fallacy; hence the nobility pretense cannot in any way validate it. Nevertheless, it is instructive to examine Solomon's take of the issue, because it further illustrates his flawed rhetoric. He claims that Beethoven's claim of nobility "at bottom was a claim of equality of birth" (119) and proffers this piece of evidence dating from the wake of the exposure of the pretense in court:

> In a Conversation Book of 1820,[*] he [Beethoven] wrote that the courts had "learned my brother was not of the nobility," and added, in apparent puzzlement, "It is singular, as far as I know, that there is a hiatus here which ought to be filled, for my nature shows that I do not belong with this plebeian M[agistrat]." In thus acknowledging his brother's non-nobility and simultaneously stating that his own "nature" was that of a noble, Beethoven *seems* to be expressing the fantasy that he and his brother had different parents—this seems to be the only way in which the "singular hiatus" could be filled. (119, my emphasis)[38]

This argument is a speculation based on a confusing text, in which the word "seems" obviously indicates the author's subjectivity. We have actually incontrovertible facts that nullify his claim. It was Beethoven's sister-in-law Johanna who initiated the "nobility pretense" when having her late husband's will delivered to the nobility court; Beethoven only tacitly acquiesced to her misrepresentation when taking his own case against her to the same court. Joanna could not have invented her husband's nobility. She must have held it from him. When Beethoven's mishap in court revealed the fraud, the judge asked Johanna directly if her husband was of noble birth and she answered, "So

---

[*] The 1820 date is very likely wrong. The entry points to a recent event; the court's finding out that Beethoven had no nobility diploma in December 1818 – therefore, it very likely belongs to late 1818 or early 1819. The so-called conversation books included piles of loose sheets (and also pieces cut from journals), on which Beethoven and his guests jotted down their entries in very large handwriting, because his eyesight had deteriorated. Schindler, who assembled them in *Hefts* (notebooks), mistakenly dated this sheet to January 1820 and the *Konversationshefte* edition preserved Schindler's original structure.

the brothers had said," which should clearly invalidate Solomon's speculation. Did Johanna lie in court? The question is legitimate and not only because we know that she was a dishonest person. The deposition continued:

> The documentary proof of nobility was said to be in the possession of the oldest brother, the composer. At the legal hearing on the death of her husband, proof of nobility had been demanded; she herself had no document bearing on the subject.[39]

This contains an obvious lie: the court could not have demanded her to produce proof of nobility when she delivered her husband's will, probably because they took the *van* particle of the name as proof. Had they demanded a formal proof, they would have sent the case to the commoner's court (as they did later), because Johanna had none to offer. However, this lie had a clear reason—to cover Johanna's own lie of claiming nobility when she delivered the will to the court.* She had no reason to lie when claiming that she heard the two brother talking about the issue. In fact, Carl had already claimed a nobility of sort much earlier: in 1800, he was recorded in his clerk job register as Carl v. Beethoven,[40] which shows that he wanted to pass as a "Herr von," like his older brother, and very likely following his advice. This must have also been a topic during Carl's final illness, when he wrote his will.

It is, therefore, very likely that, contrary to Solomon's allegation, Beethoven did not want to exclude Carl from the nobility that he claimed for himself. "The brothers" were together in the nobility pretense, as Johanna testified. Solomon seems to have realized that her testimony would do away with his speculation, because he quotes it only later in his book, in a completely different context (315). And, although he noticed that Carl wanted to pass as a "von" in his 1988 *Beethoven Essays* book, he did not include this find in the 1998 revised edition of his *Beethoven* biography of the composer ... because, I suggest, it would have undermined his thesis.

Actually, the very term "noble" is problematic, because Beethoven only euphemistically implies it in the entry. How does the sentence "my nature shows that I do not belong to this plebeian M[agistrat, the commoners' court]" qualify for his "nobility?" Solomon first gives a realistic answer to the question, namely that, in his inner conviction, Beethoven claimed "equality" with the aristocrats as justified by his great personal "nature" of a genius, a widespread belief during the Enlightenment age (117). Tellenbach, otherwise an acerbic critic of Solomon's theories, advances a similar explanation of the "nobility pretense."[41] However, Solomon's reverts to his idea that Beethoven had in mind "equality of birth." He invokes—without any comment, as if the quote was self-explanatory—an 1823 letter of Beethoven to Schindler reading, "As for the question of 'being noble,' I think I have given sufficient proof to you that I am so on principle" (119). The context, which can be found in Anderson's edition of

---

* Did Johanna lie when saying that Beethoven claimed ("was said") to have the documentary proof of the family's nobility? Very likely not – such a lie was no help. It was also to be expected that the older of the brothers have the important family documents.

Beethoven's letters from which Solomon quotes, shows that the issue was not "nobility" per se, but "nobility of character." The letter begins, "Surely it must have been clear to you that I would have nothing to do with the matter," followed by the sentence quoted by Solomon. Three Anderson notes explain the "matter": a young pianist had, following Schindler' advice, asked Beethoven to write a letter of recommendation for him, hinting that "persons of noble character were always glad to help young people to improve themselves."[42] It seems obvious that the "nobility by nature" in Beethoven's conversation book was not "nobility by birth," as Solomon maintains.

Rejecting Solomon's take of Beethoven's nobility pretense as false does not clarify the pretense itself, which is a fact during his 1815-1818 lawsuits against his sister-in-law in the Vienna Nobility Court. It seems hard to understand what pushed him to this act that seems opposed to his intimate (political and non-political) convictions. Such conflicting facts show that the "equation" of Beethoven's nobility pretense has many unknowns that make the issue hard, perhaps impossible, to solve. I will wrap it up and try to disentangle this hard knot in the next chapter, after reviewing Solomon's second take of the issue in his *Beethoven Essays* book, in which he puts the composer again on the shrink's couch.

Beethoven's relationship with his nephew

The Family Romance, re-baptized a "family constellation," holds the center stage in Solomon's approach to this issue. He announces from the very beginning that this relationship was Beethoven's "salvation," yielding to his eventual renunciation of his Family Romance delusion (297):

> The unwitting but essential ingredients in Beethoven's salvation were, paradoxically, his nephew, Karl, and his sister-in-law Johanna. His obsessive entanglement with them forcibly wrenched his emotional energies from their attachment to the outer world and focused them upon the still unresolved issues of his family constellation. Beethoven was now in the process of converting into a strange form of quasi-reality some of the fantasies that had both veiled and motored his existence, bringing into consciousness the delusions of a lifetime so that they could be faced and brought under control.

Solomon's already quoted assumption that Beethoven's relationship with his nephew was of a "paternal nature" was actually hiding more speculations to support the composer's alleged Family Romance delusion. As signaled above (see page 26-27), the custom in extended families of the time demanded the orphans to be adopted by older males (such as an uncle), who treated them like "real" sons and daughters; in turn, the children would treat their adopted parent nominally as "father." Not so to Solomon, who writes:

> For more than a decade he [Beethoven] had tried to train the boy to accept him as his true father, thus initiating a sequence of intolerable conflicts centering on the denial of the boy's real male parent. In this, Karl seems to have been the means by which

> Beethoven irrationally translated his own Family Romance into reality: he had replaced Karl's real father by a more noble surrogate—himself—and thereby elevated the boy to a noble rank. In a sense, he created an artificial Family Romance for Karl to match his own fantasies of illegitimacy and royal birth. (372)

I think it useless to analyze in detail all the speculations that Solomon advances about this subject, because they are all rooted in his Family Romance theory that I demonstrated earlier to be a baseless fabrication. I will give only a quote illustrating his scholarly fantasies that he himself describes as "dizzying":

> Karl was Beethoven himself, rescued from his false and unworthy parents by the good prince, royal father, and nourishing mother; he was Beethoven's child, narcissistically (divinely) conceived; he was also a surrogate for and continuation of Caspar Carl, whose rebirth was reenacted in Beethoven's 'rescue' scenario; he was at once Beethoven's hapless father and his partly orphaned younger brothers with whose care the adolescent Beethoven had been charged in 1887; and—even more speculatively—he may have also been a revenant of the firstborn Ludwig Maria, subject therefore, to the vicissitudes of Beethoven's fratricidal and fraternal impulses. In this dizzying series of splittings and substitutions, Carl Caspar, Karl, and Beethoven each in turn play the roles of father, brother, and son. As for Beethoven himself, he quite simply united father, mother, brother, and son in a single person—himself (328).

Solomon centered Beethoven's relationship with his nephew on the alleged Family Romance but did not forget other components of his view of Beethoven. The composer's attempt to curb Karl's youthful sexual fervor, most likely rooted in the fear of the boy's getting a venereal disease, is to Solomon far more than a foolish attempt that was doomed to fail in a teenager—as it is today, too. It was (368) "a pathological effort that carried implications of homoerotic domination, but centered on warped paternal longings and the incest fear that together had impeded Beethoven's lifelong search for a normal family existence."

Solomon acquiesced to the Sterbas' explanation of Karl's suicide attempt as a deviation of aggression towards Beethoven in one against himself (see page 48 above), with this addition (371): "A suicide sometimes seeks reunion in death with a beloved person; he may have wanted to die in order to join one from whom he has been separated. Here Karl's desire to be reunited with his mother seems fairly evident." Although Solomon lists, at page 502 of his "Selected Biography," Stefan Wolf's book *Beethoven's Conflict with his Nephew,* which argues for Karl's act as typical teen-age years behavior, like the ones so often recorded nowadays, Solomon does not mention this alternative analysis.

Solomon is so intoxicated with Freudian fantasies that he makes nephew Karl "heal" his uncle of his alleged Family Romance delusion *twice*. The first time is in 1816, when, after he got Karl's exclusive guardianship, Beethoven saw himself as "father," as he proclaimed to his friends.[43]

> In becoming Karl's "father," [Solomon writes] he was giving the lie to his own Family Romance and affirming that he was indeed a Beethoven rather than the illegitimate son of a king." (361)

The second "healing" happened ten years and twelve pages later, when Karl joined the army in 1826 after his failed suicide attempt, and

> The structure of Beethoven's Family Romance was fast disintegrating under the pressure of these events. The separation from Karl would now allow Beethoven himself to come to terms with the facts of his own ancestry. (373)

Which of the two "healings" is right? Neither, of course. They are both rooted in the same misconception. As if this incongruence within his theory was not enough, Solomon will offer yet a third "healing" in his *Beethoven Essays* book, which I review in the next chapter.

The Immortal Beloved viewed through Freudian lens

Before his 1977 *Beethoven* book, Maynard Solomon claimed to have made major achievement—solving the tantalizing mystery of the "Immortal Beloved." He first launched his theory in a 1972 article, which he obviously elaborated further when including it in his biography of the composer. His candidate, Antonie Brentano, was the wife of one of the men whom Beethoven consistently addressed as "friend" in his letters. She actually became the "official" solution of the English-speaking Beethoven scholarship, sanctioned by the 2000 *New Grove* as the "most convincing" solution in spite of some vigorous scholarly opposition. Solomon maintains that his case for Antonie is essentially based on "hard evidence,"[44] but it actually relies on the "love pattern" that the scholar assigns to the musician, which is the result of his Freudian approach. The reader can find a full rebuttal of Solomon's solution of the puzzle in my book on *The Immortal Beloved Controversy* (on this website), the only non-partisan take on the issue that one can find. I will expose here only one of Solomon's tactics in his approach to Beethoven's very letter he wrote to the unknown woman.

Solomon maintains that Beethoven displayed a consistent "love pattern" throughout his life, which would have been the expression of his "sublimated" homosexuality: always "falling for the unattainable: a married woman, like Antonie, or an aristocrat. Solomon offers as proof his reading of a fragment from the letter in which Beethoven tells his beloved about his recent travel:

> My journey was a fearful one ... the post coach chose another route, but what an awful one; at the stage before the last I was warned not to travel at night; I was made fearful of a forest, but that only made me the more eager—and I was wrong. The coach must needs break down* on the wretched road, a bottomless mud road ... Yet I got some pleasure out of it, as I always do when I successfully overcome difficulties.

---

* Solomon quotes from Thayer-Forbes' awkward translation (p. 533).

Solomon claims to discover the hidden "symbolism" of this narrative, which he gives under the precautionary label of "may be interpreted," but which is actually his essential thesis:

> We begin to feel that Beethoven is here describing no mundane trip through the rain on a daily post coach, but a symbolic journey through a Dantean *selva oscura*, a dark forest, portraying the danger of his own passage from a fearful isolation into manhood and fatherhood [...] The fear-inspiring forest and the bottomless mud road *may be interpreted* as symbolizing Beethoven's terror of Antonie's love, of an engulfing embrace to which he cannot yield because it is somehow forbidden."[45] (my emphasis)

Altman recognized this interpretation as "scholastic poppycock" of Freudian flavor[46] but failed to point its source: in Freud's theory of the interpretation of dreams, with its censure-disguise mechanism, travel is a sexual disguise. But Solomon applies the device not to the transcription of a dream but to a text written in full consciousness about something that Beethoven went through! Freud himself would have been bewildered by this misappropriation of his theory—if not enthused by the "originality" of his disciple.

4
Beethoven's second session on Solomon's couch

In his biography of Beethoven, Maynard Solomon focuses on the alleged Family Romance, but expands considerably his Freudian approach in his next book, the *Beethoven Essays*. The first part, "The Interior Dimension," is a compendium of what may be called posthumous applied psychoanalysis. We encounter here, besides the Family Romance, the acme of the Œdipal complex: "parricide" (67), Freud's theory of dreams in action, a completely novel "identification" theory, and more. The "reappraisal" of Beethoven's relationship with his nephew is basically a review of the critical (both positive and negative) reception of the Sterba couple's book (139-154), and thus of little interest: none of the presented critique goes to equal depth as chapter 2 in my book. So, I will tackle here only those issues that are (or claim to be) "new" in Solomon's psychoanalytical approach to his subject.

Beethoven's "age delusion"

Beethoven appears to have persisted all of his life in the mistaken belief that he was younger than he really was. This belief is epitomized in his rejection of his baptismal certificate, the document which certified, not explicitly but by inference, his birth date. It may seem strange, but Beethoven seems not to have seen this document until late in his life and relied on the information about his age that his family passed to him during his childhood. In 1810, when he got a copy of his baptismal certificate indicating his baptism on "December 17, 1770," which implied that he was born on the 16th (or maybe the 15th) of the month,[*] he wrote on its back, "1772," meaning the birth-year he considered right.[1] Beginning with Thayer, scholars have traditionally blamed the composer's father for this mistaken age: he wanted to make his son appear as a child prodigy comparable to Mozart and subtracted two years from his real age when presented him in public for the first time, on March 26, 1778, as "his little son of six years."[2] The same misrepresentation persisted when Beethoven published his first youthful compositions, most notably his three Clavier Sonatas (now WoO 47) issued in October 1783 with a title page presenting them as the work of "Ludwig van Beethoven, aged eleven years."[3] According to Thayer, the 1772 birth year is "the one given in all the old biographical notices and which corresponds to the dates affixed to many of his first works, and indeed to nearly all allusions to his age in his early years."[4] Beethoven seems to have taken the belief in his 1772 birth-year with him to Vienna and stubbornly stuck to it even after seeing proof of the truth in his baptismal certificate. Solomon had already

---

[*] The religious practice of the time was to baptize the newly-born as soon as possible, therefore Beethoven scholarship has, by quasi-consensus, chosen December 16 as Beethoven's birth-day, now commonly celebrated.

found fault with this view in his biography of Beethoven, in which he called the composer's seemingly odd belief an "age delusion." In his *Beethoven Essays*, he resumes the issue in the section "Beethoven's Birth Year," without recurring to psychoanalytic speculation and focusing on facts, but his argumentation is no less faulty than when on a more Freudian terrain.

Negating the obvious. Solomon takes issue with the two-year age difference from the real year (1770). He claims to find in this evidence of "a consistent pattern of deductions of one year from his [Beethoven's] age during his first two decades [showing that] apparently, Beethoven and his associates (and perhaps his parents as well) all believed that he had been born in 1771" (36). This is, to Solomon, proof that "the birth-year delusion can no longer be ascribed as rising from a deliberate falsification by Johann van Beethoven of his son's age [and that] the delusion was Beethoven's own" (42). In fact, Solomon's "downgrading" the age deduction from two- to one-year is only an arithmetic quirk associated with how one might describe one's age. He computes: on March 26, 1778, when Beethoven's father presented "his little son of six years" in his first public concert, Beethoven was seven years and four months old (that is, seven)—one year more than the alleged "six years." Similarly, in October 1783, when his three Clavier sonatas were published as the work of an eleven-year-old, Beethoven was twelve years and ten months old (that is, twelve)—again, apparently a one year difference. Solomon proffers several similar examples involving Beethoven as a child for which his date and age are known or reasonably assumed, all yielding one year difference. Even the notice that Beethoven's teacher Neefe printed, in March 1783, presenting his pupil as "a boy of eleven years and of most promising talent"[5] is, to Solomon, proof that "Neefe, here and in connection with Beethoven's earliest publications, consistently believed his pupil to have been one year younger than his actual age" (37).

Solomon's arithmetic is, obviously, correct ... but irrelevant. This is because, among Beethoven's contemporaries, age was rounded *up* rather than down. Today, a child who was seven years and four months old would be referred to as seven *because they were not yet eight*. Then, the same child would have *completed* his seventh year, and thus would be "in his eighth year." This becomes apparent in Solomon's own argument, when he states "only one notice published before 1800 specifies a 1772 birth year, [... which] appears to have been widely copied by early nineteenth-century and encyclopedia authors" (38): a biographical note published in 1790 by a certain Ernst Ludwig Gerber, certainly inspired by Neefe's notice.

> Beethoven (Louis van). Son of a tenor in the Electoral Court at Bonn, born there in 1772, a student of Neefe; in his 11th year he was already playing Sebastian Bach's *Well Tempered Clavier*. Also in the same year [1783] he had already published at Speier and Mannheim his earliest attempts at composition—9 Variations on a March, 3 Clavier Sonatas and several Lieder.

Solomon rejects Gerber's dating Beethoven's birth to 1772 (i.e., with a two-year age deduction), because it would result from "the same simple arithmetical error that has plagued so many biographers and scholars, the miscalculation which stems from overlooking the month in which Beethoven was born." In reality, Gerber's computation was right: were Beethoven born in December 1772, he would have been ten (by modern reckoning) in December 1782 and "in his eleventh year" in 1783! To Gerber, Beethoven was both "in his 11th year" (Neefe's quote) and of "age eleven years" in 1783 (as per in the note on the title page of the three Clavier Sonatas published that year).

Finally, let us note that Beethoven's own age deduction (appearing on Beethoven's baptismal certificate quoted above: not 1770 but 1772; a seemingly two-year difference) conforms to Solomon's arithmetic. Since Beethoven was born in December 1770, he would have been in his second year, that is one year old in 1772. Unless, of course, when he wrote "1772" on the back of his baptismal certificate he meant "December 17, 1772." We know that he did not mean that from the evidence that Solomon himself brings in later: the testimony of Wilhelm Christian Müller, a fervent Beethoven fan and promoter of his music living in Bremen. He visited Beethoven in 1819 and wrote a friend in 1827, soon after the composer's death: "We wanted to know from him when his birthday was, in order to celebrate him [...] he replied that he didn't know precisely either the day or the year" (41).[6] It may seem strange that, at almost fifty years of age, Beethoven did not know on what day and month he had been born and is hard to believe that he had forgotten it. More probably, he did not internalize it in his childhood, because, at that time, the birth-day was far less significant and celebrated than the name-day, which was connected to the religious calendar.[7]

All these facts invalidate Solomon's thesis of Beethoven's "age delusion." Downgrading the age deduction from two- to one-year is irrelevant: whether two-year or one-year, the age deduction would still be (to use Solomon's own term) a "falsification." Also, it was the father's "falsification" that would have been the root of Beethoven's supposed "age deduction": daddy certainly would have trained his seven-and-a-half-year-old son to always say he was six; if the child "internalized" an age, it would have been his father's falsified one. This would have been reinforced with each work that the child printed, the public advertising of which emphasized his falsified age. His teachers—van den Enden and, especially, Neefe—simply followed suit, certainly also manipulated by the father, because they were also playing a part in the promotion of a child prodigy. Beethoven naturally took the "age deduction" with him when he travelled to Vienna in 1792.

Irrelevancy of Beethoven's confusion. Continuing his longitudinal exploration of the issue, Solomon discovers that, in 1785, Beethoven began showing some confusion about his age. In 1785, on the autograph of his finished three Piano Quartets (WoO 36), Beethoven wrote, in French, "composé par Louis van Beethoven, agé 13 ans"; however, the age was initially 14, then changed to 13, which seems to indicate confusion, indeed (39)—unless, I would add, it was Beethoven's well-known poor arithmetic abilities that initially misled him. Solomon also offers a few cases in which Beethoven seems to have claimed "age deductions" varying in a wide range, from -3 to +2 years, but those extremes most likely reflect the uncertainty of the evidence. It is possible that the age deduction that Beethoven had internalized had not firmly set to one or two years, but it is hard to accept that it could vary so widely. In any case, this aspect does not support Solomon's thesis, because "confusion" is not equivalent to "delusion"—it is merely uncertain knowledge of facts, not pathological distortion of them.

Misreading the crucial evidence. Solomon's analysis relies on the "absolute" truth, Beethoven's real date of birth, which can be found, by inference but with great accuracy, in the baptismal certificate issued by St. Remigius Church in Bonn, which bears the date of 17 December 1770. Thayer mentions "several certificates of baptism" found in Beethoven's estate after his death, but reproduces only the 1810 copy that the composer's old friend Wegeler sent him, because it also includes on the verso the composer's note rejecting it as "incorrect."[*] We can stipulate that all those certificates indicated the same baptismal date; had Thayer found any discrepancy, he surely would have mentioned it. (We do not know, however, if perhaps "several" meant *more* than the three certificates that are now known to have existed.) Solomon duly quotes (40-41) all the evidence pertaining to these three known baptismal certificates:

1) The one that Beethoven's pupil and friend Ferdinand Ries obtained in 1806, without Beethoven's request. Ries' testimony records no explicit reaction of Beethoven, except a rebuke that the latter threw at his pupil in a letter for his unsolicited and unwelcomed help.

2) The one that the Beethoven's old friend Wegeler sent him, at his request, in 1810. This is the one that Beethoven formally rejected through writing a note on the verso.

3) The one that he received, in 1819 or 1820, from Wilhelm Christian Müller, Beethoven's Bremen aficionado, that I mentioned above.

Solomon has nothing to say about the first two episodes besides tersely mentioning Beethoven's rejection of the certificates as evidence of his "age delusion." On the contrary, he speculated that the Müller-provided certificate supported his thesis. As I've said before: Müller met Beethoven sometime in 1819 and wanted to celebrate him on his birth-day. When Beethoven told him that "he didn't know precisely either the day or the year," Müller took it upon himself, like Ries before him, to obtain and provide to Beethoven a copy of his baptismal certificate (41-42). This document was no different from the other two that Beethoven had seen and had rejected; therefore one would expect him to also have refuted this third certificate. However, Müller claimed that, "through us he came to know the truth, and we spoke with him about it as recently as 1820 and he jestingly said that he would not have believed that he was such an old bloke."[8] Why would Beethoven have finally given in, albeit by poking fun at himself? We have no clue, but we have the proof that Müller did not lie, in a piece of

---

[*] Unfortunately, none of the autographs have been preserved – they were lost together with all the original evidence that Thayer had gathered, therefore we only know these transcriptions.

evidence that Solomon brings in: an entry of Beethoven's nephew Karl in an 1823 conversation book (42):

> Today is the 15th of December, the day of your birth, but I am not sure whether it is the 15th or 17th, inasmuch as we can depend on the certificate of baptism and I read it only once when I was still with you in January.

It is hard to believe that Beethoven would have accepted the December birth-day, while rejecting the year in the certificate. However, Solomon quotes this entry as proof that (42)

> Beethoven had not yet, nor would he ever wholly, come to terms with the facts set forth so simply on the certificate.

In fact, what the nephew was questioning, very likely echoing Beethoven himself, was not the baptismal certificate per se, but the figure 15 versus 17 therein, which might have been not very clear in the copy.

In any case, this certainly is not proof that Beethoven had persuaded, or even tried to persuade, his nephew that the baptismal certificate was not his. In reality, it is Solomon who cannot "come to terms" with the evidence that he had gleaned, which allows a commonsensical approach of the issue.

Common sense about Beethoven's age mistake

The issue of Beethoven's "age delusion" relies essentially on his baptismal certificate, which gives us his "real" birthdate, but its role in the debate is far from simple. It was not a social status document handled to the parents of the newly born, as birth certificates often are today. The church recorded when the child was baptized in its register. When the child had become an adult he would most likely need an excerpt copy of that record to obtain a marriage license (as required in Austria) and a burial spot in a Catholic cemetery, but for no other reason. Also, anyone interested in it could get a copy of the baptism entry, under the seal of a local authority. Note that, when he went to Vienna in 1792, Beethoven had no inkling that he would never return "home." He assumed at the time that, after he had lessons with Haydn for a few years, he would return to become the Kapellmeister of the Prince Elector's orchestra, like his grandfather had been before him. Therefore, he anticipated no need for a baptismal certificate copy. As he did not return to Bonn, he got copies later. The circumstances surrounding these documents, together with the "age deduction" belief that Beethoven had developed in his childhood and youth, help us round up a reasonable, if not perfect, explanation of the composer's mistake about his date of birth.

Beethoven's May 2, 1810 letter to Wegeler, in which he asked his old friend, who was then living in Köln (near Bonn), to get and send him a copy of his baptismal certificate, contains crucial information in this fragment:

> You will not reject a friendly request if I ask you to get for me <u>my baptismal certificate</u>. [...] Something, meanwhile, is to be taken into account; namely that there was a brother <u>born before me</u>, also called Ludwig, but with the addition, <u>Maria</u>, but who died. In order to

determine my age with certainty, one has to find him first. I already know that, without [doing] this, others have made a mistake, because I was told that I am older than I am. — Unfortunately, I have lived for a while without knowing myself how old I am. — I had a family book, but it has been lost, Heaven knows how. — So, don't be annoyed if I recommend this thing to you very warmly, to find the <u>Ludwig Maria</u> and the present <u>Ludwig</u> who came after him.[9] (original emphasis)

Like many of Beethoven's written pieces of evidence, his phrasing is a bit confusing. When he writes "I was told that I am older than I am," he implies that he knows how old he is; however, in the next sentence he confesses that he had "for a while" not known his age. Reordering some of these statement helps understand Beethoven's behavior.

I have lived for a while without knowing myself how old I was. Although "while" is a vague term, the use of the present perfect tense suggests (in German as well as in English) that it must have extended almost to the very moment when Beethoven was writing his letter. This seems incongruent: the "age deduction" that he had internalized during his childhood and teenage years should have made him certain about his age; however, as I showed earlier, the "age deduction" may still have been confused in his mind. Also, as we have seen, Beethoven did not know in 1819-20 on what day of the year he had been born; it is difficult to believe that he knew it in 1810 and forgot it.

I had a family book, but it was lost, Heaven knows how (5). This further illuminates Beethoven's relative confusion: his "family-book," which he would have trusted, had been lost, and not by his doing. He never mentions the loss of a baptismal certificate as the cause of his confusion, which suggests that he had never had or seen one during his Bonn years and very likely had seen one for the first time when Ries had sent him a copy in 1806. He found it to be wrong because his "age deduction," even if still vague, certainly did not fit the 1770 birth year. And he had one more reason:

... there was a brother <u>born before me</u>, also called Ludwig, but with the addition, <u>Maria</u>, but who died. Beethoven knew, from his parents, about this dead older brother, whose date of birth he did not know and whose birth certificate he certainly had not seen (Thayer mentions no copy of his baptism certificate found in the composer's estate; he quoted it from the church registry as April 2, 1769).[10] Beethoven must have assumed that the baptismal certificate he had from Ries belonged to this brother. It may seem strange that he did not wonder why this certificate missed "Maria," the second name of this brother, but he must have taken that as a slip during the transcription.

In order to determine my age with certainty, one has to find him [the older brother] first [in the church registry]. I already know that, without [doing] this, <u>others</u> have made a mistake, because <u>I was told that I am older than I am</u> (my emphasis). So, unspecified "others" had told Beethoven that he was born in 1770, which was, in his opinion, a mistake. Revisiting the episode of Ries' supplied baptismal certificate makes things clear: as he explains, Ries did not act at Beethoven's request but was incited by some unnamed friends of the composer who wanted to know his day of birth (probably in order to celebrate his anniversaries), but Beethoven refused to talk about his age. Without Beethoven's consent, Ries got his baptismal certificate when he returned to Bonn in 1806 before returning to Vienna two years later. Ries mentions only that he sent the document to Beethoven, but he seems to have also disclosed its content to the unspecified "friends." When Beethoven became aware of it, he was demonstrably angry with both Ries and those friends in an 1809 letter to Ries.[11] Those un-named mutual friends must be the "others" who had told Beethoven that he had been born in 1770, though he was sure that he was younger. Obviously, Beethoven was certain that the baptismal certificate he had from Ries was wrong, even if he did not jot down his rejection on its verso, as he would later do on the one he got from Wegeler: one cannot be sure of it, but it is likely that he had already chosen 1772 as the "true" year! Indeed, the underlined "I was told that I am older *than I am*" implies that the period of confusion had ended and he knew his true age when he was writing.

One may wonder why Beethoven wrote Wegeler to ask for another copy of his baptismal certificate, when he was sure that he knew how old he was. It was not because, as Solomon claims, "his mind was not set at rest concerning the discrepancy between the evidence of the baptismal certificate and his own belief that he was younger" (40). Beethoven asked Wegeler to answer his request "the sooner," and his friend attributed that impatience to get the certificate to a mysterious "marriage project" that Beethoven had in that year, which was discussed amongst Beethoven's friends: Stephen von Breuning, then living close to the composer in Vienna, wrote to Wegeler in August, "I believe his marriage plans have fallen through."[12] Most scholars accept that the object of Beethoven's affection was the teenage Therese Malfatti, to whose family he had been introduced: it would have been somewhat convenient for Beethoven to produce a certificate dated 1772 rather than 1770, when asking for the hand of a teenager.

In his letter, Beethoven gave Wegeler directions how to avoid the mistake that, in his opinion, Ries had made: locate first the baptismal record of the older brother Ludwig Maria in the church registry, and look further for his own baptism date. Beethoven also repeats this direction, emphatically, in the end of his request: "don't be annoyed if I recommend this thing to you very warmly, to find the Ludwig Maria and the present Ludwig who came after him." The document he got from Wegeler, the one transcribed by Thayer, bore the baptism date "December 17, 1770," and also included the names of the godparents—his grandfather and (because he was a widower) a woman, "Gertrud Müller, named Baums."[13] We do not know if Wegeler followed the instructions and had first located the Ludwig Maria sibling—he probably did—but he must not have assured Beethoven that he did so in his letter accompanying the certificate (not extant, like most letters that Beethoven received). Therefore, Beethoven persisted in his mistake.

His rejection note on the back of the certificate reads, "1772" and adds, "The baptismal certificate seems to be incorrect, since there was a Ludwig born before me. A Baumgarten was my sponsor [godparent] I believe."[14] Did Beethoven refute only the year 1770, as a copyist's mistake, or the whole certificate as "incorrect?" The reference to the name of the godmother, which Beethoven also threw doubt on, clearly shows that he rejected the document per se, assuming that it was his older brother's certificate, even though the middle name Maria was missing; he must have again considered that the copyist slip.

The third baptismal certificate, provided by Müller almost ten years later, and the evidence surrounding it, raise two questions:

1) If Beethoven was sure, after he got the second baptismal certificate, that he was born in 1772, why did he tell Müller that "he didn't know precisely" the year? The most likely explanation is that he was still not sure about the year.

2) Why did Beethoven finally accept the baptismal certificate as his, even though it was identical with the previous two that he had rejected? He must have realized that three different copyists could not make the same mistake—omit his older brother's middle name.

Summing up: Beethoven's "age delusion" was an honest mistake, explainable primarily by the two-year deduction initiated by his father that the son internalized during the Bonn years, as Thayer surmised. There was, however, a delusional element in Beethoven's persistence in this mistake, in spite of the repeated proofs he received that he was wrong.

There is some more interesting information in the evidence that Solomon quotes but never explores. For instance, Ries, who was very close to Beethoven during his thirties, wrote that he "never wanted to speak about his age" (40). Was this refusal related to his alleged "age delusion"? Later on, Solomon brings forward the testimony of Bettina Brentano, who met Beethoven in July 1810: that is, after he had rejected his baptismal certificate, conjecturing that he had been born in 1772. Bettina wrote a friend that "he [Beethoven] does not know his age himself but he believes he is thirty-five" (41). This figure, three years lower than the age he had just proclaimed, may be related to his unwillingness to disclose his age publicly; rather, he was ready to misrepresent it for the sake of a charming young lady. He also did not miss the opportunity to rejuvenate himself—and he succeeded, because Bettina's full statement was, "He does not know his age, but thinks he is thirty-five, though he hardly looks thirty."[15] There is room here for speculation, but I have pledged to stick to the facts.

The nobility pretense—more of the same

Solomon expands the scope of his research to add more support to and even reach beyond the two new theses in his biography of Beethoven that I examined and debunked in the previous chapter. He recurs less in psychoanalytical speculations and focuses on facts, but his presentations, albeit not void of certain merits, almost always sidestep any exploration that would risk weakening his main theses.

The pre-1815 nobility pretense. Solomon quotes, in support of his thesis, two testimonies from people who knew Beethoven well, Wegeler and Schindler, albeit in very different periods of his life. "Wegeler," Solomon writes, "was fully aware of his friend's nobility pretense" (45) and quotes:

Louis van Beethoven passed from time to time for a noble, because people regarded the Dutch particle "van" as the equivalent of the German "von." In Vienna, this lasted three years. Indeed a lawsuit of Beethoven lasted for this time at the Landrechte.[16]

The "fully aware" adjective is only Solomon's implication. Wegeler's statement, taken from his "supplement" to the "Biographical Notices" about Beethoven that he co-authored with Ries, is both very vague and confusing: the phrase "from time to time" implies repetition, but only the example of those "three years" in Vienna follows. Even more relevant is the fact that Wegeler never mentions his friend's passing as an aristocrat in his first version of the book published in 1838, but only in the "Supplement" to the 1845 revised edition of the book (a year after he had introduced it in 1844 in a very short notice in the Munich newspaper *Kölnische Zeitung)*. It is obvious that his alleged "awareness" happened only after Schindler published his biography of Beethoven in 1840, in which he narrated the composer's battles in court (1815-1818) for the custody of his nephew.

The Schindler quote invoked by Solomon is an equally succinct and general statement (45):

> Had the nobles not believed him [Beethoven] to be one of them, neither his genius nor his works of art would have won him the favored position he had enjoyed [; …] the little word "van" had exercised a magic power.*

This does not indicate a time frame directly but implies that it applied not only to the 1815-1818 court dealings but also to Beethoven's early career in Vienna, when his enthusiastic reception in the aristocratic salons smoothed his path to success. Thayer quickly pointed out the precariousness of this statement, deploring that "Schindler was not as well informed as he was ought to have been in the premises [… and provided] not exact knowledge but an amiable bias in favor of his hero."[17] Indeed, Schindler was very close to Beethoven during the so-called "exposure" of the nobility pretense in December 1818 and testified about its devastating effect on him, but did not try to scratch beyond the surface of the issue. Admittedly, he might have avoided questioning Beethoven himself so as not to upset him; however, Schindler could have asked privately Count Moritz Lichnowsky, an old-time friend of Beethoven whom Schindler knew, if he was aware of any assumption of the composer's nobility in the early 1800s. He did not or at least did not choose to report it.

Without such clarifying evidence, Schindler's explanation of the "imposture" is just baseless speculation, and one that defies the facts: why would the Viennese aristocracy need the spur of the *esprit de corps* to appreciate

---

* In an endnote attached to this quotation, (10 at p. 310), Solomon adds: "a tiny manifestation of this deception lies in the substitution of the abbreviation *v* for *van* in Beethoven's correspondence." This was no newly developed deceptive trick: Beethoven had practiced this shortening before his arrival in Vienna, for example in his first known, 1787, letter (Anderson 1). He also signed L. v. Beethoven his November 2, 1793 letter (Anderson 7) to his teenage friend Eleonore von Breuning, whom he could not deceive, since she knew his humble social status all too well.

Beethoven as the one destined—according to the formula coined by Count Waldstein—"to receive Mozart's spirit from Haydn's hands," two commoners whose excellence they (the aristocracy) were now fully acknowledging?

A second explanation of Beethoven's imposture. Emphasizing that Beethoven was not indifferent to awards and distinctions, Solomon then maintains that Beethoven's nobility pretense "is expressive of that simple need for status and recognition which is so marked in Beethoven's personality" (50)—a commonsensical conclusion that seems incongruent with Solomon's thesis that the said "pretense" was a way of "living out the Family Romance." Nevertheless, he does not seem aware of the incongruity and tries to add more evidence in support of his thesis.

The Family Romance connection. Solomon begins his new strategy for validating his thesis by claiming to prove that, even after he acknowledged in the nobility court that he had no documentary proof of nobility, Beethoven continued to believe in his "noble origin," as Solomon puts it, without trying to explain what Beethoven meant by what he called "nobility by nature." Solomon further invokes (53) a letter the composer wrote, in July 1819, to a magistrate in the commoner's court, to which the lawsuit had been redirected, to inform him about the incident in the nobility court: "the discussion turned on the little word 'van'; and I had sufficient personal pride to declare that I had *never* worried *about my nobility*."[18] Solomon then notices that Beethoven's referred declaration in court did not acknowledge lack of nobility but lack of *proof* of nobility (true!); he also finds a similar statement in a memorandum draft that Beethoven prepared for the court in February 1820, in which he wrote about the unfortunate "lack of a title [proof] of nobility" of his nephew and added: "The same can be said too of myself." In the context of these statements that avoid conceding non-nobility, Solomon concludes (53) that the 1819 letter "gives the impression that his [Beethoven's] nobility was so certain that he would not debate it with those who required proof of it." And this "impression" alone—not supported by any corroborating evidence—leads Solomon to reiterate the alleged link between nobility pretense and Family Romance (54-55) that he had proffered in his biography of Beethoven (which I rebutted in chapter 2). An impression is no proof, especially when based on a single word, "bekümmert" in German, which is not unequivocal; it could also mean "concerned" or even "grieved," a meaning frequent in the eighteenth and nineteenth centuries.

Did Beethoven's nobility pretense prohibit him from getting the real thing? Turning his attention to the larger topic of "ennoblement" of commoners during Beethoven's time, Solomon speculates that the latter's "imposture" actually prevented him from getting a title (47)—how could he request one, when he had let everybody think he had one? The inference is reasonable, but the premise that he could have gotten one is as doubtful as claiming that he had made everyone think that he was of noble origin. Solomon offers this interesting quote in support of his assertion (48):

> Joseph II made financiers into noblemen by the dozens," noted W. H. Bruford, to which Arthur Loesser added, "Wealth was not the

only gateway to aristocracy, talents, too, were rewarded with ennobling recognition: botanists, librarians, physicians, and archaeologists acquired the beneficent "von" when their achievements were sufficiently noted.

Solomon fails to notice that musicians are conspicuously missing in the list of the ennobled, even though, when one thinks today of the great achievements of the age in the German world, music is the first one that comes to mind. In the whole index of Beethoven literature there are only two names of musicians bearing a legitimate *von*, Ignaz Ritter von Seyfried (1776-1841) and Karl Ditters von Dittersdorf (1739-1799), but they are not perfect examples of recognition of outstanding merit. Seyfried inherited his *von* from his father, who was the councilor of the Prince of Hohenlohe-Schillingsfürst[19]—one could buy such functions that had a *von* attached, as the father of the great poet Goethe did. Dittersdorf got his *von* himself when his patron, Count Schaffgotsch, prince-bishop of Breslau, wanted to offer commoner Karl Ditters a compensation for keeping him isolated in the provincial city of Johannisberg (Silesia, now in Czechia): he had the Empress Maria Theresa appoint him *Amtshauptmann* (district administrator) of Freiwaldau, a function that required a title.[20] One cannot help wondering why Prince Nikolaus Esterhazy did not do the same for Joseph Haydn, a much more auspicious talent that he kept isolated at his domain in the Hungarian marshes. Real merit seems not to have counted too much, even though the Habsburg nobility was reputed to be the most dedicated to music in the whole of Europe.

More explorations and misses of Solomon. Solomon finally tackles Ries' testimony that I quoted in the previous chapter, the episode in which an un-named "old countess" clearly did not treat Beethoven as her equal (66). He speculates further (54-55) and proposes two alternative reactions of the aristocracy to Beethoven's alleged "imposture:" 1) some "segments" of the nobility, namely the recently ennobled ones after the vicissitudes of the seventeenth century Counter Reformation that decimated the class, "suffered from a sense of impostorship, of shared deception, which would have predisposed them to acceptance of Beethoven's claim" (54-55); 2) "it is also conceivable that the aristocracy, or portions of it, tolerated the great composer's pretense with a fine combination of tact and secret amusement" (55). Both suppositions are reasonable, but they ignore one simple question: how did Beethoven "enact" his pretense nobility? When he was not sitting at the piano in their salons, did he behave like one who wanted to claim to be "one of them"? The fact that he considered taking dance lessons when he arrived in Vienna[21] suggests that he wanted to put on some aristocratic airs. However, there is unavoidable evidence, already presented in the previous chapter, that Beethoven "was unmannerly both in demeanor and behavior"—how could he expect to be accepted as an aristocrat?

Solomon finally discovers Vienna's "craze" for titles (45-46) not in Pezzl's work, but in the book of the English memorialist John Russel, who visited Vienna around 1820 and wrote in the book he published that, "It is common for both sexes to prefix *von*, the mark of nobility, to their surname," but missed Pezzl explanation of the fact.[22] Noticing that Beethoven's brother Carl was recorded in his clerk job register as "Carl v. Beethoven," Solomon claims that the latter had his own "nobility pretense" (46-47). On the same page, Solomon tries to resuscitate, with new speculations, an old and never corroborated "Beethoven family tradition," launched by Frimmel, according to which the composer's brother Johann would have also pretended Netherlandish nobility. The implication is that all the Beethoven brothers claimed nobility. Given Carl's modest achievements, one can be certain that he was not nourishing his own Family Romance, which works only with exceptional men, and he got his "von" either by virtue of his menial official position of "Kasse-officier" (teller) with a prominent bank or, even simpler, by deceptively shortening the *van* in his name. We know little about the youngest Beethoven brother, besides that he was a successful businessman, so he was probably recorded, in his own city, Linz, as a "v. Beethoven," like "our" Beethoven was listed in his State government tax letters.

Unaware of Pezzl's work, Solomon does not have all the facts. Eventually, he did not include Vienna's "title craze" in his 1998 revised biography of Beethoven, possibly because he became aware that it did not serve his thesis.

Summing up. Solomon's second attempt to interpret Beethoven's nobility pretense does not offer any new and convincing arguments to his original take of the issue, with its two essential theses—that the pretense was an "imposture" starting when Beethoven settled in Vienna, and it was his way of "living out" his Family Romance. On the other hand, the pretense itself is a fact during his 1815-1818 lawsuits against his sister-in law in the Vienna Nobility Court. Unfortunately, the facts evidenced in these last two chapters make up such an entangled knot of contradictions that the issue may never be solved. Why did Beethoven claim, albeit implicitly, to be of noble birth, although he knew that he was not of noble birth and he did not exhibit any desire to pass as an aristocrat in society? Why was he very distressed when the case was demoted to the commoners' judiciary, but not because he was exposed as a liar? His acceptance of the "Herr von" status was to him simply the public acknowledgement of the value of his "nature" of genius, of which he was fully aware—but that did not bestow a noble title. Could he have judged it enough to justify his claim to access the same judiciary body as the aristocracy? Some scholars, including Solomon at a certain point (see p. 69 above), have proposed that Beethoven rationalized that his "nobility by nature," which made him a "notable" of his times, entitled him to some of the respect and privileges of the aristocracy. The question becomes, why it materialized only in this episode in courts? Schindler may have been right, after all, to cut this Gordian knot by claiming that what was at stake, the custody of his nephew was uniquely important for Beethoven and he did not trust the commoners' court as equitable and reckoned the nobility court as more "appreciative of his importance."[23] All in all, this is a euphemism for "corrupting the court," as the Sterba couple maintained (see page 37), the proof of a "moral fracture" that is hard to explain in a person who was, in spite of some drawbacks, an honest person.

Trying to disentangle the nobility pretense issue

How did it happen? As I pointed out in chapter 3, it was Beethoven's sister-in-law Johanna who claimed nobility before him, by taking her case to the Nobility court. Beethoven only tacitly acquiesced; he must have been, directly or indirectly, responsible for her belief that she was entitled to do so. A scenario based on the opposite is incompatible with his well-documented distress when the Nobility Court sent the case to the lower commoners' court. [24] The process was complex and the scholarly world took it for granted, without trying to draw on it, because there is no other evidence than the bare facts: on November 14, 1815, Beethoven persuaded his dying brother Carl to make a will designating Beethoven as sole guardian of his nephew after Carl's death and appointing a certain Dr. Schönauer, a court lawyer, as the will's "curator" (executor); the same day, after Beethoven left, Carl's wife Johanna persuaded him to add a codicil to his will, designating both Beethoven and her as her son's guardians. On November 17, one day after Carl died, Schönauer delivered both the will and the codicil, under seal, to the Nobility Court;[25] Beethoven was summoned to the court for November 22, when he learned that, according to the will and codicil, he will share his nephew's custody with his mother.[26] Obviously, it was Beethoven's sister-in-law Johanna who decided to deliver the will and codicil to the court, and do it without having Beethoven involved, because she did not want him to discover the existence of the codicil that was practically rescinding the will. Was it her decision to address the Nobility court? It was, actually, not she who delivered the documents, but her lawyer, who was certainly aware that only the nobility had access to the Nobility Court. She must have assured him that Carl was of the nobility—but why? As seen in chapter 2, Johanna was a vain person, but it is hard to believe that she invented her nobility. Of course, she knew that her husband had been a "Herr von"—she would not have married an ordinary commoner, because she came from a family of "considerable wealth"[27] and was probably a "Jungfrau von" before marrying, according to the Viennese "title craze." However, she must have known that Carl's "von" was not proof of nobility. As I showed in the previous chapter, she was very likely truthful when testifying in court that she held the belief in the family's nobility from "the [Beethoven] brothers." A scenario in which the nobility pretense originated with Johanna, to which Beethoven only tacitly acquiesced after the fact, is incongruent with his distress when the lie was discovered and the case was demoted to the commoners' judiciary. Beethoven was certainly the active side of the pretense: he had been the head of the family for a long time and would have been the repository of the alleged (actually nonexistent) proof of title.

Why the Nobility Court? Distrust of the commoners' court might have been a reason, even though, as I showed in chapter 2, corruption has not been evident as an issue in the Habsburg courts. The lawsuit against his sister-in-law Johanna was not Beethoven's first rub with law. He had had two other cases that were settled out of court: with the *Artaria* publisher (1802) and with Mälzel, the inventor of the metronome (1814), both about what we call now "intellectual rights." Later, he had to go to court when two of the guarantors of his annuity-contract stopped paying their shares: in 1812, Prince Kinsky died and his heirs refused to assume this obligation and, in 1815, after Prince Lobkowitz became bankrupt and did not provide payments for years, Beethoven again had to go to court to eventually obtain this right.[28] In both cases, he understandably took his case to a Nobility Court (in Vienna and Prague, respectively), because the defendants were noble and it was their, not his, social status which mattered.[29] He might have liked how these courts dealt with the case (the last one only after his appeal), but he did not interact with the court directly; his devoted lawyer Johann Kanka, whom he repeatedly called "friend" in his letters, handled it. This time, Beethoven knew he was going to act in court and on a much more difficult matter, in which he tried to deny a mother her right to motherhood. This was an entirely different situation.

I think that Beethoven was confronted with an existential question: to be or not to be a "plebe"? There is no evidence that he effectively claimed to be of noble birth, but he left plenty of written documents in which he complained after losing the status because of his misstep in the Nobility Court, which sent his case to the commoner's judiciary. His basic complaint: he did not belong to the "plebs," as he deprecatorily called the commoner's world in his 1820 (or 1819) conversation book entry quoted in the previous chapter. He did not want to be treated like a commoner in front of an audience of commoners. This may seem incongruent with his lofty proclaimed principles, but is true: Beethoven, the man who set to music the "All men shall be brothers" ode of the universal "brotherhood" in his *Ninth Symphony,* actually believed that some shall be more "brothers" than others. "I don't write for the galleries!"[30] he angrily retorted to the opera house director who had explained to him that his *Fidelio* did not appeal to everyone.

He certainly did not feel he was the "brother" of his servants, who could only afford gallery tickets. The category of servants may be the epitome of the "plebs," and gives some food for thought: for hundreds of years, musicians had been servants living in the suites of aristocratic and ecclesiastic authorities whom they entertained, and had been treated and many times mistreated, as Mozart was at the hands of his master Archbishop Colloredo. Haydn, the son of a humble wagon-maker, wanted not only his genius but also his human dignity to be respected like one belonging to a "Herr" and even a "Herr von," and he made that a clause in his renewed 1895 contract with his employer.[31] Beethoven was born into the same condition and, as a boy, must have known well the difference between his status and the one of a "Herr." Becoming increasingly aware of his genius, he must have developed a "superiority complex" that can be perceived in his ambiguous relationships with the nobility later in his life. "Kings and princes are able, no doubt, to appoint professors, create Privy Councilors, award [nobility] titles and affix order ribbons," he wrote to Bettina Brentano, "But they cannot create great men or minds which rise above the rabble of this world."*

---

* This statement is the beginning of a spurious August 1812 letter of Beethoven to Bettina Brentano (Anderson, vol. 3, p. 1357). It introduces the narration of a famous incident in which Beethoven taught a lesson in dignity to Goethe, who behaved obsequiously to a

According to the recollections of Gottfried Fischer, a witness of Beethoven's childhood years, he was already certain he would become a "Herr."[32] Nevertheless, even after having become a "Herr von" (i. e., higher than just a "Herr") he had his moments of humiliation such as the one narrated by Ries, when he felt treated like a servant. He hated the prospect of sitting, in the court bench, next to a servant who would witness the washing of his dirty family linen. I do not find it impossible that he asked Schönauer, the executor of Carl's will, to deposit it in the Nobility Court. He might have even had a mitigating circumstance for his lie.

A mitigating possibility: Lost nobility. This is actually not a new issue—it was launched by Belgian scholar Raymund Van Aerde in a 1939 article that "complemented"[33] his 1928 book *The Flemish ancestors of Beethoven* in which he had established Beethoven's roots. This article traced further back into the history of the van Beethoven family, connecting the name to the Betho locality (surviving today as the Betho Castle in the city of Tongeren) and suggested, without offering any palpable evidence beyond similar happenstances, that the old (thirteenth to fifteenth centuries) van Betho ancestors may have been of low ranking nobility attached to a greater landlord, but they were impoverished during the wars and had to become field laborers, losing their status. Solomon buries his quote of van Aerde's supposition in an endnote disconnected from the text that refers it (note 8 on page 310) and does not explore it at all.

The lost nobility supposition actually deserves exploration: if it is true, the Beethoven family might have kept the memory of lost nobility alive as a legend until it reached young Beethoven, who would have also passed it to his brothers. And there is an entry in the early 1819 conversation books that has, to my knowledge, escaped notice so far and that bears witness that the "lost nobility" was discussed within Beethoven's circle at the time. Oliva, one of his friends, suggested in that entry, "You could initiate it [a lawsuit] as if you were merely restoring your family's older nobility."[34] Unfortunately, we do not have Beethoven's answer and the next entries depart from the issue; perhaps he thought it was futile to pursue it. Toward the end of the year, Beethoven explained to another friend (probably Bernard) in his conversation book that "<u>Van</u> means nobility <u>only</u> when it is placed between two last names, for instance Bentink van Diepenheim or Hoof van Vrenland, etc."[35]—a rule that clearly excluded himself. The entry shows up quite unexpectedly, but Beethoven's closure of it may be relevant: "In the Netherlands, one would get the best understanding of this <u>meaningless</u> meaning"; the final pun that he underlined (in German "Unbedeutende Bedeutenheit") suggests that he attached little, if any, importance to his *van* as possible proof of nobility. He was very likely right: historical examples show *van* plus place-name forming well-known family names of commoners stretching from the fourteenth century to the twentieth century—Jan van Eyck to Kies van Dongen, including even more famous individuals like Rembrandt van Rijn and Vincent van Gogh. However,

---

royal retinue. As I show in my *Immortal Beloved Controversy* book (chapter 10), Bettina fabricated this letter but based it on a real episode that Beethoven himself narrated to her.

Beethoven's lassitude might also mean that he, or his family elders, had investigated the possibility and had come out empty-handed.

One can speculate even further: Johanna's marriage to Carl had not been the modern-day romance-to-marriage kind, even though their son was born five months after the wedding;[36] her wealthy father must have demanded some assurances about the status of his future son-in-law and it is possible that he received such assurances in the form of the alleged ancient, since lost, nobility. I do not claim that the "lost nobility" supposition solves Beethoven's nobility pretense issue, but it might have been a part of it. And I will stop speculating, because I have promised to offer facts and not opinions in this book. One certainty I can, however, offer: the issue cannot in any way support Solomon's theory about Beethoven's alleged Family Romance.

The dreams of Beethoven

Beethoven narrated a few of his dreams in letters to four of his friends, for the very simple reason that they were involved in those dreams. Solomon could not miss examining them through the typical Freudian lens in his *Beethoven Essays*, re-discovering therein his old favorites—Family Romance, homosexuality, Œdipal inclinations (including parricide and incest), nobility pretense, etc. The first clue that Solomon extracts from these four dreams is a connection between their addressees—Ignaz Gleichelstein (in 1807), Archduke Rudolph (1819), Tobias Hasslinger (1821) and Karl Holz (1826): all of them were men younger than the composer (the oldest, Hasslinger, was 34). He immediately infers that Beethoven's reason for narrating to them dreams in which they appeared must have been ... his "sublimated homosexual feelings" (64). The homosexuality connection is, however, only the beginning of Solomonian exertions and a collateral diagnosis. He strings up these four dreams in chronological order, as if he would put Beethoven on his couch in four successive sessions (over an interval of nineteen years!), at the end of which he makes his patient diagnose his own psychopathy and thus helps him cure himself (64-73). He begins with an authoritative quote stating that everybody has a "core dream"—one that reflects the essence of his or her personality and, of course, their psychopathy; the task of the psychoanalyst is to identify this core dream. Proceeding further, Solomon lets himself get carried away by his Freudian zeal and his rhetorical abilities, shrouding the issues in airy eloquence (each addressee of Beethoven's letters gets biographical pages, and frequent digressions, plus psychoanalytical tortuous "demonstrations") intended to overwhelm the reader and prevent them from stopping to ask the simplest question.

I will not follow Solomon closely into his applications of the Freudian dream symbolism, which is, as I have said, wildly speculative—and likely tedious and frustrating to the reader. I will, however, reveal his many scholarly errors that appear to be deliberate misrepresentations intended to legitimize his tactics.

The Gleichensteim dream, the first one, is a perfect illustration of this approach:

> The night before last I had a dream in which you seemed to be in a stable, where you were so wholly bewitched and captivated by a pair

> of magnificent horses [...]
>
> Your purchase of a hat has been a failure, for yesterday already, as I came out here early in the morning, it got *a rip* in it (57-58, Solomon's italics).

Solomon transforms the phrase "a pair of horses" into a stallion and a mare enacting "a primal scene"—that is copulating (65). Marie-Elizabeth Tellenbach, a native German speaker, exposed this already in 1993: Solomon "revised" Anderson's version of the letter (as he acknowledges in note 9 at page 58), changing the word "couple" to "pair," to imply that the pair was one male and one female, which were mating. In fact, the original German phrase "ein Paar Pferde" means "a couple of horses," that is two horses, with no gender involved; to indicate a couple consisting of a stallion and a mare German uses the compound word "Pferdepaar," but even this term does not imply that the pair were mating.[37] Further, Solomon sees in the torn hat mentioned in the next sentence as a dream-symbol of "feelings of anxiety and castration in the presence of a primal scene" (65). In fact, as Tellenbach points out, the hat is not part of the dream narration—the composer had moved away from the dream and told now his friend that an actual hat that the latter had bought for him was torn.[38] Solomon applies Freud's dream symbolism to a sentence uttered in full awareness, a practice that he inaugurated, as we have seen in the previous chapter, in his reading of the letter Beethoven wrote to his Immortal Beloved!

The "Archduke dream" appears towards the end of Beethoven's October 15, 1819 letter to his royal pupil Rudolph:

> Steiner already has Y. I. H.'s [Your Imperial Highness'] Variations; he will thank you himself for them. As for the title page, it just occurs to me that the Emperor Joseph traveled under the name of Count von Falkenstein.
>
> As I see in the *Diarium* [a Viennese newspaper], Baumeister has built for himself a house in eternity. Without making the slightest claim as a recommender, I would know someone who would fill this place with Y. I. H. to perfect satisfaction.
>
> I am greatly looking forward to being with Y. I. H. tomorrow. Last night I dreamed about Y. I. H. Although no music was played, yet it was a musical dream. But in my waking hours too I think of Y. I. H. The Mass will now soon be finished — May heaven empty the cornucopia of its blessings daily and hourly upon your illustrious head (59).[39]

As one can see, the dream itself occupies only two sentences in the last paragraph: "Last night I dreamed about Y. I. H. Although no music was performed, yet it was a musical dream." Solomon could hardly find an adequate Freudian dream symbol for this "musical" character, but he was right to connect it with the continuation of the letter. Beethoven was working at his *Missa Solemnis*, which he had promised to compose for the investiture of the archduke as archbishop of Ölmutz in March of the following year, but was afraid, at the moment when he was writing, that he would not be able to finish the work in due time and the dream reflected his worry (66). This time, I find Solomon's inference persuasive: indeed, as neuroscience has found, most of our dreams express not wish-fulfillment, as Freud claims, but our "angsts."

However, the shrink was not satisfied with that plausible find—which is not quite what he is interested in—and appeals to another couch technique: "free association." Describing his explorations as far-fetched would be an understatement. Beethoven's reference, in the second paragraph, to Baumeister, the Archduke's private secretary and librarian, who "has built for himself a house in eternity," a pun ("baumen" means "to build" in German) meaning that the man just died, may seem a little callous, but Solomon sees much more in it: he parallels it with Beethoven's act of "parricide" in Bonn, thirty years before, when he petitioned (and obtained) that half of his father's pension be handed to him. Solomon supports this association with the "Diarium" reference in the letter: the newspaper that announced Baumeister's death had been renamed *Wiener Zeitung* in 1780, hence the use of the old name would show Beethoven turning back thirty years and remembering his then wrongdoing, that was an even worse mark of disrespect for his father, an act that must also have left him with strong feelings of guilt (67). That Beethoven had guilty feelings toward his father is very likely, far less so for his alleged "parricide" than for leaving him in very poor health when he left for Vienna in 1792 (the old man died the next month).

It is, however, hardly credible that the composer's subconscious feelings of guilt would have chosen a letter to his imperial pupil in which to pop up; in fact, Beethoven simply wanted to recommend someone for the job that Baumeister had had with the archduke. Moreover, the link that Solomon claims to establish between Beethoven's guilt feeling with the *Diarium* word in the letter is far-fetched at best. This name of the newspaper was changed in 1780, and it is very unlikely that a ten-years old would have internalized the old *Diarium* name and used it forty (not thirty, as Solomon claims) years later. Beethoven most likely adopted the old name that was still used be the Viennese.Solomon speculation is just a subterfuge allowing him to utter again the Freudian buzzword "parricide," with a hope that it could serve to reveal Beethoven's never-proven Œdipal behavior.

Yet this claim is "mild" when compared to what Solomon builds around the oncoming publication of the set of variations of his pupil Archduke Rudolf. The Archduke had told Beethoven that he intended to publish them under a nom de plume, Count Falkenstein. Beethoven's sentence in his letter, "[…] it just occurs to me that the Emperor Joseph traveled under the name of Count von Falkenstein" occasions one of the wildest speculations in the whole book. The simple appearance of the word "Emperor" is the proof that Beethoven was "activating the constellation of [his] family romance and nobility pretense fantasies" (67), followed by another amplification: Beethoven's alleged "quest for the father" would link him to Emperor Joseph II himself, which would make him his imperial pupil's cousin—and even "brother" in a parenthesis (68)! And then—another surprise—Solomon goes back "to the very beginning," that is to the Gleichenstein dream, which he describes as "[…] the primal scene in which Beethoven's conception has taken place, but the picture is dim, there is no sound.

Sexual intercourse is sublimated (repressed) into 'music' but Beethoven cannot identify the 'performers'; that is, he cannot see his parents because it is too dark" (68). I leave it to the reader to comment this interpretation.

The Haslinger dream appears at the end of a September 1821 letter to a young man whose first name was Tobias. The full text runs:

> Yesterday, as I found myself in the carriage on the way to Vienna, I was overcome by sleep, all the more so, since I scarcely ever (on account of the early rising here) have had a proper sleep. While thus slumbering, I dreamed that I was taking a very long journey as far as Syria, as far as India, back again in Arabia; finally I came, indeed, to Jerusalem. The Holy City prompted thoughts of Holy Scripture, and small wonder that the man Tobias occurred to me, and naturally that our little Tobias and the pertobiasser[*] should enter my mind; now during my dream journey the following Canon came to me:
>
> [Canon theme "O Tobias" (15 bars) follows]
>
> But I had scarcely awakened, when away went the Canon, and nothing of it would come back to my memory. But when, next day, I was on my way hither in the same conveyance (that of a poor Austrian musician), while awake, the dream journey went on, and, behold, according to the law of association of ideas, the same Canon came back to me. Now, fully awake, I held it fast, as once Menelaus did Proteus, only allowing it just to change itself into three voices
>
> [Canon on 3 voices (15 bars) follows]
>
> Farewell. Personally I will send you something on Steiner to show that he is not a stony heart. Farewell, very best of fellows [... a passage follows containing several puns of no consequence for the present topic]. Sing the epistles of St. Paul every day, go every Sunday to Pater Werner, who will show you the little book by which you may go to heaven in a jiffy. You see my anxiety for the salvation of your soul, and I remain with the greatest pleasure from everlasting to everlasting, your most faithful debtor Beethoven (60-62).

As one can see, only the first paragraph deals with the dream and includes elements (travel, departure, foreign exotic land, the city of Jerusalem, etc.) to make any Freudian scholar happy. It comes as no surprise that Solomon here meets again his well-known favorite themes, but he also brings in a new idea: the dream

---

[*] This strange word has puzzled all translators, including Solomon, who adopted several renderings (see his note 16 at page 62). The correct word is "pertobiaserl," a combination of the Italian *per* (for), Tobias name and the German suffix *erl*, used to create diminutives as terms of endearing; it means "something for little Tobias," that is the very Canon included in the letter. The solution is actually suggested in the very fragment, "*little Tobias* and the *pertobiasser[l];*" it is obvious in the original German, which reads, "unser *Tobiasserl* and das *pertobiasser[l]*." The issue is, of course, irrelevant in the topic discussed here, but illustrates Solomon's dubious knowledge of German (or Italian, for that matter).

is a wish fulfillment (70-71)—the return to "the Bonn infancy-Eden converted into the prospective image of Paradise," which is symbolized by Jerusalem, the Holy City. This is actually not a novelty—old age (Beethoven was now fifty, old at the time) is known for a penchant for traveling back in time to childhood, and he had expressed his wish to revisit his birth town several times in the 1820s. Therefore, Solomon has to discover "another route to the interior of this dream. Driving and traveling are universal symbols of sexual union [in psychoanalysis], and Beethoven's 'long journey' is the wish fulfillment of an incompletely realized heterosexuality." He does not explain the meaning of completing one's heterosexuality (having sex? marrying? having children?) and reproducing his half-page argument (71), would be far too tedious and not at all illuminating.

It is much more interesting to note that Solomon brings in again elements completely separate from the dream and follows their "free associations"—the Freudian technique for dream interpretation and a favorite of his. In a real coach session, the technique is an interaction with the patient but, in his Beethoven endeavor, Solomon's fantasy roams unbridled to take him where he wants and we know very well what that is. In the analysis of this dream, he quotes Beethoven's farewell advice to Haslinger, "Sing the epistles of St. Paul every day [etc...] you see my anxiety for the salvation of your soul," and triumphantly concludes: "The homosexual component is suggested by references to anxiety and to a cleansing religiosity" (71). In fact, it is hard to miss the underlying sarcastic tone in the St. Paul reference, especially when one knows (which Solomon apparently does not) the reputation of the said Pater Werner, whose life story is narrated by John Russell, the Englishman (mentioned above) who toured Europe and visited Vienna in 1822, later publishing a narration of his tour. Werner was a former dramatist and carouser who joined the Protestant church in Prussia and turned into a mystic writer before converting to Catholicism in Vienna and being rewarded with an ecclesiastical appointment. "It is doubtful whether he be more fanatic or hypocrite," writes Russell. "Public opinion, however, among well-educated persons, runs most generally for the latter."[40] The latter was also the opinion shared by Beethoven's circle: his friend Oliva entered a short note in an 1820 conversation Book about "[...] Father Werner [with] his gross idiotic manners."[41] Solomon could have guessed the apparent sarcasm even without knowing Russell's work and Oliva's entry because he explored Beethoven's religiosity further in the same book, concluding that the musician "had little use for organized religion" (220), but his Freudian fervor overcame him.

And there is more of the same free association. In the second paragraph of his letter, Beethoven describes how the next day, again riding in a carriage, "[...] the same Canon came back to me. Now, fully awake, I held it fast, as once Menelaus did Proteus [...]." The story of Menelaus and Proteus is simple: Menelaus, best known as the cuckolded husband of Helen of Troy, went to Proteus, who had a reputation as an oracle, to ask a prophesy while turning back home from the Trojan war. Proteus, however, was a very shifty creature who was able to change shape every second into a different animal—probably to get rid of the annoying visitor. Menelaus was, however, able to grasp all the shapes that Proteus changed into, and eventually got what he wanted. What Beethoven meant is obvious: the Canon theme almost escaped him, but he held fast, "only allowing it just to change itself into three voices." Yet again, Solomon applies the "free association" panacea to this fragment, deciding it has "similar [that is homosexual] implications" to the St. Paul statement, although "the Oedipal aspects are more decisive" (71). By such a criterion, anyone that writes about Menelaus and Proteus is a homosexual or, more likely, a parricide.

But wait! Solomon offers us two for one! He has something to deduce from the very name of the addressee of Beethoven's letter—Tobias Haslinger. According to the free association recipe, the name must also point to some place in Beethoven sub-consciousness, otherwise he would not have associated it, in his dream, with the Holy City of Jerusalem! And Solomon adds more ingredients to his psychoanalytic borsht:

> The contours of this mythic pattern [Tobias' life] are those of Beethoven's dream itself: exile [Vienna?], quest, escape from phallic dangers (Proteus), conquest of the exotic witch-bride (Helen, wife of Menelaus), return to the homeland (Jerusalem, Ithaca, Bonn), reunion with the mother, and ultimately recognition of the father, which permits the hero to take his place among the elders" (71-72).

Remarkable but pointless erudition.

Can we make any sense of the "Haslinger dream," without cooking up a Freudian recipe? Of course, dreams are, by their very nature, elusive to understanding, especially when one knows nothing about the dreamer's daily life at the time, but we have a few guidelines from neuro-science, common sense and personal experience that can help us in a rather simple case like this one. Dreams are based on intimate, old or recent, life impressions, usually—but not always—tainted by feelings of apprehension. Although this one may not point to Beethoven's "return to Bonn-Eden" that the scholar shrink builds, it is quite possible that the composer's desire to revisit his native city, often expressed by him during the 1820-ies, should have inspired him a travel dream. The exotic places (Arabia to India) of his travels may have been spawned by his interest in the Oriental philosophy, for which Solomon himself brings in some evidence in a note (46 at page 71, page 318 of notes). And I think one can easily explain the association between Haslinger and Jerusalem. Tobias is a first name that shows only once in the list of Beethoven's correspondents, therefore it must have struck the composer; being an Israelite name, the association with Jerusalem must have been immediate to him.

The Holz dream happened in the summer of 1826. Beethoven wrote his young friend Karl Holz the following:

> I dreamed last night that your parents were begetting you for this world, and how much sweat it cost them to bring such an amazing piece of work into the light of day. I congratulate you on your existence — how? why?! And so forth, the riddles solve themselves — (63)

Solomon assumes without any discussion that this is an openly sexual message: Beethoven dreamed that he was watching the parents of Holz having sex, to which the phrase "how much sweat it cost them ..." adds some tangy authenticity. A Beethoven scholar cannot fail noticing that this text is quite unique in Beethoven's over 1500 letters; while he likes and practices the sexual innuendo, he avoids overt references. Why would he write a sexually loaded letter and why to Holz? It is true that Beethoven loved this new friend for his youthful freshness as well as for his devotion to his music (Holz was a good violinist) and to his very person (he was acting like a kind of non-paid secretary to replace Schindler); Beethoven had, at a certain point, even deemed Holz the best person to write his biography after his death. However, none of the over thirty messages that the composer had sent him since August 1825, some short, some longer (mostly concerned with printing his music) contained anything comparable. If we re-read the message, we notice that the term "beget" does not mean "copulate," but simply having a child. Also, the "sweat" may be a general description of the long-time parental toil to raise a child.

Solomon does not care about such semantic subtleties and goes forcefully into the reading he proposes, pointing out that Beethoven does not use the term "I dreamed," as it appears in the above translation, but the verb "I know," which would show that the text was "no 'dream,' no imagining, but direct perception— 'knowledge'"—which, foreseeably, leads the shrink to the Family Romance again, via the Freudian dream disguise of his own parents into those of Holz. However, he has a surprise in store for us: this dream would mark Beethoven abandoning his fantasy, as proven by his admission that he "knows" now that these were "his" parents. Moreover, he solves the "riddles" in Beethoven's final line: "in the Holz dream [...] the oneiric riddle of existence—the Delphic riddle—is posed and deciphered. Birth and rebirth are one.

Beethoven has restored the primal triad of infancy: he has no further need to fear, kill or compete with his father, whom he freely acknowledges, desiring only that he be permitted to share the mother with him" (73). And so, at the end of the fourth couch session, the shrink has healed his patient! However, the conclusion that Beethoven had finally abandoned his Family Romance fantasy in 1826 should puzzle whomever had read attentively Solomon's first Beethoven book, in which he clearly states that "in becoming Karl's 'father,' he [Beethoven] was [...] affirming that he was indeed a Beethoven rather than an illegitimate son of a king"[42]—which would have happened long before 1826.

Solomon's interpretation of the Holz dream has a big problem besides the psychoanalysis model that he faithfully follows and exuberantly elaborates upon. The original German, which he gives after Kalischer in a note, (19 at page 63), does not read, "I know," as Solomon claims, but "I could." The German text runs,

> Ich *könnte* diese Nacht, da ihre Eltern sie auf die Welt beförderten,
> und wie viel Schweis er sie gekostet, ein solches erstaunliches
> Machwerk ans Tageslicht zu bringen. (my italics)

Its literal translation, "I could last night, when your parents brought you into the world [...]," does not make any sense. *Ich könnte* means I could; *Ich kenne*—I know; "I would know" is, in German, *Ich kennte*. Whether Solomon's mistake is poor mastery of language or deliberate misunderstanding is hard for me to say, but it is clear that without the "I know" language scaffolding, his Freudian interpretation of this dream implodes: Beethoven could not "know" the truth about his conception.

Can we arrive at a better solution to this linguistic jumble than the simplest one adopted by Anderson and taken over by Solomon himself, "I dreamed that"[43]? There are two acceptable variants:

1) Adding some words that Beethoven slipped out after "I could" which would give "I could *tell you that I dreamed* last night how your parents brought you into the world [...]." This reading is fundamentally the same as Anderson's translation.

2) By dropping the "I could," that is by assuming that Beethoven stopped after beginning this way and resumed later his letter about a different issue, forgetting to cross out those two introductory words. What he wanted to say was, "this night, when your parents brought you into the world [...]." Obviously, Holz had not been born the previous night, but this wording seems a good metaphor for "this is your birthday anniversary." Kalischer must have arrived at this solution of the puzzle, because he mentions "Birthday letter" (Geburtstagsbrief) in a note at the end of the letter.[44]

With either of the two possibilities, I cannot claim to elucidate the meaning of the "riddles" in the final lines. As I wrote, they are a mystery that only the context of some unknown previous communications between the two protagonists might clarify.

Of all of Solomon's psychoanalytic interpretations in his chapter on "The dreams of Beethoven," only one offers a valid find: that "concert in which one could hear no music" in the letter to Archduke Rudolph very likely reflects the composer's uneasiness at not having been able to keep his promise and deliver the *Missa Solemnis* to its dedicatee on schedule. Beethoven's wish to return to Bonn probably inspired his fourth dream, but this find is old news and all the Freudian wrappings around it are untenable. Every other proclaimed find is a fabrication based on ignoring or distorting facts, using incorrect translations of the original documents and making groundless inferences.

Another alleged Beethoven fantasy:
"identifying" with his dead elder brother Ludwig Maria

At the end of his take on the Holz dream, Solomon claims emphatically, "One riddle remains" (74) and launches himself on a new path: the hero of a dream, he says, quoting a scholarly authority, is either the actor playing in it or a "mere onlooker"; however, the scholar pursues, both the actor and the onlooker are only "introjects" of the dreamer's own "ego," which makes three participants. And then he introduces another character in Beethoven's Holz dream:

> The fourth character, observing the birth of the hero, *may* be the lost brother Ludwig Maria, who lived for six days in April 1769 and who

Beethoven consciously believed was the rightful possessor of the baptismal records that constituted the only evidence of his own birth (75, my italics).

Applying his typical tactics of transforming a *may* (italicized in the above quote) into an *is*, Solomon elaborates another wild speculation—Beethoven dreaming of being observed by his dead brother—on top of the previous wild speculation—Beethoven dreaming of seeing his parents conceiving him—into an incredible new chapter of his book: "The posthumous life of Ludwig Maria." To put a fifteen-page chapter in a nutshell: the first born of "our" Beethoven's parents, Ludwig Maria, was "the brief happiness of the young married couple" for the six days that he lived, while Beethoven, the second born, was "unloved and unwanted" (76); therefore, he developed a "central" fantasy in which he "identified" with the "loved, wanted" first born (82).

Solomon builds his argumentation by resuming a shorter version of the same case on which he based the other alleged Beethoven's "central" fantasy—the Family Romance, which is, as I showed in chapter 3, Solomon's own scholarly delusion. This time, the same case yields to this new, radically different and "compensatory" fantasy. Solomon does not bring any evidence to support the two assumptions on which he founds his theory—the "wanted, loved" first born and "unwanted, unloved" second one. He only offers his own speculations taking his psychoanalytical approach to a new height, in which he fuses all of his theses—Family Romance, age delusion, parricidal impulses, etc.—supported by flamboyant erudition—the Enlightenment, Napoleon, German Romanticism, van Gogh, Francesco Guardi, Salvador Dali, Edgar Allan Poe, William Faulkner, etc.—yielding a construct with an inconsistency of which he is utterly oblivious. Indeed, this new theory does not replace the Family Romance theory in Solomon's whole construct of Beethoven's life but complements it: the identification with his dead brother would help Beethoven "compensate" for his "disturbance in identity" by "holding fast to his tenuous family ties, by allying himself with—even 'becoming'—Ludwig Maria, who was, without any doubt, a Beethoven" (85).

I will not follow all Solomonian variations on his "identification theme," amplified into a *unio mystics* (85) with the "oedipal brother" (87), in which music is involved via the line of Don Fernando in the finale of *Fidelio*, "the brother seeks the brother," which would be a "sublimation" of Beethoven's direction to Wegeler, "search out Ludwig Maria" (86-87). Almost every line of Solomon would require a long comment, changing this sub-chapter into a very tedious and virtually useless book. Elementary logic can take us via a far shorter path to the same verdict when analyzing only the essential evidence that Solomon proffers. His crucial "demonstration" begins:

> Beethoven's birth-year delusion [...] was the plainest confirmation of his deeply rooted family romance; and this delusion was itself founded upon a confusion of identity between Beethoven and the dead Ludwig Maria. (82)

Solomon does not realize that the two fantasies—Family Romance and identification with his older dead brother—are not "compensatory," as he claims, but incompatible: if Beethoven was convinced he was not his father's son, he could not identify with another son of the same father, unless he suffered from a "split personality" symptom that would have certainly labeled him as insane, a logical inference that Solomon, however, never proposes.

Solomon's demonstration continues:

> In the crucial document that makes this [identity] confusion manifest, Beethoven insists: "But one thing must be borne in mind, namely, that there was a brother <u>born before me</u>, who was also named Ludwig with the addition Maria, but who died. To fix my age beyond doubt, this brother must first be found." (82, Beethoven's emphasis)

He does not mention that the quotation is extracted from the May 1810 letter Beethoven wrote to his friend Wegeler, living in Cologne (Köln, close to Bonn), to ask him to get and send him a copy of his baptismal certificate. I have already analyzed this letter (page 78ff), showing that it displays no birthdate confusion: Beethoven was sure to know how old he was, but he also knew that "others have made a mistake [about it], because I was told that I am older than I am"; therefore, he needed his baptism certificate to make it clear that he was right, once for all; and he also needed it, because he had a "marriage project," for which such an act was required. The phrase "this brother must first be found" is but a direction to Wegeler what to do to make sure he finds the right entry in the church register, which was ordered by date: find this Ludwig Maria first and look further for the next Ludwig. Solomon takes this phrase over to make it into an "existential" quest of Beethoven a few lines further: "This is not a mere slip but an expression of his [Beethoven's] inner conviction that Ludwig Maria, though somehow present, remained to be discovered" (83). If the little phrase had been found in a Beethoven sketchbook or in his *Tagebuch* diary or in one of his conversation books, one could, by a long stretch, advance such a speculation, but in these circumstances it is only a scholarly delusion.

Solomon then reaches the second "crucial" document, the baptism certificate that Beethoven received from Wegeler in 1810:

> On back of the authentic copy of his certificate, Beethoven notes: "The baptismal certificate seems to be incorrect, since there was a Ludwig born before me." In wrongly asserting that his own birth certificate belonged to Ludwig Maria, Beethoven was yielding up his own identity. He no longer had a baptismal certificate or a birth date, both of these being the property of another. At the very least this displacement disclosed *his inner certainty* that a substitution had taken place, which left him bereft of the basic insignia of selfhood. (83, my emphasis)

This is actually the core of Solomon's "demonstration": contesting the certificate, Beethoven would have assumed the identity of his brother—not even "metaphorically," but in "his inner certainty." I previously explained Beethoven's reaction: because Wegeler did not make it clear that he had "located" the dead brother first (of course, it would have been even better to send copies of both certificates), he stuck to his incorrect conviction that he was born in 1772. He was simply rejecting—albeit for the wrong reason—a date of birth that he believed was that of Ludwig Maria, therefore he proclaimed his "OWN identity," distinct from that of his dead brother.

One more thing is relevant. The "identification" that Solomon advances is not exactly Freudian—in fact it is quite a novelty. All the various kinds of identification in the psychoanalytic literature, from Freud himself to Melanie Klein (whom Solomon quotes in a different context, 89-90), apply to living people with whom the subject, a child or youth, interacts and whose behavior he takes for role model. To the Sterbas, Beethoven identifies with his mother, at least in her "motherly love" for her children. How could he "identify" with a brother that he had never seen? Solomon's "demonstration" of his thesis is as logical as a certain kind of dreams that some parents get from their child: "I dreamed last night that I was not myself, I was my brother" (or sister, if you will).

Beethoven's deafness à la Freud

The little that is known about Beethoven's deafness and the results of his autopsy have not helped old or new medical science to throw much light on the subject. Being completely out of the field, Solomon has not much to say about it beyond platitudes like "a form of magical asceticism, a rite of passage, a prelude to an ecstatic and 'holy' state from which emerged the masterpieces of his maturity" (95) or "he perceived his deafness as a wounding, a punishment, a retaliation" (96)—which appear somewhat contradictory. Everybody has agreed that "deafness was Beethoven's main rationale for his withdrawal from society" (97); the addition "from sexual relationships" is in line with Solomonian thinking but is not true: we know from his letter-exchange with Josephine Brunsvik-Deym, with whom he was in love between 1804 and 1807, that he constantly pressed her for what she termed "sensual love," and her refusal eventually put an end to their relationship.[45] Even Solomon accepts later that the composer was able to compensate the physical defect and "explore in reality the geography of the feminine" (98)—whether "geography" means psychological or carnal is not clear.

Predictably, Solomon cannot abstain from taking Beethoven's deafness in his Freudian dream interpretation, in which the ear has "phallic attributes," so that losing one's hearing is a symbol of castration; on the other hand, the ear can be "a nourishing female principle" (96-97)—psychoanalysis always finds ways to explain two opposites with the same apparatus or the other way around. There is no need to refute a thesis based on the Freudian delusion, which is, moreover, applied completely off its alleged scope: diagnosing illness based on interpreting a dream that never was—a triple misjudgment.

I want, however, to say this: it seems that we all—denigrators as well as devotees—having for such a long time intruded in Beethoven's mind and soul, have become so desensitized that we cannot grasp the magnitude of his tragedy and its intense impact on his psyche. We like to measure him as a human with our linear scale and we cannot realize that suffering can increase exponentially and reach the point when the soul may snap—at least occasionally.

Solomon's spawning

The enthusiasm generated by Solomon's theories has stimulated more such approaches, but I will not tarry to deal with fantasies rooted in the mother of all fantasies. I will only quote one such elaboration, illustrating both Solomon's delusion-laden authority in the Beethoven scholarly circles and the extravagant zeal of his disciples:

> Beethoven consistently disavowed the year of his birth, a delusion that Solomon convincingly interpreted as motivated in the desire to merge his identity with that of a brother, named Ludwig Maria, who died before the composer Ludwig's birth. Most notably, late in his life for a period of over fifteen years, Beethoven did nothing to suppress the rumor that he was the natural son of King Frederik Wilhelm III of Prussia. The rumor surfaced in 1810; after repeated queries, Beethoven admitted its falseness in a letter of December 1826, and then failed to post the letter. Significant in this delusional filiation is not only the formulaic family romance about royalty, but more specific the projection of north German Protestant filiation. The figure of the Prussian king may be displacing several fathers, from Johann van Beethoven to Ludwig's Habsburg patrons, but the projected musical (and thereby also cultural) paternity of another Johann—J. S. Bach—must be suspected to contribute to the compromise formation.[46]

This incredible quote is, ironically, from a book titled "Listening to Reason."

Parting with all the psychoanalysis-based views of Beethoven is certainly one of the best homages that the scholarly world could pay to poor old Ludwig who has enriched our lives.

PART II
BEETHOVEN'S MENTAL HEALTH FILE

The interest in Beethoven's mental health is and is not a novelty. It was actually more intense during his lifetime than after. His "eccentric" behavior shocked many of those who saw him and the epithet "crazy" was attached to him long before his death. However, people tended to exonerate him, accepting such behavior as the natural result of his well-known particular affliction, far more harmful for a musician than for the any other profession. This restraint held on for a century after his death, unless we count as "mental" Beethoven's well documented love of wine, which was not an uncommon inclination in the lives of the artistic minds. Then Ernst Newman took on "the Unconscious Beethoven" in his eponymous book, which hinted to the composer's displaying psychological "obsession bordering on the insane." And then, as we have seen in the first part of this book, Freud's disciples claimed that Beethoven lived with various "delusions," a term clearly pointing to some form of psychopathy.

Psychiatry, the discipline proper dealing with mental illness, has never accepted psychoanalysis as a scientific discipline and did not participate in the debate on Beethoven's mental health for a long time. It was only after the beginning of the new millennium that two physicians brought it into the conversation and, invoking the criteria set by the APA (American Psychiatry Association), transformed "love of wine" into "substance abuse" and also diagnosed Beethoven with other psychopathic disorders.

Common sense would ask us to trust the physicians to diagnose. However, this case is special, because it is a post-mortem examination, in which the physicians have to rely on the existing evidence. We have seen in the first part shrinks ignoring and/or distorting the evidence, and there is no certainty that the physicians and psychiatrists do not do the same. Not being a physician, let alone a psychiatrist, I will not touch on purely medical arguments, but I will address the biographical and logical aspects of the arguments advanced by Davies and Mai. For instance, one does not need to be a specialist to reject the argument of a psychiatrist who collects a dozen episodes involving wine spread over a quarter of a century and claims they prove Beethoven's alcoholism based on APA criteria, whose first condition is that all such events happen during twelve months. This is the kind of argumentation that you will meet time and again in the second part of this book.

5
The Case for Beethoven's alcoholism

The issue of Beethoven's drinking habits has been recently revisited by several physicians from a medical prospective. Peter J. Davies, a gastroenterologist and a music scholar well known as the author of *Mozart as a Person*, published in 2001 a similar pair of volumes dedicated to Beethoven, one of which tackles the issue, among many others, concluding that the composer had a "drinking problem," but stopping short of calling him an alcoholic.[1] François Martin Mai, a professor of psychiatry with the *University of Ottawa* took this extra step in 2007, in his book *Diagnosing Genius—The Life and Death of Beethoven*, in which he claims the composer to have been a "likely" alcoholic.[2] The same year, another physician, Dr. Michael Lorenz dropped the "likely" adjective in an article in *The Beethoven Journal,* proposing "the image of an addict who has to consume his drug until the very last moment of his life."[3]

The issue is not a novelty. Beethoven's fondness of wine has been known for a long time from several pieces of evidence, but successive generations of scholars have not considered it of much import, for reasons that will become apparent later. They trusted the testimony of the composer's friends who had known him for many years, like Wegeler and Schindler, who published the first authentic biographies or memories of him and maintained that he liked wine but "lived moderately." Furthermore, Beethoven's well-known creative pattern required continuous painstaking, day after day (and even night after night), lucid work on his musical material—"I still live by the saying *Nulla die sine linea*—no day without [having written] a line" he wrote to his friend Wegeler in 1826[4]— and would have been incompatible with alcoholism. Ober summed up in 1971 the quasi-unanimous opinion that "neither his [Beethoven's] work habits, nor his conduct, supported the idea of alcoholism."[5]

The debate was rekindled during the last few decades by several physicians that are also music lovers, not because of some new biographical findings but following the accumulation of medical proof that cirrhosis of the liver, the disease that likely killed Beethoven (advanced as diagnosis by Frimmel a hundred years ago),[6] was intimately linked to alcohol consumption. These physician-turned-scholars revisited the existing evidence, chief of which is Dr. Wawruch's account of Beethoven's medical condition and death published in 1842, but written in 1827 shortly after the composer's death. Wawruch was one of the physicians that treated him during his last months and his wording is clear and blunt: Beethoven had showed a "predominant inclination" towards alcoholic beverages almost all his adult life. This later scholarly generation took Wawruch's account seriously and contended that Schindler, already discredited for destroying or altering some evidence in order to promote his own image of Beethoven, had also lied about his drinking habits. Such was the claim made in 1981 by John O'Shea in a book investigating the health problems of several famous musicians;[7] according to him, Beethoven had a "drinking problem" that caused his death by cirrhosis, but he stopped short from calling the composer an alcoholic. His one-and-a-half-page analysis relies on only one argument, namely that Thayer, the most prominent of the nineteenth century biographers of Beethoven, would have "strongly suspected" that alcohol consumption had caused the composer's final illness and death. It is impossible to know what Thayer suspected or not, but he never intimated such a thing; his careful documenting the composer's wine purchases was just the expression of the scholarly mission that he had assumed, namely to collect every piece of evidence about Beethoven that was available.

We should start the scrutiny of the argumentations of these three physician-turned-scholars with a presentation of the historical perspective, which they completely ignore.[*] This will help both evaluate their views and then revisit the issue for a dispassionate analysis, based on the existing evidence.

A very short history of wine

For thousands of years, wine has been a staple of Western and non-Western cultures. From Egyptian mysteries to the Christian Eucharist, wine has played an important part in religious rituals. Almost four thousand years ago (around 1750 BC), the Code of Hammurabi, a set of laws of the Babylonian kings, regulated its trade.[8] A 6th century BC Hindu text described it as "the invigorator of mind and body, antidote to sleeplessness, sorrow and fatigue ... producer of hunger, happiness and digestion."[9] Ancient Greeks had a strong attachment to wine and the "father of [Western] medicine," the Greek Hippocrates, included it in almost all of his recipes for various illnesses.[10] In the Islamic world, banning wine met with the opposition of famous doctors (such as Ibn Seena, better known as Avicenna) who thought it essential to good health care;[11] it seems that drinking wine was still allowed in some parts of the ancient Muslim world, like Spain.[12] During the Middle Ages, wine (diluted with water) was given to soldiers for "staving off sickness within armies."[13] Actually, up until the second half of the 19th century, wine was the only known antiseptic (used for bandaging soldiers' wounds) and was added to water to make it safer to drink.[14]

Wine was much more than a medical prescription ingredient; it was deemed to be an excellent nutrient. Because of the similar appearances of red wine and blood, it was thought to be the best prevention cure against blood diseases. Medical writers recommended it as a source of nutrition and a basic medicine during the early modern period (14-18th c.);[15] it was thought to help digestion, prevent digestive diseases and even cure them.[16] Such views survived well into the 19th century. According to a Dr. Robert Druitt's bestseller medical book, wines (especially the French ones) "were ideal for children (sic!), the old, the sick, and for anyone who needed to use their brain."[17] Dr. Pasteur, the founder of modern medicine, did extensive research about wine (he discovered the process

---

[*] In his ten-page bibliography, Mai includes the same two books from which I have drawn the historical context, but he only retained therefrom the discussion about lead intoxication from consumption of adulterated wine.

of fermentation of the grapes) and concluded that it was "the healthiest and most hygienic of drinks."[18] Such views may seem exaggerated nowadays, after the advent of preservation through pasteurization and freezing, disinfectants and antibiotics, but they were largely justified at the time. Actually, modern science has proved that they had a certain factual basis. We know now that wine kills the microbes that carry the typhoid fever,[19] the reason why medieval armies relied on it; we know that wine helps digestion (especially that of proteins), which explains why doctors had recommended it as a nutrient for centuries; we also know now that, in moderate amounts, red wine is good for the heart.[20]

During Beethoven's time, the Austrian Empire was the second largest grape cultivator in Europe, after France,[21] and wine was on everybody's dinner table, be they rich or poor—the difference consisted in quality—simply because it was a much safer drink than water. Servants in the households of wealthy people received an amount of wine as part of their "benefits."[22] Lorenz himself discovered the custom in one of Beethoven's conversation books,[23] but he did not draw the right inference that Beethoven did not drink all the wine that he bought. There was one more, seasonal, Viennese factor that made wine very popular— the Central European summer heat, combined with the typical rusty smog of the city;[24] during an age when water was notoriously unsafe, the only cure of dehydration was beer or (diluted) wine.

It comes as no surprise, therefore, that the statistics of the time (1808) give the per capita consumption of the Viennese of 185 quarts of wine and 165 quarts of beer.[25] Given the population demographics and its drinking pattern (with men doing by far the most of it), one can estimate that any Viennese adult male consumed almost one quart of wine and almost as much beer per day. Were all Viennese men alcoholic? The mentality of the age was different from the one of our modern SAMHSA;* the alcoholic was the man who got drunk and forgot his social standing and family duties; the man who could drink without getting inebriated was actually proving his manhood. Actually, this human "sub-species" has survived at least in France, the country of wine *par excellence*: it is called "consommateur régulier" in the statistics: he—but also, albeit to a lesser extent, she—drinks around 200 liters wine per year (225 for males), that is nearly one 750 ml bottle per day, almost always with their meals.[26]

Davies' claims of a conspiracy of the witnesses

Of the three authors, Davies presents the most substantial argument, which includes evidence collected from Beethoven's letters, his conversation books, and testimonies from his friends and visitors illustrating the frequent occurrence of wine in his life. On the space of four pages (100-104) he collects some four dozen brief references to wine, beer, taverns, inns, alehouses, merry parties found within the evidence beginning 1797. Chief among them is the testimony of Karl Holz, a young violinist who "usurped" Schindler's position as the composer's close friend and private secretary in the years 1825-26, thus arousing the latter's jealousy. Holz testified later that the composer "was a stout eater of substantial

---

* Substance Abuse and Mental Health Services Administration.

food; he drank a great deal of wine at table, but could stand a great deal, and in merry company he sometimes became tipsy."[27] None of the other pieces of evidence presented by Davies goes further than Holz did, but their number gives the image of a reveler rather than that of a consummate composer who claimed to "live by the saying *Nulla die sine linea.*"

This image of Beethoven is, however, inconsistent with other testimonies that Davies himself quotes. Wegeler, who had known the composer since his teen years and had been close to him in Vienna between 1794 and 1796 (when Wegeler finished medical school there), acknowledged that his friend "lived moderately" in his memories about him, which he co-authored with Ferdinand Ries.[28] It is possible that Beethoven had changed a lot in thirty years and "took to the bottle" later, yet Davies himself quotes the testimony of Johann Sporschil, historian and publicist, who met the composer in 1826 and noticed that "he partakes of wine moderately."[29]

Davies dismisses Wegeler's account as part of the conspiracy led by Schindler to hide this dark side of the composer. He quotes from the letter that Schindler sent Wegeler immediately after Beethoven's death, which mentions the latter's concern about rumors claiming that Beethoven had drunk himself into death and asks Wegeler to take care that "his moral life would not be sullied." However, it was only after the publication in 1842 of Dr. Wawruch's article about Beethoven's medical condition and death, which claimed that the composer "loved alcoholic beverages,"[30] that Schindler's letter achieved, in Davies' words, "its desired effect"—that is, initiating the alleged conspiracy. Wegeler included the following paragraph in his supplement of the second, 1845 edition of his memories of the composer:

> By and large Beethoven lived moderately, and as far as I know, not one of his friends and acquaintances ever saw him intoxicated. Dr. Waurauch's [Wawruch's] statement that Dr. Malfatti had prescribed iced punch for him when he suffered from dropsy because as an old friend he knew Beethoven's strong taste for alcoholic beverages, is therefore completely unfounded. Causes for dropsy were unfortunately abundant.

That Schindler has walked many extra miles into forgeries to defend his proprietary image of Beethoven has been known for a long time but, as far as we know, it is the first time that Wegeler's good faith is challenged. In fact, his paragraph continues with a sentence that has, curiously enough, escaped the attention of the medical scholars whose opinion we are now investigating:

> The accusation—which Livius had long ago leveled against musicians in Rome, when he called them *vini avidum ferme genus* [a species firmly addicted to wine] and with which I frequently teased my friend—should be treated with considerable reservation.[31]

It is clear that Beethoven used to drink more than Wegeler thought wise, even though the latter never saw him intoxicated. That could have referred to a period only up to 1796, the year when Wegeler left Vienna (he never met his friend again); he could be referencing an even earlier period, during the Bonn years (i.e., until 1792), when he was quite often in the young musician's company. Obviously, Wegeler was not participating in any conspiracy—he simply said what he knew, without hiding anything.

As for Sporschil's testimony that Beethoven used to drink wine moderately, Davies simply forgets it and insists on making Holz's statement credible above all others. "Schindler wasted no opportunity to sully Holz's reputation," Davies writes. In fact, it is Schindler who provides Davies his crucial argument: in a conversation book entry at the end of February 1827, Schindler tells Beethoven that Holz "recently said to Breuning that you always drink more than a quart [Mass] of wine at lunch, and other untruths" (98).[32] That gives Davies the opportunity to quantitatively estimate the amount of wine that Beethoven allegedly used to drink on a daily basis—a German *Mass*, which is about a liter (a bit over a quart). Davies assumes that Beethoven did so for his whole life, although he does not give any evidence for that (because there is none), which allows him to conclude that Beethoven "very likely" belonged to the high risk category of "drinkers who regularly imbibe more than fifty to sixty grams [of pure alcohol] a day," twenty percent of which "will ultimately develop cirrhosis of the liver" (104).[*]

However, like O'Shea, Davies stopped short of diagnosing alcoholism: "It is to be emphasized," he wrote, "that Beethoven was not an alcoholic in the sense that he was unable to control his intake" (104). He does not mention any other "sense" in which the "A" letter would have applied. As I showed two pages above, even if Davies' estimate of Beethoven's wine consumption through all his mature life were real, he would have been just a "regular" Viennese.

Lorenz's case, based on Wawruch's testimony

Lorenz's claim to have proven Beethoven's alcoholism is based on Dr. Wawruch's testimony, which he hails as "a turning point in Beethoven biography [...] the authentic voice of a medically qualified witness [... giving] with much credibility [... a testimony ...] without parallel" (L 92).[33] The essential statement in Wawruch's testimony is that, in his thirtieth year, following the onset of deafness and some digestive illnesses and, because

> Not really being accustomed to taking medical advice seriously, he [Beethoven] began to enjoy alcoholic beverages. (W 88)[34]

Wawruch further claims that Dr. Malfatti, who later joined the team of physicians treating the composer, "as Beethoven's long-time friend, was able to acknowledge Beethoven's predominant inclination towards alcoholic beverages" (W 90). And Lorenz pursues relentlessly his goal of proving the composer's alcoholism down to his last breath: he gleans evidence extracted from the composer's letters and conversation books showing large amounts of wine being bought for his household during his fatal illness (L 97-98) and ends his argument quoting from a letter that Schindler wrote to the publisher Schott, who had sent

---

[*] Davies adopts a very conservative content of alcohol (2%), in the range he quotes "between 5 and 20 percent by volume" (97).

Beethoven a bottle of wine, "He enjoyed your *Rüdesheimer* [wine] by the spoonful until his death,"[35] which would convey "the image of an addict who has to consume his drug until the very last moment of his life" (L 98).

Dr. Lorenz's argumentation appears judicious, but a closer scrutiny of it and of Wawruch's account on which it relies reveals serious flaws.

Evaluation of Wawruch's account. Wawruch's is a disconcerting testimony. On the one hand, it is a precious document about Beethoven's final illness and death; it is the one from which we know about the mysterious incident that switched Beethoven's ongoing recovery into aggravation of his illness (51). It is not only a detached, seemingly objective, tableau of Beethoven's health issue; the cold observer makes room sometimes for a compassionate visitor who bears witness of human inner strength and dignity in the midst of agony and death. This conveys credibility, but one feels unsettled when reading, "The lives of rare talents of his [Beethoven's] kind are generally full of interesting moments until their passing but no one else can collect them better than a physician friend" (W 87).* Wawruch claims to have been Beethoven's friend, although, by his own admission, he had met the composer for the first time at the onset of his fatal illness. Inevitably, Schindler publicly attacked Wawruch's account immediately after it was published in 1842, emphasizing this misrepresentation.

Lorenz actually avoids tackling this particular claim of Wawruch, about which we have the interesting evidence given later by the son of Beethoven's friend Stephan von Breuning, himself a physician. Gerhard von Breuning was fourteen years old in 1827 and the almost-daily visits he paid Beethoven were the composer's happiest moments during his long agony. Memories of those visits left a strong imprint on the teenager's mind (they were also the main impetus for his decision to become a physician) and they appear quite fresh and unadulterated in the book that he published almost fifty years later, which I have already quoted several times. He wrote that Beethoven disliked Wawruch so much that he would turn in his bed facing the wall during his visits, mumbling "O, that ass," and eventually refused to talk to him at all, while he was quite open towards other physicians.[36] Lorenz simply ignores Breuning's testimony, although he could have resorted to Maynard Solomon's rebuttal of it in the preface to Breuning's book, published in English translation in 1992. Solomon shows that Breuning met Schindler when preparing his book and concludes that the former "naively" took over many of the latter's "most spiteful fabrications" about Beethoven's sister-in-law Johanna, his nephew Karl, and his brother Johann, including the "vengeful attacks on Dr. Wawruch." In fact, Solomon's argument is weakened by his own bias in favor of anyone Beethoven thought ill of, such as his sister-in-law, who was in fact (see chapter 2) a dishonest person. Moreover, Solomon himself acknowledges that Breuning "maintained an independent position on some issues," for instance when mentioning Johann's constant presence at the sickbed, which Schindler denied. [37] It seems that Breuning faithfully recorded what he witnessed, while trusting Schindler's

---

* Wawruch's account referred directly in text in this chapter as (W [page]). Lorenz's own article is also referred in text as (L [page]).

opinion about what he did not himself witness. Therefore, he may have written the truth about Dr. Wawruch, whom he saw quite often interacting with Beethoven.

The issue becomes even muddier when we learn that Schindler acknowledged to have seen Wawruch's account soon after Beethoven's death, asked him not to publish it, because "protest would be raised" against its sullying the image of the glorious dead (L 95), and Wawruch complied. In fact, he never published his report—Wawruch's wife published it after his death, when she found it among the papers he left.[38] One may further wonder why he did not destroy it, as doctor Bertolini did, to observe the physician-patient confidentiality rule.[39] It is difficult to assess Wawruch's credibility about his crucial statement that Beethoven "loved alcoholic beverages," one has only the account itself to work with, without corroboration. Even so, this text, specifically the crucial fragment about the "love for alcoholic beverages," when closely scrutinized, raises serious doubts about its objectivity. The way it begins, with many accurate details about Beethoven's life and health, makes it clear that Wawruch's source was the composer himself:

> Ludwig van Beethoven affirmed that from his earliest youth he enjoyed a robust and stable health [...] but] ... when he entered his 30th year, he developed a hemorrhoid condition together with an annoying noise and ringing in both ears [...] almost at the same time Beethoven realized that his digestion began to be afflicted; irregular appetite resulted in indigestion, vexatious belching, sometimes persistent constipation, sometimes frequent bowel movements. (W 88)

The continuation is the very incriminating statement at the core of the debate:

> Not really being accustomed to take medical advice seriously, he began to enjoy alcoholic beverages.

This seems tangential at best, as well as somewhat baffling. First, alcohol was not new to Beethoven's life in 1800—his love of wine during his Bonn years was, as I showed, documented by Wegeler. The claim that Beethoven drank because he rejected medical advice is also puzzling. He may not have trusted his physicians very much—they had not been able to help him with his losing his hearing—but it is hardly credible that he would have told Wawruch, "my physician told me I shouldn't drink, but I knew better." As I showed, nineteenth century medical science held wine as an excellent stimulant of appetite and digestion and even as a nutrient. According to Pezzl, the chronicler of Viennese life *circa* 1800, the city's water was notoriously bad, inducing diarrhea—one of the conditions that Beethoven constantly complained about—therefore "doctors prescribed wine for the aged and for those with stomach troubles, *and seldom to no effect*" (my italics).[40]

This was Beethoven belief, illustrated in his July 1804 letter to Ries, in which he described wine as "so necessary and beneficial to my health."[41] He must have been advised to drink wine rather than water by a physician, probably by Dr. Schmidt, under whose care he was at the time.[42] Wawruch (Lorenz sketches a biography that presents him as a respected professional) must have been aware of what medical science held to be true at the time; therefore, one concludes his "alcoholic beverage" must have meant not wine, but rather a stronger alcoholic beverage. What beverage it was becomes clear in a more careful translation of the original German, in which the paragraph continues uninterrupted but which Lorenz splits in two sentences at the wrong point. The correct translation reads:

> Not really being accustomed to take medical advice seriously, he began to love alcoholic beverages to stimulate his declining appetite. In order to remedy the weakness of his stomach—that had been caused by the consumption of strong *punch* and too much ice cream—he began taking long and strenuous walks.[43]

Obviously, the *punch* in the second sentence was the alcoholic beverage that Beethoven had "started to love," but to which he recurred with a specific purpose—to stimulate his declining appetite (in the first sentence). He even needed no medical advice to do so, as popular wisdom all over Europe held that a sup of stronger alcoholic drink (such as wine brandy) would increase one's appetite; the French, the grand masters of gastronomy called it "apéritif," a word that entered all the other languages, including English and German. The specifics of the apéritif itself varied in different countries. It happened that punch had become an English "craze" in the German lands towards the end of the 18th century, to the point that the "punchlied" (punch-song) became a landmark in poetry (illustrated by exalted names like Friedrich Schiller) and in music. Twenty-year-old Beethoven wrote a "Punchlied" (WoO 111) that was certainly sung at a party where the beverage was passed "around from hand to hand," as the lyrics say.

Was punch a strong alcoholic beverage? The answer is "sometimes, sometimes not." It was not what we call hard liquor now, but a kind of cocktail: a mixture of water, lemon and spices with brandy (distilled wine), therefore with a slightly higher content of alcohol than wine; it was mostly served warm, but also cooled with sherbet (a variant called ice-punch or frozen punch). In Beethoven literature, it also appears in his 1810 letter to Therese Malfatti, in which he advised her, "please do not take punch to help you" when reading/playing some mysterious (and as yet unidentified) music that he sent her.[44] The recipe was flexible and allowed punch to be weak enough for teenaged ladies to drink without serious risks; there was even a child-punch variant.

The second sentence of the Wawruch quote is irrelevant to the issue of alleged alcoholism. It must have been Beethoven who told Wawruch that drinking "frozen punch" eventually caused "weakness" of his stomach. However, he could not also tell him that, in order to correct that, he "*began* to take long and strenuous walks," simply because the long walks had been his pastime since his early Bonn years, when he loved to roam around the Rhineland hills.[45] This doubtful link must have been the physician's speculation resulting from misunderstanding—how could a walk restore an upset stomach? Beethoven must have told the physician that he had replaced punch with longer and more strenuous walks to increase his appetite, but Wawruch twisted his statement. Wawruch goes further in his incriminating paragraph:

> It was exactly this change of his [Beethoven's] way of life ["loving alcoholic beverages"] that almost brought him into his grave seven years ago. He contracted a violent enteritis that responded to medical treatment but subsequently caused repeatedly intestinal inflammation and attacks of colic that contributed to the later development of his final illness. (W 88)

Obviously, what he means to argue is that Beethoven had become an alcoholic around 1800 and that this was the cause of all his health problems, and ultimately his death. The seven-year-ago illness "that almost brought him into his grave" could have been only the 1821 violent attack of jaundice[46] that Wawruch learned about from Beethoven. It is hard to understand how the physician could diagnose jaundice—Beethoven must have used the term, as he had done in an 1821 letter mentioning his illness[47]—as enteritis. It seems that Wawruch did not suspect cirrhosis as the cause of the dropsy (edema) that was the most dramatic aspect of Beethoven's agony and wanted to connect the 1821 episode to Beethoven's frequent digestive illnesses. However, there is no evidence that Beethoven had made any connection between that jaundice and alcoholic beverages. There is similarly not a single piece of evidence to prove that he turned into a heavy consumer of strong alcoholic beverages. Granted, there are plenty of stories about parties where wine flowed, but he was just one of the many merrymakers and only one of these (Holz) admitted to have seen him "sometimes tipsy," and only in 1826.

Schindler seems to have correctly identified punch as the alcoholic beverage Wawruch designated as Beethoven's "love"; indeed, his attack against the physician's account insisted on the punch treatment prescribed by Dr. Malfatti during Beethoven's last illness. However, Lorenz's rebuttal of Schindler's argument—probably misled by his mistaken translation of the text—sees the punch only as a "mere mention" that did not justify Schindler's "lengthy apology of Beethoven's drinking habits." Lorenz is right to call that apology pathetic, but it *is* irrelevant to the issue, because Schindler tried to negate the obvious: Beethoven's love of wine, though wine was not what Wawruch would have included among "alcoholic beverages." Moreover, Lorenz's rhetorical conclusion, "Why defend Beethoven against an accusation that Wawruch did not make?" (L 93) is twice wrong. First, Wawruch really did launch an accusation, based on Beethoven's drinking ice-punch, in the 1800 episode. Second, Schindler was right to claim that a post-factum (Dr. Malfatti's setting Beethoven on a regime of frozen punch in January 1827) could not be proof, as Wawruch claimed, of an ante-factum—that Malfatti had been for a long time aware of the composer's "predominant inclination towards alcoholic beverages." The 1827 treatment Malfatti prescribed was not an attempt to placate an addict with withdrawal symptoms but an (ultimately unsuccessful) effort to address a worsening medical condition, which was considered an "inflammation" of the bowels and was treated, like any inflammation, with "cold"—hence the frozen punch.* Ironically, Wawruch agreed to the treatment at the time, as Schindler testifies in his 1840 biography of Beethoven, which can be trusted as the physician was at this point not yet his nemesis; he "esteemed Dr. Wawruch." One can read therein that the treatment was decided "by agreement of both doctors."[48]

Summing up: Dr. Wawruch's account launches a diagnosis ("love for alcoholic beverages") that he fails to support. I do not imply that he was malevolent nor that he lied: there was no conscious misrepresentation, and Wawruch was convinced that he was telling the truth as he knew it. He may have had an inflated ego—proven by his desire to be regarded as "Beethoven's friend"—and inflated egos easily persuade themselves that their perceptions are true representations of the facts. His certainty that Beethoven "loved" liquor, however, does not support Lorenz's thesis, which is based on the composer's "love of wine," and that is the evidence on which Lorenz finally focuses in his relentless pursuit to prove that Beethoven was an alcoholic to his last breath.

Lorenz's own contribution to the "A" diagnosis. Turning to another element of Lorenz's analysis mentioned above, the physician-turned-scholar gleans evidence extracted from the composer's letters and conversation books showing large amounts of wine being bought for his household during his fatal illness and ends his argument quoting from a letter that Schindler wrote to the publisher Schotts, who had sent Beethoven a bottle of wine, "He enjoyed your *Rüdesheimer* [wine] by the spoonful until his death,"[49] which would convey "the image of an addict who has to consume his drug until the very last moment of his life" (L 98).

The great number of such wine episodes during Beethoven's last months is undeniable, but exceptional circumstances breed unusual behavior. Lorenz does not acknowledge that Beethoven lived his last months and died in horrible pain— "He lay in bed suffering terribly," "He [...] seemed to suffer great pains," visitors noticed[50]—and his doctors reasonably would have decided to let him continue to drink wine daily as he had been accustomed to do, simply to make his agony more bearable. He also accepted some control by his doctors, asking them to agree about certain wines.[51] It is strange that they did not put him on opium, the only painkiller known at the time; indeed, the analyses of the composer's hair lock, carried on at the request of the Beethoven Center with the San José State University, showed no trace of opiates.[52]

And there is more to the *Rüdesheimer*. It was a Rhine wine, a token from Beethoven's native land, where he had been dreaming to return during his last years when, like any old man—to say nothing of a dying man—he travelled back in time to his childhood and youth. That spoonful of wine could not fill the need of an addict—wine is not heroin. Rather, it was like Proust's madeleine, a taste

---

* Interestingly, according to the independent testimony of a benevolent visitor, the treatment also included "rubbing of the abdomen with ice-cold water, a remedy with which Malfatti is said to have completely cured a similar patient" (Thayer-Forbes, p. 1030). Medical practice recommended fighting bowel inflammation with cold both on the inside and the outside.

that made Beethoven re-live the "time lost" of his youth in the native Rhineland. Lorenz's claim that Beethoven's wine "spoonful" was evidence of alcoholic addiction is saddening proof of lack of empathy.

Mai's diagnosis based on modern DSM-IV criteria

François Mai takes the extra step of declaring Beethoven a "likely" alcoholic by the modern standards of the American Psychiatric Association. His credentials as a professor of psychiatry as well as his relying on the authority of APA standards confer his diagnosis a distinct weight and requires close scrutiny.

Mai presents evidence (collected from letters, testimonies of contemporaries and Beethoven's conversation books) about eleven episodes relating to the composer's consumption of wine, in chronological order:[53]

1. The already-quoted testimony of Wegeler, the composer's friend from his teenage years, given here to its full extent, is unequivocal: "By and large, Beethoven lived moderately, and as far as I know, not one of his friends ever saw him intoxicated."[54] Mai dismisses this evidence (143) because Wegeler could not have known his friends' "lifestyle during the latter part of his life" when the other episodes happened.

2. 1804, July: Beethoven's letter to Ries: "It is hard to forgive my worthy brother for not ordering the wine sooner since it is so necessary and beneficial to my health."[55] To Mai (145), this sentence is proof that 1804 was probably the year when Beethoven began walking the path to alcoholism.

3. 1807, July 22: Beethoven's physician Dr. Schmidt wrote him: "drink moderate amounts of alcoholic beverages" (145).[56]

4. 1811, February 10: Beethoven wrote to Bettina Brentano: "I did not get home until four o'clock this morning from a bacchanalia, where I really had to laugh a great deal, with the result that today I have to cry as heartily."[57]

5. 1820, January: there are 11 references to wine in the conversation book during this month alone (146).

6. 1820, March 21: Bernard (a friend) writes Beethoven in a conversation book: "You drink too much wine."[58]

7. 1825-1826: the account of Holz, given here in full: "He was a stout eater of substantial food; he drank a great deal of wine at table, but could stand a great deal, and in merry company he sometimes became tipsy. In the evening he drank beer or wine, generally the wine of Vöslau or red Hungarian. When he had drunk he never composed. After the meal he took a walk."[59] This is an important piece of information on which Mai seems to rely heavily when diagnosing Beethoven of alcohol dependency. (I say "seems" because he never indicates it explicitly but lets us guess.)

8. 1825, April: during his visit when Beethoven had "inflammatory fever," Dr. Braunhofer enters in the conversation book: "No wine, no coffee, no spices." Karl, Beethoven's nephew, adds a few lines further: "Dr Staudenheim also banned all wines." Then Dr. Braunhofer again: "I bet if you take alcohol, you will become weak and faint within a few hours."[60]

9. 1825, August: Beethoven's letter to Danish composer Kuhlau after the latter's birthday party: "I must admit that the champagne went too much to my head also, yesterday, and *again* I was compelled to experience that such things retard rather than promote my capacities. For easy as it usually is for me to meet a challenge of the instant, I do not at all remember what I wrote yesterday" (my italics).[61] To Mai (145), this episode seems indeed an eloquent example of Beethoven's "misuse of alcohol"—since he had drunk so much that he could not remember what he had done and that "such things" were not happening the first time but *again*.

10. 1825, September: the testimony of London musician George Smart, who paid a visit to the composer: "I overheard Beethoven say, 'We will try how much the Englishman can drink.' *He* had the worst of the trial" (Smart's emphasis).[62]

11. 1826, date unknown: Schindler wrote in a conversation book: "You should not drink today."[63] To Mai (143), this implies that Schindler was "at times" concerned that Beethoven drank daily.

Mai never discusses any of these pieces of evidence in depth, assuming that they speak for themselves, but actually they do not. For example, according to Mai, the "bacchanalia" in item #4 must have been a drinking binge. In fact, Beethoven liked to use the word "bacchanalia" as a metaphor rather than a descriptive term. In a letter to Goethe, Bettina Brentano puts these words into Beethoven's mouth and they sound very like him, indeed: "music is [...] the wine which inspires one to new generative processes and I am the Bacchus who presses out this glorious wine for mankind and makes them spiritually drunken."[64] In 1815, Beethoven thought that the Ancient World's god of wine was worth "a grand lyric opera," from which a few sketches have been preserved.[65] Three years later, he jotted down his first ideas for a couple of new symphonies in an 1818 notebook, mentioning, next to the idea of introducing human voices, "in the *allegro*, feast of Bacchus"[66]—a foreshadowing of his *Ninth Symphony*. It is obvious that, in Beethoven's mind, the prime goal of a bacchanalia was "spiritual," not physical drunkenness and so possible was the party mentioned in #4 above. In fact, the next sentence in his quoted letter to Bettina, but omitted by Mai, makes the episode look very different: "Exuberant jollity often drives me back most violently into myself," writes Beethoven. It is clear that he did not have a very bad hangover the next day, but he felt sad, which was hardly surprising. Any "normal" human being would have asked himself in his stead, "how could I laugh so heartily, when I am so wretched?"

The "No wine today" advice of the physicians (items #3 and 8) were probably occasioned by Beethoven's being ill and were just medical recommendations, not admonitions to someone who drank heavily, as Mai intimates. Indeed, as Thayer documented, the composer "was so accustomed to take wine at his meals, that his physicians found it difficult to make him obey their prohibition of wine and heating spices when he was ill."[67] The similar pieces of advice of his friends (#6 and 11) were most probably reiterations of such medical advice. That childish drinking competition with George Smart (item #10) was just a way of testing their "virility," the ability to stand wine. There might also have been another explanation: during the last part of the reign of the Stuarts, before the end of the eighteenth century, a time of very "loose" social behavior, heavy drinking spread among the males of the English upper classes; the famous playwright Sheridan and the prime minister William Pitt Jr. were notorious "six-bottle men"—the bottles were of port;[68] this reputation of the Englishman as a heavy drinker survived the age and might have piqued Beethoven's curiosity. If this episode proves anything, it is that inebriation was not Beethoven's desired effect of drinking.

Finally, Mai invokes the criteria for alcohol dependence and abuse developed by the American Psychiatric Association and concludes, without any further discussion (147):

> It is likely that Beethoven had at least three (the required minimum) of the seven criteria of 'dependence': increased tolerance, use of larger amounts over a longer period, and unsuccessful efforts to cut down the intake, but he did not meet the criteria for alcohol "abuse."

Invoking the authority of APA seems to confer the aura of objective science to Mai's argument, but its flaws appear obvious when we do what he did not: actually check the proposed evidence against each individual APA criterion. We discover immediately that none of the claims about Beethoven's alcoholism satisfies the APA requirements. The DSM-IV defines two kinds of alcoholism—dependence (a kind of lesser level) and abuse—and sets specific criteria in order to differentiate between them. The language is somewhat confusing to the layman, but can be simplified as follows: the dependent shows *tolerance* for alcohol (i.e., the ability to "stand" drinking) and/or *withdrawal symptoms* (pathologic behavior when the alcoholic is deprived of his drink) while the abuser shows neither of them. Other differences (such as individual and social impairment) are less marked and overlap substantially. Here follow the APA criteria, (as described in the DSM-IV) slightly modified by Mai to particularize them for wine, on which he bases his diagnosis of Beethoven and which he includes in the Appendix 3 of his book:

Criteria for Alcohol Dependence[69]

A maladaptive pattern of alcohol use, leading to clinically significant impairment or distress, as manifested by three (or more) of the following, occurring any time in the same twelve-month period.
1. tolerance, as defined by either of the following:
   a. a need for markedly increased amounts of alcohol to achieve intoxication or the desired effect
   b. markedly diminished effect with continued use of the same amount of alcohol.
2. withdrawal, as manifested by either of the following:
   a. the characteristic withdrawal syndrome for alcohol
   b. the same (or closely related) substance is taken to relieve or avoid the withdrawal symptoms
3. alcohol is taken in larger amounts or over a longer period than was intended.
4. there is a persistent desire or unsuccessful efforts to cut down or control alcohol use.

5. a greater deal of time is spent in activities necessary to obtain alcohol, or recover from its effects.
6. important social, occupational, or recreational activities are given up or reduced because of alcohol use.
7. alcohol use is continued despite knowledge of having a persistent or recurrent psychical or psychological problem that is likely to have been caused or exacerbated by its use.

Criteria for Alcohol Abuse:

A. A maladaptive pattern of alcohol use leading to clinically significant impairment or distress, as manifested by one (or more) of the following, occurring within a twelve-month period:
1. recurrent alcohol use resulting in failure to fulfill major role obligations at work, school, or home (e.g., repeated absences or poor work performance related to alcohol use; alcohol-related absences, suspension, or expulsions from school; neglect of children or household)
2. recurrent alcohol use in situations it is physically hazardous (e.g., driving an automobile or operating a machine when impaired)
3. recurrent alcohol related legal problems (e.g., arrest or alcohol related disorderly conduct)
4. continued alcohol use despite having persistent or recurrent social and interpersonal problems caused or exacerbated by its use (e.g., argument with a spouse about consequences of intoxication, physical fights).

B. The symptoms have never met the criteria for alcohol dependence.

Let us see how the evidence advanced for Beethoven's "dependence" on wine fits the criteria. First, we find that Mai disregards a basic requirement of the APA criteria: **the qualifying events must be "occurring within a twelve-month period."** The items of Mai's evidence stretch over almost a quarter of a century (#2 in 1804, last items in 1827). Moreover, even if we stipulate that all the items pertained to the same year, Mai's conclusion still does not hold. Consider his claim that Beethoven "likely" showed tolerance to alcohol. The DSM defines tolerance by either "increased [amount]" consumed or "diminished [effect]" of the same amount. This implies a comparison—something has increased/diminished during the interval—and Mai's evidence does not allow for any such comparison. The "bacchanalia" in #4 might imply a considerable amount of wine, but was it an increase (or even a decrease) compared to the one in #2 (seven years before) or #6 (nine years after) or #7 (after another five years)? There is no way to answer and therefore no way to claim that Beethoven meets this criterion.

Mai also ignores the main ingredient of APA's criteria of tolerance—the "desired effect" of drinking. He simply eludes the essential question—what was the *desired effect* that Beethoven was trying to achieve? The typical, desperate, purpose of the alcoholic is inebriation into oblivion. None of the evidence advanced bears proof that Beethoven ever got drunk and Mai himself acknowledges that the composer was not a "drunkard." Item #7 mentions only "occasional tipsiness," which suggests that Beethoven "knew when to stop," which is quite the contrary of the behavior of an alcoholic. Even if we accept that items #4 and #9 might include inebriation, two such cases in 14 years (1811 to 1825) can hardly be evidence of a habit. Some people are dependent on the "eye opener"—a drink in the morning, in order to start a day.

There is no proof that Beethoven practiced this; in fact, the eye opener is usually strong liquor, not wine, the drink he preferred. Some other people may rely on alcohol to overcome inhibitions that hinder socializing. Beethoven was a very outspoken person that needed no such stimulus and there is no testimony that his notorious "gaffes" ever involved alcohol consumption. Finally, as many examples demonstrate (from Edgar Allan Poe to French symbolist poets and beyond), drinking (and use of other drugs) may stimulate artistic inspiration—or, at least, the artist may believe this to be true. However, testimony points to the very reflexive and laborious manner of Beethoven's composing, incompatible with inspiration induced by alcohol. "When he had drunk he never composed," says Holz (#7). There is, therefore, no evidence that Beethoven aimed at a specific "desired effect," and would thus fit the APA criteria of tolerance.

Mai goes on to maintain that Beethoven fulfills another APA criterion—**alcohol is taken in larger amounts or over a longer period than was intended**. Again, he does not indicate which of the quoted items support his claim and we cannot see any. Just like in the case of *tolerance*, comparison of amounts and duration is needed and the evidence does not contain any such information. Did Beethoven drink more in September 1825 (#10) than in August of the same year (#9)—or in 1811, or 1804, for that matter? How can one base a diagnosis on such flimsy evidence?

The third criterion of alcohol dependence that, according to Mai, Beethoven fulfills, is **a persistent desire or unsuccessful efforts to cut down or control alcohol use.** There is no hint in any of the eleven pieces of evidence (or in any other evidence, for that matter) that Beethoven himself wanted to stop drinking, let alone tried and failed. The closest that one can get, but only by stretching the argument very far, is #9, in which the composer acknowledges that "such things [drinking] retard rather than promote my capacities." But how can one see in it a "persistent desire or unsuccessful effort?"

Common sense and knowledge of Beethoven's life help us better understand the two more general pieces of evidence that Mai brings forth to strengthen his argument:

1) The hereditary factor: "Beethoven had both familial and psychological predisposing factors that could have contributed to a tendency to overuse alcohol." This is a true statement (both his father and paternal grandmother had been alcoholics), but it could only explain *why* Beethoven was an alcoholic, not *if* he was one. The so-called "alcoholism gene" that might have been pinned-down by scientists[70] is not automatically inherited. Beethoven's conduct as a whole, even though it involved drinking wine, was very different from his father's, who

could not function professionally (as a singer) nor socially, and had to be put on a financial restraint order.[71]

2) Beethoven's behavior—his poor self-care, his irritability and his lack of social grace, particularly in the later stages of his life (Mai, 144)—was consistent with alcoholism. Mai offers, as a supporting example, the 1821 episode in which Beethoven was arrested for "vagrancy." He got lost during one of his long walks on the outskirts of Vienna and in the evening was arrested as a "ragamuffin," because he was dressed in "a miserable old coat" and had no hat and the police did not believe that he could be the celebrity he claimed to be; he was eventually released when a witness recognized him.[72] Mai acknowledges that, according to the testimony, alcohol was in no way involved, but quotes the episode because it illustrates Beethoven's "poor self-care," a trait normally shared by alcoholics. This is circumstantial at best: poor self-care usually accompanies alcoholism indeed, but is not limited to it—many elderly men, especially bachelors, share it. That Beethoven, a man so thoroughly absorbed in his music, would have behaved this way is not surprising at all. His "irritability" and "lack of social grace" has also been known for many years and older scholars have found the explanation in his devastating illness—deafness. His friends had noticed that losing his hearing had changed his personality: for example, Ignaz von Seyfried, who had been Beethoven's friend for over thirty years, draws a fine flattering portrait of him but adds the final caveat, "I am speaking here of an earlier time, before the misfortune of deafness had come upon him." Medical research has indeed shown that losing one's hearing later in life frequently yields the kind of behavior that Beethoven displayed beginning with his thirtieth year: irritability, a suspicious mind, fits of unjustified anger, etc.[73] Admittedly, Beethoven displayed quite often "irritability and lack of social grace," but he was also able to show a quite different side of his personality, which Mai seems to ignore. The wife of his friend Stephen von Breuning, who had met Beethoven during his last years, recalled his eccentric behavior but also that "he was always gallant towards women."[74] And if one thinks that Beethoven had a special way with ladies, here is the much plainer testimony from a male, our acquaintance George Smart: "No one could be more agreeable than he was."[75]

It is obvious that Beethoven's behavior does not fit DSM-IV criteria for alcoholism invoked by Mai. In fact, Mai himself seems aware of the incongruity of his diagnosis with the composer's already-mentioned creative pattern, which is highly incompatible with alcoholism. Eventually he concedes (150), "it is clear that he [Beethoven] was not a 'drunkard'," but he finds a subterfuge to maintain his diagnosis: "it is possible for a susceptible individual to drink alcoholic beverages in sufficient amounts to cause liver damage without taking so much as to cause serious behavioral or neurological effects." In the final analysis, Mai's diagnosis simply reiterates O'Shea and Davies' less categorical conclusion. However, he soon forgets his own "alleviated" verdict and makes constantly use of Beethoven's alleged alcoholism to support his further diagnoses of alleged psychopathic behavior by the composer, which would have, in his opinion, been aggravated by alcoholism (164). I will deal with this issue in the next chapter.

Beethoven's love relationship with wine

While none of the evidence and of the argument advanced by these three physicians justifies a diagnosis of alcoholism, one cannot deny that Beethoven liked wine (beer, too, as item #7 proffered by Mai suggests) and drank on a regular basis. There is other evidence that these authors ignored or were not aware of. Ironically, some of this evidence would have better served to support their argument, as this from Thayer's *Life of Beethoven*:

> Beethoven was accustomed to drink wine from youth up, and also to the companionship which he found in the inns and coffee-houses of Vienna. [...] We know that he was so accustomed to take wine at his meals that his physicians found it difficult to make him obey their prohibition of wine and heating spices when he was ill.[76]

Obviously, even though he was not an alcoholic, he consumed wine on a regular basis and in substantial (if not quantifiable) amounts. That was nothing out of the ordinary in Vienna—or in Germany—at the time. When he was writing to Ries that wine was "so necessary and beneficial to my health" he was just following the medical advice of his time. He had also to order large amounts of wine for the current month to provide for his servants (he usually had two, a valet and a cook) and for his occasional guests.

It is obvious why the first generations of Beethoven scholars did not pay much attention to his drinking habits: they grew up in the same culture as he did, which considered wine the safest drink and an excellent medicine and nutrient, so his behavior would have elicited no comment. Only after the advent of the sacred monster of the twentieth century, the car, did it become obvious that much smaller amounts of alcohol than needed for inebriation are sufficient to weaken the reflexes of the person behind the wheel; thus, alcoholism criteria became more aggressive.

Holz's testimony and a tentative diagnosis. I think that Schindler did tell the truth when he wrote that Beethoven drank more than usual during eighteen months in 1825-26, when he befriended Holz.[77] Yet we must also consider the circumstances of that period. The composer was old (fifty-five was old age at the time) and, as one knows very well, the old enjoy and seek the company of the young, so much the more when they are entertaining persons. Holz was such a guy (very unlike the sour and pedantic young Schindler) and he also took upon himself, in Thayer's words, "[the] charitable act to drag him [Beethoven] out of his isolation into cheerful company."[78] I must remind the reader that Beethoven was not, by nature, a morose recluse that cared only about his inner daemon. He was in fact as extroverted as his music is; he liked company, merriment, jokes and laughter; he described himself in his Heiligenstadt testament as "susceptible to the diversions of society."[79] His deafness forced him to gradually close his commerce with the world around him, first to hide his infirmity and later because of the pain that the communication barrier inflicted on him. Holz gave him the opportunity to enjoy company again when, even though the sound barrier was still there, he could at least enjoy the sight, the movements, the gestures, the lips forming sentences and even participate, to some degree, thanks to his conversation books. It is not surprising that he might have drunk more than usual in such episodes, when Holz had even occasionally seen him "tipsy." It seems, however, that such moments happened only (or especially) in Holz's company, since another witness who met him around the same time (1826) saw him drinking moderately (see page 106).

Holz's testimony is the only one on which Mai could have invoked (but did not) as a proof that Beethoven had developed a tolerance to alcohol: he could "stand a great deal [of wine] at table." Unlike Mai, I think that this evidence is worth a deeper analysis. As I have already shown, we cannot find proof of tolerance, as required by the DSM-IV, in Beethoven's case, because we do not have any timeline comparisons of his resistance to drinking and no evidence of any "desired effect"—besides that of a gourmet—that he would have been attempting to achieve. Nevertheless, we cannot help asking why Beethoven did not get drunk during those escapades with Holz. Although of an athletic build, Beethoven was a rather short, slim man[80]; therefore, if both men were consuming at the same rate, he should have become intoxicated much faster than his friend Holz, who was so stout that the composer nicknamed him "Sir John Falstaff."[81] One explanation could be that, according to Holz, Beethoven used to eat a lot, too, and food delays absorption of alcohol.[82] Yet, if he was also a "stout eater," how could he remain slim all his life?

Modern medical researchers, having noticed that Beethoven suffered from many ailments that seemed to have set in at the same time with his first symptoms of deafness (see Dr. Wawruch's testimony, as described on page 109 above), suspected that all of them may have been the result of a systemic disease. As early as 1932, Tremble suggested that the gastrointestinal disturbances damaged the composer's auditory nerve causing his deafness.[83] In time, various systemic diseases were proposed: systemic lupus erithematosus, sarcoidosis, Whipple's disease.[84] Such postmortem diagnoses are, of course, very uncertain and none of these three covers all of Beethoven's symptoms, but it is interesting to note that malabsorption—a deficient absorption of food nutrients as well as alcohol in the small intestines—is present in all of them. Malabsorption seems a likely explanation of Beethoven's "heavy drinking" not being accompanied by inebriation, which is normally associated with it.

We have now a much clearer picture of Beethoven's "affair" with wine. He was no different from the vast majority of the Austrian males (or European ones, for that matter) of his time, who consumed wine daily. And it is likely that a systemic disease that caused malabsorption allowed him to drink substantial amount of wine without becoming inebriated, as Holz noticed. Inebriation was not the "desired effect" when he drank. He simply enjoyed wine, used to have it mostly with his meals and, apparently, enjoyed it especially in merry company.

Wine, lead, cirrhosis and death. Was Beethoven's drinking habit responsible for his death? For almost two centuries, scholarly and medical authorities have advanced diverse diagnoses, of which alcohol-induced cirrhosis has gathered most support.[85] It gained more credibility when the analysis of Beethoven's hair, the results of which were made public in 2000 and created a stir in the media, revealed a huge concentration of lead. Russel Martin, who brought the issue into Beethoven scholarship, offered the only reasonable explanation of his lead intoxication: the consumption of adulterated wine.[86] Adding lead salts to wine to delay its alteration (the salts kill some bacteria that turn the wine sour) and to sweeten spoilt wine was a practice known to the Ancient Greeks and Romans.[87] Early in the eighteenth century, the medical world had already begun to link lead-adulterated wine with what was called "colics"—an umbrella term covering a wide range of gastro-intestinal ailments, which was the name given to the illness that bothered Beethoven most of his life. The physicians knew that, depending on the seriousness of lead poisoning, the symptoms extended from "extreme stomach pain, complete constipation, *jaundice*" [our italicizing, a reminder that Beethoven had suffered a bout of jaundice in 1821] to much graver conditions like "loss of control in the hands and feet, blindness, loss of speech and paralysis."[88] Schindler appears to have been aware of this when he wrote in his Beethoven biography, "Unfortunately, he especially liked the adulterated wines which were very bad for his weakened stomach. He would heed no warning."[89]

After the results of the analysis of Beethoven's hair, the theory that his cirrhosis was alcohol induced was challenged. Philip Mackowiak, a medical professor at the University of Maryland in Baltimore, claims that Beethoven's cirrhosis, as described in his autopsy report, presented symptoms specific to lead intoxication rather than to alcohol consumption.[90] In his latest biography of Beethoven, Morris also dismisses alcohol as the cause of the composer's cirrhosis, stating, without quoting any source, that "autopsy disclosed that [he] died of macronodular, post-hepatic cirrhosis of the liver [...] not the kind of cirrhosis that derives from alcoholism, although he was certainly a heavy drinker."[91] Whether Beethoven's cirrhosis was the result of the wine or the lead in his wine is still not, and may never be, clear, but wine seems to have been involved in his too-early demise.

The hair analysis results have raised more questions than it answered. There is now an ongoing debate among medical scholars about the validity of the assumption that lead intoxication has detrimental effects on health (the reader may find more in the 2007 and 2008 issues of *The Beethoven Journal* as well as in social media). If a layman is allowed to contribute to this speculative field, I would say that, since Beethoven's apparent tolerance of wine was likely caused by malabsorption, his liver was not as highly involved in the metabolism of alcohol as has been claimed. Strangely enough, the composer's fondness of water (he used to drink a lot, as documented by Schindler)[92] may have done some harm, as water was quite often contaminated (hence Dr. Pasteur's quoted recommendation about wine as the best beverage). According to Pezzl, Vienna's water was notoriously bad, inducing diarrhea,[93] one of the conditions that Beethoven constantly complained about.

One final note: the only thing that is certain about such issues is that people respond differently to the same conditions, and sometimes against statistics—a difference that we like to call *Fate*. The anecdote about the drinking contest between Beethoven and George Smart is illustrative in this respect. The Englishman could *stand* wine better than Beethoven, so he must have been a much more notorious alcoholic (by Davies or Lorenz or Mai's standard) in his own country. However, one can find no trace of such suspicion in his biography. Sir George Thomas Smart (he had been knighted before he met Beethoven) was born in 1776 in the family of a music seller and, through talent and hard work, rose to prominence in England's musical life. He held the position of conductor of the London Philharmonic Society for over thirty years (1813-1844), in which capacity he was a great promoter of Beethoven's music. In 1838 he was also appointed composer to the Chapel Royal and, according to his published memoires, was a frequent guest of the royal family during the very strict Victorian age. It is hard to believe that he would have ever been introduced to Her Majesty, let alone be appointed her composer, had he been known as an alcoholic.[94] Ironically, George Smart, who seems to have been the heavier drinker of the two and thus more at the risk of developing cirrhosis, lived to the venerable age of 91, while Beethoven died at 56.

*

Beethoven certainly loved wine—and, to a lesser extent, beer—but no more than his contemporaries. Measuring his habits by our modern standards, as did these three physicians, is misleading. Moreover, as I showed in my analysis, their case is marred both by internal contradictions and by conflicts with the known facts. Certainly, Beethoven was taking too high a risk of harming his liver, but he did not do it like the modern day alcoholic, to get drunk. He simply liked to savor a drink.

However wrong in their diagnosis, the endeavors of Davies and Mai have a certain merit. They concentrate the largest amount of evidence ever gleaned showing that Beethoven lived in physical pain on a daily basis—on top of the spiritual agony of his deafness. Such amounts of suffering could have easily pushed a weaker human being towards alcoholism, as the path to oblivion, so much the more since Beethoven liked wine. IT DID NOT. Against their own argument, the three or four doctors bring forth another proof of Beethoven's inner strength.

6
The Case for Beethoven's psychopathy

Beethoven was certainly an "eccentric" whose behavior shocked many of those who knew him and the epithet "crazy" was already attached to him during his lifetime. A family legend passed to us much later but pertaining around 1800, claimed that a young woman whom he had courted and proposed to, Magdalena Willmann, turned him down because he was ugly and "half crazy."[1] Some twenty years later, Zelter reported to Goethe before meeting the composer, "... some say he is a lunatic."[2] Indeed, Beethoven used to pour bucketsful of water on his hot head and chest, while bellowing scales like a raging bull, without caring about the people living on the lower floor.[3] He would wake up at 5 in the morning and work on his music, with feet thumping and shouting.[4] When walking in the streets, he shocked people by his loud strident voice and laughter and many "took him for a madman."[5] He dared treat his aristocratic friends and patrons as no emperor would have, while also using them to make a living and basking in their adoration of him. He was ruthless and disingenuous in his deals with his publishers. And he sometimes treated his friends worse than his publishers. Can this behavior qualify him as mentally diseased? When examining the issue, the scholarly world did not agree. It seemed to have observed Zelter's caveat added to his statement to Goethe: "It is easy to talk. God forgive us all our sins."

The issue has been recently revisited by the two physicians discussed above, Peter J. Davies and François Martin Mai, who had diagnosed Beethoven with alcoholism—a theory that I debunked in the previous chapter. Dr. Davies diagnoses Beethoven with paranoia, and Dr. Mai—with personality disorder. Obviously, trying to diagnose a dead person, however numerous the testimonies that we may possess about his life, is a very delicate attempt and both scholars appear conscientious of the risks involved. They want to convince the reader that their approach is objective and entirely scientific, based on the criteria (so called "axes") of the APA's Diagnostic and Statistical Manual system of classifying mental illness (the DSM-IV).

Not being a physician, let alone a psychiatrist, I will not touch the purely medical aspects of the arguments advanced by Davies and Mai but will consider biographic and logical evidence. This is sufficient to show that many—almost all—of the episodes in Beethoven's life that they claim to display symptoms of psychopathological behavior distort or ignore well-known facts that can justify these actions. Also, one must not be a psychiatrist to evaluate some elementary diagnostic criteria as stated in the DSM-IV of the APA, which Davies and Mai constantly invoke. The most important of these criteria is the one included in almost every psychotic disorder: any such episode must be "not due to the direct physiological effects of a general medical condition." We know too well that Beethoven lived most of his adult life with a certain medical condition that weighed heavily on his inner balance, a fact that Davies and Mai rarely take into account; moreover, they don't even mention that such a "not due to ..." diagnosis criterion. Of the two argumentations, Davies' is more substantial, but Dr. Mai's being a professor of psychiatry with the University of Ottawa confers his diagnosis a distinct weight so we will begin with his argument.

Mai's failed case for personality disorder

Personality disorder is a very large umbrella of less severe forms of mental illnesses, which actually go undetected in many individuals or appear as simple "eccentricities"—and we could easily describe Beethoven as an eccentric. Mai invokes (161) Axis II of the DSM-IV, which defines the following characteristics of the disease:

A. An enduring pattern of inner experience and behavior that deviates markedly from the expectation of an individual's culture.
B. The enduring pattern is inflexible and pervasive across a broad range of personal and social situations.
C. The enduring pattern leads to clinically significant distress or impairment in functioning.
D. The pattern is stable and of long duration and can be traced back to adolescence or early adulthood.

Another important condition is that the enduring pattern be not the result either of another mental disorder or of substance abuse.

Beethoven "likely meets criteria A, B and C, but not D," Mai says, acknowledging that "his characterological problems started around the time of the Heiligenstadt testament"; that is, they were related to his devastating hearing loss. Eventually, Mai concedes that "[Beethoven] did not have a personality disorder per se, but his progressive character difficulties were the psychological and social consequences of his increasing deafness and his misuse of alcohol as he grew older" (161). Thus presented, however, the whole argument does not make any sense: Beethoven "likely" meets the criteria, but does not have the illness—but kind of has it, because he was an alcoholic. In fact, as we have shown in the previous chapter, Mai's claim that Beethoven was an alcoholic is plainly wrong.

Even though Mai eventually clears Beethoven of a "personality disorder (per se)," his argument about the four criteria of the illness is interesting as they reveal his approach. Just as in his diagnosis of the composer's alleged alcoholism, he does not support his statements with any example, probably assuming that the psychiatric symptoms in Beethoven's life gathered in his table 3.3 (shown on the next two pages), containing evidence from Beethoven's own letters, notes and conversation books; other information in the previous chapters of his book support his assertion.

In fact, the information in this table is largely irrelevant. The 33 examples cover a forty-year span (1786-1826) and range of proposed symptoms from "asthma" to "death wish"—but examined individually, many have clear causes outside Beethoven's will or brain that should exclude them from consideration. It is not a sign of mental disorder to react negatively to his brother's death, or a scene with his nephew, or heavy prolonged illnesses.

TABLE 3.3   PSYCHIATRIC AND PSYCHOSOMATIC SYMPTOMS

Date	Age	Letter	Symptoms
Sept. 1787	16	1	"Plagued with asthma,"[1] fears this will turn into consumption; also "melancholia" which is "almost as great a torture as my illness"
June 1801	30	51	now and then has a "raptus"[2]
Spring 1805	34	110	"private grief" (likely his hearing loss) "which has robbed me for a long time – of my usual energy"
June 1805	34	119	becoming more peevish every day
July 1809	38	220	"We have been suffering misery in concentrated form."
Dec. 1809	39	232	"Winter depresses me greatly – melancholy reminders."
Feb. 1810	39	250	poor "fitful" sleep, prefers wakefulness to any kind of sleep
Spring 1810	39	254	"Your news has again plunged me from the heights of the most sublime ecstasy down into the depths."[3]
May 1810	39	256	"I would have left this life long ago, what is more, by my own hand." (distress because of hearing loss)
Dec. 1812	42	394	"Since Sunday I have been ailing – mentally more than physically."
Jan. 1813	42	402	"moral factors" affecting health
May 1813	42	426	"A number of unfortunate incidents occurring one after the other have really driven me into a state bordering mental confusion." (likely financial difficulties)
Dec. 1813	43	441	"I am on the verge of despair."
Summer 1815	44	550	"peevish, sensitive, tormented" (by poor hearing) "I often feel only pain in the society of others."
Nov. 1815	44	571	"exhausted" because of "exertions" associated with death of brother

continued on next page

1 written shortly after the death of his mother from tuberculosis. Because there is no further reference to "asthma," it is likely that these were attacks of hyperventilation associated with his fears of contracting tuberculosis.
2 an episode of loss of control and absent-mindedness (see chapter 2, p. 34)
3 written after he was rejected in love by Therese Malfatti

TABLE 3.3 (CONT'D)

Date	Age	Letter	Symptoms
Feb. 1816	45	615	"My brother's death has affected my spirits and my nerves."
May 1816	45	633	"For the last six weeks I have been in very poor health, so much so that I have thought of my death."
1816	45	710	really ill, suffering from a nervous breakdown
1817	46	740	"I am angry, angry, angry."
July 1817	46	790	poor hearing and conflict with servants "drive me to despair"
Aug. 1817	46	805	"I often despair and would like to die ... I can see no end to all my infirmities ... if the present state of affairs does not cease next year I shall probably be in my grave."
1817	46	866	insomnia
1817	46	877	often thinks of death
July 1818	47	904	"heart attack" after conflict with nephew and with servants - likely chest wall pain associated with anxiety and frustration of situation
Jan. 1819	48	933	terrible event in family (nephew ran away to his mother), "For a time I was driven out of my mind."
June 1819	48	948	"despondency and several distressing circumstances" made him lose courage
July 1819	48	952	very unwell - worries about nephew
Sept. 1821	50	1056	difficulty sleeping, somnolence, dreaming
May 1822	51	1078	"I am very sensitive and irritable."
May 1825	54	1377 1379	anger (toward nephew)
June 1825	54	1387	conflict with nephew is having a bad effect on health
June 1826	55	1489	insomnia (anxiety re nephew)
Sept. 1826	55	1521	worn out and unhappy

While we could easily agree that Beethoven's well known "eccentricity" may satisfy criterion A, we have strong evidence that his "pattern" was not at all "inflexible and pervasive" (criterion B): he was quick to get into fits of anger versus his friends, but also as quick to regret and humbly apologize. Wegeler acknowledged that Beethoven was "highly sensitive" and quick to overreact but also that "after the first explosion, he could listen to remonstrances with a willing ear and a conciliatory heart. As a result he always apologized for much more than he was guilty." Ries also testified that "he also tried to compensate for the injustice he had done as quickly and effectively as possible."[6] One can hardly call this "inflexibility."

Neither does Beethoven meet condition C: there is no evidence that he ever showed "clinically significant distress" or "impairment in functioning." He not only maintained intact his essential "functioning"—that is, composing masterpiece after masterpiece—but he was not an anti-social person, in spite of his eccentricities. The verdict, according to DSM-IV criteria, is obvious: Beethoven may have been eccentric, but didn't have a personality disorder.

Davies' failed case for paranoia

Davies builds his case in the second of his 2001 twin volume,[7] also following DSM-IV criteria, which include (135):[8*]

A. A pervasive distrust and suspiciousness of others such that their motives are interpreted as malevolent, beginning by early adulthood and present in a variety of contexts, as indicated by four (or more) of the following:
1) Suspects, without sufficient basis, that others are exploiting, harming, or deceiving him
2) Is preoccupied with unjustified doubts about the loyalty or trustworthiness of friends or associates.
3) Is reluctant to confide in others because of unwarranted fear that the information will be used maliciously against him.
4) Reads hidden demeaning or threatening meanings into benign remarks or events.
5) Persistently bears grudges, i.e., is unforgiving of insults, injuries, or slights.
6) Perceives attacks on his character or reputation that are not apparent to others and is quick to react angrily or to counterattack.
7) Has recurrent suspicions, without justification, regarding fidelity of spouse or sexual partner.

Davies omits, in his discussion, the B item in the APA manual, which is particularly important, as we will see later. He also adjusts the seven above criteria by combining the first and the third. He basically collects some fifty-odd examples of Beethoven's behavior (135-143) in which the composer's allegedly unwavering mistrust in people damaged his relationships with the most important human beings in his life—his brothers and his nephew, his best friends, his patrons and his publishers. These examples appear to fit well five of the seven DSM-IV criteria above (#1-4, 6), which would thus qualify Beethoven as a paranoid. Davies also dwells (143-167) on the few "litigations" in which

---

* All references to Davies' book are indicated in text in this chapter. Devies quotes American Psychiatric Association, *Diagnostic and Statistical Manual of Mental Disorders,* 3rd edition, 1987, pp. 337-339.

Beethoven was involved and in which, according to him, the composer was "at the mercy of his paranoia" (143). Strangely enough, even the suit that Beethoven initiated about his annual stipend promised by three aristocratic patrons, after the financial bankruptcy of Austria reduced its value to one fifth, appears to Davies to be a symptom of Beethoven's paranoid fears.

This bulk of evidence looks impressive, but a closer scrutiny reveals a strange undertone that creates a feeling of uneasiness. I do not object to the "clinician's" coldness that Davies displays but, on the contrary, to the fierceness of his relentless pursuit in finding faults in his patient, when a dispassionate approach would have found some reasonable explanations for the latter's behavior in certain episodes. Some of Davies' allegations appear really strange, like Beethoven's "masochistic tendencies"—a clear misnomer, since the examples he offers could only (and only with a great deal of exaggeration) qualify as sadism or, much better, as childish mischievousness ("he took delight in throwing the players into confusion at rehearsals, especially at sudden changes of tempo in the scherzos of his symphonies" [171]). Davies applies a second misnomer to diagnose Beethoven with hypochondriasis, too (169-171): he quotes a physician, Karl von Bursy, who visited Beethoven and talked to him in 1816 and discovered in him the "exact sygnum *diagnosticum of hypochondraism*" (original emphasis). Hypochondria is the delusion of suffering from imaginary illnesses, but, as Davies himself amply documents, Beethoven's many illnesses besides his deafness were quite real.[9] In fact, the term "hypochondriasis" covered much more diverse symptoms during the nineteenth century, including those for paranoia.[10]

Here is another example, the meaning of which Davies stretches to make his case for Beethoven's mistrust of his friends. He would reproach Zmeskall, in a letter, for refusing to recommend his own servants to him (136). In fact, Beethoven's somewhat clumsy wording was about the recommendation letters of his servant that his friend refused to send him, as is clear from another letter to the same, in which we also find out that Beethoven suspected his new servant to have committed a theft.[11] This may be evidence that he distrusted his servants, but not his friends.

Other allegations of Davies border on the ridiculous. "It seems likely," he asserts, "that Beethoven's mistrust may also have been partly responsible for his rejection of Alexander Kyd's arrogant though generous request to commission a new symphony, which was to be short, simple and composed in his earlier style" (138). Can anyone be surprised that Beethoven felt deeply offended by the proposal and turned it down?[12] What has that to do with "mistrust?" Such an example shows Davies' desire to amass a huge quantity of data, without caring to scratch beneath the surface of any datum. These few quoted examples are by no means unique, but due to the limited editorial space, we can deal here only with the cases that played a major part in Beethoven's life.

Beethoven's confession to his friends about losing his hearing. The strangest such instance is Davies' reading of Beethoven's confession to his closest friends, Amenda and Wegeler, about losing his hearing. Because he asks them, "treat what I told you about my hearing as a great secret to be entrusted to no one,"[13] Davies assumes that it was because of Beethoven's paranoid fear that "such information would be used against him" (136). The most "normal" human being would not have behaved differently and Beethoven loss was much more devastating than it is to the typical person—he was losing the most precious sense of a musician, at the very moment when all the other Vienna musicians shared one thing, their "hatred of Beethoven."[14] Davies' inference is an astounding proof of insensitivity.

The case of "worthy" Baron von Brown illustrates Davies' rush to judge without knowing the facts. He quotes testimonies about Beethoven's feeling cheated because of the low profit he had from the premiere of his *Fidelio*'s second version in 1806, and concludes that he paranoidly mistrusted the director of the opera house, the "worthy" Baron von Braun (135-6). Later on, Davies also quotes (138) a previous Beethoven letter (written to Sonnleithner in 1804) in which the composer complains, "ever since we met, his [Braun's] treatment of me has been persistently unfriendly,"[15] as more proof of the composer's paranoid mistrust of well-meaning people.

In order to understand Beethoven's relationship with von Braun, we must get a closer look at the Viennese concert life at the time. Vienna might have been the musical capital of Europe, because Haydn, Mozart and Beethoven (and, later, Schubert) lived there, but when it came to the quality of the concert life it lagged far behind cities like London, Paris, Berlin or Leipzig, that could not claim any such genius as their own. The latter cities had well-established professional orchestras and public concert venues, while Vienna relied mainly on private aristocratic sponsorship of instrumental music. When a musician like Beethoven wanted to reach to a wider audience he had to rent an opera-house hall, assemble a makeshift orchestra with instrumentalists from all over the city and, of course, pay for everything.

Therefore, the opera-house halls were essential and the two most important ones in Vienna, the imperial theaters *Burgtheater* and the *Kerthnerthortheater*, were in the hands of Baron von Braun, who was the lessee of the theaters between 1794 and 1807.[16] The Baron let Beethoven have the *Burgtheater* for his first concert (called "Academy") in April 1800, when he presented his first grand symphonic pieces (the first Piano, the Septet Op. 20, the first Symphony), besides his improvisation. But von Braun turned down two similar requests by Beethoven in 1801 and 1803,[17] while he rented out his opera-houses to mediocre musicians, among whom the favorite was the lady pianist Josepha Auernhammer, who held no less than nine concerts between 1795 and 1806. This blatant discrimination made the Viennese magazine *Zeitung für die elegante Welt* wonder in 1806 "why has this theater to stay closed and not used, instead of being rented to our great masters like Beethoven, Eberl and others? Why must the fate of so many artists that excel in the most diverse fields depend on only one person?"[18] It is obvious that Beethoven was not paranoid when he complained that "his [Braun's] treatment of me has been persistently unfriendly." He was probably wrong during the 1806 *Fidelio* episode, but that was just the straw that broke the camel's back.

Beethoven's relationship with Haydn was, in Davies' view, one of the most illustrative examples of Beethoven's suspicious mindedness, but his quotes from other scholars about "ambivalence," attitude towards the "father figure," etc., fail to convince us of the veracity of the case. In reality, a scratch under the surface of the story shows us that Beethoven had some good reasons to feel belittled by Haydn. The issue was, first of all, Haydn's reception of Beethoven's Piano Trio in C minor from his Opus 1, of which he was particularly proud and which he expected to launch his career as a composer and an heir to the Haydn-Mozart tradition. Not only was Haydn reticent to "bless" this work—he advised Beethoven not to print it, as we learn from Ries —[19] but he also abetted the envious derogatory comments of the other Viennese composers, united, as we have already learned, in their "hatred of Beethoven." This is the story that they had spread:

> Speaking of Beethoven [his C minor Piano Trio particularly], Kozeluch said to Haydn: "We would have done it differently, wouldn't we, Papa?" and Haydn answered, smilingly, "Yes, we would have done that differently."[20]

Haydn was endorsing the now-forgotten Leopold Kozeluch (1747-1818) over Beethoven! Another anecdote, reported by Aloys Fuchs (1799-1853), a much younger Beethoven contemporary, shows that Haydn's low opinion of Beethoven extended far beyond the latter's trio.

> In 1801, he [Beethoven] was met by his former teacher, the great Joseph Haydn, who stopped him at once and said: "Well, I heard your ballet [The Creatures of Prometheus] yesterday and it pleased me very much!" Beethoven replied: "Oh, dear Papa, you are very kind; but it is far from being a *Creation*!" Haydn, surprised at the answer and almost offended, said after a short pause: "That is true; it is not yet a *Creation* and I can scarcely believe that it will ever become one." Whereupon the men said their adieux, both somewhat embarrassed.[21]

Beethoven's sincere reply—also tainted with his usual use of puns—was simply intended to say, "Please wait for me doing something really great to praise me," but Haydn felt it an impudence to have his masterpiece compared with a second-hand piece and his answer went far beyond saying that that ballet music was a decent but forgettable work: it translated into, "I can scarcely believe that you will ever write a masterpiece like my *Creation*." Obviously, this story, which circulated in the small world of the Viennese musicians for quite some time (until Aloys Fuchs, born in 1799, could collect it), could not have pleased Beethoven, who had, by that time already surpassed Haydn's mastery in at least two instrumental music genres—the piano sonata and the concerto—and was going to do the same with the symphony and string quartet in just a few years. He naturally expected the older master to acknowledge him as his successor, but Haydn clearly refused to do so. He lavished the attribute "one of the greatest geniuses that I've ever met" on another now forgotten musician—Joseph Martin Kraus (1756-1792)![22] In spite of his understandable bitterness, Beethoven dedicated his Opus 2 to Haydn, and they appeared in several concerts together, at the very time when this alleged rift happened, between 1795 and 1801.[23] Beethoven continued to esteem and revere the older master until the end of his own life.[24] Of the two, the reputedly amiable Haydn and the allegedly paranoid Beethoven, the latter appears the more human and forgiving.

Beethoven's quarrel with Prince Lichnovsky, whom he was visiting in 1806. Davies' account (141-142, after Thayer-Forbes)[25] is bare, as if it would be telling on its own: "Although the prince repeatedly pressured Ludwig to play the piano for some visiting French officers, he stubbornly refused. When he [Beethoven] was jestingly threatened [by the Prince] with imprisonment for his refusal, he suddenly lost his temper, making a hasty exit [...]" and practically putting an end to this friendship. There is more to this story, that Davies omits— the personal, historical and psychological perspective, which explains why Beethoven had an overblown response to the prince's poor-taste joke.

Prince Karl Lichnowsky was a decent person and Beethoven's loyal friend and patron but, not unlike the composer, he was good at committing blunders and had bad taste in jokes, of which a few are recorded in the composer's biography. Sometime in 1804, when Beethoven visited him, the prince insisted on playing to him something on the piano of his own invention and, to the musician's amazement and eventual anger, he produced a partial but faithful rendition of Beethoven's yet unpublished and never yet publicly performed *Andante* in F major (now known as WoO 57). It was Lichnowsky's practical joke, of course, as he immediately confessed: he had learned the piece from Beethoven's friend Ries, to whom the composer had played it after finishing it and who had been sufficiently enthused to go play it to the Prince from memory. Beethoven seems to have forgiven Lichnowsky—whom he still called "one of my most loyal friends and promoters of my art" in a January 1805 letter,[26] but not Ries, whom he punished by never again playing in his presence, even though the Prince tried to appease him, taking all the blame upon himself.[27] Beethoven's reaction may have been excessive, but we should try to understand him: his music was both his reputation and his bread-earning and it was not unusual, at the time, for fellow musicians to try to get a "sneak preview" of their competitors' musical ideas to get ahead of them.[28]

A year later, Josephine was at the center of another Lichnowsky blunder, this time with Beethoven's own help: he left the manuscript of his song *To Hope*, that he had composed for Josephine, in full view on his table. The visiting Prince had a look at it and noticed that it bore an affectionate dedication to her. Moreover, Lichnowsky made a discreet inquiry about the goings-on, which was not discreet enough—the lady got wind of it and was annoyed. Beethoven hurried to reassure her in a letter and almost invoked Lichnowsky's indiscretion as a kind of "blessings" for their close intimacy.[29] Yet, even though Beethoven forgave the princely blunder, it is quite possible that he, a very private person who kept all his love affairs secret, was not at all pleased with it. And, as we learn from another of his letters to Josephine, there had been "many rough passages which we [Beethoven and the Prince] encountered on the path of this friendship."[30]

As one can see, the 1806 incident at Prince Lichnowsky's palace was not a first fracture in Beethoven's relationship with him and, again, must have been the "last straw." It had also a very special and painful meaning for the composer and partially explains his ambivalent attitude about the nobility, which was deeply rooted in his humble birth and his social status. Musicians had been for centuries servants to the rich and powerful who employed them and sometimes abused them. Less than a hundred years before (in 1717) Bach had been actually imprisoned (albeit not for very long) by the Weimar Archduke, because he had asked to be relieved from his service. Mozart had been treated like a servant by his employer, Archbishop Colloredo, and was thrown out of His Eminence's palace with blows. Haydn had been lucky to be promoted from the rank of servant to the higher level of "house officer," which meant that he did not share the table with the servants and was sometimes even invited to his employer Prince Esterhazy's table. Haydn had accepted his position, probably with a sense of humor. Mozart rebelled and started the career of a freelance musician, for which he paid dearly, with struggle, pain and an untimely death.

Beethoven benefitted from the feeling of guilt that the Viennese aristocracy developed after the death of Mozart, whose genius they had not known how to support during his life, but which they soon recognized afterwards. They treated young Beethoven with both enthusiasm and great respect, not like a replaceable servant. He was a welcomed guest in their palaces, not only as a musician but also as a friend. He, however, could not forget his humble roots, his lack of education (even though he had caught up, at least partially), or his lack of worldly manners—which he delighted to infringe upon. He indulged in their company, but he knew he was not one of them, even when they treated him as something better than themselves, as a genius. And he learned, through such incidents as the one with Lichnowsky, that they were occasionally able to make him feel the distance between their statuses. The princely joke displayed more than bad taste—the vestige of an arrogance that the noble class could never get entirely rid of. Beethoven's angry reaction was not even disproportionate, only perhaps childish: he could have disarmed and humiliated his host by just saying, "Prince, I can hardly wait to get food and board on your house," but one cannot diagnose him with paranoid mistrust because of missing such an opportunity.[31]

This episode helps us understand Beethoven's ambivalence towards his aristocratic friends and patrons, which included appreciation *and* mistrust, and even blasts of anger. The remark about the Archbishop Rudolph that Davies quotes in support of his thesis, "Owing to my unfortunate connection with this Archduke I have been reduced to beggary" from an 1818 letter[32] is of a different nature. Beethoven gave vent once more to his dissatisfaction with his contract with the three aristocratic patrons who had lured him into staying in Vienna by offering him an annuity, because the latter had lost some 15% of its value (even after adjustment for the devaluation of the Austrian currency)[33] at a time when he was more than ever incurring expenses, such as for the raising and education of his nephew. He would have liked to be free to move to England, the country with a parliamentary regime he greatly appreciated—and where his music was very popular, and which had copyright laws that protected his published scores. In England, he could hope to secure his future, as Haydn had done before; his annuity, however, chained him in Vienna.

Beethoven's mistrust of his own brothers is also quoted by Davies in his diagnosis of the musician's alleged paranoia. He invokes several illustrative examples, but fails to note the evidence that Beethoven had in some cases solid reasons to be disappointed with them. Beethoven had a deep sense of his duty towards his family, soon reduced to his two younger brothers and, while he acted sometimes as a tyrannical father, he was also well meaning and helpful. He very likely supported them in Bonn financially after he moved to Vienna in 1792, and he brought them to Vienna soon enough after he had settled there. He trusted Carl (Carpar Carl) with his whole music business, his dealings with publishers for over ten years (1794-1806) and he certainly helped his other brother, Johann, to finish his apothecary apprenticeship.

That both brothers in time turned into big disappointments to him is another story. Carl's performance as his private secretary was far from stellar. His status as the brother of a great genius inflated his ego and he clearly overstepped his authority in dealing with the publishers, which often led to conflict between the two brothers, quickly followed by Beethoven forgiving the trespasser.[34] And after Carl got a clerical job, sometime around 1804, Beethoven learned from his friend Stephen von Breuning that his brother was suspected of embezzlement,[35] which resulted in an angry scene and a temporary break-up with Stephen. The outcome of this episode is not known, but Carl was able to keep his job, very likely due to his older brother's pulling some strings.

The other brother, Johann, evolved in a manner that Beethoven must have found even more repugnant: he grew his pharmacy store into a successful business and became rich through what his brother must have deemed as dishonest speculation—selling medicine to the French army, which the composer saw as the enemy. Then Johann started displaying both the arrogance and stinginess of an upstart. In one of the conversation books, he offered to host Beethoven, but asked him to pay rent;[36] obviously, Beethoven's calling him "my brother Cain" in an October 1824 letter[37] (Davies' example, page 152) is too strong a claim, but it has to be taken metaphorically.

The most vulnerable point in Beethoven's relationship with his brothers was probably their commerce with women, which he wanted to monitor to ensure the moral standing of their family. We have already seen what kind of a woman Carl married. In Beethoven's eyes, Johann chose even worse than Carl. In Beethoven's eyes, Johann chose even worse than Carl. He first lived with his housekeeper, a woman who had an illegitimate child, and then married her, in spite of (or maybe just because of) Beethoven's well-meant but childishly obdurate wish to prevent his brother from making such a mistake. Davies does not miss the opportunity to see again Beethoven's innate mistrust in people as the root of his low opinion of his sister-in-law, but the composer proved to be right: Johann discovered later that his wife cheated on him and eventually made a marital arrangement equivalent to a "civil divorce"—because a religious one was impossible in Catholic Austria.[38] It is obvious that Beethoven's mistrust of his brothers was not just a whimsical fantasy, but had some solid roots in reality.

Beethoven's mistrust of his nephew is also quoted by Davies as further evidence of the composer's paranoia. Beethoven's very complex relationship with his nephew is far beyond the scope of the current analysis, but it is not hard to discover in his biography plenty of reasons to be disappointed in his nephew's development as a human being. It is quite true that the musician's own behavior was responsible for many of the flaws in his nephew's character: his obdurate attempt to separate the child from his mother certainly justified the young boy's lying to his uncle; the latter's inconsistent attitude, with severe scoldings followed by repentful displays of affection, certainly made the teenager into a skilled manipulator. But this does not justify his other flaws that became stronger and stronger over time. The young Karl was lazy, did not want to learn in school, liked to schmooze with "good-for-nothings" like himself; as a young man he became a habitué of the coffee houses and his main talent was the pool. No wonder that his uncle, who wanted to see him grow into "a true Beethoven," was very disappointed to discover him as mediocre as his brothers—even worse than them from an ethical perspective. In short, his mistrust was not an *a priori* position, but followed the growth of the boy into a young man.

And then came Karl's attempt to kill himself at the end of July 1826—which looks almost like his most successful attempt to manipulate his uncle. (After two gunshots to the head, incredibly, he got out almost unscathed from the incident and explained his gesture as resulting from his uncle's treatment of him.[39]) This act shattered Beethoven so much that he aged practically overnight and he was never to be the same man again.[40] A few months later, he fell ill one last time and Dr. Wawruch, the first physician to attend him, left us the telling testimony that I have already presented (see page 51): after being treated for a week, Beethoven seemed to have recovered, but he abruptly and dramatically relapsed because of a mysterious incident in which he suffered "ingratitude and undeserved insults" from a never named suspect that could only have been his nephew. From that moment on, as Wawruch writes, "sickness progressed with giant steps."[41] It is very likely that Karl hastened Beethoven's death a second time.

More dubious examples of Beethoven's paranoid mistrust. Davies also invokes episodes in which the issue is very little known, if at all. One cannot simply surmise that it was Beethoven's paranoid mistrust that made him behave badly (yet in an unknown manner) towards his teenage friend (and, possibly, sweetheart) Leonore von Breuning, before he left for Vienna (137). Wegeler, who mentions the fact only as proof that Beethoven was able to recognize when he had been wrong (not exactly the trait of a paranoid), does not give any details, and actually downplays it, commenting, "It demonstrates first of all the contention that Beethoven always apologized for more than he had committed."[42] Similarly, one does not know anything about Beethoven's incriminated no-longer-extant letter to the Giannatasio del Rio family, which Davies calls "denunciatory" (138) based solely on Fanny Giannatasio's very vague description of it in her diary.[43] We think it is a scholarly duty to retain judgment when the facts are not known.

Beethoven's alleged psychotic episodes: the poisoning angst. In final analysis, Davies acknowledges (266) that, in spite of the evidence he presented, "it is absolutely clear that Beethoven's sanity was intact for most of the time. However, there do appear to have been several frankly psychotic episodes during his life." He quotes first of all the musician's frenzied hatred of his sister-in-law Johanna and his relentless pursuit of his goal to sever her relationship with her son Karl. Beethoven's consistent behavior has baffled and even dismayed his posterity, who could not find a satisfactory explanation. The only one, offered from a Freudian angle by the Sterba couple and by Solomon, was not "reasonable" (let alone satisfactory), as I showed in my previous essay. Davies does not tackle the issue in its entirety; only the "poisoning" episode. He quotes Beethoven suspicion that his sister-in-law had poisoned his brother, and continued in this belief even after a "post mortem examination" did not confirm his suspicion.[44] As I've argued, Johanna was a morally corrupt person and he could not forgive her for dragging the Beethoven name through the mud. Suspecting her of having poisoned his brother was probably excessive, but not excessive enough to warrant a diagnosis of paranoia.

In the elaboration of the "poisoning" theme, Davies goes awry again. He claims (267) that Beethoven had developed "an apprehension about being poisoned"—which would have been a clear sign of delusional behavior. He further quotes an August 1825 letter Beethoven wrote to his nephew mentioning the everyday "risk of being poisoned" and claims that "in order to prevent this he [Beethoven] employed Karl and other friends to taste his soup, food, and wine." He offers two pieces of evidence to support this latter allegation: a note in an 1822 conversation book in which Karl wrote that the wine Beethoven was drinking at a pub was stronger than another one he had before and an 1825 letter to Karl asking him to make sure that his servant buys pure soda water, not "who knows what." Also in support of his interpretation, he quotes the Sterbas' "likely hypothesis that Beethoven's delusion about poisoning by a woman traced back to unconscious ambivalent hostile feelings towards his mother during his childhood," a futile speculation that I debunked in chapter 2 (page 20).

When we examine closer the evidence invoked by Davies, we discover a different reality. The original 1825 Beethoven letter that uses the word "poisoned" complains about the quality of the food that his servant/cook prepared or that he could find in a restaurant:

> today there was not soup, no beef, not even an egg—finally I got a small cut of a joint from the inn [...] However little I may need to be fully fed with the lower type of food, as you know, yet all this is really to bad; and, what is more, every moment of the day to run the risk of being poisoned.[45]

It is obvious that Beethoven had in mind "food poisoning" and nothing more. This was a normal concern at a time when refrigeration was not known, there was little notion of food hygiene and, consequently, food (especially meat) was quite often rotten, particularly during the summer heat. Digestive diseases were common and Beethoven himself was pestered with them for most of his life, as Davies himself acknowledges. Common sense tells us that Karl's 1822 note that compares two wines Beethoven drank is no proof that the latter used to have his nephew test his drinks before drinking himself; it is simply proof—if proof is needed—that a party shared a drink in a pub. Finally, another sentence in the 1825 letter to Karl (Davies' timeline itself is all over the place: first 1825, then 1822, then again 1825) helps us understand Beethoven's concern: "dear son, see to it that we get the pure soda water, *not the artificially produced kind.* Do get with her [his servant] or else I might be given who knows what.[46] We know that the composer used to take mineral water cures and it appears that counterfeit mineral water is not a modern invention.

All in all, the "poisoning" episode advanced by Davies is no proof of Beethoven's psychopathy. That being said, it is true his relationship with his sister-in-law Johanna cannot be dismissed as the major symptom of Beethoven's psychotic behavior, an issue I dealt with in chapter 2.

Genetic predisposition. Like Mai, Davies (268-270) claims that Beethoven's ancestry had a long history with mental disease, which could easily explain the composer's psychotic problems. His father's alcoholism and the paternal grandmother's alcoholism—both of which developed late in life—are indeed convincingly documented, but that is not proof that Beethoven was an alcoholic himself (see chapter 5). Davies also invokes (270) the Sterbas' claim that "Beethoven's mother was subject to depression,"[47] which was never proven. All these are intended to show that such genetics, which may also involve mental diseases, must have passed to Beethoven's own generation. Davies fails, however, to find symptoms of psychotic behavior in the composer's brothers, Johann and Carl, and he concludes with the following weird argument: "[…] in Beethoven's family two of his brothers […] and also his two sisters […] died during the first three years of life. Had they survived into adulthood, some of them may have developed and manifested evidence of bipolar or depressive illness or some other mental disorder."[48] With this kind of argument one can prove anything. Finally, the statistics invoked as an argument of transmissible genetic traits do not prove anything: statistics do not apply to individuals but to groups. Davies' genetics connection argument fails.

The Family Romance. Davies not only accepts that Solomon's theory "is convincing" (168), but also makes it into an argument for his paranoia diagnosis. In reality, his heavy reliance on Solomon or Sterbas' fabrications becomes proof of the falseness of his approach.

Summing up. Davies distributes his examples to four DSM-IV criteria of paranoia, concluding that Beethoven suffered from it. I have showed that a closer look at many of the most important examples of the composer's supposedly paranoid behavior reveal that he had at least some legitimate reasons to feel harmed or offended. Moreover, almost all of these examples do not pertain to the first DSM criterion—mistrust and lack of confidence in other people, including his friends and his siblings—but to a somewhat similar criterion for the paranoid disorder set by the World Health Organization, worded as "excessive sensitivity to setbacks and rebuffs." Indeed, in most such cases, Beethoven's reactions appear as an overblown response to someone's words or acts. At the same time, his behavior shows that he was not "fundamentally" a suspicious mind. This is the paradox of his behavior: he confided in people and then felt, sometimes correctly but many times incorrectly, that he had made a mistake in doing so. The "suspicious mindedness" that Ries noticed after 1802, when he first met Beethoven in Vienna,[49] was an *a posteriori* rather than an *a* *priori* condition. Distinguishing the *a priori* mistrust from the *a posteriori* one is not always easy, but I have shown that it can be done in several instances. The *a priori* suspicion-minded person, the real paranoid, tends to withdraw from society; Beethoven did indeed withdraw, but against his own nature, and only after his growing deafness became a real, cumbersome and handicapping communication barrier.

This connects to another and very important side of the matter.

The impact of Beethoven's deafness

DSM-IV criteria for paranoia includes a second B group, which Davies omitted from consideration in his argument:

B. Does not occur exclusively during the course of Schizophrenia, a Mood Disorder with Psychotic Features, or another Psychotic Disorder and is not due to the direct physiological effects of a general medical condition.[50]

This B group raises a new question: what role did Beethoven's deafness—obviously an essential trait in his life—play in the development of his personality and his alleged mental illness? Was it the cause of the illness or only an aggravating factor? If it was not the cause, what *was* the cause?

Davies offers answers to such questions (163-167, 168-169), but they are unreliable, because they rely heavily on opinions of scholars like Rank, the Sterbas (Editha and Richard) and Solomon, who tackled such issues from a Freudian perspective. Recurring to Freud's theory in 2000 is almost like trying to build a nuclear reactor based on Democritus's theory about the atoms. Like the ancient Greek philosopher living 2500 years ago, Freud was a worthy predecessor, but, as I showed in chapter 1, the only valid precept he left us is the commonsense idea that early childhood is essential in the development of the adult personality, albeit in different ways than those postulated by Freud and his followers (such as infantile sexuality, noble birth delusion or Family Romance). We must set ourselves free from Freudian illusions/delusions when dealing with the issues at hand.

The reality is that we know little about Beethoven's childhood—we have vague images of a stern but loving mother, a very authoritarian father who forced his son to practice the violin for hours on end with a hope to mold him into a second Mozart and who punished him for failing. Beethoven was rather reluctant to talk about himself or his parents, but he wrote about "a good, kind mother to me and indeed my best friend,"[51] and he never complained about his father's "tyrannical coercion" (Davies' syntagm, 166). There has been, however, plenty of psychoanalytical speculation, based on which we would expect Beethoven to be a reclusive, uncommunicative child and youth. In reality, a neighbor, Frau Karth "[...] remembered Ludwig in his youth as always 'gentle and lovable'" and very unlike his brothers Caspar Karl ("proud and presumptuous") and Johann ("a bit stupid but very good natured").[52] A certain Carl Ludwig Junker, a dilettante composer who met Beethoven in 1791 and listened to his extemporizing, wrote enthusiastically about this experience in a letter to the Bossler's journal *Musikal*, presenting the twenty year old as an "amiable, light-hearted man [...] exceedingly modest and free from all pretension."[53] Contrary to the Freudian expectations, young Beethoven seems to have been very different than the (supposedly) paranoid man of thirty-something. In spite of financial hardship and suffering due to the death of two siblings and then of his mother, Beethoven's childhood offers little that could have been the root of his alleged paranoid disorder.

Wegeler was a close friend of Beethoven throughout his early and teenage years, beginning with the time when they were part of the von Breuning family circle who had unofficially adopted Beethoven and gave him a second home. Wegeler's memories of his friend mention his "youthful exuberance," though he was "frequently stubborn and unsociable."[54] Unsociability was also relates to what Mrs. Breuning dubbed his "raptuses," the moments when he was "abducted" (the meaning of the Latin word "raptus") by his musical inspiration and withdrew from the social interaction.[55] Neither stubbornness—quite common with teenagers—nor the "raptuses" seem to relate to any paranoid traits.

Wegeler further introduces what appears as Beethoven's main human flaw during his youth: he was "highly sensitive and consequently easily provoked"—a symptom of a choleric personality. Yet Wegeler adds this highly mitigating trait: "However, if one waited for the air to clear after the first explosion, he could listen to remonstrances with a willing ear and a conciliatory heart. As a result he always apologized for much more than he was guilty."[56] As we have shown, many of Davies' examples of Beethoven's paranoid mistrust of people were in fact his exaggerated reactions when he was too easily "provoked" by the actions or just the words of those people.

Let us note now that only two examples advanced by Davies as proof of Beethoven's paranoid traits belong to the period before 1800: the quarrel with Leonore von Breuning, of which we do not know any details and which appears as not really important; and his relationship with Haydn, that I dismissed above as Davies' rush to judgement. It appears that all these paranoid traits manifested only after the onset of the composer's essential disease—losing his hearing. This is consistent with the recent findings of the medical fields, which show that losing one's hearing later in life frequently yields the kind of behavior that Beethoven displayed beginning with his thirtieth year: irritability, a suspicious mind, fits of unjustified anger, etc.[57] For Davies, deafness would have only aggravated the musician's already well-developed paranoia,[58] but there is evidence that supports the opposite contention—that the disease onset marked a huge difference in Beethoven's behavior. Here is testimony of Seyfried, who had been close to Beethoven since his arrival in Vienna until his death:

> "Beethoven was much too straightforward, open and tolerant to give offence to another by disapprobation or contradiction; he was wont to laugh heartily at what did not please him and I confidently believe that I may safely say that in all his life he never, at least not consciously, made an enemy; only those to whom his peculiarities were unknown were unable quite to understand how to get along with him; *I am speaking here of an earlier time, before the*

misfortune of deafness had come upon him" (my emphasis)

If one thinks that Seyfried exaggerates his friend's qualities, here is the continuation of his description, which points to what is usually seen as Beethoven's "dark side":

> "if, on the contrary, Beethoven sometimes carried things to an extreme in his rude honesty in the case of the many, mostly those who had imposed themselves upon him as protectors, the fault lay only in this, that the honest German always carries his heart on his tongue and understood everything better than how to flatter; also because, conscious of his own merit, he would never permit himself to be made the plaything of the vain whims of the Maecenases who were eager to boast of their association with the name and fame of the celebrated master. And so he was misunderstood only by those who had not the patience with the apparent eccentric."[59]

Here is a second testimony, from Stephen von Breuning, who had been Beethoven's friend since his teenage years and met him again in 1801,[60] when he moved to Vienna. In 1804 he wrote to Wegeler about the "dreadful effect" that the loss of hearing had on the psyche of their friend:

> *You would not believe, dear Wegeler, what an indescribable and, I should say, truly dreadful impact the loss of his hearing has had on him.* Imagine the feeling of being unhappy — and with such a vehement nature as his. Add to this his shyness, distrust (often of his best friends) and general indecisiveness! For the most part, except for the occasional moments when his original affection expresses itself freely, association with him is a real strain, and one can never be quite off one's guard.[61] (my emphasis)

One can recognize in Breuning's testimony a description familiar to the clinical experience of the psychiatrist: "the tendency to place the blame outside of themselves represent a paranoid reaction and is similar (possibly identical) to the well-recognized paranoia seen in patients with acute acquired deafness."[62] It is very likely that Beethoven's deafness, also aggravated by his precarious general health, was the main cause of his paranoid traits in the second half of his life. Its development may also have been favored by his choleric personality, but the deafness must have been the defining factor.

Bipolar Beethoven?—Not Quite

As the link between genius and this particular mental disease has become a fad of late, it comes as no surprise that both Davies and Mai argue that Beethoven also suffered of bipolar disorder (formerly, manic-depressive disorder). Of course, they take care to emphasize that this diagnosis in no way diminishes Beethoven's stature as a musician and quote extensively psychiatric opinions which would attest that creativity in diverse fields, including music, is significantly correlated with psychopathological behavior, and especially with bipolar disorder (Mai dedicates a special chapter to the possibility). Both authors proceed in a two-step strategy: first collect evidence of many depression episodes in his life as proof that he had a depressive personality, then elevate the latter diagnose to bipolar disorder. However, they approach the issue with two different tactics: Mai, a psychiatrist, refers consistently to the DSM-IV, while Davies acts more like a music scholar, searching for proof also in Beethoven's music. As we will see, the two approaches have one thing in common—they thoroughly fail.

Mai's failed case. A manic depressive person lives alternate periods of depression and euphoria. To diagnose Beethoven with depression episodes, Mai invokes the Axis I of the DSM-IV, which defines a major depressive episode as meeting at least five of the criteria and including either the first or second of the following characteristics, over a two-week period:
1. depressed mood most of the day nearly every day
2. diminished interest and pleasure
3. weight loss or weight gain
4. insomnia or hypersomnia nearly every day
5. agitation or retardation
6. fatigue
7. feelings of worthlessness and guilt
8. impaired concentration and decisiveness
9. thoughts of death

In addition, the symptoms must impair social functioning and are not caused by another medical or psychological event.

The thirty-odd episodes in Beethoven's life in Mai's table 3.3 (124), which supposedly bear proof that Beethoven suffered from recurrent depression, spread over thirty years (1787-1826)—clearly off the "two-week period" required by the DSM-IV. They vary from simple "ailing" to "melancholy" to "poor fitful sleep" to "mental confusion" to "thoughts of death" and even suicidal thoughts (May 1810, and possibly August 1817). The only missing characteristics are the weight loss or gain and the feelings of worthlessness and guilt; the latter is worth noting because Mai claims that Beethoven "experienced [...] guilt" (162), even though he does not offer any evidence in his tables (or in his whole book for that matter). In fact, many of these episodes can hardly be called depression symptoms (who has not been "angry, angry, angry" from time to time, like Beethoven in 1817?), but this is not the main flaw in Mai's argument. He fails to consider (he only briefly mentions it [162]) the condition that the symptoms "should not be caused by another medical or psychological event." Many, if not most, of the episodes had a very definite cause and Mai himself seems to acknowledge it, because he eventually concedes (169) that there are only four clear depressive episodes in Beethoven's life that he cannot link to painful events: 1809, 1813, 1817 and 1822.

It is now the right time to fill this gap in Mai's knowledge of his patient's life. In the spring of 1809, Beethoven was anguished over his break-up with Countess Marie Erdödy. Relying only on Maynard Solomon's opinion, Mai thinks that the countess was only a friend of the composer,[63] so that his breakup with her could not explain such a deep depression. In fact, other scholars have deemed the composer's relationship with Countess Erdödy to be a love story; I present their case, together with my own persuasive arguments for it in my *Immortal Beloved Controversy* book. A break-up with his loved one was certainly a good enough reason for an episode of depression. The 1813 depression (which actually began towards the end of the previous year, as illustrated in Mai's Table 3.3) was the result of Beethoven's even more painful break-up with his *Immortal Beloved.* This depressive episode lasted a very long time and translated into a long creative slump, which is beyond the scope of the present analysis. In 1817, his depression was clearly caused by another medical condition—he was very sick (as results from Mai's own tables 3.3 and 3.4). As for the 1822 episode, the only trace of it in Mai's own table 3.3 is one entry saying, "I am very sensitive and irritable," which can hardly qualify as depression. Based on this evidence showing less than one alleged depressive episode per year, Mai emits this strange argument (162): "Although we cannot be certain whether his depressed episodes lasted two weeks or more, in the event that they did, his diagnostic criteria for major depression would be met." Elementary logic would have required him to write, "because we do not know how long his depression episodes lasted, we cannot say that Beethoven was a depressive person," but Mai takes it as a proof of the opposite. He goes on to write about Beethoven's depression as a solid diagnosis, not a rare episodic occurrence, as if he had proven it to be a fact ("his depression had a seasonal pattern, etc.") and ends up invoking again the composer's alleged addiction to alcohol. He elaborates on the combination of the two— depression and alcoholism—in a paragraph (164) that combines well-known but trivial general truth ("Depression and alcohol dependence commonly occur together in the same individual," etc.) with misrepresentations about Beethoven's case that I have already rebutted, such as the alleged depression during his youth and his later "alcoholism." Mai forgets that he had accepted that Beethoven "was not a drunkard," (150)—that is, he did not drink to deal with his depression.

Mai's argument about Beethoven's depression has also the same major flaw as the one about his alleged personality disorder: it ignores the DSM-IV condition that the major depression symptoms be "not caused by another medical or psychological event." Never does Mai consider that Beethoven's deafness was enough reason for him to "feel blue" quite often and even feel suicidal! He ignores recent findings in his professional field, the research that has found that "the prevalence rate of clinical levels of depressed mood among people with profound AHL—acquired hearing loss—was found to be 4.8 times higher than in the general population."[64] If ordinary people losing their hearing can get depressed, how much more depressed should Beethoven, a musician, have been! It is indeed amazing and arguably a proof of his extraordinary mental strength that he did not succumb to suicidal thoughts.

Convinced that he had identified Beethoven's depression episodes, Mai only needed those of euphoria, medically known as hypomania, to diagnose his patient with bipolar disorder. He invoked again Axis I of the DSM-IV, which defines a hypomanic episode as having the following characteristics (162):

A. A period of elated, expansive or irritable mood lasting at least three days.*
B. The elevated mood is accompanied by at least three of the following symptoms:
1) inflated self-esteem or grandiosity;
2) decreased need for sleep or insomnia;
3) increased talkativeness;
4) racing thoughts (expressed in words or writing);
5) distractibility;
6) agitation;
7) increased pleasurable activities that may have painful consequences
In addition, the episode is accompanied by a change of functioning that is observable by others but is not severe enough to cause marked impairment of social functioning and is not the result of another medical or psychological condition.

Mai's table 3.3 includes four sleeplessness episodes between 1810 and 1826 but no other of the seven characteristics above; moreover, some of the sleeplessness episodes were clearly caused by painful events in Beethoven's life (likely financial difficulties, anxiety caused by his nephew, as Mai himself mentions). In fact, Mai's diagnosis relies exclusively on a few letters in which, in his opinion (163-64), Beethoven clearly displays racing thoughts—the condition d. Let's examine this evidence.

1) 1816 letter to publishers Sigmund Steiner and Haring, which begins:

> Most excellent General, the following letters are for Schlemmer and Haring. [...] Please deliver them at once, in the greatest haste, prestissimo, as speedily as possible; and sell those <u>sows</u> immediately.

Mai disregards the note 2 to the letter in the Anderson's translation of Beethoven's letter that he quotes;[65] it says that the word *sows* is just a guess of several ink blots (Brandenburg 967); it could well be another word. Even if "sows" was the word, we should not rush to judge, because we do not know the context of the letter. Take, for example, this other letter that Beethoven wrote to his friend Ries on July 24, 1804, which ends quite weirdly, "Do not do too much tailoring, remember me to the fairest of the fair, send me half a dozen sewing needles!"[66] Racing thoughts? Ries explains: he was renting a house owned by a tailor who had three beautiful (but "absolutely irreproachable") daughters.[67] In another letter to the same, Beethoven tells him bitterly that he had sent King George IV of England a copy of his *Battle of Victoria* with his dedication and had not received even a thank you note. "The King might at least have presented me with a butcher's knife or a turtle," he concludes. A knife or a turtle? Poor ol' Ludwig must have lost his marbles—right? Wrong again—as Ries let us know: "the King loved rich and delicate foods."[68] Such examples show how difficult it is to draw conclusions from texts without knowing their context. Those

---

* The DSM-IV (169) requires "at least a week (or any duration if hospitalization is necessary)."

"sows"—if sows they were—quoted by Mai as typical Beethovenian racing thoughts very likely had a special meaning for both parties ... possibly based on a pun, a genre of which the composer was so fond.

2) 1802 letter to Beethoven's close friend Zmeskall:

> My dearest Baron, Barone, Baron!—Domanowitz, Please sacrifice one friendship to another today and come to the Schwan—You will therefore greatly oblige, Your etc. Count Bthvn
>
> Baron?—Baron—ron—aron—ron—etc. Hail und happiness and hail and hail and happiness, happiness, hail, hail, happiness etc. Baron Baron Baron Baron.[69]

Notice that Beethoven signs his message as Count, which is no sign of "grandiosity" (one wonders whether Mai saw it this way, since the DSM-IV Axis I includes it among the illness symptoms). Other earlier letters to the same addressee clear the mystery further. In one of them (Anderson 29), Beethoven sets the two syllables of "Baron" on music. He ends his next letter (Anderson 30), "Adieu Baron Ba ... ron ron/nor/orn/rno/onr (voilà quelque chose [here's something] out of the pawnshop)." More racing thoughts? No, as Anderson explains in a note, Beethoven makes a pun on the word "versetzen," which means both "pawnshop" and "transpose" in German. It becomes clear now that the 1802 letter quoted by Mai was a musical pun, one of those *canons* that were sung at merry parties and of which we have quite a few items from Beethoven's hand. Here "Baron" is the theme on which Beethoven "extemporizes" (ron—aron—ron—etc) before attacking the cannon, which, as usual, is based on the repetition of a few words (Hail and happiness). He simply pokes fun at his friend's title of baron, which was almost meaningless.[70]

3) Mai mentions other Beethoven letters that could also display racing thoughts, but does not care to indicate where and how. Anderson letters 33 and 34 are two short notes to an unknown person who may have been the musician Hummel or Beethoven's friend Gleichenstein. The first note says angrily, "Don't come to me any more! You are a false dog and may the hangman do away with all false dogs!" while the next one makes amends: "You are an honest fellow and I now realize that you were right. So come to me this afternoon [...] Kisses from your Beethoven, also called dumpling."[71] They are illustrative of the composer's changing moods, perhaps, from anger to remorse, but not of racing thoughts. Anderson 57 is a sarcastic letter to Publisher Hoffmeister in Leipzig, which introduces some puns again, but nothing that could suggest racing thoughts. Neither can we find any such suggestion in another letter quoted by Mai, which begins "Your news has again plunged me from the heights of the most sublime ecstasy down into the depths" (Anderson 254, 268-9), which may be regarded as a bad taste tear-jerker at best.

Mai's claim (164) that such examples "strongly suggest that Beethoven may have had transient hypomanic episodes, in which case it is likely that he suffered from what now would be called manic-depressive or bipolar disorder" is plain wrong.[72] And, since the racing thoughts are the most important symptoms on which he bases his diagnosis, we can conclude that nothing proves his case.

Davies' failed case. Davies attempt to find depression episodes in Beethoven's life is even less successful than Mai's. One can even dismiss it from start, because all the episodes in the list that he draws (see table below) have obvious causes indicated (the mother's death, the father's dismissal from his job, etc.), which means that they do not fulfill the mentioned DSM-IV criteria for a pathological episode not to be the result of an important event in the patient's life.

Davies' table of Beethoven's crises (7.1, p. 218)

Date	Age	Event
17 July 1787	16	His mother's death
20 November 1789	18	His father's dismissal
18 December 1792	22	His father's death
6 October 1802	31	The Heiligenstadt Testament
Winter 1804–5?	34	Rejection by Josephine Deym
6–7 July 1812	41	Immortal Beloved letters
1812 or 1813?	42	Suicide attempt?
15 November 1815	44	Death of Caspar Carl
6 October 1816–April 1817	46	Protracted illness & depression
17 September 1819	48	Magistrat Court appoints Johanna as Carl's guardian
6 August 1826	55	Nephew Carl's suicide attempt

It is normal and healthy for the death of his mother to have had a deep psychological impact on seventeen-year-old Beethoven; his depression, which he termed as "melancholy" in a letter (Anderson 1), could in no way qualify as psychopathy.

The only episode that may need an explanation is the one described as "suicide attempt?" (1812 or 1813), mentioned by Schindler only in his second biography of the composer. Schindler claims that, after the breakup with his Immortal Beloved (in his mistaken opinion, Giulietta Guicciardi, in 1803), the composer would have hidden in the park of Countess Erdödy's estate in Jedlersee, trying to "starve himself to death." Schindler also added "this incident remained for a long time a close secret and only after several years did those familiar with it confide it to Beethoven's nearest friends."[73] The testimony is very unreliable: none of Beethoven's known "nearest friends" corroborates it. Schindler claimed to have learned it from Cherubini, the French musician and contemporary of Beethoven, who traveled only once to Vienna, in 1805, and was no intimate of Beethoven's mysterious "nearest friends," from whom he could have learned the story. In any case, even if his story was true, it would point to a data before 1805, not to 1812-1813, when the Immortal Beloved story happened.

Davies' forays in the composer's use of minor tonalities, intended to diagnose Beethoven as a depressive personality (219-228), are totally misguided. In fact, a survey of the frequencies of the main keys (e.g., C major for his *First Symphony*, C minor for his *Fifth*) in Beethoven's music[74] clearly shows the predominance of the major mode (see table); in spite of appearances, his preferred key was C major (16.7%) and C minor (7.9%), the first minor key comes as a distant sixth; the overall frequency of the minor mode is only 19.6%.

Frequency of key use by Beethoven and J. S. Bach

	Beethoven						Bach			
Major	Cts	%	Minor	Cts	%	Major	Cts	%	Minor	Cts	%
C	40	16.7	C	19	7.9	G	40	10.6	D	35	9.3
E flat	37	15.4	F	6	2.5	C	36	9.6	C	33	8.8
D	29	12.1	G	6	2.5	D	24	6.4	A	33	8.8
G	23	9.6	A	5	2.1	F	22	5.8	G	31	8.2
F	21	8.8	D	4	1.7	A	17	4.5	E	22	5.8
B flat	18	7.5	C sharp	2	0.8	E flat	13	3.5	B	17	4.5
A	17	7.1	E	2	0.8	E	13	3.5	F	9	2.4
A flat	4	1.7	E flat	2	0.8	B flat	13	3.5	F sharp	3	0.8
E	2	0.8	B	2	0.8	D flat	2	0.5	C sharp	2	0.5
F sharp	1	0.4	F sharp	0	0.0	F sharp	2	0.5	E flat	2	0.5
C sharp	0	0.0	G sharp	0	0.0	A flat	2	0.5	G sharp	2	0.5
B	0	0.0	B flat	0	0.0	B	2	0.5	B flat	2	0.5
Total	192	80.0	Total	48	19.6	Total	186	49.4	Total	191	50.6

If music is a true expression of a composer's inner self—which seems to be a truism—Beethoven's choice of tonalities bears proof of a tonic, optimistic personality, for whom suffering, which can be hardly avoided in life, is but a step towards joy—as his favorite motto *durch Leiden Freude* (through suffering to joy) said. And there is more to Davies' faulty inference: Bach (included in the table above for comparison) used minor keys more than the major ones—does this make him a depressive personality? If we want to discover pathology, we have to look elsewhere.

There is also no logic in Davies' intimation (263-264) that the agitated or sad or tragic movements in Beethoven's pieces that he may have created when he was depressed, would be proof of psycho-pathological behavior. He gives several examples of movements that would illustrate this thesis: *La Malinconia* of the String Quartet Op. 18 No. 6; the C sharp minor Piano Sonata Op. 27 No. 2 (better known as the *Moonlight Sonata*) and so on up to the last piano sonatas and string quartets. He usually supports his interpretation with quotes from various scholars no less subjective than him, whose opinions are sometimes conflicting. For instance, on page 239, the *Adagio* of the *Hammerklavier Sonata* is characterized both as "[...] unmeasured wail over the ruin of all happiness" and "[...] so noble, so elevate, so dignified [...] completely out of touch with the everyday world." Davies forgets that many of these pieces (including *La Malinconia*!) end in optimistic major keys and that expressing various states of mind and heart was an essential part of any composer's skills.

Unlike Mai, who tried to add Beethoven's alleged hypomanic episodes separately from the depression ones, Davies attempts to cut the Gordian knot, avoiding specific DSM-IV criteria entirely and relying primarily on

Beethoven's well-documented, frequent, fast, and often dramatic mood swings, which would seem to allow one to diagnose him at least with "significant bipolar tendencies" (255-262). The inference seems logical but it is not: such "fast" swings do not fit the pattern of bipolar disorder, in which the depression episodes are typically two or more weeks long, with manic episodes that can last for several days or weeks.[75]

Then Davies muses about Beethoven's "raptuses"—a term used by the Breunings to describe Beethoven's odd behavioral episodes during his teenage years—in an attempt to make them support his argument for a bipolar diagnosis. He claims (257) that "there is insufficient info to formulate an accurate diagnosis of raptus," therefore it might have been "the spell of his creative powers" but also "a manic or hypomanic phenomenon." A well-informed Beethovenian knows the answer: there were no pathological hypomanic episodes. Wegeler—a friend of Beethoven and the Breunings and a witness of those encounters in the Breuning house—tells us that the raptus was—a "stroke of genius."[76] Years later, Beethoven himself gave a similar testimony passed by Bettina Brentano, in a letter to Goethe recalling her 1810 meeting with the composer. After one of their meetings, she had written down some of Beethoven's thoughts—"music is the mediator between the life of the mind and the senses ... melody is the sensuous life of poetry ... music is the electrical soil in which the mind thinks, lives, feels," etc.—and when she read them to him next morning, he remarked: "Did I say that? Well, then I had a raptus!"[77]

Of course, my rebuttal of the theory would not prove that Beethoven was *not* a bipolar person. The link between creativity and madness is old and has received some new impetus lately—googling for it displays hundreds of thousands of sites. But it would take a better psychiatrist and Beethoven-informed person than either Davies or Mai to present a convincing argument about the issue. My next attempt only scratches the surface of the issue.

Before that, let us conclude the rebuttal of our two physicians' theory with a merrier note. Beethoven's well-developed sense of humor is a guarantee that he was not, by nature, a depressive person. Indeed, clinical research has confirmed the popular wisdom that humor and depression do not go together,[78] another scientific finding that escaped Dr. Mai and Dr. Davies' attention.

Diagnosing Raptus

Although all of Mai's and Davies' diagnoses are wide of the mark, I agree that Beethoven had a "personality disorder." Its name is, simply, "genius." Mai had the opportunity to clarify this point in his chapter dedicated to "Illness and Creativity" but, in spite of the interesting information that he has gathered therein, he missed the main point: being a genius is such a rare thing that it is not the norm in any culture—it is a personality disorder. Cultures have learned to pay a certain price—accepting the eccentricities that accompany genius more often than not—for the benefit they get from this kind of personality disorder. It is the genius himself who has to pay a much higher price for it, because he usually still is a "social animal" and suffers because of his own inability to behave successfully as such. So was Beethoven, who described himself as "susceptible to the diversion of society," in his "Heiligenstadt testament,"[79] but acted against it more often than not.

One can say that there are two kinds of creative geniuses: the one that possesses his art/craft and the one that is possessed by it. The former can draw the perfect line between their creative and their social functioning. For the latter, this is an almost impossible task,* even though he may not be a misanthrope. Beethoven is probably the best musical embodiment of a genius of the second kind. We have no reason to doubt the sincerity of his above-quoted description of himself as "susceptible to the diversion of society"; on the other hand, he was so totally absorbed in his music (and this became more so with his advancing deafness), that it was very hard for him—and felt like an annoyance and a distraction—to connect to the world around him when his music was invading him—and music was there all the time.

We must recall here the already introduced "raptus," to which Beethoven succumbed so often and about which Davies avoids a verdict. Mai, however, is again misguided. He claims that the original Latin-derived term means "seizure" because it suggests "uncontrollable behavior" (34 and 107—note 2 to table 3.3). As we know, this is not true: the raptus was Beethoven's "stroke of genius," the moment when he was abducted (again, the exact translation of the Latin term) by his inspiration, when he unconsciously withdrew from the social environment into his inner musical realm. The raptus moments were quite frequent and must have become more so as he grew older, because his deafness cut him more and more from the outer world.

One could actually describe Beethoven's life like an immense raptus—a life-long moment of total absorption into himself, from which, paradoxically, the most extroverted music burst out. Such a "raptus" may be termed as a "mental disease," the best medical description of which would be, probably, that of "Obsessive-Compulsive Creative Disorder." One can find no such disorder in the DSM-IV, but Beethoven meets five of the symptoms proposed by the DSM-IV for the non-specific "Obsessive-Compulsive" disorder, which would be sufficient to diagnose him as suffering from it: he was a perfectionist that toiled on his scores; he was excessively devoted to his work; he was over-conscientious, scrupulous, and inflexible about matters of morality (recall his puritanical principles and expectations of his brothers); he showed rigidity and stubbornness from his early youth;[80] at least in his older age, he viewed money as "something to be hoarded for future catastrophes."[81]

Is such "obsessive-compulsive creative behavior" associated with other psychotic traits, such as paranoia? Beethoven certainly displayed frequent

---

* This statement implies, of course, some simplification, as there are plenty of "in-betweens." However, even artists that appear in full control of their craft may succumb to such fantasies that cross the line between reality and fiction. Take the example of Balzac, the great 19th c. French master of literary realism. A friend that drops by finds him with tears rolling on his chubby cheeks. "The poor thing," cries the stocky man, falling upon his friend's breast, "she killed herself!" He was talking about the heroine of the novel he was writing.

paranoid behavior—even more than those evidenced by Davies and Mai—in his everyday life, the kind named "everyday paranoia." Even though it would not suffice to qualify him as being a paranoid personality according to APA criteria, this fact cannot be dismissed from his overall psychological profile. I have, in chapter 2, also "diagnosed" him with what I named the "Sarastro symptom," which overlays, at least partially, with a narcissist personality disorder. Beethoven seems to have clustered several psychotic tendencies. Psychiatry tends to throw various mental problems in the same boiling pot, which is probably right. I feel tempted to invoke Eysenck' theory of "Psychoticism as a Dimension of Personality," that he presented in his eponymous book, according to which personality is defined by a number of "dimensions" that expand on large "scales" between "normal" and "psychotic"—for example, dedication to one's work can be normal but also a symptom of obsessive-compulsive behavior when goes beyond a certain (fluid enough) limit.[82] But I will not speculate further beyond my limited knowledge.

PART III
BEETHOVEN POLITICS

The unusual title of this part intends to point out that it does *not* deal with Beethoven's involvement in the political issues of his time in his attitude and musical output; nor does with the later "politicizing" of his music, mainly by the right or the left twentieth-century totalitarian regimes. It deals with the politics of musical life itself, namely the ones that implicate Beethoven's music. Indeed, although clear evidence about it emerged only relatively late in the Western World (in the thirteenth century Florence, when the *dolce stile nuovo*, the new sweet style, was born in poetry as different from the old medieval style), some kind of struggle that can be called political has always been part of the art world in general. Any change of style or school has always turned into "artistic politics" that fracture the field into opposing factions, pitting the New versus the Old; for instance, in music we had the fight between the *stile antico* and *stile moderno* in the early seventeenth century.

Such "internal" musical politics had sometimes expanded beyond the proper world of music and musicians, involving the public at large or, at least, the social elite setting the rules of the game through their patronage. "Political parties" of the opera have always been known in the genre, of which the rivalry between the "Gluckists and the Piccinists" in late eighteenth-century Paris has remained the most frequently quoted example. Less known but even more "colorful" is the cabal against Händel in London some fifty years earlier, when his success with the public inspired xenophobic feelings testified to by the memorialists of the age, who mention "the tenacity with which certain ladies gave tea parties, entertainments, and theatrical performances—which were not usually given in Lent—on the days when Händel's concerts were to take place, in order to rob him of his audience."[*] Beethoven, by himself, embodied an important moment of change in the history of Classical music and had his share of opposition and even loathing, but nothing in his biography suggests a colorful cabal similar to the one against Händel. He also won his battle within his life-time and was raised to the Canon soon after his death.

Beethoven was also involved in similar politics posthumously, as a prow figurehead, in a similar battle between the first Romanticist generation and the "philistines" still attached to the classicism of the old school illustrated by, among others, Haydn and Mozart. Later on, he was again a pivotal figure in another battle within the German Romanticism between the partisans and the opponents of Wagnerian "art of the future." To its partisans, grouped into the so-called "New German School," Beethoven's *Ninth Symphony* had reached the highest possible level of the genre and, therefore, music could only move ahead Wagner's way (his musical drama); opponents, grouped around Brahms,

---

[*] Romain Rolland, *Essays on Music*, David Ewen ed. (Dover Publications, New York, 1959), p. 219, quoting Viscount Henry Bolingbroke (1678-1751) and the writer Tobias Smollet (1721-1771).

argued that, notwithstanding Beethoven's greatness, the symphony was not an exhausted genre but one that could still be pursued. The polemics burst out in the media, because of a leak (how modern!) and created a long-time split within the German musical life.

Before the nineteenth century ended, Beethoven turned into a mythical central figure, a kind of Prometheus who gave music a renewed (artistic) fire and, therefore, split its history in two: before and after Beethoven. In this central position, he attracted veneration but also incited antagonism, especially after the setting in of post-modernism. It was inevitable that some new kinds of "Beethoven politics" arose.

7
Enrolling Beethoven in the cause of the Twentieth Century musical Avant-Garde

The grand rhetorical question

The history of twentieth century classical music and, by extension, of the beginning of our new century is dominated—albeit only unconsciously—by a rhetorical question formulated again in Beethovenian terms by the German scholar Harry Goldschmidt almost fifty years ago:

Why is Beethoven *so beautiful* and the modern music *so ugly*?

Of course, one must make sure what we understand by "modern music"—a term that Goldschmidt himself fails to define—but one can guess that it includes what is called the "Avant-Garde," the post-WWI atonal/polytonal "isms" and serialism. Goldschmidt does not share the opinion that such music is "ugly" and most of his fellow scholars do not either, yet he has to tackle the grand question because it sums up the quasi-unanimous opinion of the music lovers. He actually repudiates the grand question by invoking Beethoven himself as a posthumous promoter of the Avant-Garde, in another typical post-modernist argument.

Goldschmidt's argument

Harry Goldschmidt (1910-1986) was a prominent figure of the twentieth century German musicology who offered valuable, if sometimes controversial, contributions, especially in Schubert and Beethoven scholarship. In his 1974 book dedicated to the latter *The Beethoven Phenomenon*,[1] he made the composer into another prow figurehead, this time for the latest battle within the Classical, for the advancement of modern music. Indeed, modern music was, at the time, rejected by the public at large as well as by the classical music performers; and, even though modern music has diversified in the meantime, the public's attitude has not substantially changed so far. Therefore, the issue has not lost interest.

A few details about Goldschmidt's life may prove helpful to better understand his stance. Born in Switzerland, in his youth he joined the self-proclaimed communist "Partei der Arbeit" (Party of Labor) and after WWII he moved to Eastern Germany, the communist half of the country that was part of the Soviet empire. Although he did not find there the freedom that he expected and experienced some professional setbacks, he remained there and his remarkable contribution to musicology reflects to a certain degree the ideology that he could not afford to affront.[2] And Goldschmidt had something in his agenda, promoting modern music, which was not as easy as presenting Beethoven as an exponent of the progressive ascent of man that was to eventually establish the communist paradise on Earth, a thesis in line with the communist doctrine. Promoting the Avant-Garde was not easy because—an inheritance from the very first years of the Bolshevik Revolution, whose father Lenin had little penchant for the new "-isms" but was a Beethoven fan[3]—the Avant-Garde had been viewed as an expression of "bourgeois decadence." However, after the destalinization of the Soviet empire in the sixties, in both the central U.S.S.R. and the satellite countries, the ban on these "-isms" was revoked and musicians could now espouse them without fear of repercussions. Nevertheless, audiences did not respond enthusiastically to this kind of "liberation" and performers followed suit, which Goldschmidt found appalling. He hoped that invoking the authority of Beethoven, a national glory in support of Schönberg & Co. would help their cause with both the public, the performers and the Communist ideology. Goldschmidt presents his thesis in the first essay of his book, somewhat misleadingly titled "Beethoven and Progress." Both this title and the longish introduction suggest that this is just another variation on the old and many-times-varied-upon theme of Beethoven as a devotee of the ideals proclaimed by the French Revolution and a herald of the "emancipation of the human race" in a new world where liberty, equality and universal solidarity would reign supreme. This introduction is a mixture of biography, musicology and philosophy (Marx with a Hegelian touch), whose main originality consists in relying not on the *Ninth Symphony* cliché, but on *Fidelio*, where Goldschmidt points to the mixture of "action" and "lyricism" embodied by the opera's heroine. He can thus present Beethoven as a master of the heroic v. lyric synthesis "dialectics" (the Marx-Hegel touch) and finally state on page 20:[*]

> The emancipation of the human race is the ultimate preamble, the denominator under which Beethoven's progress ideology must be understood. He solves for us the impenetrable contradiction between dramatic and lyrical expression of activity, between heroic action and fulfilling love.

This ideology is, of course, reflected in his music, but this interaction is very complex, with music performing a social activist function:

> The same idea of emancipation is also the denominator for Beethoven's dialectical creative way for the described integration of the parts in the whole. To keep the whole in view means to understand music musically and, at the same time, not only musically. This attitude engenders the imperious drive of universality, the double commitment to changing the art and with the art the world.

Elaborating further, Goldschmidt assigns to Beethoven—that is, to his music—an exceptional social role during the nineteenth century:

> Therefore, Beethoven must have been a first degree influence not only from the musical but also from the social and cultural standpoint. That is what his own contemporaries thought. The

---

[*] All references to Goldschmidt's book are given within the text in this chapter.

challenge was monstrous. Goethe and Hegel, both concerned about stability, deliberately stayed afar. Even the young ones, with Weber and Schubert as flagstaff, failed to follow him for years before they realized what brazen doors he had opened to them—and to himself.

Goldschmidt could have improved his case by quoting here rather than in the end of his essay another statement of the composer:

> My music should free people from the misery in which they are slouching through. (24)

In spite of the exceptional social and musical role he assigns Beethoven, Goldschmidt thinks that its impact was limited and even discomfiting:

> And yet it remained more of a premonition than comprehension. It took a whole century and, as the current reception of Beethoven shows, it has not happened yet. Knowledge and understanding will not agree even in the future, although they condition each other. (20)

With an unexpected "on the other hand," on the same page, he introduces three ominous "dangers" embedded in Beethoven's legacy:

> On the other hand, the handing down of his art has brought undeniable dangers about which we must not close our eyes. I see especially these three ones: standardization, flattening and conservatism.*

Goldschmidt does not offer an explanation of why a "progressive ideology" like Beethoven's could have implied such dangers but elaborates on each of them. An examination of his take reveals some significant flaws of judgement that we will encounter throughout his essay.

Here is Goldschmidt's view of the *Standardization* danger, reproduced with some elisions that do not affect their meaning:

> In the practice of musical life in years and decades, an amazing narrowing of Beethoven's repertoire has undergone. This fact alone, affecting not only Beethoven, but consistently all masters of the past, would be worth a sociological study. Should it perhaps lead to the conclusion that only these works of his or any other master that have been again and again performed have resisted the ravages of time? Or does it mean that these standard works are particularly close, much closer [than others] to our times, while most of the other works are not in a position to enter our own music culture? Such a trend, such an attitude of our performers in their cossetting the standard works shows an undeniable alienation, a persistent

---

* My translation. The terms that Goldschmidt uses need some "interpretation" when translating. "Gefahren" may be "dangers," but also "risks;" because he constantly uses the present tense, I assume that danger, as materialized risk, fits better. I also translated his "Konservierung," (literally "preservation") as "Conservatism" (its literal German term is "Konservatismus") because it fits better his meaning, as will become clear later. I also preferred "Flattening" to "levelling" for the German "Nivellierung."

estrangement [Fernerrücken], which cannot be concealed by a zealous Beethoven cult. [Examples follow of neglected Beethoven pieces, including some youthful works like *Joseph Funeral Cantata* but also later compositions like some unnamed piano sonatas and the Op. 9 String Trios.]

Of course, excluding works from the concert repertoire involves the risk of losing real value, but this does not seem to have been the case for Beethoven, where quality was the essential selection tool; his youthful cantata speaks eloquently about his budding talent but does not compare with his mature work quality-wise. And, if the quality criterion was consistently applied to all other musicians, it would not have yielded to any real loss of value. The case of Vivaldi's music, which was completely forgotten for almost two centuries, has nothing to do with this risk resulting from Beethoven's "standardization;" it was a consequence of the development—or rather the lack of it—of the canon after Vivaldi's death. I do not see what is the "danger" (and for whom) involved in this "standardization," as long as the criteria was the perceived value of music. That perception may be wrong, of course—and the history of music shows us plenty of Salieris outdoing Mozarts—but that had nothing to do with Beethoven's "standardization." On the contrary, fewer of his works preserved would have meant more room available for other composers.

Goldschmidt's description of *Flattening* reads:

> The described standardization inevitably results in a flattened [without relief] standard image of Beethoven as a memorial, which has, however, only the embarrassing quality of revealing less and less of the real dimensions of Beethoven. Even the most shining cliché remains just a cliché! And only the confrontation with the entire Beethoven can save us from producing flat reproductions. (21)

Goldschmidt's inference is wrong again: we may, indeed, not know the whole of Beethoven (or of any one of his fellow composers because, according to Goldschmidt, standardization affected "consistently all masters of the past"), but we certainly know the best, if the standardization selection process has worked right. If Goldschmidt thought it had not and we have the wrong, impoverished, image of Beethoven, he should have presented us improved criteria and the results of their application. He invokes a line from Beethoven's youthful *Joseph Funeral Cantata,* a piece excluded by the "flattening," as proof of the composer's "progressive ideology," but that does not add any relief to the Beethovenian ideology that the "standardization" offers. Also, none of the other essays in his book brings alive a "new" Beethoven. They are meticulous musicology studies, but they only emphasize some details of the "old" Beethoven that we have known for generations. The claim that excluding such works from the current repertoire would "reveal less and less the real Beethoven" is a clear misrepresentation that "the sake of the argument" cannot justify.

Finally, *Conservatism*, a direct consequence of the previous two dangers, would be, in Goldschmidt's view, the worst of the ominous trio. He states it in a rhetorical question, one of his stylistic marks, ending with the grand one that I quoted above:

> How did it happen that we see Beethoven today, both in public writing and in public taste, as the reason to object to the real novelty in modern music?
>
> Why is Beethoven *so beautiful* and the modern music *so ugly*? (21)

Having reached this "widespread" (his term) rhetorical question, Goldschmidt does not try to offer an answer but proceeds to demonstrate the opposite: modern music is not ugly and Beethoven should be invoked not to reject but to endorse it. Goldschmidt phrases his case in more rhetorical questions (21-22):

> Doesn't this pervasive question prove that one hears no longer the novelty in Beethoven [himself]? Doesn't it show us how unrealistically and conservatively he is received today and how little we, experts, have so far made to counteract this fatal disfigurement? Perhaps he was not the one to say: "The art does not accept to be forced into flattering molds and goes its own ways." Or: "our age requires powerful spirits who castigate these mean, devious, wretched human souls."
>
> One has to bemoan the fact that today, two hundred years after his birth and less than two hundred years after his death, we have so thoroughly forgotten to notice the really New in his music.

In other words, the attitude of modern-day audience at large and of the professionals (performers), both of whom do not respond appreciatively to modern music, is proof that they do not really understand Beethoven's music either, that they perceive it "conservatively." They forget that Beethoven himself was the Avant-Garde of his time and proclaimed the very principles (not "flattering" the public, "castigating" its small-mindedness) paraded by modern Avant-Garde. Therefore, Goldschmidt proclaims a new agenda: "One must open the man's eyes—i.e., ears—to the New, which came in music thanks to Beethoven." And to illustrate that "New" that Beethoven brought in music, Goldschmidt quotes the composer's artistic credo items:

> "Art demands of us not to stand still." […] "Freedom, moving forward is the purpose in all of creation as in the art world." "Here we see his progressive maxims indissolubly linked with the concept of freedom. And to the never-ending objection that he did not respect the rules of music, he had the dialectical answer at hand: "There is no rule in art that could not be annulled by means of a higher rule." (22-23)

Implying that the opposition to modern music is similar to the "vehement resistance" and even "sheer defamation" that Beethoven had to cope with, of which there is plenty of evidence but which he overcame because he was sure of being right, Goldschmidt concludes:

> No, one cannot invoke Beethoven against the Avant-Garde. Avant-Garde must be free to engage in reflecting the world at large [Weltweide], in the spirit of the humanistic engagement and the universalism of Beethoven. (23)

Granted, we may call Beethoven the Avant-Garde of his time: he never stopped searching for novelty; he wanted to be "free" to say whatever he wanted and however he wanted in his music; and he broke music rules when they impeded on such "freedom." After the initial enthusiasm for the virtuoso, his public at large gradually became estranged and did not follow him along his innovative paths. He met strong criticism (I will illustrate it further in Table 1), some of which persisted after his death. Nevertheless, that does not prove that he would have heralded and welcomed our modern Avant-Garde. One must take into account the "nature" of the novelty that the two allegedly similar avant-garde phenomena brought forward and Goldschmidt has very little to say about it, and only when wrapping up his case in the ending of his essay (24):

> Beginning with Beethoven, music turned darker. He challenged it to bluntly, realistically express the dark, the unresolved, the forbidden and the razor-edged destructive conflicts. But all this for the sake of liberation.

This description is questionable, like anything that pertains to the intensely debated concept of the "meaning" of music. It is easy to argue that, in fact, "light" rather than "dark" is a much better description of Beethoven's essential message; certainly, the "standardization" of his repertoire that Goldschmidt complained about has put an excessive emphasis on his works in minor keys, but even they end in triumphant majors, as an illustration of what may be called the composer's essential program of his music: "through suffering to joy."

Anyhow, Goldschmidt stops short of claiming that the alleged "dark" Beethoven would have presaged the modern day Avant-Garde. He emphasizes that this "darkness" was only a means to achieve the "liberation [Befreiung] from the chains of tyranny, from the self-inflicted nonage, [that is to] the emancipation of the human species" (24).[*]

In fact, Goldschmidt's approach was only a Beethoven-tailored installation of the "standard" defense of the musical Avant-Garde of the twentieth century. Others had voiced it before him and would so again. Although the issue is somewhat marginal in the scope of this book, I must touch it at least to the extent to make clear if Beethoven could or could not be invoked in support of the Avant-Garde ideology.

Slonimsky's "Unfamiliar" argument

The "standard" defense of the of the twentieth-century musical Avant-Garde was first theorized by Nicolas Slonimsky in his 1953 *Lexicon of Musical Invectives*. In an introduction titled "Non-acceptance of the unfamiliar," he states his purpose:[4]

> to demonstrate that music is an art in progress, and that objections leveled at every musical innovator are all derived from the same

---

[*] Goldschmidt added that Beethoven's "liberation" was the opposite of the "salvation" [Errlösungsbegriff] ideology promoted by Wagner, who was not exactly "in line" with the Communist ideology (remember, the author was living in Communist Germany).

psychological inhibition, which may be described as Non-Acceptance of the Unfamiliar."

Slonimsky's "Unfamiliar" is actually another name of Goldschmidt's "New." His book illustrates the reaction of the audience, made manifest mostly by musicians claiming to speak for everybody else, to the "non-familiar" appearing in the music of almost every noted musician in the nineteenth and twentieth century. This would constitute, in the author's view, abundant evidence of the rule that every "musical innovator" was first rejected by his public. Beethoven appears therein as an emblematic figure, because the "invectives list" begins chronologically with him.

In fact, placing Beethoven in that special position of super-revolutionary is an oversight. With a little diligence, one can extend the *Invectives* list back in time even though the evidence might be scarcer than after 1800. What an anonymous reviewer wrote, in 1737, about Johann Sebastian Bach sounds very much like what Beethoven critics will says about him a hundred years later:

> This great man would be the admiration of whole nations if he had more amenity, if he did not take away the natural element in his pieces by giving them a turgid [schwülstig] and confused style, and if he did not darken their beauty by an excess of art. Since he judges according to his own fingers, his pieces are extremely difficult to play; for he demands that singers and instrumentalists should be able to do with their throats and instruments whatever he can play on the clavier.[5]

Slonimsky's *Invectives* show indeed some striking similarities between the criticism of Beethoven's music and that of some of the most prominent members of the Avant-Garde, of which only a few examples are given in the next table.

Criticism of Beethoven's music by his contemporaries and of music of modern composers (after Slonimsky)

Beethoven's music	Modern music
Second symphony (1804): "crass monster, a hideously wounded dragon that refuses to expire" (42).	**Arnold Schönberg** (1907, 1910): "cacophony elevated to law" (p. 148); "methodical negation of all heretofore accepted musical rules [...]" (149).
Leonore No. 3 overture (1806): "[...] never was anything as incoherent, shrill, chaotic and ear-splitting produced in music" (42).	**Stravinsky** (1922): [...] one more horrible jargon from the start to finish, sheer discord with ho right to a place on the same program with true music (199).
Seventh symphony (1825): "[...] a great deal of disagreeable eccentricity [...] we cannot yet discover any design in it" (44).	**Alban Berg** (1925): "tortured mistuned cackling, a pandemonium of chopped-up orchestral sounds, mishandled men's throats, bestial outcries, bellowing, rattling, and all other evil noises" (53).
Ninth symphony (1825): "[...] so much rambling and vociferous execution [...] without any decisive effect or definite meaning [...] obstreperous roarings of modern frenzy [...]" (45).	**Anton Webern** (1929): "[...] suggested nothing so much as a cat that moaned or growled or spat" (250).

Perusing Slonimsky's list of the victims of the *Invectives* is enough to realize that not only the radical "innovators" inspired them. Almost the whole Romanticist generation is present, many times disparaged by their peers and competitors. Brahms was certainly not a "great innovator," but he shows no less than twelve pages in Slonimsky's book, more than Beethoven himself (11) and second only to Wagner (27) and Schönberg (20). That makes the "Unfamiliar" argument rather tenuous.

It is also worth noticing that all the vilified nineteenth century composers found acceptance sooner or later and few died without a recognition concurrent with or premonitory to their induction into the Canon. In contrast, the Avant-Garde has been with us for more than a hundred years—its first memorable occurrence being the 1913 premiere of Stravinsky's *Rite of Spring*—but it has never been accepted beyond the minuscule world of the so-called connoisseurs.

This last statement is not an opinion, but a fact. Although, to my knowledge, statistics about the preferences of the audience at large have never been gathered, we have a reliable source for them in the Classical Radio stations spread both over Europe and North America, whose playlists are available on Internet. These stations also draw every year a "Top One Hundred Countdown" list that sum up the preferences of the music lovers. Of course, such surveys are not drawn with observance of the rules of statistics and they show some local variance but, judging by my limited American experience in a few areas of the United States—Seattle (KING FM 83.1), Portland (KQAC 89.9 FM), Central California (KDFC 103.9 FM) and Dallas (WRR 101.1 FM) at various times—they display the same general picture: the predilection for eighteenth and nineteenth century music, with Beethoven as a central figure,[*] and a few, marginal twentieth-century names still attached to tonality (for instance, Vaughan Williams), to the jazz age (Gershwin, Copland) or to music for movies (John Williams, Ennio Morricone). No member of the Avant-Garde (such as Schönberg, Berg and Webern) ever makes it to the top 100—unless one counts a little still-tonal Stravinsky like a *Russian Dance* from his *Petrushka*. One hundred years after its birth, the Avant-Garde music is still alien to the audience at large. Over a similar period of time, between 1700 and 1800, the history of music has recorded three or, arguably, four different "styles" or "schools": the High Baroque of Vivaldi, Bach and Händel; the early Classical known as Rococo style (or "style gallant" in France or "empfindsamer Still" [empfindsam means "sensitive," pertaining to feelings] in Germany); the Viennese Classical Age of Haydn and Mozart and Beethoven, who raised it to a new level and also announced Romanticism. The long-lasting (and not yet revoked) rejection of "modern" music makes it clear that the newness it proffered, namely the dissolution of tonality, was something far more than "non-familiar."

---

[*] His *Ninth Symphony* usually topping the list (the only exception: on WRR 2017-8 top 40, it is at #2, after Vivaldi's *Four Seasons*!); with other three-four symphonies in the top 10.

The New-Old dialectics that the New/Non-familiar argument ignores

The quest for that "far more" begins with the conflictual New-Old connection that the habitual argument for the Avant-Garde ignores, which I have termed "dialectics" to match Goldschmidt's predilection. In reality, society, and especially Western culture, never rejects "newness"—it welcomes and calls for newness. Newness is the engine of what we call "progress" since the beginning of our historical trajectory. Progress in any domain, including the one of our topic, music, is not linear, but generational, an aspect that is usually ignored, possibly because it is too obvious. Society re-news itself in human "material" with each generation and that calls for newness in all areas. The inevitable cohabitation of the two (even three) generations often results in imprecations on all sides. Slonimsky has gleaned only the invectives of the old about the young, but there have also been plenty of the young about the old. There were certainly many in the past, for instance those that Robert Schumann, an exponent of the Romanticist "innovation," threw at the "philistines" in the music magazine *Neue Zeitschrift für Musik* in the 1830s.

Generational change—in conjunction with technological advances, which are usually related to it—explains much of the changes in history, including the ones in music. This has been the mixed blessing of the Western world—for each generation to be driven by the search for novelty that it could call its own. Each of them would do it sitting on the shoulders of their parents, but would not care for their elder's legacy if their own product took the world to an entirely new direction. The reader may understand better this "generational" progress based on this example: in less than a century, between WWI and 1989 (the limit is, granted, arbitrary), the pop music genre has known three different schools: jazz, rock and rap, each of them with several subdivisions. The process was similar, albeit a bit slower, in the Classical: each generation born in barely over a hundred years between 1685 and 1797 developed its own musical style embraced by their contemporaries—high Baroque, Rococo (early Classical), Classical and the Romantic.

This pattern of dialectics is, however, more complex than simply newness rejected by the older generation while embraced by the young one. There was, for example, a time in the 1930-40s when Sibelius symphonies were very popular, rivaling Beethoven's in the concert repertoire.[6] The young generation of concert-goers wanted to listen to "their" music. That popularity was, however, historically short lived, because of the new-old dialectics at work—the drive to achieve "objectivity," not slighted by the "generational" bias, when evaluating successive novelties. When a third generation arose, Sibelius was already "old" to them and this "old newness" proved to them far less important than Beethoven. Such temporary success invalidated by posterity in this dialectics game happened to some of the Avant-Garde, too. Stravinsky's *Rite of Spring*, the first modern music that created an uproar when it premiered in 1913, became a staple of the repertoire a few years later; it fell from grace with the next generation, for whom it was no longer challengingly "new." The new generation did not care for his old newness; it wanted its *own* newness. These dialectics also explains the selective accretion of the Canon; successive generations push therein their own newness, but also test the old "newness" against the established Canon and, when finding it unsatisfying, purge it. Other nineteenth-century musicians not included in Slonimsky's *Invectives* had their own heydays as newness during the nineteenth century, but successive generations blocked them from the Canon. It also happened with the Avant-Garde of the next century.

I have introduced a term really abhorred by post-modernism—objectivity. Can we really attain objectivity? The very word hints to a connection: science.

What science can teach us ... with the help of rats

Science—prototypically, physics and math—had been part of musical practice almost from the very beginning, but within limited confines. Musical instruments have always been applied physics and math; physics and math also underlied the development of the ancient Greek modes and the tempered scale and tonality during late Renaissance.

The *perception* of music was, however, a mystery up until the end of the nineteenth century, when clinicians, neurologists and physicians worked together to decipher the perception of sound in the inner ear and had a first functional glimpse into the brain, discovering the first cortical centers governing human acts like speaking and hearing. Knowledge was very vague, but scientists could not help speculating and one of the topics they tackled was the resistance to the "modern" music of the times. German neurologist Richard Wallaschek (1860-1917) even theorized about the cause of that resistance. According to him, perception of music involved a dual process of "mental representation": one involving pitch and harmony, which he called, very German-like, "Tonvorstellung" (Ton=pitch, Vorstellung=perception); and the second one, named "Musikvorstellung," the holistic perception of higher-level musical structure, resulting from the combination of tones, intervals, chords, rhythms, etc. People differ in balancing the two processes and those who rely primarily on the "Tonvorstellung" would not be able to understand a modern piece as a whole, and would find such music incomprehensible." [7] This may explain some entries in Slonimsky's *Lexicon*—for Wallaschek, who was writing in 1894, "modern" meant Wagner—but does not have a bearing on the current issue, because Wagner, although he substantially enlarged harmony, was not "modern" in today's acceptance of the term.

Science could not illuminate the issue any further until they asked the help of the rats, who are genetically, biologically and behaviorally close enough to humans to offer some specific insights into the matter. Some fifty years ago, a team of psychologists designed an experiment intended to show how rats respond to "imprinting and exposure learning" through music, with a hope to also learn something about humans. Albino rats of the same strain were split in three groups (each of 24 specimens) who were raised from birth in the same conditions but with different sound environment: one group was exposed to selection of Mozart for 12 hours a day during 52 days; the second group to selections of Schönberg music; the third, control group had no musical exposure. In the proper test, the rats could select the music they preferred and the result was interesting, if expected: the Mozart rats showed a "significant preference" (20 of

24) for Mozart, while the Schönberg rats showed no preference, the same as the control group.[8] A translation into laymen's language is actually more telling: half of Schönberg's rats shifted allegiance to Mozart!

Obviously, rats are still not humans but their reaction is reminiscent of the attitude of the human audience and can teach us something. One incontrovertible inference is that, like humans, rats have different personalities, but there is more to infer. That the large majority (83%) of the Mozart rats stuck to Mozart is proof that exposure created habit. If half of the Schönberg rats shifted allegiance, in spite of exposure, they must have had a reason that was not "cultural" but "physiological." Indeed, experiments made in 1998 by another team of scientist showed that rats raised with Mozart music displayed enhanced abilities in the traditional rat maze tests, which hints to a physiological effect of music.[9] Once again, there appears to be more than New/Unfamiliar to the issue under debate.

What neuroscience can teach us

A few decades later after the "rat connection," neuroscience provided new insights into the brain's perception of music that have been popularized, at the beginning of the new millennium, by Daniel Levitin and Oliver Sacks, authors of two remarkable books.[10] Both are ("was" in Sack's case) well-seasoned professionals: Levitin is the director of the "Laboratory for Musical Perception, Cognition and Expertise" at McGill University, where he also teaches; and Sacks was a neurologist and a well-known author in the history of science. Neuroscience revealed the intricate neuronal network and cortical centers and chemical neurotransmitters governing the "mental perception" of music in general, with a special emphasis on the Classical. They frequently use the music of the great masters of the past to exemplify the findings of neuroscience, but modern "art music" is conspicuously missing in the experiments, as if it would be a completely distinct art. Only Levitin has something to say, very tersely, about the matter. He assigns "expectation" a key role in music: rhythm consistently creates expectations of the "beat"; the moving-on of a piece is "a game of expectation with pitch [the tonic of the key]."[11] It is the subjective feeling that what comes next in both an Elvis song *and* a symphony by Beethoven is a fulfilled expectation, which explains in a large measure the pleasure of listening. In that respect Levitin tersely notices:

> Modern composers such as Schönberg threw out the whole idea of expectation [...] thus creating the illusion of no home, a music adrift, perhaps as a metaphor for a twentieth-century existentialist existence (or just because they were trying to be contrary)."[12]

If you think that Levitin's "expectation" has finally answered the grand question, you are wrong. Like in almost any other field of behavioral disciplines, neuroscience was invoked to support the opposite points of view. Jonah Lehrer claims to find therein evidence justifying the Avant-Garde products. Jonah Lehrer is not an established scholar in music or the humanities, and is a controversial author, who has motivated both eulogies from Oliver Sacks himself and indictments of plagiarism and misuse of facts and quotes, by reason of which two of his three best-selling books have been withdrawn by his publishers.[13] Nevertheless, I found in his first (not withdrawn) book, *Proust was a Neuroscientist*, the best case, based on modern-day science, for the twentieth-century Avant-Garde in music as well as literature, painting and even gastronomy (the art of the sense of taste).[14] Compared to the Sterba couple and Maynard Solomon's contributions to Beethoven scholarship that we have previously met—as well as to more such examples to be presented later—Lehrer's *Proust* book seems a fully professional investigation. He is young and can be, therefore, biased towards "newness" in the arts. On the other hand, he has some strong assets recommending him for such an enterprise: he is not a musicologist, therefore not a prisoner to a long-standing tradition either towards or against Avant-Garde; he majored in neuroscience at the Columbia University and worked, as an undergraduate, in the lab of the Nobel Prize-winning neuroscientist Eric Kandel and co-authored articles in that field.

In his Proust book, Lehrer maintains that the modern evolution of the arts finds specific support in the advances of the sciences of the brain. We are here particularly interested in chapter 6 ("Igor Stravinsky. The Source of Music"), in which the author maintains that the human brain is aptly built to find beauty in the modern music that has destroyed tonality for the sake of "emancipating dissonance." He brings in the case of Stravinsky, although he was not the first to fully achieve this particular "emancipation" (Schönberg can claim this title); Stravinsky was, however, the first one to bring it brutally into the public ears in 1913, with his *Rite of Spring* ballet music.

Lehrer's thesis can be summed up relatively simply:

> As neuroscience now knows, our sense of sound is a work in progress. Neurons in the auditory cortex are consistently being altered by the songs and symphonies we listen to. Nothing is difficult forever. [...] Stravinsky knew that the audience would adapt to his difficult notes and discover the beauty locked inside his art.[15]

The author develops his argument beginning with an overall view of the sense of hearing (the anatomy and physiology of the inner ear), which has been known for over a hundred years) before getting to the findings of neuroscience. Here he discovers that the source of music is a "desperate neuronal search for a pattern [of pitches or notes]" and that "by listening for patterns, by interpreting every note in terms of expectations, we turn the scraps of sound into the ebb and flow of a symphony."

Lehrer never calls this "pattern" melody, but we can. Lehrer also discovers the brain's need for diversity leading to varying and alternating patterns, then returning to them before finally achieving the cadence in the tonic. Here, he stretches this discovery to an extreme that is hard to accept: this diversity and delay would prove that "music is a form whose meaning depends upon its violation." He needed the term "violation" to introduce Stravinsky's credo that "the engine of music is conflict, not consonance."[16] And Lehrer makes another hard-to-accept inference, continuing: "The art that makes us feel is the art that makes us hurt." Music can, indeed, make us feel "pain" and neuroscience may have shown that psychological and physical pain share some commonalities in the brain, but one cannot simply equate them as Lehrer does, an assertion that simply annihilates centuries of Western art music aiming to create not physiological pain, but pleasure.

The next step in Lehrer's argument is neuroscientific discoveries about the learning process. Science has known for a long time that the individual is the result of a "process" of continuous learning and neuroscience has shown that "learning" is actually continuous brain re-structuring due to its interactions with the world. Stravinsky, Lehrer claims, would have intuited this and concluded that over time the dissonance of newness would become a form of consonance. And this is, Lehrer claims, what actually happened: "The mind learned how to interpret the obscure noise" (135), realizing that "music is man-made, a collection of noises that we have learned how to hear" (138); "audiences were able to hear its [Stravinsky's music] delicate patterns and found the frightening beauty buried in its undulations."[17] The brain mechanism explaining this process looks like a rigmarole (a "corticofugal network" with an "egocentric selection" function, and with the help of "feedback from higher-up brain regions" "reorganizes the auditory cortex," a process that is "largely the handiwork of dopamine, which modulates the cellular mechanisms underlying plasticity," and ultimately puts "experience" in charge of "our sensations" but can be worded in a more palatable conclusion:

> While human nature largely determines how we hear the notes, it is nurture that lets us hear the music. From the three-minute pop song to the five-hour Wagner opera, the creations of our culture teach us to expect certain musical patterns, which over time are wired into our brain.[18]

Lehrer offers, as factual proof of his theory, the very example of Stravinsky's music, which the audiences came to appreciate after the first shock produced by its novelty. He stops short of multiplying such examples, most likely because there are none. Stravinsky is actually a different case than the one presented by Lehrer: he "emancipated dissonance" but took care to wrap it in pregnant rhythmic "patterns," and these are the ones that got "wired" into the audience's mind. Even so, Stravinsky's days of glory were short and the other "moderns" never had any. Contrary to Lehrer's assertion, Avant-Garde music has failed to be "wired in the brain" of the audience of classical music over the past century. During this time, we could see, indeed, many "musical patterns" wired in peoples' brain on a huge societal scale, but those were the several successive waves of "pop" genres. The far-smaller audience of the Classical has consistently continued to reject productions of the Avant-Garde.

Lehrer simply ignores this reality. Granted, as a result of the defense mechanisms of the human mind, the audience has not been willing to let itself be exposed to a systematic ingurgitation of modern music. Moreover, because the learning process is most intense during childhood, that exposure should have begun with babies, which was clearly against both pediatric and popular wisdom.

Studies have shown that one-year-olds react expressively to "happy" and "sad" music passages,[19] but experiments about how they would receive Stravinsky's *Rite of Spring* or a Schönberg serial piece have never, to my knowledge, been carried out. The very existence of this conscious or unconscious refusal of the audience to embrace such musical-societal experiments is another proof that there is more than the New/Unfamiliar at stake in this matter.

Lawrence Kramer answers the grand question

Lawrence Kramer, a younger post-modernist colleague of Goldschmidt, may have best synthesized why the twentieth-century Avant-Garde and its apologists are wrong: they ignore the very nature of classical music, and of music in general. The "nature" of classical music seems to be a hard-to-break musical nut on which many scholars have lost their teeth, but Kramer came probably the closest to giving an answer in his book *Why Classical Music Still Matters*. Surveying the place of music—music in general, not only the Classical—in the history of humankind, Kramer discovers an essential need of the human soul—the melody. Moreover, he finds that a musical block becomes a melody only through its, unchanged or varied, repetition.[20] He aptly defines the essential "narrative" of a Classical music work as a "drama"—the story of melody's Fate in a succession of its returns, concluding:

> So rooted, so culturally fraught, is the principle of melodic return that its own return is virtually irrepressible. It seems like the force of nature itself, of a piece with traditional conceptions of cyclical time.

The corollary of this principle allows us to understand the irremediable rupture between the old Classical and its modernist version:

> By the same token, foregoing melodic return, sometimes by foregoing melody altogether, really presents itself as a way of breaking with tradition. For this reason it became one of the chief traits of aggressive modernism in the twentieth century.[21]

Kramer thesis makes it clear that the "newness" promoted by the Avant-Garde is of a completely different nature than the one the Beethoven promoted. Beethoven's freedom to break a rule for the sake of a "higher" artistic expression of melody was the opposite of the goal of the Avant-Garde—the *destruction* of melody. Melody was the essential engine in Beethoven's music.

This last statement needs clarification because of a frequently quoted statement by a prominent member of the Avant-Garde, Igor Stravinsky, who decreed that Beethoven lacked the gift of melody and that his music was but the result of "hard labor." Indeed, Stravinsky wrote in his 1942 book *Poetics of Music* that "the capacity for melody is a gift [... and Beethoven] spent his whole life imploring the aid of this gift which he lacked."[22]

This assertion is the result of a misconception: Stravinsky defines melody as the musical singing of a cadenced phrase,"* that is as a vocal tuneful phrase

---

* Stravinsky explains that he uses the word "cadenced" in its general meaning of "rhythmical."

and it is true that vocal music was not Beethoven forte (and he was the first to acknowledge it). He invented an impressive body of tuneful phrases—of which the theme of his *Ode to Joy* is probably the best-known melody of classical music—but his forte was the "instrumental" phrase, for which he preferred the term of "musical idea." It is in this sense that we must understand what Kramer calls "melody": as a pregnant phrase, usually not very long (as a vocal melody that should sustain a whole verse or stanza) but also a striking and memorable "musical idea." Wagner, an authority in the matter even higher than Stravinsky, saw Beethoven's most important lesson in his "restoring" the melody to its "natural simplicity."[23] The mentioned concept of "memorability" is essential to Kramer's thesis, although he does not explicate it: in order for the "melody" to return, it must be recognized after being "memorized" in the previous hearing. "Memorability," not mere tunefulness, also illuminates Beethoven's secret, which is also the secret of all great music preserved in the Canon: all great music is great because it is "memorable," both in the figurative and the literal sense of the term. The most famous and world-wide-known example of such memorable musical idea is the four-note motive that opens Beethoven's *Fifth Symphony*: it is not a tuneful phrase but, once heard, it fills the soul with emotion that imprints it forever in the brain. Avant-Garde music has simply killed "memorability." Some of Stravinsky's music still can claim remnants of it, because of it pregnant rhythmic formulae, but serialism cannot. Schönberg's dream of having the listener hum his series during his waking was delusional. As the experimental research has found, even the well-versed musicians could not recognize the initial series in the development of a serialist piece.[24]

Kramer's conception of "melody's Fate" provides the answer to Goldschmidt's initial, grand-rhetorical question. It also makes it clear why Beethoven's music could not be a premonitory endorsement of the twentieth-century Avant-Garde. Any further discussion of the latter phenomenon, however interesting, is far beyond the scope of this essay. The best that can be found is still the old, 1955 book by Henry Pleasants, *The Agony of Modern Music*, a lucid analysis that the "official" musicology killed by silence, even when it borrowed from it, as does Richard Taruskin in the latest (2010) history of Classical music, in which he sums up Schönberg's credo: "The highest of all values, in his view, is technical innovation, provided that (1) the innovation in question can be viewed as an emancipation, (2) it was "influential" (in other words, that it inspired imitation, or at least turned up in a lot of later music), and (3) it placed the innovator beyond the comprehension of his contemporaries (or beyond all but an initiated elite)."[25]

Beethoven himself saw the "danger" of his legacy

It is, therefore, misguided to claim that Beethoven would have saluted Avant-Garde as his heirs. One the other hand, he was, indeed, aware of a certain "danger" hidden in his achievements. Sometime in 1817, he wrote in his *Tagebuch* (diary):

> Unfortunately, mediocre talents are condemned to imitate the faults
> of the great masters without appreciating their beauties; from thence

comes the harm that Michelangelo does to painting, Shakespeare to drama and, in our day, Beethoven to music.[26]

This entry is, apparently, the transcription of some criticism that he read in the media, the original of which has not been traced back, and the very fact that Beethoven copied it into his diary shows that he found it pertinent. He certainly did not share the critic's opinion that his daring breaks of established rules were "faults," yet he seems to have accepted that his example had set an uneasy precedent: in less-gifted hands than his, the freedom to break the rules could open the door to anarchy and nihilism in art. This "danger" was not one of those alleged by Goldschmidt, but it was far more ominous, because it actually materialized a hundred years later with the advent of twentieth-century Avant-Garde.

8
Tia DeNora's Beethoven
as a socio-political construct

In 1995, Tia DeNora, then a young lecturer in the Department of Sociology at the University of Exeter, UK, published the book *Beethoven and the Construction of Genius*, subtitled "Musical Politics in Vienna, 1792-1803."[1] The book established her as an up-and-coming Beethoven scholar and one of the promoters of the relatively new discipline of "socio-musicology," in which she identified and explored a distinct new niche—"musical politics."

Musical politics should not be confused with politicizing music, an area that had previously been inspected by several researchers. In DeNora's view, musical politics is not simply the environment in which a musician lives, which may eventually condition his recognition during his life, but an important ingredient in the definition of his very talent. As she puts it in her preface, she sees "talent and Genius as fundamentally social [not individual] achievements" (xiii).[*] She claims that the Beethoven literature was wrong to "isolate the quality of Beethoven's works as the cause of its recognition," a misconception that "leads to over-idealized and musically imperialistic conceptions of the compositional process, which sidesteps the issue of social circumstances" (6).

At first sight, such a stance should not stir controversy. Even a layman (or just Anyone?) would accept that an individual with innate musical qualities similar to Beethoven's but born in the African savanna would certainly not have produced Beethoven's music; the latter was the product of a few thousand years of European (particularly German) civilization. And even if Beethoven had been born in Bonn but two centuries later, he would not have become the Beethoven we know. Contrary to DeNora's statement, traditional musicology had always relied on the premise that genius is a social (or, better said, "cultural") product, but had never made a fuss about it.

At first sight, such a stance should not stir controversy. Anyone would accept that an individual with innate musical qualities similar to Beethoven's but born in the African savanna would certainly not have produced Beethoven's music; the latter was the product of a few thousand years of European (particularly German) civilization. And even if Beethoven had been born in Bonn but two centuries later, he would not have become the Beethoven we know. Contrary to DeNora's statement, traditional musicology had always relied on the premise that genius is a social (or, better said, "cultural") product, but had never made a fuss about it. DeNora makes more than a fuss in her book: she takes upon herself to build the right "sociology of Beethoven's reputation" (5) based on "the particularities of Viennese musical culture [that] were crucial to the shape

---

[*] References to DeNora's book are indicated in the text in this chapter.

of Beethoven's success" (3-4). More exactly, she claims to prove that the aristocracy's sponsorship of him during the first ten years after he settled in Vienna would have been crucial both in assuring his position in the history of music and in shaping his very genius. Indeed, she confines the scope of her work to that decade only, claiming that, "neither Beethoven's middle-period popularity nor his ultimate recognition as the greatest of musical masters could have occurred without his lionization by aristocratic society during the 1790s and early 1880s" (9).

DeNora's Beethoven, an overview

DeNora's argument extends to two hundred pages, which makes it diffuse and repetitive, much of it consisting of re-inventing the wheel without adding much to her argument beyond some interesting episodes of the Viennese music politics around 1800. A ten-time shorter article would probably have been more articulate. In a nutshell, DeNora's "sociology of Beethoven's reputation" claims that:

1) Beethoven was lucky to have chosen to settle in Vienna, a unique, exceptionally propitious hub for new talents among all major European cities.
2) Vienna's "exceptionalism" was due to a sizable part of the high aristocratic class, which was supporting a "reorientation of musical taste" and guessed that Beethoven would have been instrumental in promoting it.
3) This aristocracy faction carried out an intense advertising campaign for him.
4) It also helped him in other ways, financially as well as in developing his genius.
5) The aristocracy's help was not entirely motivated by their real love of music: their patronage of Beethoven was also intended to justify and enhance their privileged social status.

The weight that DeNora assigns to the role of the Viennese aristocracy in the development of Beethoven's career and genius leads her to propose an unprecedented sixth point, a what-if question:

6) *What if* another young aspiring musician would have settled in Vienna instead of Beethoven, getting the aristocracy's support?

Wouldn't he have become the one who changed music instead of Beethoven? This is not a rhetorical question. DeNora develops the issue at length, to hint to a non-Beethoven alternative in the history of music.

Critical reviews of DeNora's theory

It was particularly this last assertion that made a few prominent musicians and musicologists take a stand against DeNora's theory. Michael Broyles presented a very good summing up of DeNora's lengthy and rather diffuse text, accepted that her account was sometimes "important and exciting" and that she "makes a strong case for much of it." He was, however, not ready to go to the same extreme as to accept that Beethoven was a simple, even replaceable, "pawn" in the social game played by the Viennese aristocracy, that would have eventually defined the music Canon as it is known today; he could not see how a now-forgotten contemporary of Beethoven like Louis Spohr (1784-1859), who had the same opportunities in Vienna but certainly less talent, could have entered the Canon.[2]

The late respected pianist and musicologist Charles Rosen was even less convinced than Broyles. His short review entitled "Did Beethoven Have All the Luck?" in *The New York Review of Books* praised DeNora's book for giving "a fascinating picture of important aspects of musical life in Vienna and of the complexities of musical politics," but rejected her claim that "Beethoven's genius was 'constructed' by his society, above all the upper class." Rosen recalled that the comparison of Beethoven's music with the products of his contemporaries clearly attests his superiority in every aspect—"originality, breadth of thought, or structural sophistication"—therefore his gaining the audience's acceptance was not just a matter of "luck."[3]

The controversy grew. The following year, Mary Sue Morrow answered to a similar critique of DeNora's book (without naming its author), taking the defense of her colleague. She disliked "the excess of sociological jargon" in DeNora's work; she thought that a few statements needed more nuances added, but found the essential argument about the role that Beethoven's aristocratic patrons played in "constructing the narrative of his genius" to be well justified.[4] Rosen's review also triggered short polemics with DeNora in a 1997 issue of the same publication:[5] she argued that she did not deny Beethoven's genius but that her purpose was to show that "[his] talent was a necessary but not sufficient cause of his subsequent acclaim"[6] and that the support of his aristocratic patrons was instrumental in his eventual victory in Vienna's "musical politics" at the beginning of the 1800s. In his reply, Rosen wrote, "I never denied that genius is a social achievement," but claimed that, "a single class—like the Viennese aristocracy—cannot permanently affect the course of music. It can only give someone five years—or fifteen minutes—of fame. The history of music is an interaction of individual talent, social pressures, and the musical system already in place," a good summing up of the approach of good, traditional musicology.

I think there is more to say about Tia DeNora's contribution to the Beethoven literature, beyond Broyles and Rosen's critiques. One can, without too much effort, discover that she is mistaken in her attempts to push the simple thesis that genius is a "construct" of his time and culture into a particular, very restricted, realm of the "social." Both her analyses and her inferences are too-often incorrect and her final assessment of Beethoven and his position in the history of music is misconstrued.

How DeNora's being right turns into being wrong

One can easily accept DeNora's particularizing the statement "genius is a social achievement" into a "success equation" that includes the genius and his audience (or what DeNora calls "reception"). The main fact on which DeNora founds her theory is well documented: it was the Viennese aristocracy (or, at least a large part of it) who embraced Beethoven and launched his career when he showed up as a new talent in the city. DeNora is also right that the artist-audience symbiosis is a matter of "marketing." An artist has to "sell" himself and, in this regard, she argues that Beethoven was lucky to launch himself on the most propitious market—Vienna. He found there the best marketers to act for him: the Viennese aristocracy. That the favorable reception by his audience stimulates the artist and thus contributes to the development of his talent seems a commonsense statement that does not need demonstration. One can, therefore, accept that Beethoven's membership as a founder of the music Canon owed something to the initial enthusiastic reaction of the aristocratic salons in which he played in the last decade of the 1790s.

This "something" is both self-evident and imponderable, but DeNora claims to have clarified the matter: it meant everything! Without it, Beethoven would not have become Beethoven. "I argue," she unequivocally claims, "that Beethoven's talent was a necessary but not sufficient cause of his *subsequent* acclaim" (my emphasis). What does "subsequent acclaim" mean in the case of Beethoven (or any other creator, for that matter)? It can mean three things, depending on how fast the "subsequent" takes place: immediate success; or success and recognition during the artist's life; or, finally, posthumous consecration in the Canon. Beethoven actually went through all the three phases but in a more complex timeline: he enjoyed immediate success after he arrived in Vienna and was the favorite virtuoso-composer of the aristocratic salons; after 1800, when he started opening new avenues as a composer, his music was met with mixed reviews before "putting him on the [European] map" towards the end of the decade; after 1812, he entered a period of creative "eclipse," for causes that have never been fully explored, including the collapse of his "Immortal Beloved" love story and the arrival of another "conqueror"—Rossini; Beethoven's last, very productive ten years re-established him as the greatest living musician and he was quickly "canonized" after his death by the Romanticist generation, who saw in him one, and actually the greatest, of them.

DeNora's "necessary but not sufficient" clause is precarious for a second reason. She holds this clause as a general rule, which she particularizes to Beethoven as the most conspicuous illustration. There are, however, notable exceptions to the alleged rule. The first one that comes to mind is that of another "van"—van Gogh; he could not sell a single painting during his lifetime, but he has entered the visual arts' Canon posthumously as one of the greatest luminary of his age. In music, Schubert (whose name Charles Rosen alluded to in his critique of DeNora's book) is "almost" as good an example that DeNora disregarded: he could sell only a few of his many works to the publishers and was unknown beyond the narrow circle of his friends, yet he made it to the Canon quickly enough after his death. Obviously, his talent was sufficient for that. Why would Beethoven have needed a "political" support to achieve what Schubert did with none?

The "Schubert factor" manifests another flaw in DeNora's theory. I mentioned already her statement, "Neither Beethoven's middle-period popularity nor his ultimate recognition as the greatest of musical masters could have occurred without his lionization by aristocratic society during the 1790s and early 1880s" (9). She never proves this assertion and Schubert's example proves that recognition during life is not indispensable for induction into the Canon.

These fundamental flaws in DeNora's argument are rooted in her methodological premises. Although she does not explicate them upfront, one gradually discovers that they are, typically for a post-modernist view, grounded in a Neo-Marxist approach to arts. I do not object to this approach *per se*—I share many of its points and assumptions—but to its unbending application, as if it were a rigorous formula of the $E=mc^2$ kind—a rigidity that is missing in Marx and Engels' original. One can easily accept the thesis that "talent and genius [are] fundamentally social achievements," but the "social" is an extremely complex determinant that can include cases so apparently conflicting as van Gogh and Schubert's. Reducing it to the political maneuvers of Viennese aristocracy lasting only one decade is an over-simplification, the kind of which Marx and Engels were careful to avoid.

A second essential premise of the post-modernist approach is what I would call "absolute relativism." This oxymoron is intended: relativism is the only absolute principle that postmodernism accepts. If everything is a "social construct," there are no values or criteria that could cross cultural lines in space or time; we will see this principle in action repeatedly in DeNora's book. Granted, the discipline of ethnomusicology has revealed the diversity of the musical worlds of the planet; however, it has also showed that at least two elements exist that provide a common ground: the rhythm (either in exacerbated or in a subdued form) and the appeal of consonance. To stay on topic, it is easy to accept that "our" Beethoven is not identical to the one of the Viennese aristocrats *circa* 1800; there must be, however, some deep commonality, otherwise we would not still find him "great" two centuries after those aristocrats did. These two lines of thought undermine substantially DeNora's approach, but they are not the only flaws of her argumentation. As I will presently show, she also misinterprets her data; she misconstrues logics; and, worst of all, she disregards well-known facts that do not fit her theory. Let us proceed in scrutinizing her six major points enumerated above.

An overblown claim: Vienna's musical "exceptionalism"

DeNora particularly insists on what she proposes as the two essential circumstances that Beethoven benefitted from the most: Vienna's appreciation of "high" or "serious" music, not only that of Haydn and Mozart but also that of Bach and Händel (3-4); and an influential group of aristocratic Maecenas devoted to this "high music." She delves into this on some 50 pages spread across several chapters, including statistics tables (19-23, 31, 32, 34, 35), charts (28), minute details, as well as anecdotes and quotes to demonstrate what Thayer had done long ago in a couple of pages, concluding that, when Beethoven arrived in Vienna

> all the conditions precedent for the elevation of the art [music] were just at this time fulfilled at Vienna, and in one department—that of instrumental music—they existed in a degree unknown in any other city.[7]

Indeed, Thayer, the first and foremost in the long lines of literature that DeNora blames for promoting "musically imperialistic conceptions," had similarly pinpointed Vienna's exceptionalism.

In a larger perspective that DeNora misses, one must take this Viennese exceptionalism with a grain of salt. The city shared characteristics with all the German lands during the eighteenth and nineteenth centuries: instrumental music played an essential part in everyday life, as other scholars have noticed, based on the testimonies left by the memorialists:

> In Vienna, music is embedded in the heart of the city. She regulates its beat; she enters into the humblest houses, down to the narrow roads of the rural suburbs. It happens also and almost to the same measure, one could say, in virtually all the towns in Germany and Austria. There is no German town, no matter how little, where, if one strolls in the evening, after the daily traffic noise has ceased, one does not hear, coming out through an open window, a phrase from a trio of Haydn or a quartet of Mozart, or a septet of Beethoven, played, not without mistakes and awkwardness, by the parents and the children united by the same passion around their music desks.[8]

Vienna was indeed, at the time, "the capital of music," but that was essentially due to the presence of Haydn, Mozart and Beethoven (and Schubert, later), all of whom issued from the German musical tradition. The city owed its exceptionalism to them, not the other way around.

Moreover, Vienna was lagging *behind* other major European cities in a musical feature that was no less important to Beethoven than his success in the salons—public concert life. Paris had, since 1725, the Concert Spirituel society that organized public concerts, where good orchestras played a large variety of music. In 1778, during his visit to Paris, the Concert Spirituel commissioned from Mozart a symphony which he obligingly supplied with his No. 32 (dubbed "Paris"); Haydn had a set of *six* "Paris symphonies" commissioned (1785-1786). In Berlin, the royal Capella was one of the best orchestras in Europe since 1740. Leipzig had its Grosses Concert society (later famous as the Gewandhaus Orchestra) since 1743. Vienna relied only on aristocratic "cappellas," which were, as DeNora herself documents (29, 42-43) disappearing by the time Beethoven arrived in the city. It took him almost ten years to find a venue and give his first public concert, then called "Akademie." Vienna's "exceptionalism" applied only to the salons (which mostly but not exclusively, aristocratic), where piano and chamber music was played, primarily by virtuoso-composers.

DeNora's second claim to Vienna's exceptionalism, the presence of an aristocracy uniquely devoted to "high" music, is also an exaggeration. Nobility all over Europe was a fervent supporter of music, from Saint Petersburg—which sent Count Razumovsky, Beethoven's future patron, to Vienna as ambassador—to Lisbon, which dotted for nine years (1719-1727) on Domenico Scarlatti, before the latter moved to Madrid. DeNora claims that England, at the time the most socially advanced country, possessed of a strong middle class, had no aristocracy capable of promoting a pianist, because "the piano was, for many aristocrats, tainted with the new commercial musical values"

(173). Other researchers give us a different picture. Julian Rushton wrote this about London at the time when the Mozart family visited to promote their child prodigy in 1764-5:

> There was relatively more mingling of aristocratic and mercantile [middle] classes than elsewhere. Musicians relied mainly on the patronage of the former, but the latter class was more numerous, more influential, and no less cultured, than its continental counterparts. The situation favored instrumental music and song, which were popular in the pleasure gardens, and concert series such as the one recently established by J. C. Bach and his countryman K. F. Abel.[9]

This version of reality is far more convincing than DeNora's. It explains why many musicians born in continental countries (the young Bach and his friend Abel were not the only ones) followed Händel's example and settled down in London. As one can see, DeNora's construct of Vienna's exceptionalism as uniquely able to foster the development of an innate talent such as Beethoven's is rather dubious, which seriously undermines the foundation of her theory. The city had certainly strong attractions for a young aspiring musician, which could easily explain why Beethoven decided to settle there and not to move out, in spite of some misgivings that he had later. Certainly, the reception he received from the high aristocracy was one of them, but that alone does not justify the weight DeNora attributes to the city's "exceptionalism."

The graft of "high music" on Viennese aristocracy: a thesis based on misinterpreted statistics

There is another point on which deNora's argument falters. The combination of the two traits of Viennese exceptionalism, the appreciation of "high" music and an appreciative aristocracy, plays a crucial role in DeNora's theory. According to her, in the decade before Beethoven settled down in Vienna, the Viennese aristocracy "reoriented" their musical taste towards the "high" or "serious" music, becoming *connoisseurs*. Van Swieten initiated the movement by opening his music library, brought from Berlin, to musicians. This library contained works by Bach and Händel, but his followers, most of them musically educated aristocrats, were still a minority in the 1780s (15). The audience at large requested lighter genres, which explained the decline in Mozart's popularity after his initial success during his first Viennese years. DeNora may be right to link it with the increased complexity of Mozart's works, which would have been mainly the result of his own "reorientation" towards the "serious" under the influence of his foraging in van Swieten's music library (14-15). She is, however, wrong in her further speculation. Soon after Mozart's death, the city that had uncaringly watched him die in misery suddenly awoke to the realization that they had lost a great genius; his popularity sprang up in the concerts. Of course, the aristocracy, who would have been in the best position to help the indebted Mozart, shared in this collective feelings of guilt. DeNora sees in this occurrence proof of a sudden "reorientation" *en masse* of the aristocracy towards the "serious," in which the middle class did not participate (30). Thus "re-oriented," the Viennese aristocracy embraced Beethoven, in whom they saw the seeds of the "serious" ready to grow. As we will soon see, DeNora's conferring to the aristocracy a proactive rather than a reactive role introduces a ground-breaking theory that is supposed to replace the traditional view of Beethoven as the exponent of the ideals of a new social, and implicitly needed, musical age, the promoter of which was primarily the middle-class.

DeNora builds her argument on the sparse statistics gleaned by other scholars about the concert life in Vienna between 1791 and 1810, presented in several tables, of which Table 5 is the most essential. It shows the number of pieces by various composers played in about 370 concerts at the city's five major venues that she allotted to the aristocracy and the middle-class. Jahn's was actually a restaurant where classical music was played (33) and DeNora does not allot it to any group, but this can be dismissed as it weighs little in the statistics.

TABLE 5
COMPOSERS MOST OFTEN LISTED AT FIVE MAJOR LOCATIONS, WITH NUMBER OF PERFORMANCES OF THEIR WORKS AND THE YEARS DURING WHICH THEY ARE LISTED FOR 1791–1810

Jahn's	Leopoldstadt	Wien	Universitätssaal	Burgtheater
Mozart (11), 1791–	Haydn (6), 1800–	Beethoven (22), 1798–	Beethoven (9), 1807–8	Haydn (79), 1791–
Eberl (6), 1804–5	Mozart (5), 1801–	Mozart (13), 1791–	Haydn (3), 1807–8	Par (23), 1800–8
Cimarosa (6), 1795–1802	Cimarosa (5), 1795–1804	Cherubini (12), 1804–		Mozart (22), 1791–
Haydn (5), 1798–	Müller (5), 1796–1808	Haydn (10), 1791–		Beethoven (20), 1795–
	Kauer (5), 1798–1809			Weigl (13), 1791–1807
				Mayer (12), 1802–8
				Paisiello (11), 1791–1804
				Eybler (11), 1794–1804
				Cherubini (11), 1805–
				Salieri (9), 1795–1809
				Auernhammer (8), 1795–1806
				Winter (8), 1796–1810
				Süssmayr (8), 1797–1809
				Handel (8), 1792–1807
				Cimarosa (8), 1793–1810

Source: Morrow 1989, 258–364.
Note: The Liebhaber concerts at the Universitätssaal featured, in addition to performances of Beethoven and Haydn, those of Mozart, Himmel, Cherubini, Rode, and Müller. These composers appeared on Liebhaber programs only once, at the first concert in the series; subsequent concerts were devoted to music of Beethoven and Haydn.

DeNora, Beethoven and the Construction of Genius, page 34

Leopoldstadt was "the most distinctly middle class theater, located in Vienna's suburbs" (31). The Theater an der Wien and the Universitätsaal were managed by the GAC ("Gesellschaft des Associierten Cavaliere"), which was "exclusively aristocratic" (30). The GAC also managed the Burgtheater, which DeNora describes (slightly more nuanced) as "predominantly aristocratic" (30).

Discussing Table 5 data in conjunction with the few concert programs that researches have been able to locate, DeNora writes

> Genres [of music] which from our twentieth-century preconceptions and stereotypes we characterize as lighter (that is shorter pieces, or

more overtly virtuosic pieces, songs, arias, and overtures) appeared primarily at the Leopoldstadt theater, while the GAC controlled Theater an der Wien and the Universitätsaal concerts featured symphonies, cantatas, unstaged versions of opera and Mozart's *Requiem* instead of (or in addition to) the genres offered at Leopoldstadt (33).

DeNora concludes:

> It seems fair, then, to suggest that a serious music ideology, which took as its exemplars Beethoven and reconstituted, more explicitly "learned" and grandiose versions of Mozart and Haydn, emerged during the 1870s in Vienna, and that this ideology was primarily subscribed by the old aristocracy, not the middle class. This view runs counter to what Arnold Hauser (1962), Henry Raynor (1976), Theodor Adorno (1976), and a host of other scholars have had to say, on the basis of scarce evidence, about the origin of serious music ideology and, as such, it challenges received sociological wisdom and Beethoven mythology concerning the origin of musical Canon. (35-36)

In other words (38-39), the change happening *circa* 1800 in the musical landscape, in which Beethoven played a major part and which defined the musical Canon we now know, had nothing to do with the ascent of a democracy-promoting middle-class, as the traditional view of music history holds, either from Marxist, Neo-Marxist or Romanticist perspectives. It was the Viennese aristocracy—or, at least, a faction of it—that promoted the change, primarily by taking advantage of the arrival of Beethoven and supporting him, at least in his first decade in Vienna. Indeed, this is a concept that turns the table on previous "Beethoven musical sociology."

It may seem indeed a remarkable achievement to apply the Neo-Marxist socio-historical theory in order to prove the opposite of what that theory sees in the socio-politic position of Beethoven in the history of music. It is, however, very unlikely that Viennese aristocracy shared the ideals of the French Revolution, which are typically associated with Beethoven. Granted, some of the most ardent supporters of Enlightenment ideology were aristocrats and Emperor Joseph II was an "Enlighted Prince," but they did not carry their allegiance nearly so far as the French Revolution did at the end of the century. DeNora had to come up with a different argument about how a relatively large portion of the Austrian aristocrats became supporters of a "revolutionary" like Beethoven. She first contests the term "revolutionary" because "imprecise as an indicator of Beethoven's place in music history" (2), a statement going against traditional views epitomized in a biography of a composer published almost a hundred years ago.[*] She does not offer any argument to support her rebuttal and proposes the allegiance of a sizeable part of the Viennese aristocracy to "high music" as the explanation for their choosing Beethoven to support and of their managing a

---

[*] Robert H. Schauffler, *Beethoven: The Man Who Freed Music* (Doubleday, Doran & Co., New York, 1929).

"political" campaign in his favor. Their commitment would have also pursued a second, purely political and far less honorable, goal that I will reveal in due time. All in all, according to DeNora, the pro-Beethoven political game of the aristocracy would have greatly contributed to the crystallization of his genius and to his role in shaping the future of music.

There is, however, a serious problem with DeNora's theory. Examining her Table 5, one notices immediately that the repertoire of the Burgtheater, supposedly expressing "predominantly" the aristocratic taste, is similar to the one of the "middle-class" Leopoldstadt—a mixture of great and minor masters, with the latter (Pär, Weigl, Mayer, Eybler, etc.) actually quantitatively dominating slightly (130 pieces of 251); almost all of them wrote mostly opera (only Paisiello ventured in the instrumental genre, with eight keyboard concertos and many dances for the orchestra). It seems fairer to me to suggest that Table 5 shows that the tastes of the aristocracy and the middle class shared largely one and the same—and not exclusively "high." In fact, DeNora will admit later (86-87) that the "serious music" concept "was not yet a pervasive part of aristocratic Viennese musical life" at the time.

While the inferences of DeNora's analysis (high-taste aristocracy v. low-taste middle class) are false,[*] her conclusion—that the aristocracy launched Beethoven's career in Vienna—is still right. This is a well-known fact, but has a much simpler reason than the "reorientation" of taste: since the Renaissance, the aristocracy had viewed support of the arts as one of their strongest justifications for claiming their privileges. One must also acknowledge that significant segments of the aristocracy had, historically, embraced "progressive" lines of thought that conflicted with their social power and privileges, siding with the rising middle class. Emperor Joseph II, the prototypical "enlightened Prince," was the most exalted such example, but even he certainly did not wish to see a revolution happen, though he wanted the privileges of the nobility the be restricted and *gradually* abolished.

Unaware of the discrepancy between her thesis of the aristocracy as the flagship of "high music," and the data she supplied to support it, DeNora goes further to explain how and why the Viennese aristocracy allegedly "reoriented" their musical tastes. She dwells for over twenty pages (37-59) on various aspects of the musical life in the city, to prove that the aristocracy had "reoriented" their tastes towards "serious" genres in order to set itself apart from the rising (allegedly low-taste) middle-class, so that they could "identify their own level in the social sphere as an aristocracy of taste" (57); supporting Beethoven would have been just another proof of their good (i.e., distinct) taste. As one can see, DeNora's "musical politics" are more than the generic art/science of politics applied to the field of music; it is intrinsically mixed with politics aiming to power. And Beethoven would have been one more pawn maneuvered on the national (perhaps also international?) stage. In the process, DeNora drops a hint about the Canon of the Classical, quoting approvingly Don Randel (49): "canonic

---

[*] The critics of DeNora's book missed her argument about the statistics in Table 1. It is true that they were musicians not statisticians, but neither is this author.

ideology [...] is built in to the analytic strategies that music scholars employ," which results in tautological reasoning. She does not insist on this point here, but we will see her at it later, targeting Beethoven again.

The Beethoven–Wölffl duel as musical class warfare

DeNora tackles the 1799 piano contest between Beethoven and Joseph Wölffl, another prominent virtuoso of the time, later in her book (Chapter 7), but its logical place is here, after she had split Viennese society both socially and musically: on one side the high aristocracy, devoted to the "high" or "serious" or "great" music; and on the other what she calls "the second society," the lesser rank nobility and middle class, adepts of the "lighter" music. DeNora's twenty-odd-page argument (147-169) meanders through various topics, only conjecturally related to the issue. In a nutshell, however: Thayer "clearly politicizes the contest," because he paralleled it with the fight between the Gluckists and Piccinists on the French opera stage a quarter of a century earlier (148), one of the many "new vs. old" rounds in the world of art. The narrative account of the contest left by Beethoven's contemporary and friend Ignaz von Seyfried (1776-1841) confirms it, by stating that "the many friends of art in the Imperial City arrayed themselves in two parties," for Beethoven and Wölffl respectively; it names "the amiable Prince Lichnovsky" as the head for the Beethoven party and "among the most zealous patrons of Wölffl [...] the broadly cultured Baron Raymond von Wetzlar" (155-156), a prominent member of the "second society" who hosted the contest in his luxurious Vienna villa. Because her four-page (162-165) exploration of the back-stages of Viennese "musical constituencies in 1799" did not reveal any close connections between Beethoven and Wetzlar's circle, similar with his deep involvement with the high aristocracy, DeNora concludes that the two worlds did not overlap in their patronage of music. She found another argument: Beethoven had lately had reviews blaming him for his penchant for "mysteriousness and gloominess" that only the connoisseurs could fathom—which suggests that high aristocracy stood behind him. On the other hand, Wölffl, "trained in the school of Mozart, [was] equable, never superficial but always clear and accessible to the multitude" (156, quoting also from an anonymous 1799 review in the *Allgemeine Musikalische Zeitung*). DeNora's final verdict,

> Within the high culture music world, the Beethoven-Wölffl duel placed at stake relations between an upward aspiring middle class or second society and Vienna's old aristocrats (169),

is strikingly similar to her thesis of the musical-political split of Viennese society, which she takes further into a musical class warfare, trivializing the Marxist view on arts, which is far subtler than such rigid schemes.

DeNora's argument has several major flaws. First, the opposition of high aristocracy vs. middle class as reflecting the "serious" and "light" music dichotomy is false; I showed earlier that, according to the very evidence advanced by DeNora, both classes shared the same musical taste: an equal mixture of "high" and "light." Her delineation of the two parties, relying here only on anecdotic examples of Prince Lichnovsky and lower-nobility Wetzlar, is arbitrary. One knows, in the Beethoven literature, examples of high aristocrats who were not Beethoven fans: Ries tells the story of a certain "Count P [who] spoke so loudly and freely with a beautiful lady" while Beethoven was playing in an aristocratic salon.[10] One also knows a baron, von Zmeskall, who became Beethoven's devoted friend soon after the latter's settling in Vienna.[11] Let us also notice the inner conflict in DeNora's theory, in which Mozart is an important component of the "high" music, together with Haydn and Beethoven (see page 174); in her take of the Beethoven-Wölffl contest, the Mozart school unaccountably represents the "light"!

There is also a significant detail in the very evidence that DeNora quotes (156) that she misses, which throws a different light on the episode. It is this sentence from Seyfried's testimony:

> [...] the interesting combats of the two athletes *not infrequently* offered an indescribable artistic treat to the numerous and *thoroughly select gathering* (my emphasis)[12] (152).

Obviously, "not infrequently" does not necessarily mean "frequently," but it shows that there was no one-time duel, as DeNora assumes all throughout her argumentation, but several contests—how many it is impossible to say—when the two contestants met and played, separately and even together ("at two pianofortes [... in a kind of] four-hands Cappriccio," as Seyfried writes). All happened in front of "thoroughly select gatherings," which again suggests the presence of both "societies"—which means that, contrary to DeNora's claim, they overlapped quite a bit.[*] The serious-light opposition on which DeNora speculates, seeing in the contest "an important moment in music history [...perhaps] the earliest emergence of the nineteenth-century ideology of serious music as a debatable issue and as in contrast to more conventional dilettante values" (168), is a very tenuous construct.

By and large, DeNora's thesis of musical-social warfare between "two societies" does not hold water. If he was indeed a representative of the "school of Mozart," the contest was just another example of the inter-generational fight that explained Beethoven's rise to notoriety. I am not familiar enough with the music of Wölffl, but, judging by the few samples of his music that can be heard on *YouTube*, he, too, was trying to "say" something musically newer than Mozart—he was not of the latter's generation, either—but he was not a creative genius. A comparison between Beethoven's *Pathetique* (composed about the time of this "duel") and Wölffl's *C minor Piano Sonata* that he composed a few years later, is sufficient evidence of that.

---

[*] It is not relevant here who won the contest. According to Seyfried, "It would have difficult, perhaps impossible, to award the palm of victory." The *AMZ* review claimed that "opinion is divided [... but] it would seem as if the majority were on the side of the latter [Wölffl]" (Thayer-Forbes, pages 206 and 205, respectively).

Why did aristocracy really support Beethoven

According to DeNora, the Viennese aristocracy endorsed Beethoven because they saw in him the fulfilment of their desire for "high music." One question is immediate: Did they discover the "high" in Beethoven, or, rather, they chose him above one of his competitors, because they saw his potential and then educated him towards the "high?" DeNora claims from the very beginning that, when Beethoven arrived in Vienna,

> [...] one could easily envision his continued success—a career not unlike that enjoyed by his teacher Neefe, his grandfather Ludwig, or any other of the many successful but now forgotten musicians of the late eighteenth and early nineteenth centuries. One could also imagine that, in the later words of his teacher Haydn, Beethoven might eventually "fill the position of one of Europe's greatest composers." What was not so clearly foreseeable was the unique way Beethoven came to be identified during the subsequent decade and a half as the author of unconventional, often "difficult," and sometimes unprecedentedly lengthy works [follows the list of his 1803-1806 major works] (2).

In other words, the realization of Beethoven's promise would have been rather modest, not much better than his competitors; either the Viennese aristocracy showed unusual keenness or he was just lucky to be chosen.

DeNora is mistaken: Beethoven's future was already "clearly foreseeable" in his 1790 *Cantata on the Death of Emperor Joseph II*, in which Brahms saw, when the work was published much later, "Beethoven through and through! [... with] all the characteristics which we may observe and associate with his later works."[13] The cantata was never performed during Beethoven's life, but Count Waldstein, his first aristocratic supporter and a music connoisseur, must have known it, because he was a prominent member of the *Legegesellschaft* association in Bonn, which planned the memorial celebration of Joseph II;[14] he certainly saw great promise in this work and wrote in the autographs album of the youth who was leaving his native city to go to Vienna to learn further his craft, "With the help of assiduous labour you shall receive *Mozart's spirit from Haydn's hands*."[15] I would also recognize a "juvenile masterpiece" in Beethoven's *Piano Quartet in E flat* (published posthumously as WoO 36 with two similar quartets) that he wrote when fifteen, a piece revealing a dramatic tension that he would not match for fifteen years! It is obvious that the Viennese aristocracy saw far more promise in Beethoven than DeNora assumes in order to give the aristocracy a far greater weight in the development of Beethoven's genius. He might not have been a better piano player than his competitors, but far surpassed them as a composer and, at the time, the two sides of a musician were inexorably linked in the judgement of the audience.

There was, however, a second and more important reason for Viennese aristocrats to love this newcomer above all others: the "generational change" that I have introduced in the previous chapter as the engine of "Newness." A quick look at Beethoven's Viennese aristocratic patrons—not to mention his less-elevated friends like Gleichenstein or Oliva—shows that, with one exception, they were all about his age: Count Waldstein, his first important supporter and Prince Lichnovsky, his most ardent (male) supporter were 8-9 years older, but every other aristocratic devotee was younger: Count Moritz Lichnovsky (b. 1771), Count Fries (b. 1777), Prince Lobkowitz (b. 1784), Prince Kinsky (b. 1781); and Archduke Rudolph, Beethoven's pupil and most important patron after 1800, eighteen years his junior. Born in 1733, Van Swieten was the exception representing the older generation, which may explain why he was the advocate of the previous Baroque musical style. Beethoven was the greatest Novelty in town that this new aristocratic generation wanted to claim for its own.

Can one identify Beethoven's novelty as the "high music" allegedly promoted by the Viennese aristocracy? The answer is not obvious, because DeNora's "high music," which includes Haydn and Mozart as well as Bach and Händel, was not exactly a novelty at the time. The high-low dichotomy is different from the old-new. The former pertains to quality or "seriousness," not to style or school. Haydn and Mozart practiced the same style as the exponents of the "light," but they were better or more "serious." It is very likely that Beethoven's novelty that conquered the aristocratic salons was both "high" and new. In fact, DeNora noticed (124-125, 129ff.) that, while we tend to see Beethoven's production before 1800 as still within the "classical mold," it must have sounded as a breach with that tradition to the Viennese.

The alleged "Haydn's hands" scheme

After introducing Vienna's musical exceptionalism, DeNora tries to illustrate and consolidate her thesis in a chapter with an unassuming title, "Beethoven's social resources," that does not do justice to its importance in her book. It launches the already-mentioned unprecedented "What if?" question that is actually the core of the theory, but I will put off analyzing it, because it will be easier to evaluate it from the perspective of all the "politics" that, according to DeNora, the Viennese aristocracy set up for the "construction" of Beethoven's genius. Those politics would have been directed in two ways: to help establish him and then to preserve his reputation. Both were necessary for him to be "canonized" before he died; but they also indirectly helped him to grow as a musician.

Promoting Beethoven as Haydn's pupil was the first means of establishing his reputation. DeNora needs six pages (89-95), containing the biographies of several other Haydn pupils that do not add anything to her argument, to reach the commonsense conclusion that being a pupil of the most celebrated composer of the day was an excellent marketing technique. However, she wanted more from Haydn—to become an active player in the "promoting Beethoven" politics of the Viennese aristocracy. The first of their endeavors would have been to encourage a myth that linked him indestructibly to Mozart and Haydn, as bearers of the high music standard. The already-mentioned entry of Count Waldstein in Beethoven autographs album introduced the lengthy-named myth "receive Mozart's spirit from Haydn's hands." DeNora claims that the Viennese aristocracy not only accepted Beethoven as Mozart's heir, but also coopted Haydn in a "marketing campaign"—Broyles calls it "almost a grand conspiracy"[16]—intended to disseminate the phrase all over the city and beyond and transform what has been generally considered a "prophetic" appraisal of genius into a powerful marketing tool. DeNora spends pages to prove this last assertion and comes up with three more documented cases (besides Waldstein's) of the slogan "Mozart's spirit from Haydn's hands," but they spread over four years (1793-1796). She may be right to claim, "it is reasonable to suggest that, over the previous three years, there had been talk among aristocrats about Beethoven's relationship with Haydn, and that this talk functioned as a means of registering Beethoven's special promise" (87), but three private communications over a four-year interval cannot bear proof of a relentless "marketing campaign." DeNora also overdoes it when spending three pages (98-100) to prove the obvious—that Haydn also benefitted from being Beethoven's teacher, so he had an interest in promoting his pupil: the brilliance of a pupil naturally reflects on his teacher.

DeNora fails to recognize that Haydn's support of Beethoven did not last long. Her lengthy description of the relationship between the two (pages 95-110), which claims to analyze it "in the context of the changing occupational and cultural climate of musical life in late-century Vienna [… from] the old (patronal) to the new (quasi-freelance) models," embodied by Haydn and Beethoven, respectively (106-110), abounds in interesting and relevant topics but misses a few well-known facts and their implication. Quoting old biographers (Carpani) and modern scholars (Landon, Solomon), DeNora agrees that the relationship was "more complicated" and "more ambiguous" than traditionally beheld, and even accepts that "from about 1796 to around 1803 the two composers behaved openly like rivals" (106). The statement is misleading: rivalry presupposes the mutual acceptance of equal footing by the opponents, when in truth Haydn refused to fully acknowledge Beethoven's value. DeNora is also wrong when claiming that "whatever Haydn may have thought of Beethoven, he could hardly contradict any imagery of Beethoven as his prodigy that was projected onto their relationship by such august patrons as van Swieten, Waldstein, Lichnovsky, and Lobkowitz" (110-111). In fact, Haydn was not shy of voicing his disapproval of Beethoven, at least within Vienna's music world, which was certainly an important "marketing" venue. When Beethoven published his Opus 1, including the C minor Piano Trio of which he was particularly proud, not only was Haydn unwilling to "bless" this work—he advised Beethoven not to print it, as we learn from Ries[17]—but he also abetted the envious derogatory comments of the other Viennese composers, united in their "hatred of Beethoven"—the phrase used by Dolezalek, a younger musician who reported the story:[*]

> Speaking of Beethoven [his C minor Piano Trio in particular], Kozeluch [a Viennese musician] said to Haydn: "We would have done it differently, wouldn't we, Papa?" and Haydn answered, smilingly, "Yes, we would have done that differently."[18]

---

[*] I am repeating here two stories that I already presented in chapter 6, which also commented Beethoven's relationship with Haydn. Redundancy is sometimes better than cross-reference.

Haydn was endorsing the soon-to-be forgotten Leopold Kozeluch (1747-1818) over Beethoven!* This may come as a shock but it should not. Haydn's opinions about his contemporaries were not exactly stellar: he exalted not only Mozart, but also a certain Joseph Martin Kraus (1756-1792), as "one of the greatest geniuses that I've ever met."[19]

Dolezalek could have gotten the story only in 1800, when he arrived in Vienna as a young aspiring musician; that he could collect this anecdote five years after the fact shows that the story was legendary in Vienna. Another anecdote, handed by Aloys Fuchs, an even younger Beethoven contemporary, shows that Haydn's low opinion of the latter extended far beyond the disputed piano trio.

> In 1801, he [Beethoven] was met by his former teacher, the great Joseph Haydn, who stopped him at once and said: "Well, I heard your ballet [The Creatures of Prometheus] yesterday and it pleased me very much!" Beethoven replied: "Oh, dear Papa, you are very kind; but it is far from being a *Creation*!" Haydn, surprised at the answer and almost offended, said after a short pause: "That is true; it is not yet a *Creation* and I can scarcely believe that it will ever become one." Whereupon the men said their adieux, both somewhat embarrassed.[20]

Beethoven's sincere reply—also tainted with his usual penchant for puns—simply wanted to say, "Please wait for something really good to praise me," but Haydn felt it an impudence to have his masterpiece compared with a second-hand piece and his answer went far beyond saying that that ballet music was a decent but forgettable work: it translated into, "I can scarcely believe that you will ever write a masterpiece like my *Creation*." As late as 1801, which is within the period covered by DeNora, Haydn clearly refused to acknowledge Beethoven as his successor.† If he had partaken in the alleged pro-Beethoven "conspiracy" during the latter's first Vienna years, he withdrew after his pupil launched his career as a composer (1795), which makes DeNora's theory untenable.

In spite of such flaws of her argumentation, DeNora is basically correct about the main point. Every artist goes on a "market" to sell a "product"—the concept of the artist creating for posterity is a myth invented by the twentieth-century Avant-Garde. Beethoven needed a marketing policy, however different from that of a Jimi Hendrix, with whom some modern writers have compared him.‡ He needed allies, sponsors, promoters in the "media" of his time, which

---

* DeNora discovers the episode in a later, not related chapter, in which she discusses the mixed reception of Beethoven's music before 1800 (159).
† Beethoven's reaction was subdued and not resentful. He refused to inscribe "Haydn's pupil" under his name on the cover page of his Opus 1, telling later a friend that "he had some instruction from Haydn but had never learned anything from him." (Wegeler-Ries, p. 75). Nevertheless, he dedicated his Opus 2 to Haydn and continued to esteem and revere him until the end of his own life.
‡ Harvey Jay Smith, a writer turned into amateur scholar, in a fantasy novel titled *Beethoven in Love, Opus 139: Concerto Quasi Una Fantasia* (Yes Quickly Books, 2016).

consisted primarily in "word of mouth." It is unlikely, however, that Beethoven had an unfair advantage over his competitors in this regard. There was certainly more talk about him in the city than about his virtuoso rivals, just because he was better than them, but they had their share. Proof of that is the publishing market. A survey of the *Musikalien* rubric (Music publishing news) of the archives of Vienna's main weekly journal, *Wiener Zeitung*,* shows Beethoven in 47 issues between 1793 and 1800. However, his competitors are also present: Wölffl (with whom Beethoven would compete in that 1800 "contest") also has 29 appearances; two other competitors can be found therein, Gelinek and Steibelt (8 and 9 occurrences, respectively), besides the many other composers of the times, from all over Europe (Süssmeyr, Cimarosa, Boildieu, Clementi, etc.)—all of them easily surpassed by Haydn and Mozart.

Beethoven as politician

Although DeNora absolves Beethoven of having been "instrumentally careerist" (113), she finds in him qualities of an able "music politician" who maneuvered the Viennese aristocracy into accepting his "innovations in the realm of the music listening setting and within the composer-patron relationship" (144-146). He was not the first great musician to live as a freelance artist and not as a servant to a patron. Händel could arguably be credited with that, in England—a far more "advanced" country than Austria in this sense. England had also launched Haydn along a similar track during his old age. Mozart had tried to live as a freelance artist in Vienna ten years before Beethoven, but failed and had to pay for that failure with poverty and, perhaps, an untimely death. Beethoven was the one who fully succeeded in imposing on his aristocratic patrons, who accepted his rules of the game: they had to show respect to him as a person and to his music as the highest form of entertainment. Gone were the days when their Excellencies had eaten and talked and flirted while a genius like Mozart played for them. Beethoven indeed succeeded to "formalize the [classical] music listening situation," for the future, into "ritualistically solemn devotion to the performance," as DeNora finely put it (146). She is also right that these innovations helped to prepare his listeners, including his closest aristocratic supporters, to receive his new and increasingly unconventional works.

DeNora also maintains that "a key resource for Beethoven was the traditional conception of privilege, namely, that some individuals (that is, nobles) were more worthy than others" (143). She reminds us that Beethoven, the man who set to music the verse "All humans will be brothers" in the final chorus of his *Ninth Symphony* was actually an elitist who looked down on the ordinary people, those who were not able to raise themselves to the understanding of his music. DeNora adds the known fact that Beethoven tried, almost twenty years later after the time frame of her argumentation, to cheat the Habsburg judicial system by taking his case for the custody of his nephew to the nobility court of the Empire instead of the court for the commoners like himself. She quotes Maynard Solomon's thesis about Beethoven's "nobility

---

* A search engine available online at http://anno.onb.ac.at/anno-suche?

pretense"—the composer's deluding himself and others into believing that he was of noble origin—and finds fault with the thesis only because it "deflects attention away from the social effects or consequences the nobility pretense facilitated" (144). In other words, duping his aristocratic patrons into believing that he was one of them, it was easy for Beethoven to ask them to give his person and his music a previously unheard of mark of respect. I tackled the "nobility pretense" issue in chapter 4, showing that Beethoven had no delusion of the sort and that there is no proof that he tried to "dupe" his aristocratic sponsors into believing that he was of the nobility. He considered himself a "notable," a person of "creative nobility," a rank even more valuable than statutory nobility; his "nobility pretense" episode in court expressed his wish not to be treated like one of the "ordinary."

DeNora's final assertion about Beethoven as a "politician," namely that his success was due to the fact that "unlike his fellow Viennese musicians, he had considerable social resources at his disposal" (146) shows again her bias. It is another reiteration of her thesis that Beethoven had been "lucky" to be chosen by the Viennese aristocracy among the many ones available at the time. In fact, the aristocracy complied with his demands only because they were really enthralled by his music and we should give them their due: they recognized greatness. As Thayer recorded, "He [Beethoven] once said that it is easy to get along with nobility, but it was necessary to have something to impress them with."[21] This statement explains his relationship with his aristocratic patrons, and also shows that he did not consider himself (socially) one of them.

Aristocratic help in developing and preserving Beethoven's reputation

DeNora devotes a full third of her book (pages 114-185) to demonstrating how the Viennese aristocracy further helped Beethoven to build and keep his reputation. In the process, she tackles various topics that are interesting and sometimes original, but which are only of marginal relevance to her main thesis. She gives only later in her argument the definition of reputation: "I see Beethoven's reputation as the product of an interaction between his own effort, his social circumstances, and the effort of others" (143). This is commonsensical but not fully illuminating, because she had never introduced the contribution of the "others" before. In fact, she seems to have adopted the plain definition of reputation as public opinion. Nevertheless, she examines it "not from a musical-analytical standpoint, for example how initial listeners may have been 'mistaken' in their assessments" (123), but from her disciplinary predilection– the "social context." Therefore, she splits Beethoven's reputation in two: the one enjoyed in the narrow circle of the Viennese aristocracy (which she estimates at about a thousand, including their extended families); and the Viennese public at large, the lower-rank nobility and the educated middle-class, which she combines into the "second society." The former reputation was the first to rise, fed by Beethoven's performances in the aristocratic salons. It preceded and also stimulated the latter one, which began to grow a few years later, about 1795, when Beethoven had his first public concert and his name began to have "strong attraction for the public at large" (134, quoting Thayer).

DeNora is most probably right when claiming that aristocratic support went beyond just the enthusiastic reception of Beethoven's music and buying his published works; they also "spread the word" in the city, by means of "publicizing stories about his talent" (121), such as those about the "contests" held in the salons opposing him to another (at the time) famous pianist, whom he "crushed" pianistically. She is also likely right that it must have been his aristocratic connections that were instrumental in getting Beethoven invited to compose dance music for the 1795 annual ball at the Redoutensaal, which made him known to a larger audience. That his music was well received is proved by his quickly publishing the piano transcriptions of the two sets of dances (twelve Minuets WoO 7 and twelve "German dances" WoO 8) that same year.

However, DeNora is wrong in over-rating the importance of this aristocratic support. She does not offer any proof of her claim that "during the 1790s, Beethoven was shielded from hostile and destructive reception" (148), obviously implying that this was the doing of his aristocratic supporters. First of all, Beethoven met "hostile reception" only later in the decade, when he began to evolve towards his definite "style" of composing. His *Sonata Pathetique* Op. 13 seems to have been the watershed, widely regarded (not only by the fellow musicians, as it had happened with his C minor Piano Trio) as "the oddest stuff possible—such as no other one could either play or understand," as the testimony of Moscheles attests.[22] DeNora herself quotes Czerny's testimony that "during the early 1800s, the 'general public completely condemned Beethoven's works'" (131), but only as an opportunity for a digression about the difference between "Mozart school" and "Beethoven school." She does not indicate any tangible step that the Viennese aristocracy took to counterbalance adverse "public opinion."

DeNora also invokes the change of attitude about Beethoven's music in the reviews of the *Allgemeine musikalische Zeitung*, the most authoritative German critical voice at the time: the negative evaluation at the end of 1788 changed to a much more favorable one only a few months later. Rejecting the justification offered by the anonymous reviewer, that, "after he has tried to accustom himself more and more to Hr. Beethoven's manner [he] has learned to admire him more than he did at first," DeNora proffers a different explanation:

> A more plausible approach is to perceive him [the reviewer] as wavering in the face of persistent musical authority from Beethoven's growing aristocratic network of sponsors. (182)

Without a single, be it even circumstantial, proof, this allegation looks only like wishful thinking. DeNora also does not notice the inexplicable failure of the Viennese aristocracy to help Beethoven's public career. One wonders why it took him almost three years to ascend the stage in a public concert. Half of the explanation consists in a peculiarity of the Viennese musical stage system that DeNora disregards. As I already stated, unlike cities like London, Paris, Berlin or Leipzig, which all had well-established professional orchestras and public concert venues, Vienna relied on private aristocratic sponsorship of instrumental music. When a musician like Beethoven wanted to reach to a wider audience, he had to organize a concert, an enterprise called "Akademie" at the time. He had to rent an opera-house hall, assemble a makeshift orchestra with instrumentalists from all over the city, have the scores copied into parts and, of course, pay for everything. Access to the opera-house halls was therefore essential. The two most important opera theatres in Vienna, the imperial theaters *Burgtheater* and the *Kerthnerthortheater* were in the hands of Baron von Braun, who had bailed their management, between 1794 and 1807. And I have already presented (chapter 6, page 129) Beethoven's long-time frustrating experience with renting a hall from von Braun. It was only in April 1800 that von Braun rented out the opera hall to Beethoven, probably because the latter "bribed" him by dedicating a piece to Braun's wife. Beethoven finally had his first "Akademy," but von Braun turned down two similar requests of Beethoven in 1801 and 1803, while he rented out his opera-houses to mediocre musicians. One cannot help wondering where was Beethoven's aristocratic support group; obviously, it was not as "crucial" as DeNora claims it to have been in Beethoven's career.

Aristocratic help in Beethoven's musical growth

According to DeNora, Beethoven's aristocratic patrons would have also helped him to find his "initial identification of his pianistic identity," by pushing him towards the "high music ideal" opposed to the "light" pianistry of his competitors and by acclaiming his production that complied with that expectation. DeNora builds this argument in the beginning of chapter 6 ("Beethoven in the Salons"), but resumes certain related issues later, without noticing some conflicting positions. She founds her case on the rivalry, resolved in a well-documented contest, between Beethoven and a popular pianist-composer, Joseph Gelinek, known at the time as "the variation-smith" (119). Beethoven's crushing victory would have been just another step in his adherence to the "serious" music as opposed to the "light" genre of his opponent (119-123). DeNora does not discuss what Beethoven's "serious" genre was, but she contrasts it with the genre of variations practiced by Gelinek, which she describes as "relatively easy to play, simple in texture, and idiomatically predictable" (119). However, thirty pages later, she finds Beethoven's numerous variation sets published during those years (a dozen sets between 1793 and 1798) "a lighter, more popular genre" with which he targeted his "musical public at large" (148). She is right in that: Beethoven's early variation sets do not fully illustrate Beethoven's initial pianistic identity, because they were—like Gelinek's—intended for the use of amateur players, not by virtuosos like himself.

Indeed, the published variations were far "tamer" than the ones the virtuosos performed in their contests. The crux of a contest was essentially the improvisational skill displayed in the set of variations on a theme given by the audience. Supplying the theme, usually taken from one of the popular operas of the time, was a way of making sure that the musician did not cheat by presenting as improvised a piece that he had meticulously prepared in advance. Beethoven's improvisations appeared to the audience as "the *non plus ultra* of the art." Highly skilled musicians who listened to him improvising, whether before 1800, like Bohemian musician Johann Wenzel Tomaschek (in 1798), or later, like Ries and Czerny, vouched for that. Tomaschek: "the daring flights in his improvisation stirred me strangely to the depth of my soul"[23]. Ries: "His improvising was the most extraordinary thing that one could ever hear."[24] Czerny: "He knew how to produce such an effect upon every hearer that frequently not an eye remained dry, while many would break out into loud sobs."[25] The very aristocrats who allegedly pushed Beethoven towards "high music" appreciated more his more accessible improvisational style than his published productions. One can understand their opinion: listening to an improvisation is a way of vicariously participating in a creative act, which the printed score cannot provide; the irrepetitiveness of an improvisation also adds to this feeling of participating in uniqueness.

On the other hand, Beethoven did not particularly enjoy the "improvisational pianistry" that his aristocratic salons adored. Maybe it served him to transgress into a different kind of "fantasy" style illustrated first in his C sharp minor Sonata "Quasi una fantasia" Op. 27 No. 2 (now known under the totally inappropriate name of "Moonlight Sonata"), but it did not infuse his work, as it happened with other piano virtuoso-composers, such as Jan Dussek. Beethoven gave a superb demonstration of what his improvisations were in the piano introduction to his *Choral Fantasy* Op. 80, (a kind of adieux to his audience in 1808, when he played for the last time in public,) but that was all. Obviously, Beethoven's "high music" pianistry is illustrated primarily by his piano sonatas, the first piano works that he deemed worthy of opus numbers—which were not stimulated by the kudos his aristocratic supporters granted him for his improvisations.

DeNora is far closer to the facts about Beethoven's indebtedness to his aristocratic friends who offered him the opportunity to master the very demanding string quartet genre (117-118). When Prince Lichnovsky engaged Ignaz Schuppanzigh for his Friday morning concerts in 1794, Beethoven befriended the young violinist and started taking lessons from him. He had had such lessons earlier, first as a child and then as a teenager—enough to approach the violin in a few of his Bonn compositions,[26] but he had never dared to go any further. These new lessons were essential to his embarking on writing for chamber ensembles and, especially, for a quartet of strings. The prince did even more: at the suggestion of Schuppanzigh, he gave Beethoven a present of a set of string quartet instruments,[27] so that the composer could have his music played at home by his music friends and thus improve his mastery of the genre. Do we owe to Lichnovsky Beethoven's set of six *String Quartets* Op. 18? The princely gesture may have speeded up the process, but it is highly probable that, even without the instruments at his disposal, Beethoven would have striven to master the genre, acknowledged as the supreme proof of musical craft, just as Schubert would do twenty years later, without similar help.

DeNora's failed *What If*

The weight that DeNora assigns to the role of the Viennese aristocracy in the development of Beethoven's career and genius leads her to propose an original "What if?" question:

It is interesting to consider what our modern musical evaluative standards would look like if a different composer had been inserted into the supportive frame [Viennese aristocracy] that surrounded Beethoven" (142).

This speculation is a reflection of DeNora's adherence to Postmodernist "relativism": if there are no absolute criteria of value, a caprice of Viennese aristocracy might have propelled a different "genius" (DeNora even proposes one or two), which would have resulted in a completely different picture of the history of music. DeNora stated from the very beginning her motivation: "Because pro-Beethoven culture is so extensive, the experience of his music can be a very rich one" and therefore "we are blinded by visions of how music history could have been otherwise." That is, "we close off from inquiry of how and why some individuals, findings, and enterprises are celebrated over others, why some are perceived as exemplary and others not" (6). She tries to "open" this inquiry in the fourth chapter of her book, misleadingly titled "Beethoven's Social Resources."*

No one has, to my knowledge, given serious thought to such a "what if," probably because common sense ascertains that speculating about what could happen on the road not taken is fruitless. Why wonder if Beethoven would have composed the *Pastoral* inspired by the banks of the Thames instead of the forested hills surrounding Vienna? DeNora aims, however, much higher than that. She doubles the question: what if Beethoven had not settled in Vienna, and another young aspiring musician, now fallen into oblivion, had chosen the city in 1792? Would Beethoven still have become the composer that we know and venerate today? Or would that other musician have filled that bold place in the Canon and thus changed the picture of the history of music? As a good candidate for her speculation, she chooses the Bohemian musician Jan Ladislav Dussek (born in 1760), who had not settled in Vienna but spent his most productive years in London. She claims to prove that

> there were numerous other musicians who, under different circumstances, could have ended up as celebrities." (69)

and that

> It is unlikely that Beethoven in London would have become the prominent figure we know, even with the support of English aristocrats. (71)

DeNora acknowledges that "Beethoven's own contribution to his subsequent recognition as a genius was crucial," but adds that "more than his contemporaries, [he] was well positioned" in Vienna by "his relation to a culturally powerful segment of music sponsors who were becoming increasingly concerned with the idea of *great* music" (82), which would spur him into greatness. Unlike Beethoven, Dussek, who was ten years older, spent his

---

* For whatever reasons, DeNora makes this case soon after she had argued for "Vienna's exceptionalism," without first developing her main argumentation about how instrumental the aristocratic support would have been in shaping Beethoven's genius, which would have (if demonstrated) strongly supported her case.

adventurous life moving all over Europe (with only one longer stable residence in London between 1789 and 1799) and, though he was acknowledged everywhere as a great piano virtuoso, he never made it to the Canon—although music history posits him occasionally as an obscure "progenitor of the romantic 'piano lyric'",[28] from whom even Beethoven might have taken some hints, for instance from Dussek's 1800 *Farewell* piano sonata.

DeNora parallels the careers of the two (62-71, including several summarizing tables), in which almost all that Dussek did could not measure up to Beethoven's successfully positioning himself for building his success. Dussek was born in a small provincial town (Čáslav in Bohemia, now Czechia), which limited his exposure to the world of music. He had only his father as teacher in his early part of his life, which again limited his exposure to the field. He had no ties to a court Capella (as Beethoven had), where he would have gotten exposure to symphonic music or opera. As a boy, he sang in a church choir (Beethoven did not), which left him less time for learning and looking for patrons. Unlike Beethoven, who never left Vienna after he settle there at twenty-two, Dussek crisscrossed Europe (Amsterdam, Hamburg, St. Petersburg, Berlin, Paris) in search of a better position, before settling in London in 1790. Because Dussek's most prolific time was his nine-year long stay in London, DeNora elaborates on it, pointing out further factors acting against his chances. His "patronage worlds" were "diffuse" and less consistent (62), because they were split between the aristocracy consistently interested in "ancient music," and upper middle class (supposedly less so). He did not have at his disposal, as Beethoven had, a privately sponsored string quartet (Count Razumovsky's private quartet headed by Schuppanzich) and an orchestra, therefore his output was essentially for the piano (71).

While some of these assertions are germane, most of them can be easily rejected with counter-examples. Dussek's early disadvantages were not that important. Mozart had only one teacher, his father, as a child; Johann Christian Bach had certainly been a formative influence too, but Dussek also benefitted from the lessons of another Bach (Carl Philip Emanuel).[29] At eleven, Schubert began to sing in the Imperial Chapel Choir and later at the Konvikt in Vienna. (Bach also sung in a choir when he was fifteen.) Dussek's later development does not fit DeNora's case either. Of course, one never knows what exactly would have happened on the road not taken, but we can have a reasonable guess based on the known facts of the road he did take. I have already mentioned (page 184) two of Beethoven's competitors living in Vienna around 1800—Gelinek and Wölffl—to whom similar opportunities offered by the city did not apparently help enough to be "canonized" like him. They simply were not good enough for that. Dussek is a similar case in another environment: he did not benefit from the strong Händel tradition of London's musical life. One more counter-example: Beethoven had for a long time wanted to get an English piano, which he considered the best, but he got his first one, a Broadwood, only in 1818.[30] Dussek had the English pianos at his disposal far earlier (he even worked with Broadwood to improve his design), but it was Beethoven's, not Dussek's music that shaped the future of the instrument. It is obvious that such hindrances as those encountered by Dussek could not prevent a greatly talented young musician to ascend to the Canon. The case that DeNora makes for her "London Beethoven" is not any better. The hindrances that she claims he would have met in London are fabricated. Her quote (from Milligan) that "the English canon was defined in opposition to contemporary music, which was conceived by its advocates as vulgar and decadent" (4) may be true but it does not prove anything: in fact, the many piano pieces published by Beethoven's minor contemporaries settled in London (Clementi, Cramer a.o.) prove that he would have had plenty of opportunities to become the hailed author of sonatas and concertos.

He also had much better opportunities to develop his mastery of the symphony in London than in Vienna. London's public concert life flourished in the second half of the eighteenth century to a higher degree than in any European capital;[31] it reached an acme in the 1790s, when Haydn presented there his last twelve symphonies, and then went into decline because there was no one to follow in his path.[32] Had Beethoven lived in London at the time, his symphonies would have made him a national hero, like Händel before; he would also have been incited into creating more than he did in Vienna, where, as I showed earlier, he could find no hall to hold a concert between 1795 and 1800. In London he would also have been exposed thoroughly to the great Händelian tradition that the city cherished and he might have had a faster and easier transition to his so-called "third style," the way it had stimulated Haydn when commissioning him to compose a great Händelian oratorio, *The Creation* (1797-8), which premiered in London to great acclaim. Therefore, DeNora's emphatic conclusion quoted above, "It is unlikely that Beethoven in London would have become the prominent figure we know, even with the support of English aristocrats" (71) is wrong! Beethoven would have certainly evolved differently, but would have been differently great.

London is not the only other place where Beethoven would have become the great Beethoven. If his talent grew into genius because it was nourished with "high music," as DeNora claims, he could have found this food in abundance in Berlin or Leipzig. Indeed, the re-emergence of Bach and Händel's music towards the end of the eighteenth century was not a Viennese accomplishment. Van Swieten had imported it from Berlin, where he lived for seven years (1770-1777) as the Habsburg Empire ambassador to the Prussian King.[33] It is actually surprising that DeNora misses the fact, because she accepts, later in her book, that such "aspects of a northern German conception of 'serious' music—van Swieten's interest aside—were not yet a pervasive part of aristocratic Viennese musical life" in late 1790s (86-87) and had to be imported. Bach was also "imported" in England, where the composer Samuel Wesley (1766-1837) managed to gather around him a "Bach junto"[34] towards the end of the century and where pianists like J. B. Cramer—a name present in the Beethoven literature, too—would play pieces from *The Well-Tempered Clavier* in "semi-public settings,"[35] that is in salons of the nobility or rich commoners.

DeNora's "What if?" illustrates, as Rosen has noticed, one of the fashionable post-modernist trends, the rehabilitation of the "little guy." It is true that a first-hand Dussek can sound like a third-hand Beethoven sometimes (only Beethoven could have written second-hand Beethoven). The "little guy" is certainly worth a "socio-musicological" approach that Professor DeNora may like to broach sometime—but she did not in her book, therefore this topic is beyond the scope of the present essay.

Contesting the Canon

In the preface of her book, DeNora assures the reader, "I will not address here the issue of which works or composers should be 'in' or 'out' of a musical canon (or whether there should be such a canon); that is a task for cultural critics" (xii). In fact, her argument is all about the Canon criteria, the value of which, as a post-modernist adept of what I termed "absolute relativism," she doubts. On the same page, she reminds us the post-modernist program:

> Even now, artistic standards and canons of taste are being debated in and outside of musical and academic fields and programs for cultural reforms abound [ranging] from suggestions for "reshuffling" personnel within the canon, to suggestions for substitutions [...] to abolishing canonic structures altogether in favor of post-modernist aesthetics and local and community arts.

She utters conforming statements time and again. Quoting approvingly Don Randel (49): "canonic ideology [...] is built in to the analytic strategies that music scholars employ," which results in tautological reasoning. DeNora does not explain the tautology, but it is easy to guess: Beethoven is great because he is in the Canon, which is based on the assumption of Beethoven's greatness. A whole "Excursus [on] approaching the study of reception" in chapter 6 (123-129) argues for the "more fundamental concern with cultural relativity, multiple realities, and the social construction of the object," which "conventional" musicology (the originator of the Canon) has replaced with "an implicit form of naïve positivism within music analysis and criticism" that "postulate[s] categories of analysis as historically transcendent" (125). Resuming her big "what if" approach, DeNora finds that "it is interesting to consider what our modern musical evaluative standards would look like if a different composer had been inserted into the supportive frame that surrounded Beethoven" and offers a second alternative, that of the Irish musician John Field (1782-1837), "whose prophetically Chopinesque nocturnes provided a contemporary alternative to Beethoven's forceful approach" (142). Quoting some initial negative reviews of Beethoven's music, based on criteria established by the older musical tradition, she notes that "If these criteria had not been subsequently exchanged for other, more flattering ones, it seems fair to say that Beethoven's place in music history might have been quite different—less prominent or, at the very least, more equivocal than it became" (181). In her final say, a subchapter titled "Beethoven, the construction of genius and the relativity of value," DeNora concludes: "To ask, Who is a genius? Or What factors 'cause' or inculcate genius? is to travel the topic with too much a priori baggage" (190). She stops short of proposing adopting *a posteriori* post-modernist baggage, at least.

I concede that some of DeNora's previously presented arguments—perhaps most, if not all, of them—raise legitimate questions. It is her answers that I objection to, because of two main flaws of her argument. The first flaw consists in not realizing that, although Beethoven achieved world-wide recognition[*] during his life-time, he was actually "canonized" only after his death, through an "international project" in which London and Paris and several important German cities like Berlin and Leipzig (cities that had, as I showed earlier, a much more developed concert life than Vienna) played the crucial role, while Vienna seems to have almost forgotten Beethoven. In his 1840 biography of the composer, Schindler wrote: "A foreign visitor might find it strange not to find any opportunity in Vienna to hear a Beethoven sonata."[36] And in the second version, printed twenty years later, he commented, "had it not been for Frau von Ertmann, Beethoven's piano music would have disappeared even sooner from the repertoire in Vienna," which was at the time embracing "the emerging new direction in compositions and piano playing introduced by Hummel and his disciples."[37] This seems really strange when knowing that the piano music had been the crux of the aristocracy's involvement that would have, according to DeNora, contributed "crucially" to Beethoven's success and even to the development of his genius. In fact, Beethoven's piano music all but vanished for decades from the European musical stage: from Paris, which had become the intellectual capital of the world; from England, with London a thriving music hub; and from all German-speaking countries, too, notably in Leipzig, Berlin and Dresden, cities with long musical traditions. Beethoven was quickly "canonized" by the first Romanticist generation, but based essentially on his symphonies, which were dominating the public concert stage. His other music, including even his piano concertos, fell into oblivion. (I will revisit this process, with details, in chapter 13, in which I deal with another DeNora theory, in which Beethoven's piano music is a pivotal element.)

All things considered, then, it is hard to see how the support of the Viennese aristocracy around 1800 would have played any significant role in this evolving Canon process per se, especially since Vienna had lost its title of "capital of the music" after 1830. As a compensation, it gained another title with the raise of another name to prominence—that of Johann Strauss, the "Waltz King." With him, the "light" genre triumphed over the "high," as the passion of all social classes.

Furthermore, DeNora fails to consider the implication of three elementary facts, although she acknowledges them: 1) the Viennese aristocrats promoted Beethoven based on their aesthetic criteria (the so-called "serious music") that they set about 1780-1790; 2) Beethoven's immediate posterity inducted him in the canon based on its 1830-1850 version of the "canonic criteria"; 3) modern musicology still holds Beethoven in great esteem, based on its own twenty-first-century "canonic criteria." The inference is immediate: these three sets of criteria must agree at least in their fundamentals. It seems, therefore, that the post-modernist "relativity" is not absolute, it is only relatively relative!

---

[*] Of course, by "world" I mean the Western world, which extended from Europe (including Russia) to the North American East Coast, where Boston's *Handel and Haydn Society* wanted to commission an oratorio from Beethoven (Thayer-Forbes, p. 834).

Summing up

The foregoing analysis, investigating in detail all the facts and arguments presented in Tia DeNora's book, confirms the globally assessed verdict issued by Broyles and Rosen: the book fails to prove DeNora's main thesis. Beethoven's genius did not owe anything essential to the "political" mechanisms or the circumstantial "unfair advantage" hypothesized by DeNora. Vienna was indeed an auspicious place for a young aspiring musician to start his career, but other great cities had their own advantages that would have suited him better in other important regards. The Viennese aristocracy was indeed very supportive of Beethoven, but the "political motivation" that DeNora assigns to it is a speculation not supported by facts. The aristocracy's endorsement within their private salons certainly stimulated Beethoven's creativity, but it was far less "crucial" in promoting his public career. It also did not help him define his pianistry, which clearly diverged from the improvisational style that the salons adored. The alleged "marketing campaign" involving Haydn is a speculation refuted by his consistent refusal to acknowledge Beethoven as his successor when the latter started opening new musical avenues. The "what if" argument claiming that another musician could have succeeded equally in Vienna, while Beethoven would have failed in another city (such as London), is another speculation rebutted by the known facts.

All is not misconstrued in DeNora's book: many of the facts and details are true, but they have been known since Schidler's biography of Beethoven, without engendering similar speculations. DeNora also revealed a few new and interesting details of Viennese life two hundred years ago, but they are not relevant to her theory. All in all, hers is a failed attempt at innovative socio-musicology.

9
Beethoven's alleged plagiarisms

Plagiarism had not been a major issue in the history of music until quite recently. Therefore, the well-known conductor John Eliot Gardiner raised quite a "stir" in the spring of 1996, when he claimed on British TV and radio that Beethoven would have "borrowed" music from some now-forgotten composers of the French Revolution and made impressive use of it in some of his most important works. The last movement of Beethoven's *Sixth* would have "borrowed from a 'Hymn to Agriculture,' written by the French composer Jean Lefebvre." Even the famous four notes that open his *Fifth*, the most famous motive in classical music, would have been "a straight lift from [Rouget] de Lisle's *Dithirambique* [hymn of the Revolution]."* Gardiner was, however, careful to mitigate his claim, stating that, "It is not plagiarism. It is the debt genius pays to the second rate. He transformed ordinary lines of music into what was sublime."[1]

Not quite!—replied Gardiner's colleague Barry Cooper, a distinguished British scholar and author of a reconstruction of Beethoven's mythical *Tenth Symphony*. He investigated further the alleged *Pastoral Symphony* "borrowing" and wrote in a letter to the editor of *The Beethoven Journal* that "every single note [in the introduction to Lefèvre's hymn] can be found in the finale of the symphony," concluding emphatically, "Could anyone find a more blatant piece of plagiarism?"[2] Dr. Cooper's obvious satisfaction of having caught Beethoven "in the act" points to another kind of post-modernist "politics": Beethoven was the "big guy" robbing the "little one."

The Pastoral "stir"

The "borrowing" in the *Pastoral Symphony* was not a novel idea in 1996. It had been known for at least eight years: in the booklet accompanying a Nimbus CD containing Lefèvre's *Hymn to Agriculture*, released in 1989, John Humphries wondered whether "Beethoven had heard Lefèvre's introduction [to his hymn] by the time he wrote the finale of the *Pastoral* symphony," but stopped short from uttering the word "plagiarism."[3] This was not a first-time find, either. Schauffler had tackled the issue of other examples of Beethoven "borrowing," including the famous four-note motive opening the *Fifth Symphony*, as early as 1937.[4] Arnold Schmitz had drawn attention as early as 1927 on the similarity of the famous four-note motive of the *Fifth* with a phrase in Cherubini's *Hymne au Panthéon*, dating from 1797.[5] In fact, the influence of French Revolutionary music on

---

* Gardiner developed later his views in the TV movie "The Secret of Beethoven's Fifth Symphony," illustrated with a beautiful performance of the music on period instruments.

Beethoven had also been acknowledged almost a hundred years ago, but nobody had seen anything unethical in his being influenced by other artists.

Plagiarism is an issue of the modern world, wary of the protection of intellectually property under the mixed blessing of technology, which allows mass-distribution of art. What we call plagiarism now was not objectionable in older generations, when the purely aesthetic point of view prevailed. Even we moderns did not "cry foul" when discovering that Shakespeare ennobled the mediocre utterances of some of his contemporaries, by chiseling them out and incorporating them into his new plays. Moreover, in music, the kind of "plagiarism" that Cooper envisages, by "every single note," was inevitable—at least in its Western tonal variant, since the diatonic scale includes only seven notes, therefore the number of combinations they can engender, even when expanded to incorporate rhythmic formulae, is very limited. Short sequences of notes, later called "motives" or "cells," seem to have been a kind of "common property" of the musical establishment since the beginning of this art. The most extreme such case was recorded over five hundred years ago, when Guillaume Dufay (1397?-1474), at the very beginnings of the Renaissance period, noted down the Burgundian song "L'homme armé" (The Man in Arms), a secular tune, very likely folk song, that became a "great hit" for half a century, inaugurating a tradition of the *L'homme armé Mass*: during the next two centuries, from Dufay to Carissimi (1605-1674), some thirty masses were composed employing its theme as *cantus firmus*, with an echo on the threshold of the next millennium, in *L'homme armé—A Mass for Peace* (1999) by Karl Jenkins (b. 1944).[6]

Plagiarism is first mentioned as a significant issue in music in the first half of the seventeenth century, when now-forgotten musicians living in England frequently complained that Händel would have stolen their melodies to make (better) use of them.[7] There was only one recorded case of what we could call "real" plagiarism, with detrimental consequences for its author: Giovanni Bononcini, one of Händel's contemporaries and rival, dared to present another musician's piece as his own and was so disgraced that he had to flee England in 1731.[8] As for Händel, he went on to do his "transformative imitations"[9] of other composer's tunes and so did everybody else, even after copyright laws were legislated all over Western Europe.[*] Mozart did it too, for instance when borrowing a theme from a now-forgotten quartet of Boccherini to develop one of his masterpieces, the Fugue in C minor for two pianos (K. 426).

Turning back to the case of the *Pastoral Symphony* that Cooper investigated, I can only agree with him that every single note of Lefèvre can be found in Beethoven's symphony, but that does not prove anything in and of itself, simply because both pieces share the same key, F major and, obviously, the same seven notes of its diatonic scale. I could locate an 1899 collection of music of the French Revolution in piano transcription,[10] which shows some slight differences from the score that Cooper disclosed. The images below show both, together

---

[*] Copyrights for books had been introduced in England in 1710. Laws were later introduced to protect printed music, but those protecting the intellectual property of the "inventors" of music arrived only at the end of the nineteenth century.

with the theme in the *Pastoral Symphony* as it is enounced first by the clarinet and then reassessed by the first violins:

The similarity is undeniable but there are also meaningful differences, notably Lefèvre's rococo ornamentation (bars 3-4), which is missing in Cooper's example. The differences are more obvious when listening to the music: Lefèvre's (on the mentioned Nimbus CD) is a naïve attempt to create a pastoral atmosphere by overdressing the short motif with that typical rococo ornament meant to imitate birdsong. (Ironically, the musician of the Revolution was unable to break with the fashion of the aristocratic salons!) His music is no more pastoral than Boucher's princesses dressed up in shepherdess' clothes were shepherdesses. What Beethoven did with the same notes is very different! If he really "borrowed" it, he did so because he must have realized the immense potential lying in that simple musical kernel, the potential of which the lesser musician had been completely unaware—or at least, unable to realize. The genius cleaned the superfluous from Lefèvre's mediocre utterance, and revealed the pure, noble melodic line, an archetypal melody of nature—a "plagiarism" for which we owe him our deepest gratitude.

Beethoven's stealing from the big guy

In fact, Beethoven robbed the big guy, too—and this was no less than Mozart! This "theft" also has been known for a long time. Gustav Nottebohm, one of the prominent nineteenth-century Beethovenians, revealed the first such borrowings in 1887: Beethoven's introductory phrase to the Scherzo of his *Fifth Symphony* is strikingly similar to the opening of the final movement of Mozart's famous *G minor Symphony No. 40,* K. 550.

Nottebohm showed that this "borrowing" must have been intentional: he discovered the 29 bars of Mozart's finale transcribed by Beethoven in a sketchbook containing also work for his *Fifth*.[11]

The similarity is, however, deceptive, because the two musicians used this phrase to build very different musical expressions. Mozart made it into the first half of the frantic theme of his finale. Beethoven changed the meter to ¾ and assigned it to the *basse* to build the mysterious nebulous portal to the resounding emergence of the famous Fate motive in the horns. It would be hard to find a better illustration of the saying, "notes alone don't make the music."

Mozart. Symphony No. 40, Finale

Beethoven. Symphony No. 5, 3rd movement

A second, and much better known, borrowing, was revealed by George Grove in his classic 1896 book on Beethoven symphonies: the main theme of the first movement of the *Eroica* would reproduce the beginning of the overture to Mozart's operetta *Bastien und Bastienne*.[12]

Did Beethoven really copy Mozart's theme? *Bastien und Bastienne* was a very simple, one-act *singspiel*,[13] and was only a short-lived fad in Vienna in 1768 as the work of a twelve year old. Robbin-Landon's *Mozart Compendium* credits it with being the most performed of the composer's early operas during his lifetime,[14] but does not list any performances. According to other sources, it was never performed again until 1790 in Berlin[15]—Thayer's *Life of Beethoven* does not mention it among the list of operas given in Bonn when young Beethoven was living there.[16] It is therefore unlikely that Beethoven's usage of this theme was a "borrowing." Discussing the issue in his landmark 1929 book *Beethoven the Creator*, Romain Rolland claims the borrowing to be from a symphony, also in E flat major, by one of the Stamitz family musicians—most likely Johann

(1717- 1757).[17] In fact, the resemblance between Mozart's and Beethoven's phrases is, like in the previous case, deceiving. Mozart's is embellished, like Lefèvre's, with a rococo flourish at the end—just a pleasant way into the next elaboration. Beethoven keeps only its essential core, the beginning notes, as a powerful motive, in which the rococo embroidery is replaced by the simplest trick (which is also a stroke of genius): the final descent, which makes this almost banal musical cell the hero of one of the most powerful dramas in music.

Wilibald Nagel (1863-1929), author of 1905's *Beethoven and his Piano Sonatas* (in German) signaled a third Beethoven borrowing from Mozart: the finale of his D minor Piano Sonata Op. 31 No. 2 is built from the notes of one of the secondary themes of the first movement of Mozart's Symphony No. 38.[18] Unlike Lefèvre's piece, Mozart's symphony was a well-established piece of the musical canon by 1800, when Beethoven wrote his sonata; therefore this borrowing might well have been intentional. But an artist like Beethoven would not simply quote Mozart. He "borrows" only the cell , changing the meter from $^4/_4$ to $^3/_8$ and the key from major to minor, transforming the expression altogether and making a soulful secondary theme into the engine of an airy, yet not always clear-sky, finale:

The Internet does its bit

The plagiarism issue has been raised to a new level in the age of the Internet, with so many music lovers listening to forgotten pieces of classical music and triggering debates in forums and chat rooms, far beyond what professional musicologists had done before. To their credit, I must say that, even though they love to signal resemblances, the amateurs more easily accept this as a non-issue, at least with Beethoven, thus showing more commonsense than some specialists that love to cry wolf.

Although Mozart (as a would-be plagiarist) seems to be the primary target of Internet-based music buffs, Beethoven does not escape their attention. His case seems the most interesting because it involves no less than his *Ode to Joy*, which was found to be strikingly similar to a motive in Mozart's *Misericordias Domini* (K 222), a short piece of sacred music that entered the repertoire just a few years ago and is easily available on YouTube. Mozart's piece is a beautiful exercise in counterpoint, which he composed after he had learned the craft from his teachers, probably from Padre Martini in Italy, during his teenage years (before he discovered Bach's and Händel's music). The resemblance of the beginning of the second section of K. 222 with the beginning of the *Ode to Joy* is obvious, even though Mozart deals in quavers and Beethoven in quarters:

The would-be plagiarism involves the initial one-bar cell in Mozart's K. 222, which is so common that it must appear in hundreds (if not thousands) of music pieces. The two masters use it for very different purposes: Mozart builds a short, four-bar orchestral introduction to a beautiful Fugue, based on a different theme; Beethoven melts the cell repetition with its mirror variant into a seamless flow to get what we know so well, probably the most fluid intonation of human voices.

Did Beethoven really take inspiration from Mozart? K. 222 was published only in 1880,[19] but sacred music circulated primarily as manuscripts and parts at the time, not as printed scores;[20] Beethoven could have heard it at a church service and even seen the parts sometime during his youth. It would have had to have happened before 1795 to qualify as an intentional borrowing, because Beethoven's "Ode to Joy" theme is already present full-fledged in his song *Gegenliebe* (Requited love), WoO 118, dated in 1794/5:

This theme had indeed preoccupied Beethoven for a long time, because he also used it one more time before his *Ninth*, to build his *C minor Choral Fantasy* Op. 80. The discovery by simple amateurs of this borrowing that no scholar had signaled before is an opportunity for reflection. Obviously, it was triggered by listening to music, not by reading it; it also involves only the opening "cell" of the musical phrase and not the whole phrase. In fact, the same can be said about all the cases here discussed: one part of the phrase that is closely similar is sufficient to create a general feeling of "sameness." This is because of the role that "anticipation" plays in the perception of music: the beginning of a memorized phrase induces immediately the remaining of it in the brain center responsible with the processing of music.[21] And anticipation is based on what neuroscience has revealed about the mechanism of memorization as the essential tools of the growth of the individual human brain—the role of the "attractors." The attractor is the constellation of neurons that corresponds to the memorization of anything, beginning with the first moment of life: the word "mama" or the face of the mother stimulates the creation of neural connections, thus creating the corresponding "attractor" that the brain will further recognize; the perception of only the beginning of the attractor triggers the entire memorized concept.[22] The role of attractors has been particularly studied in language acquisition and much less so in the perception of music, but it seems reasonable to assume that it must be similar for the latter, too. Listening to Beethoven's "Ode to Joy" easily creates an attractor; when, at some later point, the brain recognizes the beginning of this attractor in Mozart's K. 222, the feeling of sameness becomes overwhelming, although the two musical elaborations differ substantially.

All of Beethoven's so-called plagiarisms, whether intended or involuntary borrowings, are examples of his capability of making much better use of the potential hidden in the originals. We should expect that both scholars and Internet aficionados will go on looking for more such cases and we should be prepared to evaluate them under the same assumption.

Postscript: The case of the most famous motive

There is little doubt that the four-note motive that opens Beethoven's *Fifth* is the most widely known motive of classical music and, arguably, of every kind of music. Did Beethoven indeed borrow it, too, from a French or any other source? I answer the question in my essay "A Short Historytory of the Most Famous Motive of Classical Music" (available on my website *BeethovenOurContemporary*), showing that the question is irrelevant, because this four-note cell is the most widely used motive in classical music, albeit in less conspicuous manner than in the *Fifth*. I also track its usage back to the beginning of Renaissance and also forward up to the middle of the Twentieth Century.

PART IV
LATTER-DAY FEMINISM vs. BEETHOVEN

Feminism has become a main—arguably "the" main—political movement of the last few decades and has pervaded all areas of life, at least in the Western World. I have no misgivings about what I would call "real" feminism—on the contrary. I have been well aware since early adolescence that, for most of the existence of the human race, women have suffered oppression—in some cases, almost slave-like oppression—in patriarchal societies, and that their long-overdue emancipation began in earnest only some sixty years ago and only in a very limited area of the world. I know that women had been obstructed, that is practically barred, from practicing some professions, including certain fields of music, like composing or conducting. Therefore, I believe feminism is more than legitimate—it is an absolutely necessary movement for human civilization to advance.

This being said, I cannot help feeling uneasy—I might even say, worried—about the evolution of feminism in the postmodernist era, when it has at times turned into indiscriminate male bashing spurred by a feeling of revenge blind to the non-gendered logic that two wrongs cannot make a right. As one of the most iconic names in the cultural consciousness of the Western world, Beethoven has become one of the most—possibly *the* most—besieged individual male figure. Obviously, all feminist scholars have not joined in this siege. Many of them have continued to dedicate themselves to the old scholarly mission, looking for evidence, and found plenty to justify their claim that women artists, including musicians, have brought their valuable contribution to the creative corpus of humankind, without debasing male contributions. The best example is, probably, that of Professor Alessandra Comini, who has worked assiduously to promote the female painters, writers and performers of the remote past, but does not display any hostility toward Beethoven in her remarkable book centered on the birth and early growth of the Beethoven myth.[*]

Beethoven as the target of the so-called "new musicology" is the topic of the last part of this book. Like previous parts, it focuses on facts—the objective, undeniable facts that expose the fallacious scholarly apparatus underpinning the crucial defining moments of the prosecution of Beethoven as the prototypic representative of "toxic masculinity" in music. It begins with the multi-layered theory of Professor Susan McClary, which opened with an indictment of Beethoven the musical "rapist" and grew into a "sacred war" on classical music as we know it. It then follows the further elaborations of some colleagues of McClary who took up the relay of Beethoven's allegedly toxic masculinity. We will end up, perhaps unexpectedly but convergently, in the Hollywood movie industry.

In the process, Comini also brings in evidence on how the nineteenth-century feminism perceived Beethoven—as a soulmate, not an oppressor—making one wonder what happened to feminism in the meantime.

---

[*] Alexandra Comini, *The Changing Image of Beethoven. A study in Mythmaking* (Rizzoli, New York, 1987). For her feminist endeavors see her book *In Passionate Pursuit* (Braziller Publisher, New York, 2004), p. 157ff.

10
Susan McClary's Jihad
against Beethoven and Classical Music

In January 1987, Susan McClary, then a little known musicology professor at the University of Minnesota, burst suddenly to fame in her professional world and even beyond, by stating in a paper presented at the *Minnesota Composers Forum*, further made public in the forum's *Newsletter*:

> The point of recapitulation in the first movement of [Beethoven's] Ninth is one of the most horrifying moments in music, as the carefully prepared cadence is frustrated, damming up energy which finally explodes in the throttling murderous rage of a rapist incapable of attaining release.[1]

This point-blank statement elicited a wave of indignation among her peers, who had been (musically) raised as firm believers in the almost God-like quality of Beethoven and had to cope with a startling new situation—a newly-born Beethoven detractor. The outcry—still accessible thirty years later, by googling the issue—was as diverse as McClary's statement was equable, ranging from the purist Schenkerian analysis to concerns that her metaphoric descriptions were trivializing the horrific experience of actual rape victims. However, all critics—both laudatory and critical—could not fail to recognize Susan McClary's statement as part of the rising discipline of "feminist studies," of which she was to emerge as one of the prominent leaders. With her academic career thus propelled, McClary expanded her Beethoven's *Ninth* thesis in her *Feminine Endings* book[2] to build a theory indicting (Western) classical music as the emanation of oppressive patriarchal civilization and an expression of sexual violence against women.

McClary's views have, in time, become part not only of the feminist norm but also of mainstream scholarship. In spite of some critical standpoints coming from other feminist researchers, she has risen to a position of scholarly authority, so that it is enough to write nowadays "as McClary has shown ..." in support of some other bizarre idea in order to prove its validity.[3] This is unsettling. Granted, such extreme feminism will not kill classical music—Schönberg & Co. have taken care of that—but it may kill even the memory of it as a musical Paradise (irretrievably?) Lost.

As I said, I have no misgivings about feminism and I think that, since men and women differ in many ways, there must be a specific "feminine voice" both in music and in music criticism. Reading through Susan McClary's work and views, I could not help but agree with her many times. It is hard to deny that "most people have music in the center of their lives,"[4] when one sees generation after generation of young and old wearing their headphones 24/7 (or almost). I could "feel" McClary's aggravation when complaining that established formalist musicology "has prohibited the asking of even the most fundamental questions concerning meaning [of music]" (FE 4).* Nevertheless, while she is so good at asking daring, legitimate questions, her answers appear to me almost always in the wrong. In fact, they seem a typical example of the postmodern evolution of feminism into indiscriminate male bashing.

Neither the laudatory nor the negative reviews of McClary's work have explored *how* she builds up her arguments. She is an adept of the latter-day vision of post-structuralism and deconstruction, which stem from the same root as their theoretical foe, Marxism, namely social determinism. I do not dispute this approach, but the manner in which she makes use of it when invoking what she calls "the socio-historical context," as the cornerstone of her theories. The present "deconstruction" of her own deconstructive approach touches only marginally on musical aspects—and never beyond a 101 college course in Appreciation of Music—but delves deep into her "socio-historical" reasoning, exposing very serious flaws and infringements on the ethics of scholarly work, which vitiate all the basic tenets of her criticism of the Western classical music.

Taking issue with Beethoven's *Ninth*: a case of wishful thinking

When she included her original article, "Getting Down off the Beanstalk," in her *Feminine Endings* book a few years later (1991), Susan McClary slightly toned down her already-quoted indictment of the first movement of Beethoven's *Ninth* (*FE* 128), calling the episode only "one of the most horrifyingly violent episodes in the history of music." She goes on to write that "this explosive rage fuels most of the remainder of the symphony." The *Adagio* is spared as "the image of a world in which pleasure is attainable without thrusting desire, where tenderness and vulnerability are virtues rather than fatal flaws," (*FE* 128) but "the 'triumphal' end of the symphony is likewise problematic [... because] "Beethoven simply forces closure by bludgeoning the cadence and the piece to death" (*FE* 129). And the diatribe continues, engulfing almost all of the nineteenth century music, which "turns violent [...] *more often and more devastatingly* [...] *than in heavy metal*" (*FE* 130; repeated at 199, n. 23; my italics).

The absurdity of the latter statement is obvious, but even the obvious needs demonstration sometimes. While various studies of physically quantifiable loudness—the equivalence of sound violence—give slightly different levels for the musical and non-musical kinds of sounds, in all of them, the typical rock concert is three to four times louder than the symphony orchestra at its loudest. Powell gives the levels of 80 decibels for the symphony orchestra at its loudest and 100 db for the typical Rock concert; Levitin's figures are 100-105 and 120, respectively.[5] And heavy metal is not the quietest of the rock styles, on the contrary: the metal band Manowar has claimed the title of "loudest band in the world," citing a measurement of 129.5 dB in 1994 in Hanover.[6] There is also more than loudness to the difference between musical genres: research has shown

---

* All references to McClary's *Feminine Endings* book in this chapter are included in the text as (*FE* page).

that even at the same level of loudness, heavy metal levies a much higher "physiological cost of the hearing" than classical music.[7] McClary's statement (for which she also invokes the "testimony" of her students), that the music of Beethoven and other nineteenth century musicians is often more violent than heavy metal, is just wishful thinking proffered as argument. She has every right to dislike Beethoven's music, but accusing it of proliferating "sexual violence" that dwarfs even heavy metal simply defies reason.

We come across another example of wishful thinking in Susan McClary's scholarly output in her article "Construction of Subjectivity in Schubert's Music," in which she contrasts Beethoven's *Eroica* with Schubert's music.[8] She claims that in the first movement of the symphony "the subjective force of the principal theme hammers away [...]. Any distraction from its agenda—especially the tender motives that keep cropping up during the exposition—must be resisted or annexed [...]." Meredith has already pointed out the shallowness of this account, showing that the main theme itself is far from a monolithic outburst and the movement displays a large variety of dispositions.[9]

Waveform display of the first movement of the *Eroica* symphony (on *Audacity* software)

I add here an objective measure to his analysis, based on the waveform display (see figure) of an actual recording of the movement (Karajan's classic 1963 version on Deutsche Grammophon, 429036). The total duration of loud *forte-fortissimo* passages is less than half of the movement's length (400 seconds of 14 min, 41 sec). Only wishful thinking may push someone to portray such a musical construct as "hammering away."

Ignoring facts or twisting them to her advantage is actually characteristic of McClary's entire argument. One encounters many such examples throughout her articles and books. Here follow a few examples of such transgressions, when she tries to persuade the reader that the condition of women worsened in seventeenth century Italy, the country that can claim to be the birth-place of classical music. Among the alleged discriminations against women, she mentions that "[this was] a time when some thought that castrati enacted women better than women themselves" (*FE* 50) and supports her claim in a note saying that the female characters at the first performance of Monteverdi's *Orfeo* were played by castrati (*FE* 181, note 31). She even enlarges the argument in the note, asking that the use of castrati be re-evaluated—presumably as another way of discriminating against women. The use of castrati to sing female roles in *Orfeo* in fact went against the historical trend that McClary chose to ignore; it is a well-established fact that the castrati were primarily employed for the male parts and, by 1680, they had basically "supplanted 'normal' male voices in lead roles."[10] Quite characteristically, at the 1642 premiere of Monteverdi's *Incoronazione di Poppea*, an opera to which McClary dedicates many pages (*FE* 35-52), all the female parts were sung by women and all the male parts by castrati.[11]

Professor McClary also decries a 1686 papal edict forbidding women to receive any training in music, but fails to acknowledge the next sentence in her source, "How effective these papal edicts may have been we do not know. It seems unlikely that they could have effectively stemmed *the tide* of girls and women studying music ..."[12] (my italics). Indeed, in spite of the Vatican interdiction, Naples had a "conservatorio" for girls (*Scuola dell'Annunziata*)[13] and the monastery *Ospedalle della Pieta* in Venice supported a school for the musical education of the girls, where Vivaldi would teach after 1700 and whose orchestra was famous all over Europe for their performances and greatly contributed to Venice's reputation as the "Republic of Music" in the seventeenth century. Plenty of instrumentalists graduated from this school, some of whom also taught music, and at least two of whom became respected composers—Anna Bon (ca.1739-?) and Vincenta da Ponte (active in the second half of the eighteenth century).[14]

In reality, Renaissance ideas were gaining ground and generating fertile debates among the educated classes and the intellectuals during the seventeenth century. This was a time of important scientific discoveries, of which women were a major beneficiary. The seventeenth century scientists who investigated the reproductive functions of humans and other species exposed as "insulting" the view of woman as an "incomplete male" that the Church and patriarchal authorities had adopted from ancient Greek philosopher Aristotle and had used to justify the second-class citizen status they had imposed on their wives and daughters for hundreds of years. As de Graaf, one of these scientists, wrote, "Nature had her mind on the job when generating the female as well as when generating the male, for without females there would be no generation of any animal. And indeed being female is a kind of perfection of individual form."[15]

Such views spread throughout the educated classes all over Europe and generated a momentum for social change. The Italian aristocracy and the well-to-do middle class started giving their daughters private education similar, in many regards, to that of their sons, including in music. One of them, a certain Cornaro from Venice, had such a talented daughter that the University of Padua accepted her as a student and later granted her a doctorate in mathematics— Elena Lucrezia Cornaro Piscopia was the first woman ever to get a PhD, in 1678.[16] She and twenty-four other women were accepted as "honorary members" into the Paduan *Accademia dei Ricovrati* (funded in 1599), which was also promoting education for girls.[17]

The poor were not forgotten either. Comenius (1592-1670), a theologian and teacher, now considered the father of modern education, advocated universal education for both sexes.[18] That was an ideal far too advanced for the time, but the first steps towards this goal occurred in Italy, through the dedication of Rose Venerini (1656–1728), the daughter of a physician, the initiator of public education for girls, who—with the support of the ecclesiastical authorities!—founded over 40 schools for the girls of the poor.* Women also began to be accepted into professions that had been typically "male." Artemisia Gentileschi (1593-1656) was respected by her fellow male painters as an equal; Giovanna Garzoni (1600-1670) was another painter who enjoyed success during her life. It comes as no surprise that feminist scholar Sarah Gwyneth Ross placed at this moment of history the birth of feminism in her eponymous book.[19]

McClary, however, ignored all such facts and selected only the few ones that suited her theories and, when they did not, she twisted them to her purpose. We will meet again this un-scholarly approach when tackling her views on every important moment in the history of classical music, be it the birth of tonality or its death. This will also reveal another cherished technique of hers: quoting scholarly authorities in support of her theories, without checking the truthfulness of their statements or simply distorting them to her purpose. McClary's first purpose was to indict classical music with one of the three modern capital sins—sexism. Beethoven, the musical rapist, was only a first step.

The sexist Sonata form: The "demonstration" that never was

Professor McClary's second critical rocket booster takes on the musical structure that Beethoven developed to perfection, the sonata form. According to the feminist scholar, this form is based on the male-subjugate-female pattern of patriarchal societies. This quintessential form of the classical period, which carries the initial *Allegro* movement of a symphony or sonata, is a (musical) "narrative" about two contrasting themes: the principal dynamic one in the main key of the piece and a secondary, usually a contemplative one, in a different key. When, after the development of this material, the recapitulation wraps up the musical discourse, the secondary theme is resumed not in its original key, but in that of the primary theme. Since the two themes have long been described as "masculine" and "feminine," respectively, McClary claims that the re-shaping of the latter into the key of the former during the recapitulation is in fact its "subjugation."

You may have guessed who the vilest musical sexual predator is. "Many of Beethoven's symphonies," McClary writes, sending us again to listen to the *Eroica*, "exhibit considerable anxiety with respect to feminine moments and respond to them with extraordinary violence" (FE 69). It is worth mentioning in this regard that the female contemporaries of Beethoven did not share McClary reaction to his music; the most pianistically gifted among them were not only happy to play his music, they were his best interpreters, as he himself testified. He was so enthralled by Marie Bigot's performances that he ran to her to have her sight-read the manuscript of his *Appassionata* though he had barely finished, and which he gave her after publishing the sonata.[20] Baroness Dorothea Ertmann was his "Dorothea-Caecilia," the saint patroness of music; when retiring as a virtuoso, "in the more private concerts he had already long given place to the Baroness."[21] Later, he wrote Marie Pachler-Kotschak "I have never yet found

---

* Rose Venerini was canonized by Pope Benedict XVI in 2006.

anybody who plays my compositions as well as you do [...] You are the true guardian of my intellectual offspring."²² Obviously, these women had a perfect communion with Beethoven's music.

And this was not a singular case—that of his interpreters: women felt such deep affinity with his music all throughout the nineteenth century. One of them even dared to write him in her imagination, because he was dead at the time, addressing him with the unusual "thee" that one reserved for the divine or the closest "significant one" at the time. She entered in her journal, presumably after having had the opportunity to listen to some of his music:

> To Beethoven, November 25, 1843
>
> My only friend,
>
> How shall I thank thee for again tonight breaking the chains of my sorrowful slumber. I did not expect it. For months now I have been in a low state of existence [...] But thou, oh, blessed master! Dost answer all my questions, and make it my privilege to be. Like a humble wife to the sage or the poet, it is my triumph that I can understand, can receive thee wholly, like a mistress I arm thee for the fight, like a young daughter, I tenderly bind thy wounds. Thou art to me beyond compare, for thou art all I want ... Beethoven, my heart beats. I live again, for I feel that I am worthy audience for thee ... Thy touch made me again all human. O save and give me to myself and thee.²³

The author of this passionate declaration of intellectual love was the first important American feminist, Margaret Fuller (1810-1850), an abolitionist and militant for women's rights. What happened to feminism in a hundred fifty years? How could McClary ignore this simple truth: our perception of Beethoven's music might be biased towards his "masculine" fight with his unforgiving Fate, but his creative mind also included a strong "feminine" side? This is how his contemporaries perceived him, as the poet Grillparzer summed it up in his funeral oration of Beethoven: "From the cooing of doves to the rolling of thunder [...] he had traversed and grasped it all."²⁴

McClary's argument runs into another strong objection, besides musical sensitivity or lack of it: the gendered description of the two themes of the sonata form was introduced at the middle of the nineteenth century (*FE* 13), a hundred years *after* the form itself was designed by early classical age musicians and long after it was brought to perfection by Haydn, Mozart and Beethoven. There is no evidence that any of them ever thought of the themes they invented in terms of masculine or feminine, let alone understood their musical dialectics in terms of "subjugation." McClary rejects this objection (*FE* 14), claiming that the "subjugation paradigm" was there intentionally from the very beginning, because the sonata form was twice modeled upon the eighteen century opera: first, it emulated the expression of the themes substantiating the male and female operatic characters (she parallels the "sighs" in the soprano arias and the themes in the instrumental music); and second, the sonata form borrowed the typical opera narrative, in which the hero, always a male, encounters and conquers obstacles in order to achieve his manhood. And here follows McClary's demonstration of her claim (*FE* 13):

> Drawing on the structuralist work of the soviet narratologists Vladimir Propp and Yurij Lotman, Teresa De Lauretis has <u>demonstrated</u> with respect to traditional Western narrative that:
>
> > The hero must be male, regardless of the gender of the text-image, because the obstacle, whatever its personification, is morphologically female [...]
>
> Furthermore, as De Lauretis and other narratologists have <u>demonstrated</u>, regardless of the manifest content of particular stories, these two functions interact in accordance with a schema already established in advance—*the masculine protagonist makes contact with but must eventually subjugate (domesticate or purge) the designated [feminine] Other* in order for identity to be consolidated, for the sake of satisfactory narrative closure.
>
> The narrative schema is played out quite explicitly in opera. But it is no less crucial to the formal conventions of "absolute" music [...] In sonata [form], the principal key/theme clearly occupies the narrative position of masculine protagonist [...] while the less dynamic second key/theme [...] serves the narrative function of the feminine Other. Moreover, satisfactory resolution—the ending always generically guaranteed in advance by tonality and sonata procedure—demands the containment of whatever is semiotically or structurally marked as "feminine," whether a second theme or simply a non-tonic area. (McClary's italics and my underlining)

The italicized section is the crux of McClary's argument and its importance goes beyond the sonata form; even beyond music, for that matter: according to her, Teresa De Lauretis has demonstrated that in the "typical" Western narrative the hero is always a male and the obstacles in his enterprises are always female. This is a very bold sweeping generalization of a size that is, to my knowledge, a first in the history and critique of the civilization it applies to. And even though de Lauretis is not one of the famous scholars quoted by McClary—such as Levi-Strauss, Saussure, Barthes or Foucault—we must judge the merits of the thesis itself, not the reputation of its author.[25] So let us evaluate De Lauretis' "demonstration."

At the above-mentioned page 118 of De Lauretis' book, we find only the paragraph quoted by McClary (followed by a few short elaborations of it), but nothing that would resemble a demonstration: no facts, no deductions based on them, no syllogistic conclusion (see pages 118-119 of de Lauretis' book in the Appendix). The chapter containing the paragraph, titled "Desire in Narrative" (*AD* 105-158) does not demonstrate anything either. The author meanders amidst several issues, quotes other well-known and lesser-known authors, quotes Freud or scholars quoting him (she is, obviously, a devoted Freudian) and utters the statement "a story is always a question of desire" (*AD* 111), which seems to mirror the title of the chapter. The closest she comes to the issue of the hero and the obstacle is a debate (*AD* 109-110) about the gender of mythological monsters (the Sphinx, the Medusa, the Minotaur), who are "obstacles man [male] encounters on the path of life, on his way to manhood, wisdom and power" and "must be slain or defeated" (*AD* 110). Although both the Medusa and the Sphinx were female, De Lauretis does not claim that the obstacle in any story must be of female nature, apparently aware of the fact that an example is not a demonstration (there are plenty of masculine "obstacles" in Greek mythology, such as the Minotaur).

Drawing on two Soviet narratologists does not get us any closer to a demonstration. Vladimir Propp (1895-1970) was a formalist scholar who analyzed (in a work published in 1928) the basic components of the plots in Russian folk tales in order to identify their simplest irreducible narrative elements. He came up with eight characters (such as the hero, "the princess or prize" that the hero would eventually marry and the villain, whom Propp called "the antagonist") and thirty-one "functions" that the various characters can perform (within certain limits); for example, the villain will always do a "Villainy" or a "Trickery", while the hero will always receive an "Interdiction" (to do something, to go some place, etc.). Yurij Lotman (1922-1993), a student and then collaborator of Propp, was a prominent Soviet literary scholar, semiotician, and cultural historian, with special interest in cinematography, the arts, literature, robotics, etc. While his name was not associated with a thesis as specific as that of Propp, he was one of the most widely-cited authors in these fields. His cited article[26] does not advance any kind of "gendering," either before or after the paragraphs quoted by De Lauretis. She sums up Lotman's thesis accurately (*AD* 118): he divides the characters populating the ancient Western World myths into two categories: those who are mobile (can change their place) and those who are immobile and represent, in fact, a function of the "closed space" which they occupy. The immobile characters (or the place they represent) are the "obstacles" or the hero's "antagonists" (Propp's term) in a narrative, such as the Sphinx in the Oedipus myth. Lotman can now define a story as "a simple chain of two functions, open at both ends and thus endlessly repeatable: entry into a closed space and emergence from it." Then De Lauretis quotes Lotman:

> Inasmuch as this closed space *can be interpreted* as 'a cave,' 'the grave,' 'a house', 'woman'[27] (and, correspondingly, be allotted the features of darkness, warmth, dampness), entry into it *is interpreted* on various levels as 'death', 'conception', 'return home', *and so on*; moreover, all these acts *are thought of as mutually identical* (De Lauretis' emphasis)

and articulates her claim (*AD* 118-119) that McClary calls a "demonstration":

> *In this mythical-textual mechanics*, then, the hero must be male, regardless of the gender of the text-image, *since* the obstacle, whatever its personification, is morphologically female and, indeed, simply *the womb*. (my emphasis)

If one compares this statement with Susan McClary's quote (see page 210), one notices some differences: she replaces the "mythical-textual mechanics" with "traditional Western narrative," without taking any notice of the differences between the two, on which Lotman theorizes a lot in his article (pp. 161-166); she also drops the end of de Lauretis' quote ("the womb"), which would have required a more detailed explanation. Scholarly ethics require signaling such changes, which McClary did not, but let us disregard this particular point for the sake of the argument.

De Lauretis' last quoted paragraph, which basically states that "the hero is male *because* the obstacle is female," has three major flaws. First, it is an incomplete syllogism: it draws the conclusion (the hero is male) based on only one premise (the obstacle is female), while any syllogism requires two premises. Second, none of De Lauretis nor Lotman or Propp previously demonstrated the premise "the obstacle is (morphologically) female." Lotman utters the word "woman" in an enumeration of the possible embodiments of the obstacle, because the obstacle may be feminine (like the Sphinx and the Medusa), but a supporting example is not proof of the universal validity of a statement. De Lauretis seems to infer the validity of her premise from the phrase in Lotman's quotation that she italicizes: "all these acts are thought of as mutually identical." However, she fails to explain such an inference and I cannot see how she could make it. What does "identical" mean in a simplification as drastic as the one proposed by Lotman? Elements like 'a cave,' 'the grave,' 'a house,' 'woman'—an enumeration that is not exhaustive, as indicated by the italicized "and so on"—can be identical only in one way: as "closed spaces" that the hero enters (or obstacles that he must vanquish), not because they would be feminine in their nature. How could a cave or a grave be "morphologically" female, which means "having female reproductive organs" according to the dictionary?

Playing the devil's advocate, I can think of only one way in which this enumeration could have served De Lauretis as a "demonstration" of her premise that "the obstacle is female": through Freud's theory of the interpretation of dreams. She does not explicitly say so, but her insistence on the value and usefulness of the Freudian approach throughout this chapter of her book suggests that this may be the case; also her most recent book, *Freud's Drive: Psychoanalysis, Literature, and Film*,[28] is a plea for the relevance of Freudian theory. Although Freud's view of women was deprecatory, mainstream feminism—which has moved its focus towards sexuality in the sixties—relies heavily on his fantasy theories like the *oedipal scenario*. Freud's interpretation of dreams involves a "censorship mechanism" that camouflages sexuality in non-sexual objects, among which any close space (cave, grave, even a house) is the symbolic disguise of female genitalia (perhaps the mysterious womb in De Lauretis' statement!). Lotman, who in one of his essential books, *Culture and Explosion*, explicated the "radical error of Freudianism" in a couple of paragraphs,[29] certainly did not imply anything of the sort in his analysis of the ancient myths. And as I have already shown in part I, chapter 1 of the current work, Freud's whole theory and particularly his theory of dreams is a speculation without any basis.

Finally, it is impossible not to notice that the conclusion of De Lauretis's (false) syllogism is invalidated by many examples. How could a typical obstacle like the Minotaur in Theseus' myth be "morphologically" female? Hercules, the archetypal hero, had to kill or subdue no less than nine very morphologically male obstacles during his twelve labors: the Nemean Lion, the Ceryncian Hind (a deer that had antlers), the Erymanthian Bear, the Cretan Bull, Geryon and Cacus (two male giants), and the two-headed dog Orthrus, and, finally, the three-headed watch-dog of Hell, Cerberus. Examples do not prove a theory, but counter-examples do nullify it.

In conclusion, De Lauretis' statement, invoked by Susan McClary as a "demonstrated" truth, constantly dismisses facts and is a concoction of statements ideologically biased and/or based on the Freudian theory, now discredited by modern science. The seventeenth century Western narrative, including the operatic one, *did not* posture the obstacle (antagonist) in hero's path as of a universally feminine nature. Certainly, there were female antagonists in operas (such as Agrippina in Händel's eponymous opera or Mozart's "Queen of Night"), but the villain was more often than not another male. The human species belongs to the world of primates, in which both the hero and his antagonist are typically *alpha males*. McClary falls short of the scholar's duty to check the validity of the quotes she invokes in support of her own theses. De Lauretis' quote cannot in any way validate a theory about the "sexism" of the sonata form resulting from the adoption of the alleged but non-existent operatic genre bias into instrumental music.

What, then, are the roles of the "masculine" and "feminine" themes in the sonata form? The sonata form was the most elaborate structure of the "classical" musical style and had, therefore, to rival the highest Baroque form, the Fugue, which it was intended to replace. It had, therefore, to set in motion an "active" theme, apt to be treated with energy and full mastery. On the other hand, music, and especially classical music, needs diversity in order not to bore; hence, the need of a contrast, which was, at the time when the form crystallized, both tonal and expressive. It was natural to contrast the "active" theme with one displaying "sentiment," which also allowed the musician to prove that he was a versatile artist. One could, de rigueur, call these two themes "masculine" and "feminine," as the nineteenth-century musicians and critics later came to, but that had nothing to do with "subjugating" the second one in the recapitulation. Rather, it had everything to do with the need to achieving "unity within diversity," and the best option—that is, the most musically elegant—was to re-cast the second theme in the key of the first, which was the "active" element of the movement and should, therefore, be leading.[*] For the great musicians, the sonata form had no sexual connotation. How many times are Mozart's first themes a clear "feminine" character? Or, how "masculine" is the first theme of the first movement of Beethoven's Violin Concerto?

Sexual, sexist tonality: the "demonstration" that proves the opposite

The third booster of Professor McClary's musicological rocket raises her

---

[*] The reader will get a full understanding of what the sonata form is by (re-)visiting the book *Sonata Forms* by Charles Rosen, a much better authority than this author,

theory to an even higher level. It is not only that Beethoven's music is rife with sexual violence; it is not only the sonata form that is a sexist musical structure. It is the *whole construct of tonality* that is guilty of sexism:

> The tonality that underlies Western concert music is strongly informed by a specific sort of *erotic imagery*. [...] Music after the Renaissance most frequently appeals to libidinal appetites [...] expressly tied to male-defined *models of sexuality*. [...] As the shaping device of most classical music, it presents as though universal only a single kind of erotic experience: that of the male— more particularly, that of the *patriarchally invested male* [...] For most of the history of post-Renaissance Western music and in virtually all of its critical literature, the *sexual dimensions* of its mechanisms have been shamelessly exploited and yet consistently denied. (My emphasis)[30]

McClary did not explain in her 1987 article how this major change (allegedly for the worse) happened but she takes up and elaborates her theory in *Feminine Endings*.[*] She first re-states her stand in the very introductory chapter:

> [...] at the historical moment [when tonality was born] at which the legitimation of culture moved from the sacred to the secular realm, the 'truth' that authorized musical culture became expressly tied to male-defined models of sexuality. (*FE* 3)

But she loses the limpidness of this statement in a further chapter, by asserting something that seems quite different:

> like its popular counterpart, classical music presents *a wide range* of competing images and *models of sexuality*. (*FE* 54, my italics)

She then proceeds to address, in the same chapter, a few examples of such alternative models: Bizet's *Carmen* (*FE* 56-67), a case of "female sexuality in a male narrative;" Tchaikovsky's *Fourth Symphony* (*FE* 69-79), which the scholar refrains, however, from calling a gay narrative; a few other similar examples (such as Donizetti's *Lucia di Lammermoor* or Richard Strauss' *Salomé*) are scattered in her book. Finally, she describes tonality later as "most concerned with the exclusive control of sexuality by the male," (*FE* 127) which is slightly discordant: *most* concerned is *not totally* concerned and conflicts with the next *exclusive*, but let us accept that this may be just a *lapsus linguae* and move on.

The idea that tonality may be linked to sexuality—whether male or "alternative"—cannot be dismissed just because it seems absurd. As McClary points out, tonality took shape during the shift from the sacred to the secular vision of the world and it is trivia to say that "liberation" of sexuality was part of that change; it would also seem normal that male sexuality should be in many ways dominant in a patriarchal society. On the other hand, questions come to

---

[*] McClary also dropped the passage in her article about "the principle of building to climax three-quarters of the way through a piece," which she alleged to govern tonal composition; obviously, it did not fit male (or female) sexuality, whose climax comes always at the end.

214

mind that challenge the idea. For instance, the modes—which are, in McClary's opinion, the epitome of sacred music—did not express some kind of sexuality, even though they were rooted in the ancient Greek modes, which were the product of a very patriarchal society. Also, emancipation of sex was not a historical linear process, but had obvious ups and downs—why did such a radical change in music occur during the seventeenth century when, as I will show, the sexual emancipation movement was in a clear "down?"

Ignoring such complexities, McClary simply claims that tonality was born at the moment when sexuality took hold of the social discourse in the Western world, a claim that she supports by another "demonstration," that of the French philosopher Michel Foucault in his book *History of Sexuality*:

> He [Foucault] writes: "since the end of the sixteenth century, the 'putting into discourse of sex,' far from undergoing a process of restriction, on the contrary has been subjected to a mechanism of increasing incitement."[31] As Foucault goes on to *demonstrate*, even if such public discourses are intended to control and contain sexuality, the obsession always to talk—or sing—[32] about sex also has the effect of continually stirring libidinal interests. [...] To a greater extent than ever before, gender and sexuality become central concerns of Western culture in the seventeenth century, and the new public arts all develop techniques for arousing and manipulating desire, for "hooking" the spectator. Witness, for example, the brand of tonality that emerges at this time: a surefire method for inciting and channeling expectations that easily supplants the less coercive procedures of modality. (*FE* 36, my italics)

The problem with this new "demonstration" is that it appears very different in the quoted source from what Susan McClary claims. She takes Foucault's passage out of context, ignores the philosopher's train of thought and intimates things contradicted by facts fully acknowledged in Foucault's book. His quoted statement appears in Part 1, an introduction maintaining that, at the time when his book was published in 1978, we were still afraid to talk freely about sex (hence the title of this part, *We 'Other Victorians'*) because of mistakenly believing that sexuality had been repressed for hundreds of years, at least as far as public discourse went. Then comes the statement, claiming that "since the end of the sixteenth century, etc." but the "demonstration" is the matter of the second part of his book (titled *The Repressive hypothesis*), which McClary ignores. This part begins with a blunt proclamation of exactly the opposite of the previous claim:

> *The seventeenth century*, then, *was the beginning of an age of repression* emblematic of what we call the bourgeois societies, an age which perhaps we still have not completely left behind.[33] (My emphasis)

Then, in a very philosopher-like routine (thesis-antithesis-synthesis), Foucault's next paragraph appears to reverse this picture again:

> Yet when one looks back *over these last three centuries* with their continual transformations, things appear in a very different light:

around and apropos of sex, one sees a veritable discursive explosion. [...] There was a steady proliferation of discourses concerned with sex [...]: a discursive ferment that gathered momentum *from the eighteenth century onward.*[34] (my italics)

All these conflicting statements are solved by the italics in the quote: the age of the "discursive explosion [about sex]" goes back three centuries from the author's present time (1978), that is to the end of the seventeenth not the sixteenth century, as McClary claims. Foucault actually repeats this assertion later: "Toward the *beginning of the eighteenth century*, there emerged a political, economic, and technical incitement to talk about sex [...]" (my italics).[35]

Discarding all these clarifications with which Foucault complements his initial misleading statement, McClary implies that the alleged seventeenth-century "sexual liberation" in discursive terms was a new trend in the post-Medieval age of history. In fact, as she could have read in the philosopher's book that she quotes, exactly the opposite is true: the public discourse was much more restricted than before. As Foucault writes, "No seventeenth-century pedagogue would have publicly advised his disciple, as did Erasmus [who died in 1536] in his *Dialogues*, on the choice of a good prostitute."[36] The reason why the seventeenth century was an age of increased repression of sexuality and its discourse was very simple (though never stated by Foucault): the arrival of syphilis around 1500 had changed the social landscape. The new disease hit Europe with the fury of the old scourge, the plague, but, unlike the latter, did not burn itself out. It only subsided and its catastrophic consequences became gradually apparent—which put on hold, for over a century, the sexual emancipation launched during Renaissance. As the French historian Quétel stated,

> At the beginning of the seventeenth century, the wind of the religious reform [Counter-Reformation] was blowing, and social and intellectual libertinism were on the point of being indiscriminately repressed; the curiosity value which the pox had had in the previous century, was to give way, for more than a hundred years, to silence and contempt.[37]

As we can see, after summoning De Lauretis' bogus "demonstration," McClary cites another one, which asserts the opposite of what she maintains. There are more such examples to come.

... and a bizarre socio-historical argument

Susan McClary advanced a second argument in her thesis by linking music to what she calls "the specificity of socio-historical contexts." She did this in a rather scattered manner, but here is the core of her contention:

> Before the general crisis of the late sixteenth century, European culture was shaped by ideals of harmony, balance, stability [...] marked by relatively non-coercive modal techniques that delight in the present moment, rhythms that are grounded in the physicality and repetitiveness of dance, and the kind of carefully regulated

contrapuntal interplay that Renaissance theorists associated with the harmony of the spheres, of nature and humankind, of soul and body.

With the general crisis of the seventeenth century precipitated by—among many other factors—the Reformation, colonial expansion, humanism, the scientific revolutions of Copernicus and Galileo, and Cartesian philosophy, the ideal of culture changes from stability and balance to extravagant, individualistic assertion. The theatrical genres of opera, cantata, and oratorio immediately move to the center of vocal compositions; the virtuosic solo violin sonata leads to the creation of specifically instrumental forms that dispense with verbal discourse altogether and that work purely on the basis of aggressive rhetorical gestures, goal-oriented tonality develops to provide the illusion of narrative necessity that underlies the new music of the modern era. (*FE* 119-120)

Tonality is, therefore, the original sin of Western music![38] Following it, man and woman were chased from the modal Paradise of eternal happiness into the world of human exertion and suffering and change—not to mention that, like the Biblical original sin, it was caused by the discovery of sexuality. Apparently, humanism is the father of evil tonality. And capitalism must be its mother, because tonality is related to

the various excessive qualities of modernity—the capitalist undermining of more mercantile economic processes, imperialist invasions of 'primitive' societies, scientific quests that replace ecologically grounded philosophies of nature with threats of nuclear destruction, the program of urban renewal that destroy traditional communities. (FE 124)

In a bizarre paradox, the revolutionary feminist rubs shoulders with twentieth-century mystic Berdyaev (1874-1948), who saw humanism as the root of all evil in the modern world and dreamt of "new Middle Ages."[39]

And the worst was yet to come in music, from the hands of Beethoven, who took tonal evil to new heights and spawned a host of followers:

As if the thrusting impulse characteristic of tonality and the aggression characteristic of first themes were not enough, Beethoven's symphonies add two other dimensions to the history of style: *assaultive pelvic pounding* (for instance, in the last movement of the Fifth Symphony and in all but the 'passive' third movement of the Ninth) and the sexual violence. [...] The celebration of this kind of *sexual desire*, which culminates in *violent ejaculation*, becomes virtually a convention of nineteenth-century symphonic music [...]. This image has very little to do with lovemaking (which presupposes a partner and communication): it represents something closer to *masturbation*—at best. (*FE* 4)

Such an abolishment of an essential part of the canon of Western music can only happen during an epiphany. McClary's was the discovery of her ideal of feminist music, totally in opposition with the Beethovenian approach, in the piece *Genesis II* of the little-known composer Janika Vandervelde. She finds therein music that "creates a sense of existence *in* time that is stable, ordered, yet 'timeless'" and makes the listener "experience the possibility that the [musical] pattern might be replicated indefinitely, infinitely [and] resonate with the patterns of nature: seasonal yet timeless, always fascinatingly different and yet always the same" (*FE* 118-119). She claims that this piece has a strong appeal to her and many of her female students, while being rejected as boring by almost all her male students (*FE* 124). According to her, this music appeals to the feminine soul because it resorts to old medieval modes rather than the tonal approach.[40]

Professor McClary's "socio-historical context" explanation for the momentous change in the Western music is hardly persuasive. Her description of European culture before the general crisis at the end of the sixteenth century as "shaped by ideals of harmony, balance, stability" is totally misguided. Arts may have aspired to such ideals, but the real world was completely different. In his magisterial synthesis on the Renaissance, John Hale draws this succinct picture: about 1500, "Europe was doomed to be fissured by mutual hostilities. [...] France has England as a check, England has Scotland, Spain Portugal. [...] One Italian state against another, Swiss against Germans, one German prince or city against a neighbor [...]"[41] Moreover, the Renaissance had already set sexual liberation in motion—how is it possible that this was not reflected in its music, following McClary's own prescription? Furthermore, as I have shown, the seventeenth century general European crisis had yielded the Counter-Reformation and repression of sexuality. Finally, one can easily associate capitalism and imperialism with aggression, and in turn aggression with male sexuality (a favorite theme of radical feminism),[42] but aggression is far older than the seventeenth century; medieval cultures had plenty of it, even in the name of the Church, yet it had not branded music with its sexual stamp.

All these incongruences in McClary's reasoning render her inferences incredible. If tonality was indeed about sexuality, one must look for a different explanation.

Sexual Tonality 2: The Boomerang Effect

Susan McClary tries also to find a purely musical justification for her claims, but incongruences run deep under the surface and eventually invalidate her theory—without her even noticing it. She correctly connects music to sexuality through body and dance. One can easily agree to her emphasis on "music's association with the body (in dance or for sensuous leisure)" (*FE* 17) and its "uncanny ability to make us experience our bodies in accordance with its gestures and rhythms" (*FE* 23) that she describes later as "metaphors of physicality [that] can cause listeners to experience their bodies in new ways—again, seemingly without mediation" (*FE* 25). This has been common knowledge for ages and the science of anatomy has been aware for at least a century that the auditory nerve sends a fascicle to the cerebellum, which is responsible for the coordination of body movements[43]; modern neuroscience has recently discovered that the cerebellum is also an active participant in the perception of music.[44]

218

Problem arise when getting beyond Professor McClary's trivial utterances. If sexuality is the basic "meaning" of Western classical music, as she maintains, she should be able to discover "the body" therein. But she does not. In fact, she discovers exactly the opposite: "classical music [she claims] is perhaps our cultural medium most centrally concerned with denial of the body, with *enacting the ritual repudiation of the erotic*—even (especially) its own erotic imagery" (*FE* 79, my italics), a diagnosis repeated later as "the radical separation of mind and body that underwrites most so-called serious music" (*FE* 137). She goes further to generalize: "the tendency to deny the body and to identify with pure mind underlies virtually *every aspect of patriarchal Western culture*" (*FE* 54, my italics), a statement repeated later, "Western culture—with its puritanical, idealist suspicion of the body" (*FE* 136), particularized again to music: "the mind/body split that has plagued Western culture for centuries shows up most paradoxically in attitudes toward music" (*FE* 151). How can any art embody and project something that its core beliefs rejects? McClary apparently did not notice the contradiction; she wanted "it" both ways, as both sexual expression and sexual repression, an antinomy that she fails to tackle, let alone solve.

McClary revisited the music-and-body issue in a later book *Conventional Wisdom*,[45] elaborating it into an analysis of the Baroque dances—Courante, Minuet, etc.—most famously illustrated in Bach's harpsichord suites. Following her analysis and expanding it into regions that she missed, although they are part and parcel of music theory and history, will help us expose the irreconcilable contradictions in her theories.

The Baroque dances, though formalized court dances and songs, are actually rooted in folk music. Indeed, folk played a crucial role in the process of crystallization of tonality and, therefore, in the history of music, but this role is always understated in the music literature, because, unlike sacred music, secular music of common folk was not written down for a very long time. It represents what Richard Taruskin acknowledges, in his most recent history of Western music, as "the unwritten repertory many times larger than the literate repertories."[46] The classical inherited both its major and minor modes from the prevalent modes of Western world folk, the Ionian and, respectively, the Aeolian. Quite symptomatic, Taruskin places the beginning of "the tonal revolution" in the succinct chapter section (621-628) dedicated to *Dances, Old and New* and describes the latter as "the unheard and unhearable 'iceberg'." These dances took shape all over Europe between the fourteenth and seventeenth centuries, were formalized into the Baroque suite movements, and constituted the foundation of all major instrumental forms, including the sonata and the symphony. When, in the middle of the nineteenth century, Wagner looked back at the history of his art, he discovered not even tonality, but *folk* and *dance*. "The harmonized dance is the basis of the modern symphony [of Haydn and Mozart]," he wrote.[47]

The corollary is simple: if sexuality was present and quintessential at the formation of tonal music, as McClary maintains, it could have been inherited only from the folk music and should be retrieved from the Baroque suite dances. But she describes the latter[48] as not being "the authentic body" (*CW* 95).

Although she does not clearly state what she means by "authentic," we can safely guess that it designates the kind of overt sexuality in modern day pop culture, such as in Madonna's shows that the scholar praises in *Feminine Endings* (148-166). Indeed, none of the Baroque dances—I mean the dancing, not the music—shows anything similar to the "total body articulation" characteristic to African dancing or as emulated by modern pop culture. Even "innocent" sensuality was absent more often than not from Europe's dances,[49] because their important social function was not to organize sexual encounters but to sponsor the meeting of young men and women with a view to their future mating. Health was much more important than sexual overtures for this mutual sizing up; according to their destination—for courtiers or ordinary folk, with plenty of intermingling, too—dances ranged from ceremonial to athletic.[50] They embodied courtship broadly, not sexual ritual in a narrow sense. The steps, turns and hops in the pair-dance, and the coordination and integration of the group dances, were signals of physical and mental health, which were essential for ensuring healthy progeny. Darwin's suggestion that music preceded speech as a means of courtship in his theory of sexual selection was endorsed by modern neurologists in search for an explanation of the evolution of our brain.[51]

The conclusion is obvious: by McClary's own admission, Western classical music had no musical source from which to inherit sexuality. How could she not notice that this statement clashes with her previous thesis? I think she did notice, because in *Conventional Wisdom* she unexpectedly delivers a 180-degree change in her views about tonality.

The (almost) 180-degree turn

In chapter 6, titled "What was Tonality," of her second book, Susan McClary had this to say about the eighteenth century tonality:

> If conventions could ever be said to have possessed wisdom, these eighteenth-century [tonal] procedures certainly would be candidates. When we hear the words "Western values" applied to music, they usually refer to this extraordinary period when it was possible to believe unequivocally in such possibilities. (*CW* 107)

While it is almost impossible not to agree with the final sentence, one cannot help noticing the huge difference between this statement and the same author's previous opinion on page 214 of this book. The change of judgment is astounding. Of course, there is nothing essentially wrong in changing one's views over time—it happens to almost everybody—but intellectual and professional ethics demand one acknowledge and explain the change. McClary never does that—it is as if she had never written that 1987 article or her 1991 book.

In order to understand the change of scholarly doctrine, one may recur to the time frame and the "socio-historical context," McClary's favorite work-horse: in *Feminine Endings*, although she describes tonality as "the music of the modern era" (*FE* 120), she refers mainly to its beginning in the seventeenth century, which was cultivating "extravagant, individualistic assertion," and music that worked "purely on the basis of aggressive rhetorical gestures" (*FE* 119-120), expressing "libidinal appetites" (*FE* 3). When she again tackles tonality in her newer book, she deals with the next century, the eighteenth—which was, in her view, "a period of unparalleled confidence in the viability of a public sphere in which ideas could be successfully communicated, differences negotiated, consensus achieved" (*CW* 64). To anyone that has any knowledge of history, the descriptions of both centuries will look at best as exaggerated ... and at worst, grounded in ignorance and bias. The seventeenth century was a late-Renaissance period, hindered, at its beginning, by an alleged "general crisis" that included some sexual repression, but still a time of great cultural advance and a precursor of the age of the Enlightenment. The latter was certainly a period of great achievements, but not an earthly paradise: it was also marred by deep economic, social, political conflicts (national and international) in which force, not consensus dictated,[52] and which would culminate in the French Revolution, the Terror regime and the Napoleonic wars. McClary's emphasis on the "socio-historical connection" as determining the development of music—and without entering in any specificity for that matter—remains just a meaningless slogan.[53]

The real explanation of this change of doctrine is much simpler: in between her two books, McClary had another epiphany: after Vandervelde—Vivaldi. Vivaldi's name shows only once in *Feminine Endings*, in a note in which the author claims that "the Baroque repertories of Bach and Vivaldi and the nineteenth century symphonies" were based on "the fear-of-women paradigm" (*FE* 187, note 33). In *Conventional Wisdom,* Vivaldi became the very epitome of perfection: he not only "standardized the Baroque concerto into the format that set the terms of composition for years to come," but also made tonality act as "a dramatically compelling model of self/group interactions" (*CW* 80), thus incarnating "a specific kind of social world that allows equally for collaboration and individuality—an arrangement that permits both to exist, to work together toward progress, reason, consensus, freedom of expression, and long-range goals, etc." (*CW* 81)—an eleven-page eulogy, and a well-deserved one, too.

In the process of discovering Vivaldi, McClary also exonerates Bach—at least in as much as he emulated the former in his *French Suites*—and Mozart, for producing "a dynamic self with an immutable, sensitive core" (*CW* 107) (whatever that means) even though both of them still "challenge us with the occasional enigmatic episode" (*CW* 64). She had already given passing grades to Händel and Haydn, because they had "rarely invented stories that 'demand sadism' [her term for delayed cadences]" (*FE* 127). She forgets now even the (male) sexist sonata-form, which was the quintessential product of the eighteenth century and in which Haydn and Mozart indulged with great gusto.

Nevertheless, McClary's 180-degree turn does not apply to Beethoven—he is still the great villain. However, he plays a new part in *Conventional Wisdom*: he is no longer the exponent of evilly sexist tonality, but the first one who "acted against the hegemony of tonality," (*CW* 64) initiating a destructive development, the result of which was that "by the end of the nineteenth century, tonality—that guarantor of reason and shared ideals (!)—had been declared bankrupt" (*CW*

111).⁵⁴ The scholar's evidence for the indictment of Beethoven takes 15 pages in *Conventional Wisdom* (119-133, of which seven of score), in which she "deconstructs" his *A minor String Quartet* Op. 132—with emphasis on its first movement—to state:

> It is already clear in late Beethoven that the center established by eighteenth-century cultural forms would not hold, as the very devices that had appeared to resolve tensions so naturally came to be seen as artificial mediations at best, lies at worst. For the remainder of the century, artists returned again and again to the Enlightenment vision of intersubjective wholeness to try to make it work. Yet the gap between outside and inside, between the possibility of social agreement and desire for immediated individuality grew wider.
>
> Or at least it did in Germany. (*CW* 133-134)

With the last sentence, McClary concludes her image of Beethoven as "diabolus in musica," by making a whole (German) nation guilty of a premeditated crime—the killing of tonality.

The alleged German Malady: An "argument" that never was

McClary diagnoses Germany with a malady unique in Europe:

> During the nineteenth century, composers in Italy, France, and elsewhere—many of them deeply committed to progressive political agendas—continued happily to utilize this [tonality] and other conventions in order to maximize communication and social impact. But in German-speaking regions, the musical lingua franca itself was cast as part of the problem. (*CW* 111)

This malady would have culminated in a kind of attack of (musical) insanity in which the German musicians killed tonality and replaced it with diverse variants of its opposite, atonality.

As usual, McClary's "demonstration" does not rely on facts. She mentions only in passing "the emphasis on an oddly nonsocial, evolution-based history" illustrated by the likes of E.T. A. Hoffmann (*CW* 111), that could have given her thesis some credibility. Indeed, Hoffmann's discussion of the Viennese classics, particularly of Beethoven, was far too often guided through the lenses of Kappellmeister Kreisler, the fictional character Hoffmann invented as his alter ego, who was the "mad musician"—one of the incarnations of the prototypical "mad artists" of the Romantic age. McClary replaces such facts with her speculations on the "socio-historical context" in her argumentation, that covers some seven pages (*CW* 112-118) of rather scattered reasoning, including statements by other, well-known or lesser-known scholars (e.g., Adorno and Kittler) and quotes of her own stance about some momentous musical achievements like Bach's *Brandenburg Concerto No. 5*, Mozart's *Piano Concerto* K. 453 and *Prague Symphony*, as well as forgotten pieces like Alessandro Scarlatti's opera *Griselda*. She begins by reminding us that the Germans had a history of iconoclastic behavior in the name of nationalism: during the Enlightenment age, they had invented their national "Kultur" in opposition to the French "civilization," which they deemed superficial (*CW* 96, 111). She then claims that, during the nineteenth century, "a whiff of pathology clung to this [German] notion of the inner self [Kultur], right from the outset," invoking the authority of German scholar Klaus Doerner, who

> in his study of attitudes toward insanity in various parts of modern Europe, has argued that *only in Germany* was genius defined in ways that often made it indistinguishable from dementia. (*CW* 111, my italics)

That would explain how the mentioned "whiff" grew later into "[...] strangeness and estrangement of moods and drives of physical and mental disease," which lead to "the belief in a logic that does not emerge from human conventions but emanates from on high or (what may be the same thing) from 'the music itself'" (*CW* 112). The belief in the autarchy of their field, would have gradually lead nineteenth century (German) musicians to "focus on formal matters rather than banal manifest content" (*CW* 114) and, since society at large ("community" in the scholar's language) was still attached to the pleasure of the "manifest content," a chasm was born between the two halves of the musical world, that is, between the musicians and their audience, during the nineteenth century. Thus estranged, musicians reached the stage in which the "norm [tonality] became the enemy" (*CW* 117) and had to be killed. The perpetrators of this act, the consequences of which "proved to be devastating" (*CW* 118), were not just any musicians but the German ones, as McClary reminds us again: "it is important to remember that this crisis occurred primarily in Germany [...] it didn't [happen] in most parts of contemporaneous Europe" (*CW* 117).

This argument has many problematic aspects, but I will focus on those that expose McClary's obvious misrepresentations. The first crucial moment in her thesis is a very strong statement: nineteenth century Germany was the only country in which "genius [was] defined in ways that often made it indistinguishable from dementia," a verdict allegedly given by the German scholar Claus Doerner in his book *The Madmen and the Bourgeoisie*. As proof, McClary offers the following quote:

> Liberal capitalism and its economic crises were accompanied by waves of Romanticism, a testimony to the fact Romanticism was no match for rational social reality. The antirational realities were as much an expression of social refusal as of escapist movements, as much a realistic protest against all rational constriction of bourgeois existence as an irrational cul-de-sac. That held true for the evolutionary development of history, for the myth of the *Volk*, and for emanational logic, as well as for the romanticization of the sinister-mysterious, the imaginary and unconscious, the dreams and utopian wish-fulfillments, of wandering, solitude, and homelessness, of childhood and fairytales, of strangeness and estrangement, of moods and drives, of physical and mental disease.[55]

This quote may be a very apt description of certain traits of German Romanticism,[56] but it never mentions the term genius, with or without any link to madness. I became suspicious of another spurious "demonstration," a familiar weapon in McClary's scholarly arsenal. Therefore, I read the whole work in question. *Nowhere in his book does Doerner state* (let alone "argue") *what McClary claims he did, i.e., that nineteenth century Germany was a country (let alone the only one) in which genius was defined in ways that often made it indistinguishable from dementia.*

Klaus Doerner (b. 1933) is a psychiatrist; his book is a history of the development of psychiatry in three European countries (England, France and Germany) beginning with the Enlightenment until the mid-nineteenth century, when psychiatry was established as a medical discipline (science). It has a particular flavor because the author is also a "latter-day" Marxist of the twentieth century, and thus strives to incorporate Marx's theory of the "class struggle" into psychiatry.[57] Genius is of no particular interest to him and is mentioned only in passing, as just one form of an out-of-the-normal personality, following a quote from the great German philosopher Kant: "Formally, insanity is no less originality [...] than genius, which follows the dictates of an innate talent."[58] This terse statement is a far cry from the assertion that the two would be "indistinguishable." McClary's claim to support her "German malady" theory with Doerner's insights is just another of her many misrepresentations.

There was, in fact, a nineteenth century cultural undercurrent in Germany who linked genius to insanity besides the Romantic "mad artist" fiction, but McClary missed it: in the writings of Arthur Schopenhauer, the influential philosopher of the second half of the century. In the section on aesthetics of his most important work, *The World as Will and Representation*, he postulates a similitude between genius and insanity, because "every increase in intellect beyond the ordinary measure is an abnormality that disposes one to madness."[59] Nor was Schopenhauer the only European thinker to make this connection. His views were also shared by many prominent psychiatrists of the time not only in Germany but in almost any major Western country. In England, Henry Maudsley (1835-1918), a leading figure in his field wrote, "What rights have we to believe Nature under any obligation to do her work by means of complete minds only? She may find an incomplete mind a more suitable instrument for a particular purpose." William James (1842-1910), dubbed "the father of American psychology," subscribed to this idea, summing up, "the greater the Genius, the greater the unsoundness."[60] The French sociologist Henri Joly (1839-1925) shared similar ideas in his book *Psychologie des grands hommes* (1883). But it is the Italian Cesare Lombroso (1835-1909) who most closely examined the association between genius and madness: he wrote a four-hundred page book as demonstration, based principally on anecdotal evidence, that "genius is a true degenerative psychosis belonging to the group of moral insanity" or, more precisely, "a degenerative psychosis of the epileptoid group."[61]

Without Doerner's support, McClary's theory rests only on the fascination with the irrational in the German Romanticist movement, which she would have us believe led German musicians to kill tonality in a kind of insane musical fit. However, fascination with the irrational was not uniquely German but a general feature of Romanticism all over the Western world. The "irrational" irrupted first in the English literature, when Horace Walpole (1717-1797) patented the Gothic novel, the first horror-and-madness literary form, in *The Castle of Otranto* (1764), that preceded the horror stories of the German writer Christian Heinrich Spiess (1755-1799). Another English writer, Mary Shelley (1797-1851), introduced to the world the epitome of the mad genius, the famous *Frankenstein* character, in her eponymous book published in 1818. Obviously, the "malady" did not single out Germany—it was a Western World epidemic.

German musicians killing tonality: A case of withholding evidence

McClary does not advance any scenario of how this happened, nor does she name any of the culprits. Everybody knows the name of the main perpetrator, Arnold Schonberg, who set himself to completely "liberate the dissonance" and, still unsatisfied with the result, so-called "expressionist" music, replaced tonality with the twelve-tone system and also boasted his exploit in an unabashedly nationalistic claim—"thus German music came to decide the way things developed, as it has for 200 years."[62] However, McClary avoids passing an explicitly negative judgment on twentieth-century music in either *Feminine Ending* and *Conventional Wisdom*. She dared that only in a 1989 article deploring the avant-garde's "withdrawal from the public" in order to be free to write "difficult music" that the public would reject as unintelligible,[63] but she seems to have recanted, as she paid a vague tribute to "the accomplishments of the high serialists" later (*CW* 137). Because she claims that by 1900 "tonality was declared bankrupt," she must have other musicians in mind who, before Schonberg and, like passengers on an Agatha Christie train ride, took turns thrusting their daggers into the body of poor tonality. Of course, we have the list of the usual suspects: Wagner, who "enlarged harmony" (his famous *Tristan chord*!); then Mahler, who made some further steps to "liberate the dissonance," preparing the way for Schonberg's final act.

But does the Wagner-Mahler-Schonberg triumvirate speak in the name of all German musicians? The German music world was not the monolith McClary implies. About the middle of the century, a chasm opened therein regarding Wagner's proclamation of "the art [music] of the future." His disciples called themselves "the New German School," claiming to represent the whole of the national music; but other musicians, among whom Brahms was the leading figure, differed in their understanding of music and its evolution and condemned the other side's "preposterous theories" in an open letter which, together with the incensed retort of the other side, embittered forever the ambiance of the German music profession.[64] The first group opened one trajectory (Wagner-Mahler-Schonberg) towards the rejection of tonality, but the second one marched into the twentieth century and viewed themselves as fully "modern" without the need to discard tonality. Richard Strauss (1864-1949), the most prominent twentieth-century German musician, abandoned his own experiments in "liberating the dissonance" (1900-1910) and practiced tonality until his death. Max Reger (1873-1916) may not have had enough time to get beyond late romanticism, but Alexander von Zemlinsky (1871-1942) did, yet he never followed Schonberg's example, even though the two men were friends. Karl Orff (1895-1982) developed a still-tonal "modernity" (tainted by modality). Kurt Weill (1900-1950) changed fields to the musical ethos of cabaret music, where atonality could not find an audience but diverse variants of jazz could. Eric Wolfgang Korngold (1897-1957) remained a late Romanticist and became one of the founders of film music. Such outstanding examples show that all German musicians did not participate in, or perhaps even acknowledge, the killing of tonality. It is hard to believe that McClary, a musicologist, was not aware of the facts here presented, but she chose to ignore this evidence for the sake of her misconstrued argument.

This is not the only evidence that Susan McClary withheld. In fact, the "crime" was not an exclusive German act, as she claims, but the result of a world-wide "conspiracy." The French impressionists (Debussy, Satie) started subverting tonality around 1880, in the name of national specificity, a euphemism for the reaction against German supremacy in music that had lasted for almost two centuries. Russian Alexander Scriabin (1872-1915) embarked on atonality shortly after 1900, before Schoenberg, who was still a late-Romantic at the time; Scriabin's last five piano sonatas, composed between 1912 and 1915, even dispensed with key signatures. The Italians' almost exclusive adherence to the opera helped them resist attacks on tonality longer, because their genre relied much more than the instrumental music on the support of a large public that felt alienated by modernity; but even they joined in after the death of Puccini, who also took the Italian opera with him into his grave. If other national musical schools (the Czechs, Norwegians, Swedes, Spanish, etc.) deferred abandoning tonality for some time, it was because they had reached the world's music stage later and had to build their own traditions before destroying it; they were, however, quick to change allegiance after WWI (think Bartok!). And, to paraphrase Oscar Wilde, the Americans had their (musical) decadence without having even reached civilization. Charles Ives (1874-1954) began "experimenting polytonality" before 1900 in his *Psalms* and his first String Quartet before making it the basic feature in his major works, such as "Central Park in the Dark" (1906), in which two orchestras play unaware of each other, each of them mixing tonality and polytonality.[65] All this happened at the time when, as I have shown, many German composers were still firmly attached to tonality. Susan McClary's indictment of the German nation as the sole killers of tonality is another misguided theory, built on cherry-picked evidence and exclusion—whether from sheer ignorance or deliberate neglect—of indisputable facts pertaining to the history of the Western music.[*]

Killing tonality 2: More of the same scholarly transgressions

According to Susan McClary, one of the main reasons of the demise of tonality was the estrangement of nineteenth century musicians from their indispensable beneficiary, the public at large. While the latter continued to

---

[*] If I may suggest an explanation of McClary's reasoning, she thought that the twentieth-century history, with Germany responsible for the outbreak of two world wars and guilty of the acceptance of a mad totalitarian political and genocidal regime, was highly supportive of diagnosing the nation as psychopathic.

respond only to the "manifest content" of music –McClary's term for the feelings evoked or induced by music—the former became essentially preoccupied with the form, practicing the "art for the art" paradigm.[66] This would have been particularly true in Germany, where

> [...] one of the tasks critics such as E. T. A. Hoffmann, Schumann, and Hanslick took upon themselves was the production of a new kind of customer: one who would renounce the easy pleasures of sentimentality or virtuosity and gravitate toward music that rewarded what Adorno later would call structural listening. (*CW* 114)

This is very likely a unique statement in music criticism of the Romantic Movement, even more so because it is not supported by any evidence. Indeed, a quote from Steven Rumph about Hoffmann's insistence on the harmonic aspect in the latter's 1810 seminal article about Beethoven's *Fifth Symphony* (*CW* 114-115) is no proof that Hoffmann would have denied the emotional power of music; in fact, he is generally viewed as the one who discovered, in Beethoven's music, "a whole new way of experiencing emotions".[67] Neither was Schumann a "formalist" because he rejected Berlioz's "program" of his *Symphonie Fantastique* as irrelevant to the qualities of the music (*CW* 137); as Sanna Pederson, a prominent historian of musical criticism, has shown, "Schumann encouraged his readers, first, to have (and to trust) strong empathic responses to the music they heard or played, and, second, to try to explain them in terms of the composer's achievement."[68] As for Hanslick, McClary relies only on his reputation as a staunch defender of "absolute" music to make the case for his indictment. She simply ignores, willfully or not, his explicit statement in his most important book, *On Beauty in Music*:

> Far be it from us to underrate the deep emotions which music awakens from their slumber or the feelings of joy or sadness which our minds dreamily experience. It is one of the most precious and inestimable secrets of nature that an art should have the power of evoking feelings entirely free from worldly association and kindled, as it were, by spark divine. [...] Music may, undoubtedly, awaken feelings of great joy or intense sorrow [...][69]

What Hanslick objects to is the view that music actually "represents" emotions,[70] a favorite thesis of the enemies of the "absolute" music and proponents of the "art of the future," who, as common musical wisdom holds, were the initiators of the demise of tonality. When opposing them, he acted as a defender of tonality.

Summing up, McClary's argument about the Romantic musicians becoming "formalists" is another of her misrepresentations. And so is her claim that an estrangement developed between musicians and their public during the nineteenth-century. It is true that the relationship between the two sides was more complex than it had been before: the century was a period of momentous changes in European society, involving also the arts and, especially, the music. An "explosion" of public concert life happened,[71] with more and more concert halls and opera houses built and more orchestras instituted all over the Western World, in order to satisfy the demand of the rising middle class—a class that grew as the result of the Industrial Revolution, and that emulated the declining aristocracy in the enjoyment of the arts. This "democratization" of the arts was not without certain downsides. First, it led to a certain degradation of taste, because the middle class was less musically educated and had a far shorter tradition in patronizing music than the aristocracy. Second, classical music had to compete with the blossoming "light" genres like the café-concert, the variety show, the operetta and vaudeville, as well as the dance music, the forerunner of modern pop. Musicians and critics (a then newly born profession) had to educate this new public, to refine its taste, to teach it how to distinguish between the various genres and the good and not-so-good in every genre.

Paradoxically, the light genres helped promote the "serious" (also called "art") music; indeed, there was no gulf between the two sides similar to the one that would be born about the middle of the twentieth century. The nineteenth century had a very efficient "glue" that bound together the two genres: the waltz. This popular dance rose to prominence soon after Beethoven's and Schubert's deaths (largely graced by the latter's efforts) and permeated all musical forms and genres to such an extent that the century could be called the Waltz Age. It was easy to waltz one's mind and feelings from the ballroom to the operetta and then to the opera house or to the concert hall.[72] Finally, the musicians themselves had to define their inner self, split between the fashionable Romantic poses of *génie damné* or *artiste-prophète*, both intended for posthumous glory, and the natural desire of recognition. As Taruskin put it, they generally solved this "contrast between romantic theory and romantic practice [by] what psychologists call dissociation (or, more vulgarly, 'compartmentalization') that allowed romantic idealists the ability to achieve sufficient compromise with reality conditions to survive, often very happily indeed."[73]

All in all, there never was much of a chasm between musicians and their public during the nineteenth century. And German speaking countries, which McClary incriminates, were the ones where the relationship between the two was the strongest. Here is the testimony of the great cellist Pablo Casals, who toured extensively all over Europe around 1900:

> In Germany one finds immediately that music is an essential part of people's life. I have played at hundreds of concerts in the land of Bach and Beethoven and I have always been struck by the atmosphere of devotion to be found in the public. An artist tries to create such an atmosphere in order to get in more direct and intimate communication with his audience. I must say that it finds it ready to hand in Germany. [...]

> In Austria you feel that music is not the privilege of a group or class of people. Everybody has a natural need of music, just as much as the need for conversation. One day, when I was coming out of the Bristol hotel in Vienna, I noticed that the porter was humming a tune while he put letters in their boxes. I said to him, "Do you know what you are singing?" "Of course," he replied quite naturally, "the third Brahms Symphony" (sic!) And as I questioned him he told me he belonged to a music society whose concerts he attended twice a week. And he added, "So do most of the clerks and cab drivers and carpenters."[74]

It is true, however, that a sort of "malaise" began to undermine this happy relationship towards the end of the nineteenth century, involving the public reception of the music of only one (nowadays deemed) great composer, Gustav Mahler. His public was eager for novelty but was torn between the musician's "tame" side—such as his Third Symphony's Scherzo dubbed *Blumenstück* or his Fifth Symphony's *Adagietto*—and his wild utterances tantamount to atonality. But this was just the beginning of a relatively late but deepening chasm between musicians and classical music lovers during the twentieth century—and the chasm was the effect, not the cause, of the abandonment of tonality by the musicians.

Professor McClary does not miss the opportunity to inject her favorite ingredient, gender, in the misconstrued deconstruction that I am (in turn) deconstructing here. She claims (*CW* 113-4) that the alleged rift between musicians and their public was primarily a gender matter: it would have been the feminine public who continued to respond to the music's emotional strain, while the males moved to a different kind of perception, that of the form—hence formalism. That women as a group remained faithful to the emotional layer of music is very possible, but McClary could not present any evidence that the (German or non-German) males did otherwise. She claims that a similar rift happened in poetry too, but again without putting forward any evidence of such a contrast (*CW* 113). Finally, she alleges (*CW* 114) that

> [...] this gendered division still remains [to this day]. In his book *Nineteenth Century Music*, Carl Dahlhaus argues that even the greatest art can be transformed into Kitsch if played by and for women,

indicating her source at page 313 of the book of this prominent twentieth-century German musicologist.

As with her previous appropriation of Doerner's work (or at least his name, as described above), Dahlhaus (1928-1989) does not make such a statement, either on page 313 or anywhere else in his book. In the chapter on *Trivial Music*, to which this page belongs, he theorizes that during the nineteenth century, as a result of intense "commercialization" accompanying the rise of the middle class, classical music began to be "trivialized" (or degraded into mere kitsch). That happened when listeners were encouraged to be "self-indulging," that, is responding only to the emotional side of music and failing to consider the "content-form dialectics." Women were particularly susceptible to such an approach, Dahlhaus writes, because the education they received in that patriarchal society encouraged them to learn and practice music only to "touch and gladden the heart," which, in his opinion, is a form of kitsch.[75] Professor McClary could have challenged Professor Dahlhaus's claim that music "touching and gladdening the heart" would be kitsch; she could have quoted the phrase Beethoven inscribed on the head of his *Missa Solemnis* ("from the heart—may it in turn go to the heart"), but Beethoven was anathema to her. She chose to distort her dead opponent's account into a most blatant misogynistic statement.

Finally, when we mull over the bulk of McClary's theoretical work, we discover a very important inconsistency. At a certain point in her arguing over the alleged "German malady," she deplores the fact that in music "each liberatory style became the oppressive tradition from which the succeeding one had to break loose" (*CW* 116). The fact is undeniable and is a pattern in all Western arts, steered by what we like to call "progress": over a five-hundred-year span, we had Renaissance, early Baroque and Baroque, Rococo and Classical Age, Romanticism and Post-Romanticism, etc. But why does McClary lament this fact, when her own doctrine justifies it? She had previously defined tonality as a convention—"the particular cluster of conventions we call tonality" (*CW* 63, a description repeated several times later: 65, 107, 115, 136)—and affirmed that "composers did not reject conventions simply because they were conventions, [...] they also reacted against the cultural uses made of such codes during their eighteenth century heyday" (*CW* 115). It is, therefore normal, by her own assessment, to replace a convention with another one, including tonality with atonality. Why all the bemoaning? Just to find reasons to imprecate the one whom she passionately loathes—Beethoven?

Professor McClary's comrades-in-arms

In spite of her claim to the contrary,[*] McClary's doctrine stems from the firm belief that, in an oppressive society such as a patriarchal one, every social aspect is determined by that particular domineering force—in this case, male sexuality. Such an outlook of history takes socio-economic determinism to an extreme rejected even by Marxism and Leninism (although, as we will see, not by Maoism). Marxism views a society as consisting in a *basis* (by and large the equivalent of McClary's "socio-historical context") and a *superstructure* including immaterial components like law, religion, literature, art and music. According to Marxism, "Basis determines Superstructure," but the founders of the theory, men with solid classical educations who appreciated literature and art (Engels was a good amateur musician, too), knew that such simplified formulae are prone to dogmatic interpretation. Engels, whom Marx (very busy with finishing his master work, *Capital*) entrusted with defending the theory against various perils, including vulgarization, wrote most of his works and plenty of letters to explain those perils to younger and less-broadly-knowledgeable adherents to Communist ideology. Thus, he wrote to one of these ideologically neophytes:

> Political, juridical, philosophical, religious, literary, artistic, etc., development is based on economic development. But all these react upon one another and also upon the economic base. It is not that the economic position is the *cause and alone active,* while everything else only has a passive effect. There is, rather, interaction on the basis of the economic necessity, which *ultimately* always asserts itself.[76]

If one applies the Marxist formula to Western classical music in this elastic way, one can say that, while patriarchal societies certainly had a say in the development of this art (for instance, by subordinating it to the Church), music

---

[*] "[...] this is not to suggest that music is nothing but an epiphenomenon that can be explained by way of social determinism" (*FE* 21).

also played a certain part in creating the social fabric—actually one of the general statements proclaimed by McClary herself (see page 204-205). And one can also say that music did not have to be an expression of the male oppression of women just because it was the product of a patriarchal society. Actually, Herbert Marcuse, a prominent twentieth century Marxist, who was also the mentor of the New Left movement to which Susan McClary also belongs, considered art to be "largely autonomous" from social relations and not reflecting societal repression but "subverting" it.[77] McClary missed this particular lesson from her guru and chose to view society exclusively through the lens of gender.[78]

This kind of dogmatic outlook is, unfortunately, no novelty. Immediately after they seized power in Russia by means of the so-called Bolshevik Revolution of 1917, the Communists instituted an organization meant to stimulate the development of "Proletarian Culture" (culture means here artistic creativity). The Russian abbreviation, "Proletkult," came to designate this kind of Leftist tunnel vision, in which one had to demolish all existing art (because of its bourgeois foundation) and replace it with a new art, "for the proletariat, by the proletariat." This radical vision eventually clashed with more traditional views of the authorities, including Lenin (who, incidentally, loved Beethoven's music); therefore, the organization was disbanded and its ideology denounced as "leftist deviation."

A parallel "leftist deviation" manifested in a more recent and much gorier episode in Communist China. During the Cultural Revolution of the 1960s and '70s, tens of millions were sent to thousands of "re-education camps" of the *laogai* (the Chinese gulag) where many of them died.[79] One of the punished crimes was listening or playing Western music. The party daily *Jenmin Jih Pao*, in an article titled "Works of music without titles don't reflect the class spirit," explained that "Marxist-Leninists hold that all musical works, as a form of ideology, are products of the reflection in the human brain of the life of a given society," and singled out "German bourgeois composer Beethoven" for condemnation.[80]

*

The present deconstruction has conclusively shown that Susan McClary's argument in defense of her succinct yet broadly encompassing theory about the Western classical music is rife with serious scholarly errors, which nullify her basic tenets. She willfully ignored and distorted facts; she twisted other scholars' statements and arguments; she did not check the accuracy and veracity of the sources when they suited her theses—all because she was driven by a specific agenda. Ideology cannot be fully excluded from research, but it should never impair the scholar's professional judgement. Ideology did very seriously impair Professor McClary's. That her theories have been so easily adopted as an important part of the feminist outlook of the Western world is proof that feminist scholarship has still to raise its level of self-critical assessment.

Appendix. Pages 118-119 of De Lauretis' book *Alice Doesn't*

118 / ALICE DOESN'T

"precipitated" in one single or cyclical text-image. And the same would be true of multi-heroed texts, where heroes of successive generations (say, father and son) function as diachronic character-doubles of each other (while twins would be synchronic doubles). As for the totality of different characters distributed across the plot-text, this is how Lotman maps their genesis in the cyclical system:

> Characters can be divided into those who are mobile, who enjoy freedom with regard to plot-space, who can change their place in the structure of the artistic world and cross the frontier, the basic topological feature of this space, and those who are immobile, who represent, in fact, a function of this space. Looked at typologically, the initial situation is that a certain plot-space is divided by a *single* boundary into an internal and an external sphere, and a *single* character has the opportunity to cross that boundary; this situation is now replaced by a more complex derivative. The mobile character is split up into a paradigm-cluster of different characters on the same plane, and the obstacle (boundary), also multiplying in quantity, gives out a sub-group of personified obstacles—immobile enemy-characters fixed at particular points in the plot-space ("antagonists" to use Propp's term). [P. 167]

Several considerations are in order. First, in the notion of immobile characters or personified obstacles, fixed at a certain point of the plot-space and representing, standing for (on) a boundary which the hero alone can cross, we easily recognize the Sphinx (and Oedipus) and Medusa (and Perseus); but also, if less immediately, Jocasta and Oedipus, or Andromeda and Perseus. Second, by reducing the number and functions of what Propp would call the *dramatis personae* to the two involved in the primary conflict of hero and antagonist (obstacle), Lotman outlines a pattern of mythical narrative strongly suggestive of the one Mulvey ascribes to sadism. Third, as he further translates in cyclical terms the elementary sequence of narrative functions, which Propp had found to be thirty-one in the folktale plot-text, Lotman finds a simple chain of two functions, open at both ends and thus endlessly repeatable: "entry into a closed space, and emergence from it." He then adds: "Inasmuch as closed space *can be interpreted* as 'a cave', 'the grave', 'a house', 'woman' (and, correspondingly, be allotted the features of darkness, warmth, dampness), entry into it *is interpreted* on various levels as 'death', 'conception', 'return home' and so on; moreover all these acts *are thought of as mutually identical*" (p. 168; my emphasis).

In this mythical-textual mechanics, then, the hero must be male,

232

Desire in Narrative / 119

regardless of the gender of the text-image, because the obstacle, whatever its personification, is morphologically female and indeed, simply, the womb. The implication here is not inconsequential. For if the work of the mythical structuration is to establish distinctions, the primary distinction on which all others depend is not, say, life and death, but rather sexual difference. In other words, the picture of the world produced in mythical thought since the very beginning of culture would rest, first and foremost, on what we call biology. Opposite pairs such as inside/outside, the raw/the cooked, or life/death appear to be merely derivatives of the fundamental opposition between boundary and passage; and if passage may be in either direction, from inside to outside or vice versa, from life to death or vice versa, nonetheless all these terms are predicated on the *single* figure of the hero who crosses the boundary and penetrates the other space. In so doing the hero, the mythical subject, is constructed as human being and as male; he is the active principle of culture, the establisher of distinction, the creator of differences. Female is what is not susceptible to transformation, to life or death; she (it) is an element of plot-space, a topos, a resistance, matrix and matter.

The distance between this view and Propp's is not merely "methodological"; it is ideological. Suffice it to point out that in very similar terms René Girard interprets the Oedipus myth in its double link to tragedy and to sacrificial ritual, and defines the role of Oedipus as that of surrogate victim. Ritual sacrifice, he states, serves to reestablish an order periodically violated by the eruption of violent reciprocity, the cyclical violence inherent in "nondifference," or what Lotman calls "non-discreteness." By his victory over the Sphinx, Oedipus has crossed the boundary and thus established his status as hero. However, in committing regicide, patricide, and incest, he has become "the slayer of distinctions," has abolished differences and thus contravened the mythical order. "Patricide represents the establishment of violent reciprocity between father and son, the reduction of the paternal relationship to 'fraternal' revenge," which is exemplified by the enemy brothers Eteocles and Polyneices or by the brothers-in-law Oedipus and Creon. Regicide is but the equivalent, vis-à-vis the polis, of patricide. And therefore, with Oedipus in Thebes,

> violent reciprocity is left in sole command of the battlefield. Its victory could hardly be more complete, for in pitting father against son *it has chosen as the basis of their rivalry an object solemnly consecrated as belonging to*

11
Lawrence Kramer's second leg in Beethoven's violent masculinity relay

Lawrence Kramer, a Distinguished Professor of English and Music at the Fordham University in New York, is, alongside with Susan McClary, a pioneering figure of the so-called new musicology. In his 1997 book *After the Lovedeath*, subtitled "Sexual violence and the Making of Culture,"[1] he pays his dues to his predecessor only in passing,[2] and assigns Beethoven a leading role in his thesis as already made explicit in the subtitle. Therefore, one can describe him as the second leg in the relay opened by Susan McClary with the purpose of exposing Beethoven as a musical "sexual predator," the first in a short line of such musical evildoers. However, Kramer aims higher, making Beethoven into the allegorical symbol of the fundamental sin of the modern Western civilization, that is, sexual violence against women.

An overview of Kramer's thesis

Kramer's book professorially—and I am not using this term in any derogatory way—opens with a clear-cut statement of purpose (1):

> This book proposes that the forms of selfhood mandated as normal in modern Western culture both promote and rationalize violence against women.

The limpidity of this introduction is remarkable, even though it is not exactly a novelty. It positions Kramer as a forerunner of the present-day "me-too" movement, and as a further developer of Carole Pateman's theory of the "sexual contract," which would have been part of the "social contract" postulated by the Enlightenment theorists as foundation of society.[3]

New in this statement of purpose is the fact that by "modern Western culture" Kramer understands simply the world we live in at the crossroads of two millennia, which we used to credit with having made huge steps forward in correcting a misdeed that is at least as old as written history. Although he had promised in his book's subtitle to present us "the making of culture," he tackles only our contemporary society, which obviously inherited "sexual violence" from time immemorial. We will see later how he tries to fill this gap. It may seem odd that he could insert Beethoven, a man that lived two hundred years ago, into such a modern drama, but we will see that there is method to the oddness, too.

Kramer's book is loosely structured, in what he calls a "mosaic" (3); the longer introductory chapter is followed by a collection of 81 very short essays (some of them less than a page), which look like a professor's take on assignments given to his university students over the years and later assembled into a book, in order to fulfill a well-known requirement of academe. They cover and tend to coalesce the two disciplines of the professor, literature and music, and display the author's great erudition involving literary and non-literary names, from A(ndreas-Salome Lou, a first-generation psychoanalyst) to Z(ola Emile, the naturalist French writer), closely or remotely connected to the topic. This makes his argument scattered and results in some inner incongruities. (I will signal the major ones in due time.) Since we are interested here in Kramer's approach to music and particularly to Beethoven, most of his essays are of collateral or no interest, and my final evaluation refers only to this topic.

Kramer postulates that violence against women is an innate trait of male mentality, an assertion that even a cursory knowledge of the history of the (Western and non-Western) world appears to support. He is, however, not satisfied with stating facts to prove his assertion; he tries to "deconstruct" it, by appealing to a later version of psychoanalysis. He introduces a rather confusing concept that he calls "gender polarity," which would be responsible for igniting that mentality and he traces down its roots to the famous (and, as we have seen in Chapter 1, illusory) "Œdipus complex" postulated by Freud and reviewed and modified by one of his later disciples, Jacques Lacan, around the concept of "phallus," as a symbol of "absolute masculinity."

To introduce Beethoven into this picture, Kramer takes a clue from a short fragment in the writings of Robert Schumann (already invoked by McClary) describing Beethoven's music as "masculine," and extrapolates it, promoting Beethoven as "the most masculine" of the composers, therefore most guilty of "gender polarity." This way, Kramer makes "[t]his tale of the gender of musical genius" into an "allegory, the gist of this [his] book" (5).[*] However, he does not put Beethoven on the couch, as the Sterbas and Solomon did, probably because he could not find anything in the Beethoven literature to support a connection between the composer's alleged "musical masculinity" and his feelings as "the holder of phallus." Instead, Kramer resorts to an indirect association, through a once famous and now almost forgotten late nineteenth century fiction, the novella *The Kreutzer Sonata* by Leo Tolstoy, a classic of Russian and world literature. This is the story of a man that kills his wife out of jealousy, a drama in which the famous Beethoven sonata plays a certain important and yet confusing role: the wife, a good amateur pianist (as many upper-class ladies were at the time), enjoyed playing the sonata together with a (male) professional violinist that the husband saw as a would-be seducer. To Kramer, the "masculinity" expressed in the first movement of the sonata was meaningfully involved in the murderous act.

Beethoven's "masculinity": An overstated label

Kramer's "tale of Beethoven's masculinity" as illustrative of the Western world's "sexual violence" begins with ... Schubert, whose music Kramer confesses to have taken to heart from an early age, infiltrating his dreams (4)—a perfectly understandable and moving commitment. Kramer further invokes the authority of Schumann, who was also a prominent music critic during the age of

---

[*] All references to Kramer's book in this chapter are given in the text.

early Romanticism and contributed both to making Beethoven into the prow-figure of the movement and to promoting Schubert as its posthumous star. Rewording Schumann's opinion about Schubert's music, Kramer writes (4-5):

> For all its beauty, it [Schubert's music] lacked virility, at least in comparison with the masculine ideal embodied, inevitably, by Beethoven. Schumann sets out to rescue Schubert from this invidious comparison, though only at the cost of assenting to it. In relation to Beethoven, Schumann writes, Schubert was indeed a feminine composer, but in relation to all other composers he was masculine enough. Beethoven, in this reading, is a violent figure, or a figure—a personification—of violence: one who feminizes others but who can never himself be feminized. "The man [Beethoven]," writes Schumann, "commands," the woman [Schubert] "pleads." In this hypervirile role, Beethoven stands as the embodiment of musical culture itself: stern, unyielding, commanding, his name the name of the Father. Before this Beethoven, Schubert is yielding, dependent, permeable. Yet this same Schubert can himself lay claim to the name of the father if only one can forget (but one can never forget) the figure of Beethoven behind him.

The Schubert v. Beethoven comparison that Kramer invokes is only a short fragment from a longer commentary on Schubert's music that Schumann published in the June 5, 1838 issue of *Neue Zeitschrift für Musik* [The New Music Magazine][4] founded by him, that had by then become the main voice of the Romanticist generation. Kramer quotes it from a collection of Schumann's writings published (in the English translation of Paul Rosenfeld) in 1946. One can read therein, "Schubert is a more feminine character compared to the other [Beethoven]."[5] Actually, Schumann's description is more colorful: "Compared to the other [Beethoven], Schubert has the character of a very talkative girl" [ist ein Mädchencharakter an Jenen gehalten, bei weitem geschwätziger]; that is, Schubert let himself carried away by his musical drive, unlike Beethoven, who was far more concentrated, or "self-contained," as Goethe characterized him.[6]

Kramer further invents the "Beethoven commands, Schubert pleads" paradigm based on this sentence found in the same Schumann source: "to be sure, he [Schubert] brings in his powerful passages, and works in masses; and still he is more feminine than masculine, for he pleads and persuades, where the man commands." The original German is not quite unambiguous (like many others in Schumann's reviews), therefore the translator's work is not easy and can fail, as it does in Rosenfeld's awkward phrase "[Schubert] works in masses." The correct translation is:

> It is true that he also brings in his forceful side and mobilizes the masses; but it always happens like in a wife (or woman) toward husband (or man) relationship, [in which] he commands, while she entreats and persuades.[*]

---

[*] The original reads: *Zwar bringt auch er seine Kraftstelle, bietet auch er Massen auf; doch verhält es sich immer als Weib zum Mann, der befiehlt, wo jenes bittet und*

Indeed, the original has no comparison term ("mehr" in German) and the "powerful passages" make sense as the man's "command." These "powerful passages" also explain why Schumann finds Schubert "masculine enough" when compared to other composers, as Kramer himself notices. Kramer could have also noticed, in the Schumann book he quotes, a description of Schubert's *Piano Trio in E Flat Major* D. 929 as "more active, masculine [männlich] and dramatic," as compared to his *B Flat major Trio* D. 898, which was "more passive lyric and feminine."[7] The "Beethoven commands, Schubert pleads" proclamation is just another stretching of the argument. One may also notice that Beethoven himself was no foreigner to this duality—he practiced it a lot, like in his *Coriolan* overture or in the first movement of his *Piano Sonata in D minor* Op. 31 No. 2.

To sum up, in Schumann's view, "masculinity" is a relative not an absolute measure. He never declared Beethoven the most masculine of all composers, as Kramer hurries to claim in the already quoted line about Beethoven's "hypervirile role." The only comparison that Schumann extends besides the Beethoven-Schubert one is that between the latter and the "newer musicians," in comparison with whom Schubert was definitely more "masculine." Who were these "newer musicians?" There is only one possible answer: Schumann's colleagues of the first Romanticist generation. Granted, this was not a homogenous group: it comprised both composers that Schumann greatly appreciated and were actually entering the canon—Mendelssohn, Chopin and Liszt—as well as many now forgotten virtuosos who were popular and quite prolific at the time, such as Sigismond Thalberg (1812-1871), Liszt's competitor in the virtuoso arena.

Actually, in the same notice about Schubert in the *Neue Zeitschrift für Musik*, we can discover that Beethoven was not the only "masculine" composers. Before comparing Schubert to him, Schumann sketches a broader perspective of musical affinities. He writes:

> Experiences which youth has not yet achieved are necessary to the evaluation of Bach; it [youth] even underestimates Mozart's greatness. Mere musical studies are not enough to enable us to understand Beethoven, just as in certain years he inspires us with one work rather than with another. It is certain that equal ages exert a reciprocal attraction on each other, that youthful enthusiasm is best understood by youth and the power of the *mature master* by the full-grown man [die Kraft des männlichen Meisters vom Mann]. So Schubert will always remain the favorite of the youth.[8] (my emphasis)

The italicized *mature* is actually termed "masculine" in the original (männlichen); the translator had chosen a word that fits better the context, but the original shows that Schumann had a fluid usage of the term "masculine." To

---

überredet. Weib and *Mann* are ambiguous terms in German; the former can design both woman and wife, and the latter both man and husband.

him, Bach and Mozart were as "masculine" as Beethoven. Nothing in his reviews justifies Kramer's mentioned description of Beethoven as 's "hyper-virility," that he further wraps up in psychoanalytical lingo.

Beethoven's "masculinity" as allegorical "sexual violence"

The quoted beginning of Professor Kramer's book stating that senses of self in "modern Western culture both promote and rationalize violence against women" does not define its terms. It seems that "modern" means in fact "contemporary," because the author consistently uses the present tense. But what does "sexual violence" mean? The infamous "r" act, or the "sexual contract" denounced by Carole Pateman as a hidden part of a much vaster scope of oppression of women at all societal levels? The continuation of the paragraph seems to indicate the most literal kind of "violence" and draws the picture of a frightening modern world that presages the "me-too" movement:

> Even if unacted, the possibility of sexual violence ripples in the air like rising heat, visible and invisible at the same time. Far from being haunted or threatened by this possibility, normal selfhood is permeated by it. Both men and women alike are enjoined to construct heterosexual gender identities based on a mercurial love-hate relationship to whatever is understood as femininity.

The term "femininity," is also introduced, a concept that will prove essential in Kramer's argument, at least in what concerns the subject of my present book—Beethoven. As before, Kramer does not offer a clear definition of this new term, perhaps assuming that we all share his. He does not seem to need a definition either, because, as he soon claims (2),

> the predicament [the persistence of sexual violence] arises not from any particular definition of what it means to be feminine or masculine, but from the way femininity and masculinity are distinguished.

If one wonders how one could distinguish between two concepts without having them defined, Kramer has an explanation:

> The two genders may be construed, performed, and lived in any number of ways, as long are femininity constitutes the radically ambivalent polar opposite of a radically unambivalent masculinity.

One can recognize in this one of the principles of the methodological approach that post-modernism shares with libertarianism, which I termed above as "absolute relativism." Each individual—Kramer and I, and you, my reader—is free to construct his or her conception of gender the way he or she wants and then apply to it one of the two labels, on condition that he/she knows what Kramer understands by ambivalent (femininity) and unambivalent (masculinity). I confess that I have no clue after having finished his book. In fact, the two dualistic terms seem only to serve for Kramer to introduce Beethoven in his picture of modern Western culture via his "masculinity." With Beethoven indicted for occupying a unique position of "masculinity" in the musical world, as a sort of "musical Father" (5), Kramer then explains:

> This tale of the gender of musical genius gives, in allegory, the gist of this book. Bluntly stated, my argument is that in our gender identities, all of us—men and women alike—are Schuberts, none of us a Beethoven. (5)

This last sweeping generalization is really perplexing in its logical consequences. As if that would not have been enough, Professor Kramer gives us a coup-de-grâce (5):

> Between the sixteenth and the seventeenth centuries, the position in which Schumann recognized Schubert became the normative position of the subject in Western culture, and so it remains today. For both men and women, to become a subject, to acquire an identity, is to assume a position of femininity in relation to a masculinity that always belongs to someone else.

It seems that some mysterious force arose sometime around 1600 (between the sixteenth and seventeenth centuries), messing up a world that had lived in perfect sexual harmony before! Beginning with that moment up to the present, all of us, men and women—because everybody has an "identity"—had to become feminine and be subjected to the sexual violence exerted by "someone else." If *all of us* are feminine, who is that masculine "someone else?" Even Beethoven could not be it, because he was born seventy years after that alleged watershed moment.

Kramer's whole argument about us as "none of us Beethoven-all of us Schuberts" does not make any logical sense. Besides that, I showed that Beethoven's "masculinity" was nothing out of the ordinary in the Classical world; his music was arguably reflecting a "masculine" perspective on his world, but why would that made his "masculinity" into the kind that feminism calls "toxic" today? Kramer himself acknowledges that "no man, and certainly no woman, can securely identify with this masculine subject-position" (5).

The psychoanalytical approach marring Kramer's argument from start

Kramer solves this contradiction by invoking Freud's "Œdipal complex," which "authorizes and perpetuates the oppression of women" (21). He invokes the authority of Jacques Lacan, a later-day disciple of Freud and a proponent of a new version of the famous complex, centered on the "phallus." The phallus is not the penis, which every male has, but a kind of symbolic "scepter" of absolute masculinity, which no man really possesses, because he always has also incorporated into himself a feminine side; the existence of this side induces a Freudian "fear of castration" in the man and "the fiction of holding the absolutely masculine subject-position that in truth no one can hold." Although the pretense of having the only existing phallus is "unstable, sometimes even ridiculous […] it translates for some men into the privileges of a practical, manifest, functional masculinity" (6). The man's wish to be recognized as a "holder of the phallus" can be fulfilled only when he had "recuperated" it from a woman, who would now be the symbolic thief (of his phallus); of course, the man would have the right to recuperate it by force. "This symbolic function," Kramer writes, "operates in a multitude of contexts, social, erotic, aesthetic, narrative, and ideological" (7) and is as essential part of "the cultural regime of Œdipal or phallic subject-formation that canonizes sexual violence against anything or anyone coded as feminine."

Kramer adds the concept of "gender polarity" to the Lacanian theory. Gender polarity "occurs when the duality masculine-feminine is constructed around a rigid boundary, a phallic bar or barrier, in terms of mutual exclusion and masculine dominance" (9-10). Judging by the examples that Kramer gives, gender polarity, typically encountered only between heterosexual males, would consist in the exclusion/murder of the feminine side (Kramer calls it "position"), which is always present, as science has found a long time ago (the two sexes share the same hormones, in different proportions).

Gender polarity might be a suggestive description of the male personality that can effect sexual violence against a woman, but is just an empty term. Kramer never offers a real definition of the alleged "rigid boundary" between the two positions; one feels tempted to translate it with some commonsense term like "psychopathy border," but it would be a mistake: psychopathy is a disease that distorts human nature, while "the Œdipal" *is* male human nature in the psychoanalytic view.

Finally, Kramer introduces an antidote of gender polarity, the equally confusing concept of "gender synergy" that he never defines other than something that would "collapse the polarized structures that privilege an abusive virility" (12). Obviously, feminine nature is by definition "synergetic," and so is the homosexual one, but hetero males might also reach it with some mysterious effort, which would be "our best hope for a humane gender system" (16), guaranteeing a happy ending of the humankind story sometime in the future.

I will not rebut each of Kramer's psychoanalytical arguments that are spread throughout his book, for the simple reason that the whole on which his approach is based is a Freudian delusion. Kramer seems unaware of the many scientific and clinical findings that have been gleaned for over a quarter of century proving the fallacy of the Freudian theory (which I summed up in chapter 1 of this book); he only mentions this in passing (8-9) and rejects the negative appraisals of psychoanalysis that have been made from within the field itself and from philosophical perspectives. He extensively (and "gratefully") quotes the apology of the theory proffered by philosopher Thomas Nagel (8-9), who claimed that "common sense has in fact expanded to include parts of Freudian theory." As I have showed in Chapter 1, modern neuroscience and anthropology have exposed Freud's theory, including the Œdipus complex, as a scientific delusion. There were no conditions for this complex to develop in the primeval human societies in which the human species crystalized, separate from other primates.

Unfulfilled promises

Carried away by his psychoanalytical zeal, Kramer forgets to fulfill two important promises in his statement of purpose. Although he claims to present us "the making of culture," he tackles only our contemporary society, which obviously inherited "sexual violence" from times immemorial. He briefly mentions a threshold "Between the sixteenth and the seventeenth centuries" when (Western) society would have undergone a major change related to "sexual violence," without any further explanation of what and how this happened. He gives us instead a ready-made psychoanalytical recipe and he continues to speculate throughout his book, in the many disparate chapters/pages, mainly about the already mentioned "gender polarity."

Another promise that Kramer does not keep is to show how modern Western culture "rationalizes" violence against women. He claims that "normal selfhood" is nowadays "permeated" by it, although "virtually everyone regrets it, including those who inflict it (1-2). Even if this assessment was true—and it is not, as even a pioneer feminist of the sixties like Camille Paglia acknowledges[9]—that would not be proof that modern culture "rationalizes" violence against women. "Rationalizing" would imply that at least one societal factor would disseminate theoretical arguments to justify the dominant position of males, and Kramer does not cite a single one, for the simple reason that there is none. Modern society would certainly abhor such a position. In fact, the only rationalizing of sexual violence that we can encounter in Kramer's book belongs to Kramer himself: according to him, males are born within "the Œdipal," which would be the root of sexual violence; therefore, they enact it in accordance with natural law.

Tolstoy's *The Kreutzer Sonata*: The facts

I hope that the reader by now agrees that Kramer's theory about Beethoven's "masculinity" as an example of "gender polarity," in which Beethoven claimed de position of "Father" of the musical world, dominating his more "feminine" fellow composers, is just another fantasy. Nevertheless, Kramer returns to the composer's "masculinity" again and again, in a different way, by repeatedly invoking Tolstoy's novella *The Kreutzer Sonata*, because it "shows gender polarity in its most self-conscious and also its most reprehensible form [... and Beethoven's] music is somehow at the heart of the dilemmas of gender polarity" (12).

In order to understand Kramer's take on Tolstoy's novella and the implication of Beethoven's music, one must first be introduced to the characters and their lives before the crucial episode of the narrative that leads directly to the murder. In fact, we need a more thorough introduction than Kramer offers, which explores the narrative only selectively, omitting many meaningful aspects. That will help us understand how and why Kramer is wrong and right at the same time.

At first reading, Tolstoy's novella, published in 1893, appears to be case study of jealousy pushed into pathology—that is, into murder. It employs an infrequent (at the time) format that assigns the omniscient author a secondary role, restricted to commenting on the way in which the evil hero himself narrates his history to a fellow passenger during a train trip. This happens after the murderer had been acquitted of the killing—in accordance with the laws of the times (shared all over Europe) that pardoned "honor killing." His murderous act, however, had shocked the perpetrator to the point of giving him "seeing" powers that enable him to understand and describe objectively at least the circumstances surrounding the act that remains itself unexplainable. The main characters are typical of the Russian upper-class at the end of the nineteenth century, and their husband-wife-seducer triangle is, according to Tolstoy, also typical. Pozdnyshev, the murderous husband, is a man approaching middle age, nominally not an aristocrat (making him one would not have passed the Tsarist censorship) but a well-off official. He had married according to the new fashion of romantic love, or at least believes he had. His never-named wife, much younger than him, is a well-educated offspring of the rich class, therefore adept at romantic love as well as playing the piano. The marriage did not abide well, with increasing disagreements that "at last reached a stage where it was not disagreement that caused hostility but hostility that caused disagreement."[10] The third member of the triangle is an older chance acquaintance of Pozdnyshev, a violinist named Trukhachevski, who is not an ordinary "fiddler"—he, too, is a member of a reputable class and a guest of high-society salons.

Pozdnyshev's wife is now in her young thirties. After having given her husband five children—itself including much angst and suffering—she feels restored; she had learned from her doctors how to enjoy sex without risking pregnancy and is at the peak of her femininity and likes to shine. Pozdnyshev, who would later confess of having been "tormented by jealousy all his married life"[11] is "terrified" by the thought that she expects something to happen in her life that he cannot give her.[12] Nevertheless, as if stimulated by a masochist instinct, he invites Trukhachevski to their home, because his wife has rekindled an interest in the piano she had neglected due of her motherly duties, and wants to practice music again. The wife and the violinist like each other, practice under the eyes of the suspicious husband and, a few days later, play Beethoven's Kreutzer Sonata together for the guests in her husband's salon. Pozdnyshev would later confess that this sonata, particularly its first movement, was a "terrifying thing" that "had a horrible effect" on him,[13] but without being able to explain in what way. He leaves for a tour of duty in the province, but a letter from his wife mentioning casually that the violinist had paid her a visit and that they had practiced together (while the husband had thought that the violinist was going to leave the city for some time) triggers a fit of jealousy in Pozdnyshev,[14] The husband hurries back home and, during his journey, works himself up with exacerbating scenarios, imagining himself as both Othello and Iago, dwelling on details that gradually grow to great significance in his mind. When he arrives, prepared for the worst, he discovers the two just making music together, but is nevertheless certain that they had an affair (he reads "terror" in their eyes). Pozdnyshev kills his wife but fails to kill the man, who manages to escape.

Pozdnyshev's essential explanation of his murderous act, as he tells it to his "confessor":

> It was he [the violinist] with his music who was the cause of it all. [...] At the trial the case was put as if it was all caused by jealousy. No such thing, that is, I don't mean "no such thing", it was and it was not. What my wife's relations with that musician may have been has no meaning for me, or for her either. What has a meaning is [...]—my swinishness. [...] The whole thing was an outcome of the terrible abyss between us.[15]

He is not quite sure about his understanding of the facts. He accepts that he was jealous, but he eventually points to his "swinishness" as the root cause. "Swinishness" is the term that Tolstoy's translator chose here to rendered literally the original Russian ("свинство"), for which he otherwise preferred the common English word of debauchery. "Swinishness" may be more descriptive, because it recalls the dictum of the twentieth century feminist movement, "all men are pigs." Indeed, to Pozdnyshev, his murderous act was only the result of his treatment of women as objects of his sexual discharge in all circumstances, in hiring prostitutes as well as looking for "love and marriage," which was just another form of "debauchery" in his view. He extended this self-loathing to condemnation of his society and culture as guilty as it hypocritically attempts to "emancipate women in universities and law courts, but continue to regard her as an object of enjoyment,"[16] justifying, promoting and creating the conditions for general "swinishness."

Such overall societal condemnation could certainly be subsumed into Pateman's denouncement of the beforehand mentioned "sexual contract" intended to assure man's "orderly access" to a woman's body that a patriarchal culture sanctioned as a fundamental right of the male.[17] Feminism would like less Pozdnyshev's further extension of his indictment: swinishness has also perverted the female, teaching her how to adjust and become a full participant in debauchery and how to use her power of seduction to become the master of the owner of her body. This was the main cause of the "mutual hatred" that marred his marriage:

> It could not have been otherwise. That hatred was nothing but the mutual hatred of accomplices in a crime—both for the incitement to the crime and for taking part in it. What was it but a crime when she, poor thing, became pregnant in the first month and our swinish connection continued?[18]

Kramer ignores a key fact that helps one to understand *The Kreutzer Sonata*: this is Tolstoy's most autobiographical writing. Its (anti-)hero Pozdnyshev is modeled after young Tolstoy. Born (1828)* into an aristocratic family that offered him the privileges, luxury and vices due his status, the writer led a dissipate life in his youth, indulging in sex with prostitutes, courtesans and adulterous married women, as well as (the most detestable abuse of power) with maid-servants who were raised in the homes of the rich and powerful to serve the old and young masters' sexual needs. After going through a gory war experience (1854-1855) that matured him, Tolstoy tried to redeem himself through "love" (he elaborated a personal theory of Love, as altruistic expression) and in 1862 he married, for love, a young girl, just as Pozdnyshev did. This marriage worked well for some time, allowing Tolstoy to write his first major works (his epic *War and Peace* included), with his wife helping him as his secretary, besides raising their many children coming along every other year. Yet in late 1870s, Tolstoy's

---

* My main source is Hugh McLean, *In Search of Tolstoy* (Boston, 2008).

quest for redemption led him to a true "conversion," the first fruit of which was his *Kreutzer Sonata*. He put his new creed in the mouth of the novella's evil hero but did not redeem him, as he had redeemed himself. In order to make the moral of the story more poignant, he made the hero's swinishness lead him to murder.

After his novella became controversial, Tolstoy felt the need "to explain in clear and simple terms, what I think about the subject of the story,"[19] and so wrote and published (1890) its "Afterword." This afterword, which Kramer ignores, does not attempt to give a psychological explanation of how the protagonist's jealousy turned into murder; it re-states, scraping off any elements of intrigue, Pozdnyshev's view, at which he arrived after his murderous act opened his eyes. In fact, the afterword is an exposé of Tolstoy's own gospel, which included many social aspects too—including an indictment of property and its consequences. Sexual life, as it is practiced by society, in both of the apparently antagonistic forms of prostitution and of "love," including marriage for love (which he argued is only "long-term" prostitution), is an infringement on Christ's teaching and is, therefore, the great evil in history.

Love—what we call romantic love—is as great a sin as lust; it perverts the soul of both men and women (whom it turns into seducers far less moral than prostitutes) and yields to marital and general infidelity. Love must be given only to God and to your neighbor, of whom your children and parents are the closest, but not the only ones. As for sexuality, it should be practiced only for what God (as nature) instituted it—procreation; practicing it for "pleasure" is pure "depravity." The claims of (false) medical science that sex is a health need is a fraud—work (physical and strenuous) and an adequate vegetarian diet would be enough to consume and yield the energy otherwise discharged in the intercourse. Beginning in his fifties, Tolstoy lived as he preached and his relationship with his wife—whom he accused of having used practices to prevent pregnancies, as Pozdnyshev said about his wife—as well as with his grown-up children deteriorated and, as great men are greater than human in their flaws as well as their achievements, his marriage entered history (testified in the couple's diaries) as one that was not much different from the one he described in *The Kreutzer Sonata*—at least with the difference that he did not end up as a murderer.

I must also emphasize that Tolstoy never mentions Beethoven's sonata in his "Afterword," although the novella's title marks the sonata a major character in the plot. This clearly indicates that Beethoven's music was only a "cameo" incident in the plot—what we would call a "MacGuffin." As Pozdnyshev/Tolstoy told his "confessor," the essential explanation was the "swinishness" that had created an "abyss" between him and his wife. Granted, that does not explain the proximate motivation of the murder (jealousy), and it may seem strange that the "afterword" does not tackle this issue either. As the protagonist explains at the end of the same quote, jealousy was just a pretext: "If the occasion had not been jealousy it would have been something else."[20] And if jealousy was merely pretext, the catalyst for it, Beethoven's sonata, is even more incidental.

Kramer's failed reading of Tolstoy's novella

Because of the scattered design of Kramer's book, his argument about the sonata is hard to gather into a well-rounded analysis. He put together his short essays on Tolstoy's *The Kreutzer Sonata* in a second book dedicated to musicological issues as a chapter titled "Tolstoy's Beethoven, Beethoven's Tolstoy: The Kreutzer Sonata,"[21] but this is just a "re-print" that does not improve the "mosaic" design of the argument. It consists in many repetitive, complementary and at times conflicting assertions, most wrapped in psychoanalytical Lacanian phraseology as difficult to credit as the theory on which they rely. The scholarly shrink is not intimidated by the intricate psychological threads of Tolstoy's narrative, of which I have given only a simplified version above.[22] He has his Œdipal skeleton key that opens all mystery doors—the gender-polarized recipe. It would explain the protagonist's personality, the failure of his marriage, his jealousy, his murderous transformation. And, of course, it would explain how Beethoven's sonata was an accomplice to the murder. All these arguments are as many failures, usually in conflict with the facts in Tolstoy's narrative or leading to inner incongruities.

Although Kramer qualifies Pozdnyshev's "swinishness" utterance as "an impassioned denouncement of gender polarity," he claims that the man was

> an anti-feminist, tortured by a terror of female sexuality so great that he feels his identity collapsing into the liquid liquefaction of his own desire" (37)

Kramer changes his mind later, when he states that

> [g]ender-polarized men like Pozdnyshev seek to control feminine sexuality, not because they are afraid of it, but because they are afraid of life without it, which is exactly the life they are constrained to lead" (185).

Obviously, one cannot logically be simultaneously afraid of something and of the lack of it.

Gender polarity also allegedly solves the sexual dilemma of Pozdnyshev's marriage:

> [He] discovers on his honeymoon that sex is a failure at upholding gender polarity and more, that its pleasure consists in this failure. Sex continuously subverts the sexual difference it is supposed to confirm. Like music, it makes a man feel what he keeps telling himself he doesn't really feel, meaning rather that he is not supposed to feel it" (117).

How can one read this subtlety? One can speculate almost indefinitely on this statement (for instance, Pozdnyshev might have felt that he had not been up to the task of proving to his virgin bride his "manhood," but how would that have given his "gender polarity" any pleasure?), but it is better to get to the basics—what does Pozdnyshev actually tell his "confessor"? He likens his memory of "the abomination of his honeymoon" with a previous experience in Paris, when he went to a show advertising "the bearded woman," only to discover that it was "nothing but a man in a woman's low-necked dress, and a dog done up in walrus skin and swimming in a bath." Tolstoy simply could not infringe on taboos that were not removed until several decades later, and thus could not speak freely about sexuality, instead utilizing only vague euphemisms. He can only suggest his experience by way of a sentence about his young sister, who, on her wedding night "ran out of her bedroom in tears and, shaking all over, said that she could on no account, even tell us what he [the bridegroom] had wanted to do to her."[23] One must stretch the imagination quite a lot to draw Kramer's inference. But in fact, since Pozdnyshev unequivocally speaks later about his wife willing and enjoyable participation in his "swinishness," Kramer's generalizing about "sex continuously subverting ..." is plainly illogical.

Even more importantly, polarized masculinity allegedly clears two major mysteries: the murderous Pozdnyshev and the collusion of Beethoven's sonata. Remember that polarized masculinity must reject or, better, kill its own feminine side (or, to use Kramer's terminology, the feminine "position"). It would be a mistake to see this feminine side as something like "intuition" or "sensibility," which one "kills" with such sexist stereotype formulae as "big boys don't cry." Kramer's explanation is announced on page 11:

> Pozdnyshev sees Trukhachevski as a monstrosity not because he, Trukhachevski, desires Pozdnyshev's wife, but because he resembles her [...therefore] the secret that must be kept at any cost, the incorporation of the feminine position within the structure of masculinity, ceases to be a secret, it becomes transparent, even blatant. Pozdnyshev's murder of his wife is an impromptu ritual through which this revelation is reconcealed.

This is fully presented on pages 77-78, which I will try to put in a nutshell, quoting selectively but so as not to alter the meaning:

> Pozdnyshev loathes Trukhachevski at first sight yet he seemingly can't get enough of the man. He virtually seduces this object of loathing [...] virtually pimping for her [his wife]. [...] It is as if Pozdnyshev were compelled to make the archetypal Other Man, the phallic one, appear in person, perhaps in order to master him, perhaps in order to woo him. [...] Trukhachevski's red lips and bulging bottom [mentioned by Pozdnyshev] suggest that masculine desire [...] is in and of itself feminizing [...]. The man who successfully becomes the object of desire finds himself prompted to identify with the object of desire and thus paradoxically defaces himself as a masculine subject [... which] suggests that masculine desire by its very nature includes the feminine desire to be desired, to relate to the object of desire not as a proprietor but, uncertainly and ambivalently, as both proprietor and property.

In plain English: the feminine side of Pozdnyshev's masculinity consisted in being sexually attracted by Trukhachevski and could be annihilated inside him only by killing his wife. To make sure that we have gotten it right, Kramer names unequivocally this double desire later, at page 208. Any respectable psychoanalytical approach has to include at least a drop of "homoeroticism" in the cocktail it serves.* There is nothing in Tolstoy's narrative—no hint of homoeroticism—that would suggest any such double desire scheme. (And, if my McLean source is not mistaken, there is no such hint in any of Tolstoy's works.) Pozdnyshev notices the violinist's "specially developed posterior, like a woman's"[24] only once, as a feature that should diminish the violinists stature as a man; Kramer repeats it (pages 11 and 78), as if Pozdnyshev noticed it twice.

Without any further ado, after the last quoted statement, Kramer adds that Beethoven's sonata, more exactly the A minor *Presto* of its first movement (following the slow introduction)

> evokes in Pozdnyshev the same combination of desire, identification, and repulsion at both that the sleazy-charming musician does. (79)

I will return to this claim later, when discussing all of Kramer's takes of the "complicity" of Beethoven's music in the murder. The gender polarity also "resolves," via the double-desire scheme, the mystery of Pozdnyshev's jealousy:

> Jealousy is Pozdnyshev's first line of defense against desire. Trukhachevski at first is a perfect conduit for jealousy, an unparalleled stroke of good luck [...] were Trukhachevski to seduce Pozdnyshev's wife, the abused husband could rid himself of both heterosexual desire, by displacing it into jealousy, and homosexual desire, by displacing it into the other's man's heterosexual desire. (208)

It is not clear whether Kramer means hetero- or homo-erotic desire or even the double desire that he theorizes.

What does Pozdnyshev himself say about his jealousy? "During the whole life of my married life I never ceased to be tormented by jealousy, but there were periods when I specially suffered from it." He goes on to explain that the most pregnant crisis occurred when, following the doctor's advice, his wife did not nurse her first child, which, in his view, allowed "her feminine coquetry which had lain dormant within her [to manifest] itself with particular force," raising "torments of jealousy" in him. His particular reason even strikes a Shakespearian tone: as Othello thought that Desdemona, who had lied to her father about their love, could as easily lie to him, Pozdnyshev was right to "unconsciously conclude" that his wife, who had easily abandoned her moral obligations as a mother, could as easily disregard her duties as a wife. [25] It is also worth recalling that Pozdnyshev had had relationships with adulterous married women during his philandering stage, therefore it was rational to be afraid that his wife (whose relationship with him was "abysmal" by his own description) could have plenty of reasons to cheat on him. Such fear was particularly high at the time when Trukhachevski showed up; she had learned how to have sex without fearing pregnancy. Explains Pozdnyshev:

---

* As we know from chapters 2 and 3, the Sterba couple had actually made Beethoven "latent" homosexual, a label that Solomon changed to "sublimated".

> She had been brought up in the belief that there was only one thing in the world worthy of attention—love. She had married and received something of that love, but not nearly what had been promised and was expected [now] she was glad [...] and became alive again for the one thing she knew—love. But love with a husband, befouled of jealousy and all kinds of anger, was no longer the thing she wanted. And she began to look about her as if expecting something.[26]

Pozdnyshev is particularly wary because, as he says, "it is by means of those very pursuits [involving nearness, such as posing for a painting or playing music together], especially of music, that the greater part of adulteries in our society occur."[27] Given all these, Kramer's further claim,

> to become a cuckold may well be Pozdnyshev's strongest sexual desire (209)

is plainly absurd, even though moderated by the doubt-loaded "may." I will return to the issue of jealousy later, because Kramer has a second key to it, again in Beethoven's implicated *Presto*.

As I said, Kramer totally (deliberately?) ignores Tolstoy's "Afterword," which illuminates the *The Kreutzer Sonata*'s purpose and design. It also makes it clear why Kramer's psychoanalytic speculations about the novella can never find support in the text. Only a person feeding for years, like Kramer, on the Freudian-Lacanian Œdipal fantasy, could have built the fiction he claims to read in Tolstoy's text. Tolstoy, the real father of the Pozdnyshev, could not have inserted into the consciousness or subconsciousness of his character a twist of whose fantasy existence he was totally unaware.

Kramer's failed reading of Beethoven's *Presto*

The same gender-polarized recipe also "solves" the mystery of how Beethoven's sonata, particularly the *Presto* of its first movement, is involved in this intrigue—that is, how the protagonist perceives it and how this perception impacts his acts. Kramer offers us two slightly different arguments, both relying on the crucial episode: Pozdnyshev's narrative of the soirée when his wife and Trukhachevski play the Kreutzer Sonata. I already introduced Kramer's first argument two pages before, in the wake of his explanation of Pozdnyshev's turning murderous: he had to kill his wife in order to kill his own feminine position within himself consisting in feeling attracted to ... his rival Trukhachevski. Without any further analysis, Kramer claims that Beethoven's incriminated *Presto* of his sonata

> evokes in Pozdnyshev the same combination of desire, identification, and repulsion at both that the sleazy-charming musician does. (79)

Kramer does not give us any hint about how any music could achieve such a result, but this is not the only problem with his statement: nothing in the Tolstoy narrative states that the murder was caused by the sonata, or even suggests it. Let us see what Pozdnyshev actually testifies about the episode in which he heard the sonata. His account begins with an exclamation: "Ugh! It is a terrible thing, that sonata. And especially that part [the A minor *Presto* of the first movement]." The testimony continues with a full page in which Pozdnyshev rationalizes, in a self-contradictory way, his fear and mistrust of music in general, and of the *Presto* is an illustration. "What is music?' he asks. "What does it do? And why does it what it does?" He rejects the stereotype that "music exalts the soul," accepting only that it is "effective, terribly effective—but not in an exalting way." He feels that music takes him out of his own self into irreconcilable antinomies (" … feel what I do not really feel, understand what I do not understand, can do what I cannot do"). On the other hand, he proclaims that music carries him "immediately and directly into the mental condition of the man who composed it, [and] my soul merges with his and together with him I pass from one condition to another," but even if this is the fulfilment of the impossible dream of any performer, musicologist or music lover, it does not illuminate Pozdnyshev/Tolstoy. He cannot understand what put Beethoven in that peculiar condition in which he produced his *Presto*, and what "things" Beethoven did because of it; therefore, this music does not reach its goal and only "agitates" him, the listener. He gives some examples of music that he understands: "when a military music is played the soldiers march to the music and the music has achieved its goal. A dance music is played, I dance and the music has achieved its goal." Music that fails to achieve such a "goal"—like the Kreutzer Sonata— has "a terrible, horrible effect."[28]

Pozdnyshev's narrative ends with a similarly long, self-contradictory statement about the "horrible effect" that the piece had on him: "it was as if quite new feelings, new possibilities, of which I had been till then unaware, had been revealed to me. […] What this new thing was that had been revealed to me I could not explain to myself, but the consciousness of this new condition was very joyous." He felt "light-hearted and cheerful the whole evening" and everything "appeared in a new light" to him, including his wife's "shining eyes, severe significant expression while she played," and he thought that "she was feeling what I felt." For the first time, he sincerely pressed Trukhachevski's hand and thanked him for the enjoyment he had given him.[29]

Nothing in this text supports Kramer's claim about what the music "evoked" to Pozdnyshev.[*] In fact, the latter's change to an unprecedentedly *positive* attitude towards the violinist can be read only as proof that, through the experience of the Kreutzer sonata, he had put his jealousy to sleep … temporarily, at least.

Kramer's speculation has another big problem: the music "evokes in Pozdnyshev," but he fails to realize what it evokes! Kramer himself finds it "particularly striking that Pozdnyshev initially fails to recognize the nexus of sexual desire and gender positioning that the Beethoven Presto arouses in him," but he hurries to add: "He makes this recognition only in retrospect, several nights later" (79). But in fact, neither the "initial failure" and the "later

---

[*] To confirm my reading of the text, the reader is invited to use the translation of the page of Tolstoy's novella in the Appendix at the end of this chapter.

recognition" ever happened. Kramer tries to explain the former by putting the blame on Pozdnyshev's conflicting statements, which would have prevented him from realizing what the music had "evoked" in him: his "desperate need to reject the music," illustrated by his exclamation "it's a terrible thing that sonata"; that "very joyous" state of mind induced by the music that only his "feminine position" could perceive; the "movement of transcendence, a breakthrough into spirituality" that the music had wrought in him would have been "quite inconsistent with the lust, décolletage, and triviality of the drawing room" (79); "rage and resentment [at] understanding that his visionary experience [of his feminine side] can be generated only through the sleazy, illicit medium of music, the medium, above all, of the feminine, and the feminizing body" (80). One recognizes the recipe again, but this time it absolutely defies logic: Pozdnyshev's "misrecognition" happened because he understood "his visionary experience," which he did not recognize!

Kramer's case for Pozdnyshev's post hoc "late recognition" of the impact of Beethoven's music on him is as unbelievable as his initial "misrecognition." The shrink tries to explain that "recognition" by invoking a later episode in the development of the protagonist's feelings of jealousy: Pozdnyshev's memory of the "weak, piteous, and beatific smile" of his wife after playing with Trukhachevski *not* Beethoven's sonata (this is *the only time* when the sonata is mentioned in the narrative) but a small piece, Ernst's *Elegy*, that had not impressed Pozdnyshev at all at the time it was played, but which seemed to him in hindsight to have been "impassionate to the point of obscenity."[30] "Only through this little extra piece," claims Kramer, "does the element of phallic display in the Beethoven, and its effect of virtual adultery, become manifest" (79). Nothing in Tolstoy's narrative suggests any such connection; in fact, Kramer himself acknowledges later "the little extra piece that *forces the fatal outcome*" (171, my emphasis). In the final episode (at the end of which, in a fit of re-awakened jealousy, Pozdnyshev kills his wife) a few recollections from the past musical soirée are involved, especially his wife's expression after playing, which now looked very different to him, but the Beethoven sonata is conspicuously not among them. Allow me to repeat for emphasis: the only time that Kreutzer Sonata appears in the narrative is the episode when Pozdnyshev's wife and Trukhachevski play it in front of the salon gathering, in which it seems to put the protagonist's feelings of jealousy to sleep. It is not among the recollections that drive him to murder.

If Kramer's first argument for the "complicity" of Beethoven's music is about what it "evokes" in Pozdnyshev, the second is concerned with what "Tolstoy hears" in the same music. Kramer assumes (quite reasonably) that Pozdnyshev is the writer's "mouth-piece," therefore the two names are interchangeable in his analysis. This argument, too, is a reading of the episode when Pozdnyshev listens to his wife and Trukhachevski playing the Kreutzer Sonata[31] but it is wrapped up in some metaphorical silk paper supposed to enhance and clarify it:

> What Tolstoy hears in the Presto of the "Kreutzer" Sonata is the little dirty secret of gender polarity—or it would be if the secret

were not so open, like a gap or an edge in a piece of clothing that we agree not to notice as we keep surreptitiously gazing over or through it. ("How can that first Presto be played in a drawing-room among ladies in low-necked dresses?") What Tolstoy hears is the unspoken truth that gender polarity is a travesty, is travesty itself: that both of its opposing positions are feminine. (213)

As a gender-polarized male, Pozdnyshev would discover in the *Presto* the secret of his personality type: he is a sham—not only does his possess a feminine position, but even his masculine one is feminine. His secret is also "so open," which should probably be interpreted as "open to anyone." I must confess that it is not "so open" to me, in fact it is not open at all. The parenthesis about the "gap or edge in a piece of clothing" is pointless: it is just a hint to the fact that the sonata was played in a fashionable salon full of ladies' décolletés, which seemed totally inappropriate to Pozdnyshev ("such things should only be played on certain important significant occasions" he comments); and the addition of "gazing" suggests the male's attraction to the female flesh—which would seem to be not exactly a feminine "position." Moreover, how can a gender-polarized male, who is by definition "constructed around a rigid boundary, a phallic bar or barrier, in terms of mutual exclusion and masculine dominance" have both positions be feminine?

For the two arguments that Kramer extends to be consistent, the two "feminine positions" in the second argument should somehow parallel the "double desire" (hetero- and homo-) in his first argument. I cannot see, however, how that could happen: a hetero-erotic desire in a male should certainly be termed a masculine, not a feminine "position," even when "by its very nature [it] includes the feminine desire to be desired." The homo-erotic desire for the violinist who looks like a woman is also "masculine," unless Pozdnyshev is to be seen as a lesbian female, which Kramer never claims. This second argument of Kramer is as faulty as the first ... and they do not match each other, either.

This argument becomes even less credible when Kramer elaborates it by invoking Pozdnyshev's narrative, re-stating some of it, and concluding:

> When the music carries him [Pozdnyshev] away, takes him beyond himself, he is enabled to yield to this truth without speaking it, to enjoy it (in the sense of *jouissance*) without knowing it. That's why listening makes him so extraordinarily happy and why, on later reflection, it disgusts him so much: exactly the same process that he goes through with sex. (213)

One can hardly see how the same cause (being carried away by music) has two simultaneous, contrasting outcomes, enjoyment and disgust—a change justified only by "later reflection." Kramer's addition of "the same process" sends us back to another speculation of his that I debunked earlier, which claims that Pozdnyshev's frustrated memory of his honeymoon had revealed to him that "sex is a failure at upholding gender polarity and more, that its pleasure consists in this failure" (page 245-246). This second argument re-introduces Pozdnyshev's "late recognition" of the "truth" in Beethoven's *Presto* that Kramer claimed to have found in his first argument. This would also explain his change of attitude towards Beethoven's music, which had made him "extraordinary happy" when listening to it but inspired "disgust" later. We find more about the "late recognition" from Kramer's reading of Pozdnyshev's statement quoted above, "Music carries me immediately ..."

> In the immediacy of listening, music is blissful sublimation, erotic merging with a superior man; afterwards, on reflection, it is debasement. Pozdnyshev describes this debasement as a forgetting of the "true position," and so it is, but not in the sense he means. The forgetting coincides with, and covers up, the acting-out of his true position. The truth is that the masculine position differs from the feminine only in being hysterical about its own femininity. (213-14)

The "erotic merging with a superior man [Beethoven]" points to Freud's postulate that *any* attachment is erotic. The "reflection" would have been the result of Pozdnyshev feeling "debased" by Beethoven's music because it had made him forget his "true position." This seems to reflect Pozdnyshev's sentence, "Music makes me forget myself, my real position," but it is clear that "position" does not mean for Tolstoy what it does for Kramer—his "masculine side." Kramer further speculates about Pozdnyshev's "forgetting"—obscurely coinciding with both an acting-out and its cover-up—based on his two alleged feminine positions, one of which would be hysterical. Conflicts internal to the argument (i.e., not internal to Pozdnyshev/Tolstoy) render this speculation futile.

In a further speculation, Kramer finds a more likely explanation of what caused Pozdnyshev's "later reflection" that made him change his perception of Beethoven's sonata: he (Pozdnyshev) would have been listening in an "abandonment of masculine pretension, a feminine abandon. In retrospect, when the impact of listening has faded, those who need to disavow this truth about it can do so by belittling the music" (214). In plain English: on later reflection, Pozdnyshev felt that his letting himself carried away by the music was giving in to his feminine "position", which he then had to deny by changing his opinion about the music (i.e., belittling it). This explanation might sound reasonable: how many times have we felt somewhat ashamed for having given in to the charm of an overtly sentimental piece? There is a problem, however: the very idea of a "later" change of opinion does not fit Pozdnyshev's account of the sonata-playing episode, which he gave, obviously, after his alleged "recognition." Why did he belittle the music in the first half (as "terrible") but assess its positive impact resulting from "listening in abandonment" in the end? If he had decided to "belittle" the music, it should have remained "terrible" to the end.

In fact, much of the apparent conflict in Pozdnyshev's opinions of Beethoven's music are the results of the translation. Both the "terrible ... sonata" and its "horrible ... effect" descriptions are misleading. All languages contain ambiguities that render translation sometimes difficult, and Russian is not an exception. Kramer's "terrible" comes from the old 1925 translation by Louise and Aylmer Maude (that Kramer quotes), but the 1996 revision of the text by J. D. Duff[32] proposes "terrifying" instead. The two terms are related but not equivalent in English: the latter emphasizes awe and fear, while the former indicates basically "poor quality." The Russian original страшная ("strashnaya") is rendered in most dictionaries as "terrible," but "terrifying" is a much closer rendering in this case, because the whole text at pages 144-145 displays the narrator's disarray and fear when coping with music; something bad, of poor quality would not have stirred such comments, but just one depreciative word. Similarly, one cannot see how the "horrible effect" of the music could have included a "joyous consciousness" in Pozdnyshev; the Russian word ужасно ("oojasno") has dozens of possible renditions, almost all with negative connotation (abominable, horrible, terrible, wretched), but also a few contrasting superlatives (almighty, strong, terrific, or violent). I think strong/violent fits the best the context: the terrifying music had a violent effect on Pozdnyshev. Unfortunately, Tolstoy never touches the issue of Beethoven's music in his "Afterword" of his novella, which would have perhaps cleared the confusion.

Kramer submits later in his book a second vision of Beethoven's incriminated *Presto* and the whole sonata, to explain Pozdnyshev's jealousy:

> This sonata is a sexual appliance. Its performance is a sexual act [... therefore] Pozdnyshev is perfectly right to see the performance of the 'Kreutzer' sonata as an act of adultery. In its sensory fullness, emotional violence, the "Kreutzer" sonata breaks the bounds of genteel piano performance proper to women. (171)

Kramer sets forth here a theme to be developed in a further leg of Beethoven's masculinity relay—the alleged incompatibility of his pianism with feminine playing. I will debunk this thesis in due time, but I will remind here that Beethoven greatly appreciated several women pianists as the best interpreters of his music. Of course, playing his music involved passion, but passion is not sexuality.

There is also no hint in Tolstoy's novella about Beethoven's music inspiring jealousy to the protagonist. He clearly states that it was not the Kreutzer Sonata, but that "little piece," Ernst's *Elegy*, that triggered his murderous jealousy, in hindsight, because of his remembering the mien of his wife's face when she was playing. In fact, jealousy was seizing Pozdnyshev from the very moment when he watched his wife practicing with the violinist first time, not Beethoven music, but some songs without words and a little sonata by Mozart. In his own words:

> He [the violinist] behaved himself very well. My wife seemed interested only in music and was very simple and natural. But though I pretended to be interested in the music I was tormented by jealousy all the evening. From the first moment his eyes met my wife's I saw that the animal in each of them, regardless of all conditions of their position in society, asked, "May I?" and answered, "Oh, yes, certainly."[33]

The account itself is inconsistent—the two players "behaved well" but were exchanging glances confirming their readiness for an affair, possibly because of Pozdnyshev's very feelings of jealousy—but regardless, it is clear that music was not responsible for it. Feelings of jealousy follow specific (Othello based) logics that Tolstoy illustrates later in the narrative, but Pozdnyshev began to build them inside or, better to say, *re-awakened* them, at this particular moment in the plot.

All in all, the case that Kramer makes for the "complicity" of Beethoven's music in Pozdnyshev's murderous act is unconvincing. Not only is it too obscure in its Œdipal-Lacanian phraseology, but the little that can be deciphered is built on incongruent arguments.

A half-hearted attempt at absolving the Kreutzer of "gender polarity"

When Kramer the shrink falls asleep, the still-awake musicologist can provide some penetrating insights into both music and text. The best of them is a short sentence that is almost lost in its context:

> What must Tolstoy be hearing in the Presto of Beethoven's "Kreutzer" sonata? Passion and impetuosity on the surface and lots of them [...] *a degree of intimate, deeply attentive interplay that exceeds anything a Pozdnyshev, or perhaps a Tolstoy, could ever share with his wife.* It does not matter that this Presto sounds nothing at all like conventional "love music"; there is a palpable erotic script in its duo writing. (201, my emphasis)

The italicized phrase seizes the miracle of "making music," in which two performers (or even more) can achieve the sort of harmoniously ideal communion that can be reached only in perfect love making—that is, something that the novella's protagonist could never hope to achieve with his wife, the consciousness of which would have been a very palpable reason to be jealous. Viewed from this angle, one can even accept as a metaphor Kramer's addition about the above "erotic script."

Unfortunately, the shrink has an immediate comeback on the same page, adding another drop of homoeroticism:

> In Beethoven's day, with the performers presumptively male, it [the sonata] is a homoerotic script, something like a celebration of passionate friendship that at its height becomes indistinguishable from passion itself. (201)

Actually, we should not be surprised. The author had advised us from the beginning that, "the general importance of homosexual desire, even for those who don't act on it, surfaces repeatedly in t[his] book" (12); his whole idea of "synergy" is but another facet of it.

At some point, in one of the longest essays in his book ("Tinnitus"), the musicologist escapes the shrink's harnesses and manages to absolve Beethoven of the indictment of gender polarization thrown at him in the very beginning of his book. He discovers that

> what Tolstoy [through his ear-piece Pozdnyshev] does not hear in the Presto of the "Kreutzer" and could not bear to hear is the music's—in music's—gender synergy. (215)

This is Kramer's antidote to the evil male polarity. What he implies is that music itself is, by definition, "synergetic." In the *Presto,* the synergy is the doing of the movement's second theme, which "puts into question the gender polarity of the movement as a whole" and "ripples throughout the entire movement" (217).[*] Kramer seems to conclude

> The masculinity of the movement as a whole is thus framed, enveloped, potentiated, between feminine terms that set the boundaries of stability and instability; (222)

but takes a step backwards in the next paragraph:

> At the same time, however, the music's masculine energy carries it outside this frame [...] as the movement takes its course. (222)

As usual, the shrink later regains the leading role and discovers another gender-polarized moment of the first movement of the sonata. Developing his theory, he proposes four ways by which "manhood" can be attained (initiation, examination, gift and theft), which he illustrates and comments with examples from world literature. Of them, the last one interests Kramer because it means violently "stealing" another man's proof of "manhood." He illustrates this case with an example from literature in which

> the theft is indeed supported by a fantasy of Œdipal triumph, but the fantasy is still furtive even in bravado. Whitman slips one such into "Song of Myself," [...]:
> I am a free companion, I bivouac by invading watchfires,
> I turn the bridegroom out of bed and stay with the bride myself,
> I tighten her all night to my thighs and lips.

Although downplaying the poem like a "fantasy," Kramer acknowledges its "violent subtext"[†] and—after the inevitable Lacano-Œdipal extemporization—advises us that "the fantasy of theft may also inform the first movement of Beethoven's 'Kreutzer' Sonata." And he explains that the A minor Presto "steals" a two-note figure from the A major introduction, converting it "from a static warble into a fierce, pouncing gesture" of "virile energy"—which would be a perceptive description (also supported by the score as proof), if it were not be part of Kramer's general thesis that this first movement of the sonata is the musical embodiment of "gender polarity" that paralleled, even triggered, Pozdnyshev's own "polarity" and, thus, his murderous sexual violence. I am sure that Kramer the musicologist knows that the kind of musical "theft" he identified has been part of the craftsmanship of all composers before, during and after Beethoven's time. If he eventually does not really absolve Beethoven's *Presto* of (masculine) "gender polarity," Kramer finds a kind of justification of it in the balance of the sonata as a whole:

> In Beethoven's sonata, the **exaggerated** masculinity of the first

---

[*] Kramer also does not omit to pay a little tribute to McClary in passing (216), but stripping her theory of its essential indictment of the sonata form as a "male subjugate female" construct.

[†] This example actually illustrates the incongruities inherent to baseless speculations like Kramer's: he states that gender polarity is restricted to the heterosexual male (1), but Whitman was homosexual and Kramer treats him as such throughout his book.

movement and the exaggerated femininity of the first several variations of the second movement melt away into the radical heteronomy of synergy. Yet for this to happen the extremes must be fully unfolded, and not merely pro forma; they must be arresting, each in its kind, the first movement domineering in its relentless passion, the early variations (even the lyric minore) alienating in their frigid beauty. Synergy does not deny the appeal of polarity; it requires this appeal; it transforms it. (112)

In other words, "masculinity" and "femininity" require each other for the whole to be well balanced.

Tolstoy's testimony solving the Kreutzer mystery

Kramer writes that Tolstoy "does not hear and could not bear to hear" the "synergy" in Beethoven's first movement of the Sonata that he chose to involve in the plot of his novella. Yet he never wonders why a sensitive man like Tolstoy could be so blind (or deaf) although he sees Pozdnyshev as the author's mouthpiece. He had previously stated that "[m]usic spellbindingly performed is the great medium of gender synergy [and] that is what Tolstoy hated and feared in music" (108), but that is neither an explanation of the writer's blindness nor a justification of the role of the sonata in his novella. In fact, the only clue about it can be found in Tolstoy, not in the Lacanian "Œdipal" nor in Kramer's own "gender polarity."

Tolstoy's moral reformation in his fifties also involved his relationship with music, a fact that Kramer again ignores. As an aristocrat, Tolstoy received musical education, played the piano well, attended concerts and sometimes even operas (a genre he was not particularly fond of). He had a sensitive perception of music, which he poetically called "the shorthand of emotions" and "love in search of a voice," and was, occasionally, moved even to tears by music.[34] He assigned to Beethoven's C sharp minor Sonata "Quasi una fantasia"—the most popular piano piece at the middle of the century—a role of moral catalyst in his 1853 story *Family Happiness*, a kind of antagonistic complement of his *Kreutzer Sonata*: this is a story, also a first person narrative, but from a feminine perspective, describing years of struggle with her disillusion of her marriage and of her husband, as well as struggling with her own flaws.

All these changed with Tolstoy's conversion, explicated in his book titled *What is Art?*[35] published in 1897. The intransigent Christian moralist first draws a line between religious and secular art, and then he divides the latter in what he calls "universal art," which would respond to everybody's needs and comprehension, and the "upper class art," which would have been imposed by the "critics." Critics were responsible for praising

> rude, savage, and, for us, often meaningless works of the ancient Greeks : Sophocles, Euripides, Æschylus, and especially Aristophanes; or, of modern writers, Dante, Tasso, Milton, Shakespeare; in painting, all of Raphael, all of Michael Angelo, including his absurd "Last Judgment"; in music, the whole of Bach, and the whole of Beethoven, including his last period [...][36]

As one can see, Tolstoy does not take many prisoners—not even Bach: the man whom some "critics" have called "the fifth evangelist" figures again in a second "black list" that Tolstoy drew later in a October 29, 1900 diary entry about the distance between "religion of true Christianity" and the false religion, the "superstition of the cultured mob, propagated by such unjustly celebrated eminences as Hegel, Darwin, Spencer, Shakespeare, Dante, Ibsen, the Decadents, Raphael, Bach, Beethoven and (perhaps worst of all) Wagner."[37]

Tolstoy spends many pages loaded with quotes from various aestheticians and philosophers of his time to justify his criteria of "beauty," but one can far more easily grasp them from his enumeration of "bad" painting examples, which ends quite illuminatingly, "and, above all, pictures with voluptuous subjects all that odious female nudity which fills all the exhibitions and galleries,"[38] the one stimulating and simulating the sexual "depravity" that Tolstoy had previously denounced.

Obviously, Tolstoy needed a different set of criteria for the appreciation of music, and probably another one for instrumental music as distinct from the vocal music. And here *The Kreutzer Sonata* (1893) and *What is Art?* (1990) diverge. In the former, Tolstoy's mouth-piece Pozdnyshev voices his inability to understand music, although it has a strong effect on him. In *What is Art?* Tolstoy sets much less sophisticated but material and educational requirements: he essentially asked for music to flow in "free melodies [that] can be understood by everybody" and not loaded with "exclusive" harmonies familiar only to few.[39] On this basis, he draws the list of the "good" music, barely a dozen pieces:

> Bach's famous violin aria [actually the arrangement of the second movement of his *Orchestral Suite* No. 3], Chopin's nocturne in E flat major, and perhaps a dozen bits (not whole pieces, but parts) selected from the works of Haydn, Mozart, Schubert, Beethoven, and Chopin.

He also extends the list of the "bad" music to the whole of the nineteenth century to include:

> all the chamber and opera music of our times, beginning especially from [with?] Beethoven (Schumann, Berlioz, Liszt, Wagner), by its subject-matter devoted to the expression of feelings accessible only to people who have developed in themselves an unhealthy, nervous irritation evoked by this exclusive, artificial, and complex music.[40]

Beethoven is, obviously, not one of the favorites of "late" Tolstoy. He accepts a few of his early works (never specified), probably including his C sharp minor piano sonata "Quasi una fantasia," a favorite of the heroine of Tolstoy's mentioned "Family happiness" older story. However, he denounces "late Beethoven," including his *Ninth Symphony*, as "not a good work of art." And he goes further to explain that even the final *Ode to Joy* fails because "the music does not accord with the thought expressed in the verses; for the music is exclusive and does not unite all men, but unites only a few, dividing them of from the rest of mankind,"[41] a strange objection, because the "joy theme" is one the most tuneful in the history of the classical. Tolstoy's particular "ideology" was taking precedence over his musicality. It is no surprise that his wife was not able to keep up with this later-day Savonarola.*

Although Tolstoy never cites Beethoven's Kreutzer Sonata in his *What is Art?* book, one can reasonably guess why he chose it to play a prominent role in his eponymous novella. It was the best possible literary device for illustrating an evil-permeated society: it was "bad" music and also allowed to bring in the would-be seducer, the violinist, who would incite Pozdnyshev's jealousy to break loose and turn murderous. It was also a very good marketing tool: Beethoven was a world-known name. Who would have cared to buy a book titled *Ernst's Elegy*, referring the music that was really responsible for turning Pozdnyshev murderously jealous? These Tolstoy facts invalidate Kramer's psychoanalytic speculations about the novella. Tolstoy is the father of Pozdnyshev; he could not have put in the consciousness or unconsciousness of his character a twist of whose existence he was totally unaware. Only a person dreaming for years, like Kramer, on the Œdipal phallus, could have imagined anything like that—and there was no Œdipal when Tolstoy/Pozdnyshev lived.

Why is Beethoven's *Kreutzer Sonata* so "masculine?"

No matter how much I disagree with Professor Kramer's several theses, I cannot but agree with him that the first movement of the Kreutzer Sonata displays an unusually "virile concept," and that the other two movements occasionally do the same. The Kreutzer is, in this regard, unique among Beethoven's set of violin sonatas. Why? The answer is simple enough, and the same as the answer to a related question: why was Beethoven generally perceived as more "masculine" than other great composers? He introduced a new "sound" in music. History of this art generally disregards this aspect—every new style or school was actually a new "sound of music." The Baroque sound was different from the one of the Renaissance. The early Classical (the Rococo) sound was as different from the Baroque sound as the Classical Age sound from the Rococo one. Beethoven changed the sound of music again—to the ampler, symphonic sound. He went further than Mozart, whose final four symphonies, true masterpieces, were epitomes of the pre-Beethoven orchestral-still-cameral sound. Of course, the change did not happen from the very beginning. Beethoven practiced for several years the typical form of the eighteenth century sonata for piano and violin, which was essentially a piece for piano, optionally accompanied by violin. The Kreutzer was his first piano and violin sonata to be really symphonic, as pointed out in its long title: "Sonata per il Pianoforte ed uno violino obligato in uno stile molto concertante come d'un concerto"[42]—a concerto for violin and piano. Kramer actually read this argument in Charles Rosen's authoritative book *The Classical Style* but failed to grasp it (45).

I also think that even the incriminated first *Presto* of the Kreutzer sonata

---

* Girolamo Savonarola (1452-1498), a fifteenth century Dominican friar and preacher was active in Florence; he strongly criticized the Catholic Church policies, including its endorsement of the Renaissance painting; he instituted the "bonfires of vanities" in Florence, in which "sinful" books and paintings were burned.

shows a good masculine-feminine balance—a "synergy" in Kramer's terms. As I did when debunking McClary's indictment of Beethoven's *Eroica*, I present here the "wave" format of the movement, based on the performance of Isaac Stern and Eugene Istomin (CBS Records, M2K 39680).

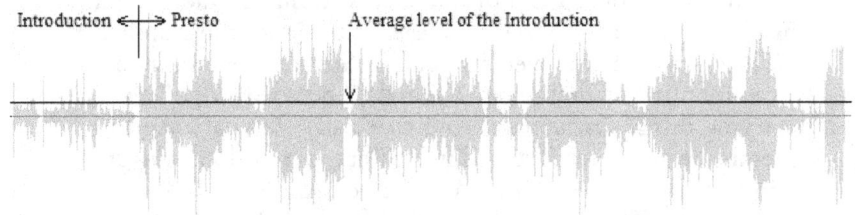

The black line represents the average wave level of the A major introduction, a good enough marker of the "synergy" level. When we count the duration over and at or less this average, we find that of the 9:03 minutes that the Presto lasts, 6:08 are over this marker—an overall indication of "masculinity;" however, there is also a considerable amount of feminine "synergy" (33%) which should be enough to absolve the movement of the accusation of gender polarity.

Summing up

The foregoing presentation has brought into evidence the danger inherent in heaping speculations founded on a baseless speculation—in this case, the Freudian Œdipus complex transmogrified by a later disciple, Lacan, which becomes Kramer's foundation for his "gender polarized" theory. He acts on it with the self-confidence of an evangelist wrapped in Freudian or Lacanian verbiage that reigns supreme, leaving the author unaware of the absurd lengths his speculations have taken him, of which I have signaled only the major ones: his "tale of the gender of musical genius" centered on Beethoven's "masculinity" is not only based on a shallow interpretation of a couple of opinions about Beethoven's music as compared with his Romanticist followers, but also ends up in an absurd "allegory" of a modern world that practices and rationalizes sexual violence against women but in which all humanity is feminine, with no one left to be an oppressing male (see page 238-239 of this chapter). Kramer's speculations about the Kreutzer sonata issue within Tolstoy's novella also end up in self-contradictory assertions about a "polarized male" made up of two feminine sides (see page 247). They are also conflicting with Kramer's own musical analysis of the sonata, which absolves Beethoven of "polarity," without, however, understanding the reason of its "exaggerated masculinity."

Granted, in a few cases when Kramer the shrink lets his inner musicologist free, he has interesting things to say, some of which indeed throw some light on the topic. It is a pity that this happens only rarely. The general picture is that of grandiose, authoritarian statements, of which the most staggering is this one:

> Music is the speech of the female body, the female genitals, [therefore] it must be fetishized, handed a prosthetic phallus, before men can tolerate it. (172)

The epitome of postmodernist feminism, indeed.

Appendix. Tolstoy's *The Kreutzer Sonata*, pp. 144-145.

The Kreutzer Sonata

Pózdnyshev paused and produced his strange sound several times in succession. He tried to speak, but sniffed, and stopped.

'They played Beethoven's Kreutzer Sonata,' he continued. 'Do you know the first presto? You do?' he cried. 'Ugh! It is a terrifying thing, that sonata. And especially that part. And in general music is a terrifying thing! What is it? I don't understand it. What is music? What does it do? And why does it do what it does? They say music exalts the soul. Nonsense, it is not true! It is effective, terribly effective—I am speaking of myself—but not in an exalting way. It has neither an exalting nor a debasing effect but an agitating one. How can I put it? Music makes me forget myself, my real position; it transports me to some other position not my own. Under the influence of music it seems to me that I feel what I do not really feel, that I understand what I do not understand, that I can do what I cannot do. I explain it by the fact that music acts like yawning, like laughter: I am not sleepy, but I yawn when I see someone yawning; there is nothing for me to laugh at, but I laugh when I hear people laughing.

'Music carries me immediately and directly into the mental condition of the man who composed it. My soul merges with his and together with him I pass from one condition into another, but why this happens I don't know. You see, he who wrote, let us say, the Kreutzer Sonata—Beethoven—knew of course why he was in that condition; that condition caused him to do certain actions and therefore that condition had a meaning for him, but for me—none at all. That is why music only agitates and doesn't lead to a conclusion. Well, when a military march is played the soldiers march to the music and the music has achieved its goal. A dance is played, I dance and the music has achieved its goal. Mass is sung, I receive communion, and that music too has reached a conclusion. Otherwise it is only agitating, and what ought to be done in that agitation is lacking. That is why music sometimes has such a terrible, horrible effect. In China, music is a state affair. And that is as it should be. How can one allow anyone who pleases to hypnotize another, or many others, and do what he likes with them? And especially that this hypnotist should be the first immoral man who turns up?

'It is a terrifying instrument in the hands of any chance user! Take that Kreutzer Sonata for instance, how can that first presto be played in a drawing-room among ladies in low-necked dresses? To hear that played, to clap a little, and then to eat ices and talk of the latest scandal? Such things should only be played on certain important significant occasions, and then only when certain actions answering to such music are wanted; play it then and do what the music has moved you to. Otherwise an awakening of energy and feeling unsuited both to the time and the place, to which no outlet is given, cannot but act harmfully. At any rate that piece had a horrible effect on me; it was as if quite new feelings, new possibilities, of which I had till then been unaware, had been revealed to me. "That's how it is: not at all as I used to think and live, but that way," something seemed to say within me. What this new thing was that had been revealed to me I could not explain to myself, but the consciousness of this new condition was very joyous. All those same people, including my wife and him, appeared in a new light.

'After that allegro they played the beautiful, but common and unoriginal, andante with trite variations, and the very weak finale. Then, at the request of the visitors, they played Ernst's Elegy* and a few small pieces. They were all good, but they did not produce on me a one-hundredth part of the impression the first piece had. The effect of the first piece formed the background for them all.

'I felt light-hearted and cheerful the whole evening. I had never seen my wife as she was that evening. Those shining eyes, that severe, significant expression while she played, and her melting languor and feeble, pathetic, and blissful smile after they had finished. I saw all that but did not attribute any meaning to it except that she was feeling what I felt, and that to her as to me new feelings, never before experienced, were revealed or, as it were, recalled. The evening ended satisfactorily and the visitors departed.

'Knowing that I had to go away to attend the Zémstvo meetings two days later, Trukhachévski on leaving said he hoped to repeat the pleasure of that evening when he next came to Moscow. From this I concluded that he did not consider it possible to come to my house during my absence, and this pleased me. It turned out that as I should not be back before he left town, we should not see one another again.

'For the first time I pressed his hand with real pleasure, and thanked him for the enjoyment he had given us. In the same way he bade a final farewell to my wife. Their leave-taking seemed to be most natural and proper. Everything was splendid. My wife and I were both very well satisfied with our evening party.

12
Sanna Pederson's third leg of Beethoven's "Masculinity" relay

"Beethoven's masculinity" has certainly become an obsession for postmodernist scholarship. After Professor McClary and Professor Kramer had indicted Beethoven's masculinity for sexual violence, Sanna Pederson, currently a professor at the University of Oklahoma, revisits the issue in an essay included in the 2000 book *Beethoven and his World*,[1] containing diverse, unconnected contributions of some twenty-odd scholars. She quotes both McClary and Kramer, describing them "as leaders of the 'New Musicology' of the 1990s [that] established gender and sexuality as central categories for musical interpretation that were more critical than affirmative of established masters and masterpieces." She then promises "to go about the immensely complex task of incorporating the categories of sex and gender into the historical understanding of Beethoven and his music" (314)[*] from a novel perspective.

Pederson begins her argumentation by quoting Romain Rolland, one of the prominent Beethoven scholars of the first half of the twentieth century, who wrote in 1927: "He [Beethoven] is the most virile of musicians; there is nothing—if you prefer, not enough—of the feminine about him" (313). What follows seems to have become the inevitable since McClary–Schumann's description of Beethoven as "masculine," as opposed to the "feminine" Schubert (313). I elucidated Schumann's "masculinity" quote in the previous chapter (see pages 236ff) dealing with Kramer's work; I showed there that Beethoven's alleged "masculinity" was a matter of age and maturity, not of gender.

Rolland's account is a similar distortion rooted in a personal metaphor: he labels the romanticist movement as "feminine" and rejects the idea, predominant at the time, that Beethoven was one of them—hence his description of him in "masculine" terms."[2] It does not matter to Pederson that this description is Rolland's subjective opinion and that, according to it, every musician before the romantic age was "virile." It is enough that she has found a second authoritative voice that had made Beethoven into a prototypical "masculine" figure. She proceeds to argue that Beethoven's "masculinity" was of the type practiced and theorized by the patriarchal society of his age, which continued oppressing women, as it had since the beginning of (historical) times. He would also have—or, to use Pederson's ambiguous terminology, "is assumed" to have—embedded this concept in his music, his contribution to "legitimizing male domination in a modern world which recognizes that all people are born equal," as she puts it in the conclusion of her essay (326). Pederson avoids it in her final verdict, but implies that Beethoven, both the

---

[*] All references to Pederson's paper are indicated in the text in this chapter.

man and his music, were guilty of sharing and promoting an ideology of oppressing women and should probably be thrown into the garbage can of history when society has finally achieved the utopia that we all have grown used to see embodied in his "Alle Menschen werden Brüder" [All men will be brothers] choir of his *Ninth Symphony*. Fortunately, as I will presently demonstrate, Dr. Pederson fails to make a credible argument for her case that Beethoven was an exponent of the wrongly "gendered" concept of masculinity.

Where Pederson is right: "Patriarchal masculinity"

Pederson begins with a long introduction covering half of her argument (314-320) with the presentation of the "patriarchal ideology" of the nineteenth century: namely its views about the position of the two sexes in society, with women subservient to men and confined to "domesticity" or, at best, to a small "intimate world." This concept, rooted in age-old historical practice and theory, was designed to help with "maintaining the patriarchal authority in the wake of revolutionary social and political change" (316) brought about by the French Revolution, which had at least introduced (albeit failing to implement) the concept of a "universal society" made up of equal people. Pederson illustrates this new-old theory from the works of several influential ideologues of the time, philosophers like Hegel (1770-1831) and Fichte (1762-1814), and polymaths like Wilhelm von Humboldt (1767-1835), who were theorizing in the footsteps of the preceding Enlightenment Age that had instituted that ideal, and who tried to revise the old theory without fundamentally changing it.[*] In a nutshell, their theory defined women as "born" and, unlike men, incapable of "becoming" through a learning process; the two sexes would have stood as "nature" (woman) versus "culture" (320), which would have justified patriarchal authority. They also claimed to support their theory with a simulant of "scientific" proof pertaining to the differences between the sexes, of which some data were true but trivial (woman is physically weaker, she has a specific reproduction function), and some, like female "illiteracy," that had been clearly disproven through history, and some that would be refuted by later scientific advances.

One needs not be a feminist to accept Pederson's presentation of this "patriarchal ideology" as historically accurate and I will not insist on dissecting the theory's main tenets.[†] They were already ridiculous at the time and they would be later fully discredited as unscientific. I will, however, introduce some details of the "patriarchal masculinity" concept when tackling its immediate

---

[*] I confess of not having checked all of Pederson's quotes from these authors. After a few checks, I assumed I could trust her integrity about it.

[†] Following McInnes, Pederson speculates about the theory of the "social contract" introducing the concept of "gender" as distinct from "sex": as "sex," women were born equal with men, but "gender," which was their social constructed femininity, sanctioned their subordinate status. In fact, the enlightenment theorists only accepted the obvious, that the different forms of historically developed "social contract" were based on the differences between the sexes; neither Locke nor Hobbes, the best-known promoters of the "social contract" theory, ever used the term gender or any equivalent of it in their writings. McInnes' speculation has actually no import on the issue here discussed.

implications in Pederson's indictment of Beethoven. In fact, the picture Pederson draws of nineteenth century German society is far from complete. Certainly, the institutions were patriarchal, and the dominant ideology, also; even worse, the ideology that shaped Germany was not the one that Pederson pictures, which had assumed the idea of equality and fraternity: the political factors that shaped society, people like Metternich, the architect of the New Europe after Napoleon's fall, and Bismarck, the unifier of Germany under the hegemony of militarist Prussia in the second half of the century, were no adepts of the slogan of the French Revolution. Nevertheless, there were also strong undercurrents that were in time to prevail.

Feminism was one such undercurrent. It had started as an idea much earlier, with a German man, Heinrich Agrippa von Nettesheim (1486-1535), a polymath and author, amidst many books on the most diverse issues, of a *Declamatio de nobilitate et praecellentia foeminei sexus* (*Declamation on the Nobility and Preeminence of the Female Sex*, 1529), a book in which he contended that men oppressed women without any justification from natural law and that women were morally superior to men. This idea grew steady during the sixteenth and seventeenth century, reaching the keyword "equality,"[3] also in Germany and even in the field of music.[4] The names involved are certainly less notorious than those of Humboldt and Hegel, but feminism was gaining ground around 1850s in Germany, too, with figures like Ottilie Assing (1819-1894), Louise Aston (1814-1871), and Louise Otto-Peters (1819-1895), to quote only the earliest ones. Beethoven died too soon to see these feminist ideas foment, but writers like Gottlob Ephraim Lessing (1729-1821) and Friederich Schiller (1759-1805), who were part of his intellectual baggage, actively defended the dignity of womanhood and the rights of women.

Failed attempts to link Beethoven
to "patriarchal masculinity"

Pederson proposes two "symptoms" showing that Beethoven would have conformed to the "masculinity" described above, one pertaining to his personality and the other to his music. The first one refers directly to Beethoven's sexuality. Quoting Humboldt, who claimed that "women seem to be permitted to a very high degree to give in to their sexual natures, whereas men must at *a very early stage* sacrifice a great deal of theirs to other human values" (319, my emphasis), Pederson speculates further: "if 'giving in' to sexuality is a feminine characteristic, it makes sense how Beethoven's renunciation of the Immortal Beloved, for instance, could actually enhance his masculinity" (320). In other words, when Beethoven gave up his dream about the mysterious woman that he named "my Immortal Beloved" in his famous July 6-7 (1812) letter, he felt it as a tribute to his masculinity.

This speculation ignores several details of both Humboldt's statement and of the known facts in Beethoven's life. As I emphasized in the Humboldt quote, this "masculinity trait" was supposed to apply only to very young men, while Beethoven was forty-two at the time of the Immortal Beloved episode. On the other side, in his twenties, he took full advantage of Vienna's very lax morality, as his intimate friend Wegeler testified later: "[he] sometimes made conquests which could have been very difficult, indeed, if not impossible, for many an Adonis."[5] In his thirties, he also gave up his only known dream love, for Josephine Brunsvik-Deym (a main candidate for the Immortal Beloved), but not before pressing her for "sensual love," a quest that she rejected,[6] which put an end to their relationship. These facts hardly fit Pederson's inference. Let us also notice the inner incongruity of her speculation: its premise is Humboldt's quote, which is false (reason and feminism both agree on this) and one cannot infer a true conclusion from a false premise.

The second link that Pederson tries to establish between Beethoven and "masculinity" is more copiously developed. It is built on a particular aspect of the patriarchal ideology that somehow softens its sexism—the "complementarity" of the two sexes, which gives Pederson hope for "understanding a subsidiary issue of Beethoven's masculinity, the gendering of the sonata form" (316), one of the basic tenets of McClary's theory that I analyzed and debunked in chapter 10. I recall here McClary's thesis: the sonata form is constructed on two themes, a masculine theme and a subsidiary feminine (and somewhat contrasting) theme; both themes are presented in two different keys and, after some "adventurous" treatment of them (the so-called development), they are again restated, but this time the feminine theme is enounced in the key of the principal theme; therefore, it is argued, the sonata is a "man subjugates woman" form. Pederson quotes Scott Burnham's objection to McClary's thesis, claiming that the two themes are complementary (317), and connects that last term with the similar one in the patriarchal ideology: according to Humboldt again, the male and female "spheres of activity complement and embrace each other—and [the] inclination which serves to endear each to each is Love" (317). Therefore, the two themes of the sonata form are just like the patriarchal marriage of love, in which "a loving, uncoercive marriage of equals must always simultaneously be the subjugation of wife to husband" (317-318). This is only a slightly different reiteration of McClary's thesis and, at the same time, Beethoven, the foremost producer of sonata form movements, is integrated into the patriarchal masculinity concept.

What I have written in rebuttal to McClary's thesis in chapter 10 obviously applies to Pederson's claim, too. The "masculine vs. feminine" labels of the two themes of the sonata form was an invention of the later Romantic period (which, ironically, was going to destroy this musical form), and there is no proof that Beethoven conceptualized his themes this way. Certainly, some of them "sound" feminine, like, for instance, the secondary theme in his *Coriolan* overture, but it all depends on what kind of contrast he desired. In this piece, he thought the sonata form was appropriate because it fit what he thought as the key moment of the play that the overture was designed to introduce: the confrontation between the ruthless male warrior and the supplications of the two women he loved, his mother and his wife. In many other cases, the two themes were indeed more "complementary" than "conflicting" and I think that there are many examples when both are "masculine" or "feminine." What is really masculine in the first movement of Beethoven's *Violin Concerto*?

On the whole, Pederson's attempt to link Beethoven to that "patriarchal ideology" is a failure. In fact, even she concludes, at the end of this section in her article, that Beethoven "can appear ungendered and his qualities universal" but reminds us that his masculinity appeared specifically when we compare him with others composers. She asks "Why does Beethoven appear more masculine than any other male composer?" (320). Leaving it to Kramer to seek an answer from a psychoanalytical angle (that I dealt with in the previous chapter), Pedersen embarks on a socio-historical investigation on two fronts that seem auspicious to her: Beethoven's involvement in the "masculine" sphere of politics and his personal "heroic narrative," that is, his fight with his terrible Fate.

Three failed arguments about Beethoven in the "masculine sphere of politics"

Pederson challenges the quasi-unanimous view of Beethoven's music as a (or we should say "the"?) embodiment of the ideals proclaimed by the French Revolution in 1789, "Liberté, égalité, fraternité!" She does not contest this allegiance, although it is hard to understand why she needs to invoke Solomon's authority to claim the obvious, that the *Ode to Joy* "celebrates the principle of fraternity." However, she invokes the argument of a feminist colleague, Carole Pateman, who claims to have identified a sexist, masculine undertone in Beethoven's commitment to the concept of fraternity.

> Our contemporary ideal of fraternity, however, has been shaken by its exposure in recent times as the bond specifically between men. Carole Pateman has questioned "why fraternity, rather than another term, should be used as a synonym for community." She argues that the concept of fraternity is part of the ideology of the "sexual contract"—that women are precluded from any discussion of the equal rights of man because of the assumption of a more basic contract that gives men the right to rule women. (321)

This justifies by virtue of a typical post-modernist feminist strategy—the quotation chain—Pederson's conclusion:

> Beethoven's strong association with the concept of fraternity enforces our perception of his masculinity because fraternity means membership in an exclusive male society; but because fraternity can also mean all-embracing community, it simultaneously covers this male identification with universal mankind. (321)

This argument would be hilarious if it were not saddening, as another proof to the extreme effects that ignorance of history can have. Because neither Pateman nor Pederson can get out of their native English box, the assume Beethoven intended his *Ode to Joy* as the anthem of universal *maleness*! I cannot claim to have explored all English language dictionaries, but I consulted dozens of them and found that, indeed, all of them give the first meaning of "fraternity" as "1. A local or national social organization of male students, usu. with secret initiation and rites." The sense of "universal solidarity," if not missing altogether, is usually the last meaning. The older and more academic English dictionaries or encyclopedias that I checked do not mention at all this meaning. The 1789 *Oxford Dictionary* specifies eight meanings, seven of which about various male associations recorded in history (college fraternities at no. 7) and the last one as "sibling"; *Webster's 3rd New International Dictionary* (unabridged) is not any better and neither is the world-famous *Britannica* encyclopedia. My 1997 *Webster's Collegiate Dictionary* is almost a non-characteristic exception, because it gives at "5. The quality or state of being brotherly; brotherhood," something that could be read, by stretching it out, as an equivalent of the 1789 French "Fraternité." This was Beethoven's concept of the word: "universal" solidarity of the human race. He got it in his youth, from the circle of his teacher Neefe, a man infused with enlightenment ideas, who also introduced Beethoven to the lectures given in Bonn, in 1790-91, by one Eulogius Schneider, who encapsulated that very catchphrase of the French Revolution.[7] German language was also contaminated: it added to the old word "Bruderschaft" [brotherhood] the French-derived *Fraternität*, exactly to define the "universal" meaning of the word, which is now common in all languages.

Pateman's claim that the word "fraternity" is part of the patriarchal ideology is technically right, because languages are part of the patriarchal heritage of the world. In this regard, all languages known to me to a reasonable extent—Romance, Germanic or Slavic—are sexist: many terms about family and community at large are masculine and have been also extended to cover both sexes. To stay within Beethoven's language, "Brüderlichkeit" (brotherhood) comes from "Brüder" (brother) and the plural of the latter word has been generally used to include persons of both sexes. The same was true in English up until the twentieth century, when the term "sibling," which had been used for century to define "relatives," was re-assigned to the current meaning in public usage. The same happened in German, where the term for sibling, "Geschwister" had existed for centuries,[*] but entered the current usage only after WWI. I must also add that patriarchal language had tried to assuage some of its sexism, probably because of the male's special relationship with his mother. In Latin (followed by all Romance languages), *Patria* (fatherland) comes from *Pater* (father), but is a feminine noun. So are most abstract concepts, like intelligence or beauty.

Let us also notice another essential argument annihilating Pederson's claim—the "Alle Menschen werden Brüder" verse in the *Ode to Joy*: the German word "Mensch" is a generic term for "human being," man or woman. Beethoven—via Schiller—clearly had universal, not male, solidarity in mind.

Much of Pederson's argumentation works by way of quoting authoritative scholars who elaborate on Beethoven quotes. She invokes Solomon again to bring into evidence Beethoven's allegedly dubious adherence to a second concept of the French Revolution, "equality."

> As Solomon puts it: "Liberty and fraternity—but not equality. It is also the issue of equality that Beethoven parts company with the slogans of the French Revolution and the eighteenth-century utopian

---

[*] Goethe even wrote a play titled "Die Geschwister" (1776).

philosophes." Solomon quotes the composer as declaring in 1798: "*Power* is the moral principle of those who excel others, and it is also mine."[8]

This yields Pederson's conclusion:

This remarkable statement and many others clearly indicate that Beethoven did not subscribe to the idea that "all men are created equal," even when only men were indicated. (322)

There is plenty of evidence that, indeed, he did not share the common belief of post-modernist scholarship that "all men are created equal." The famous phrase inscribed on the frontispiece of in the American constitution obviously refers to the fundamental equality regarding human rights; an aspect usually disregarded in post-modernism is human *responsibilities* (for instance to observe and be similarly treated by law). From all the other points of view, we are fundamentally unequal. If I may use this banal example, none of us, who are now writing or reading about Beethoven, is his equal. He was fully conscientious of this kind of inequality and held his inferiors in ways that were quite often unseemly. Not only was he rude to his servants, but he several times expressed his conviction that he had a right to treat people, even his friends, as simple tools.*

The final element in Pederson's statement ("when only men ...") points back to her claim that Beethoven excluded women from the fraternity concept, which is, as I showed, a misrepresentation. I cannot help speculate on another aspect of Pederson's statement: although she does not explicitly state it, she seems to attribute to the word "power" in Beethoven's quoted sentence a particular meaning—power over others. This implication is false: Beethoven used the German word *die Kraft*, the closest equivalent of which is "strength"—physical as well as inner (or moral) strength:[9] the "power" that Pederson and Solomon intimate would have been phrased as *der Macht* in German. It is obvious that Beethoven had in mind his inner strength, not his coercive authority over other people.

About half-way in Pederson's argument (322), after she had claimed that Beethoven's allegiance to the ideals of fraternity and equality "may break down on [her] closer inspection," she accepts that "something stronger," namely Beethoven's music, "overrides these particulars" justifying "the persistence of Beethoven as the musical image of the ideal political state." Unhappy with this apparent backtrack, she immediately introduced a new argument, stating that "a historical perspective shows that there is another reason" to eventually pinpoint the politically masculine Beethoven. She claims that "music, like woman, helped define the political sphere in the nineteenth century by being specifically excluded from it." Like woman, whom the patriarchal ideology confined to the

---

* "I regard him [Zmeskal] and S [Schuppanzigh] merely as instruments on which to play when I am inclined" (1801 letter to his friend Amenda, Anderson 53, p. 64). "Never *outwardly* show people the contempt they deserve, because one cannot know when one may need them." (*Tagebuch* in Solomon 1988, p. 256)

domestic domain, music was excluded from the political sphere and, according to Pederson, "in this context the importance of Beethoven's masculinity grew: it became a talisman that was used to ward off accusations that music had nothing to do with the real world." In support of this new thesis, she mentions that "as part of the 1848 revolutions, proposals for a musical reorganization that would make music more accessible and a more integral part of people's lives were formed by liberal and revolutionary musicians" (323).

The thesis that music was excluded from politics is also at odds with facts. While music did not go into the streets to fight for those humanistic ideals— although a few musicians, like Wagner, did—it was certainly involved in the political sphere of the nineteenth century. Ironically, it may have begun with Beethoven. In 1814, when Europe was engulfed in the last of Napoleon's wars, in which the Germans participated as in a nationalistic war of liberation, Beethoven became overtly "political." He composed two works celebrating the Allies' victories over Napoleon's army, the cantata *Der Glorreiche Augenblick* (The Glorious Day), Op. 136 and the *"Battle" Symphony* (or "Wellington Victory") Op. 91, which were tremendous popular successes and made him an instant celebrity. He was fêted by the European royalty assembled at the Congress of Vienna (autumn of 1814), which was deciding the fate of the continent after the final defeat of the "Corsican usurper." He became the symbol of German nationalism. One could even say that he opened the main political and musical landscape of the nineteenth century—the century of nationalism. Indeed, during the century, many larger and smaller nations fought and acquired the status of independent countries. Belgium separated from the Netherlands (1831), with a new Constitution that became a European model for other countries. The Italian *Risorgimento* movement united provinces under longtime foreign (Austrian, Spanish, French) rule (1859-61). Most German lands, split into a dozen larger or smaller principalities, finally united in 1866 into a German Empire, under the hegemony of the strongest of them, Prussia. In the Habsburg Empire, the only remaining German land outside the newly born Germany, the many nations incorporated by conquest (Czech, Slovak, Hungarian, Croatian) fomented various "nationalisms."

Nationalism became the war cry in music, too. "National schools" of music were born all over Europe, succeeding declining global romanticism, in Russia, Bohemia (not yet a country), Hungary (autonomous in the Habsburg Empire), Spain, Norway, Finland, and Poland (not yet a country), to quote only the first most productive examples. Music was sometimes directly involved in nationalistic movements, as well. In Italy, the most prominent such case, the opera was a symbol of the country; Verdi's choir "Va pensiero" from his *Nabucco* became a kind of national anthem; and "Viva Verdi" (Vittorio Emanuele Re D'Italia—VERDI)[*] was the salute of the freedom fighters against the Habsburg rule. If music played a less-militant role in Germany, it was nevertheless a symbolic unifying trait in the consciousness of the nation; it was a

---

[*] Vittorio Emanuelle, Duke of Savoy, was the popular figure who became the King of Italy after unification.

source of national pride and Beethoven was the foremost focus of that pride, as Wagner proclaimed, because "the German spirit has through him redeemed the spirit of humanity from deep ignominy."[10] It is worth mentioning that this last thesis from Pederson—music excluded from the sphere of politics—is also at odds with her own conviction that she had expressed only a few years before, in a 1994 paper, in which she quoted critically, as nationalistic, A. B. Marx's proclamation that the symphony genre "was virtually the exclusive property of the Germans."[11]

Summing up: the whole argumentation offered by Pederson to support Beethoven's "masculinity" by way of his active or passive involvement in the political sphere (of his time or later) does not stand scrutiny.

The "Heroic narrative": Another failed argument

Pederson is obviously right to write, "his [Beethoven's] heroic confrontation with fate put him in a category apart from other musicians" (323) and not to elaborate on the theme of "the deaf musician," which is certainly an important root of the Beethoven myth, but is not relevant in the discussion at hand. Trying to define a "specific content" to the archetypal heroic narrative, Pederson looks again for help from other scholars, this time from Burnham:

> In a letter from 1815, Beethoven wrote: "We mortals with immortal spirit are born only to suffering and joy, and one could almost say that the most distinguished among us obtain joy through suffering." Burnham comments, "it would be hard to imagine a more direct transcription of the popular view of the meaning of Beethoven's heroic style." (324)

"Through suffering to joy" (translation of the German phrase "durch Leiden Freude") has indeed become a clichéd label stuck to Beethoven's "heroic" music, but Pederson takes it into the realm of the untenable. She is right to see heroic battles against Fate as character-building processes, a concept endorsed by German Enlightenment as *Bildung*. However, she pushes her speculation further to prove that "a narrative of overcoming necessarily mark the music as masculine" (324). According to the "masculinity" concept she attributes to the nineteenth century and to Beethoven, "man becomes" while "woman does not become—she *is*," therefore a woman cannot build her character through such heroic narratives. And, Bingo!—here is the masculine Beethoven music again.

This second argument of Pederson is less amusing but is as wrong as the first, and for several reasons. Beethoven denying the woman the "heroic narrative!?" What about Leonore, the heroine of his only opera, an upside-down rescue story in which the (mezzo-)soprano saves the tenor's life by risking her own, and whom Beethoven hailed in the final choir—"Never will she hymned enough?" Clearly, Beethoven did not deny female heroism.

In fact, neither did Beethoven's Germany. Indeed, the most outstanding "heroic narrative" in the whole Western World history was that of a woman, Jeanne d'Arc, the farm girl who led the French army against the English invaders during the One-Hundred Years War and succeeded, paying with her life at the stake. Her story was well-known in nineteenth century Germany, including in the form of the tragedy *The Maid of Orleans* that Schiller wrote in 1801, and that was known to Beethoven. In his February 1811 letter to Bettina Brentano, he wrote: "What shall I tell you about myself? 'Pity my fate' I cry with Johanna." Johanna was Jeanne d'Arc, whose replay Emily Anderson, who translated Beethoven's letters into English, located in Schiller's play.[12]

And there is more to it. Schiller's play might have been the spur for real women to follow Joan of Arc. A young German woman named Leonore Prohaska, disguised as a man, fought and died heroically in the liberation war against Napoleon's armies in 1813 and inspired the eponymous tragedy of a now forgotten writer, Friedrich Duncker, for which Beethoven wrote in 1815 four pieces of incidental music in the memory of that heroine, including the orchestration of the Funeral March from his *Piano Sonata* Op. 26.[13] Granted, this WoO 69 work is little known and hardly ever played (yet available now on YouTube), but the story must have resonated in Beethoven's mind as a "specific content" of female heroism.

Even the quote with which Dr. Pederson supports her argument are evidence of the opposite. Pederson ignores the addressee and the context: Beethoven wrote it to his friend, Countess Marie Erdödy, who had left Vienna travelling abroad and had sent him news about her suffering during her journey. "I am now trying to console you," he wrote her just before the invoked "joy through suffering" sentence.[14] Therefore, the *We* in "we mortals" included the countess, who was indeed a person who, like Beethoven, had known what suffering was (and was going to know far worse pain soon). Obviously, Beethoven included her, a woman, in the "joy through suffering" heroic experience. This conclusion is one more proof that the alleged patriarchal "masculinity" of the nineteenth century that excluded women from *Bildung* is a very dubious construct. Some influential intellectuals, such as Hegel, might have thought so, as Pedersen duly documents (325), but that does not prove her case. Everybody did not think so. Schiller certainly did not think so and neither did Beethoven.

Pederson's final verdict – a misconception

My foregoing analysis has shown that Pedersons' final verdict:

> The reason why Beethoven is assumed to be the most masculine of composers is that what he and his music stand for is precisely the same ideology that tries to attain universal society in theory while maintaining male domination in practice. (326)

is a clearly unsubstantiated statement. Let us notice first of all that the assessment that Beethoven was "the most masculine of composers" in Pederson's verdict is nowhere demonstrated. Two or three quoted statements comparing him to Schubert and the latter to some unnamed "others" cannot serve as a demonstration. Yet, even if we accept it as a premise, all of Pederson's attempts to prove that this alleged masculinity reflected Beethoven's allegiance to "patriarchal ideology" are complete failures. He did not subscribe to that "ideology" in any way, either in his behavior towards women or by proclaiming or hinting at male privileges in his music. He sincerely believed in equal freedom for all and I will show that he even shared some feminist concepts.

When I debunked McClary's theories (chapter 10) I also pointed out a well-known fact in the Beethoven literature that refutes his allegedly violent "masculinity": unlike modern day feminism, Beethoven's feminine audience of his time enthusiastically embraced his music, which can be explained only if they did not feel any "oppressing" element therein. Either they did discover a strong feminine side or, if they felt a masculine one, they liked it, they felt it not oppressive but appealing, reassuring and protective.

Equally wrong is the final paragraph of Pederson's essay, which claims to justify the feminist approach to Beethoven, inaugurated by McClary:

> A feminist approach to this topic does not necessarily aim to vilify or celebrate Beethoven. Rather, as part of the debate of how to interpret the meaning of Beethoven and his music, it can expose the gendered history of the so-called universal concepts that have secured his legacy. This approach will help us to understand what keeps Beethoven at the center of the canon, as well as the forces that are unsettling his position.

This statement implies that Beethoven is still "at the center of the canon" because many people—like this author—are still, at the beginning of the third millennium, living within the "patriarchal ideology" that feminism denounces, and that the forces are justified that want Beethoven removed from his uppermost position in the canon or, maybe, thrown out of it altogether. In fact, opposition to post-modernist feminism—which is the scope of this part of the present book—does not imply living within a patriarchal ideology; it means simply refusing to replace a wrong with another wrong, and requiring any debate to accept the undeniable facts and to observe the fundamental laws of logical thinking, which cannot be wrong because they were enounced by males rather than females. They were the root of all progress of the human race, including the arrival of feminism.

13
When DeNora meets McClary: Gendering Beethoven

Professor Tia DeNora continued to engage Beethoven in her further research. He was unavoidable, because he had played such an important role in what she calls "canonic ideology"—the criteria establishing the "value" within the realm of Classical music—which cast him as a major character in the realm of socio-musicology. In most cases, Beethoven appears only as an illustration of a general concept or a development of DeNora's original thesis about the politics to which he purportedly owed his rise, which I debunked in chapter 8. Only one of these newer contributions proposes an original theory involving Beethoven directly—a 2002 article somewhat misleadingly titled "Music into Action: Performing Gender on the Viennese Concert Stage, 1790-1810."[1] In this article, she revisits the topic of her main concern, the social "meaning" of music. Again, Beethoven is a central figure, but she views him from a different angle.

The term "gender" in the title implies also a feminist angle. DeNora did not come through as a feminist in her Beethoven book (as discussed in chapter 8). She praised McClary's "analyses of music's social and ideological content" as "compelling when they focus on the ways music is mapped onto other social phenomena" and, therefore, "seductive," but found that "McClary is on less secure ground, however, when she suggests that Beethoven's symphonic works are about masculine domination."[2] The scholar seems to have "evolved" in the meantime: in her 2002 article, she accepts Susan McClary's description of Beethoven's music "'as aligned with a transgressive violent form of masculinity'" (26-27).[*] She, however, drops the adjectives "violent" and "hegemonic," because she has a different goal in line with her dedication to socio-musicology: to demonstrate that the public performance of Beethoven's music by female and male pianists between 1790 and 1810 was instrumental in defining nineteenth century concepts and "institutional practices" of "masculinity" and "femininity." In this way, a gap in the study of the sociological meaning of music would be filled by revealing "music's link to gender formation" (26).

The alleged force at work in the alleged process is, however, not the unmediated "meaning" of music—revealed in its content—but the mediating "music into action," that is, music as performed and received by the public. Therefore, her article consists of two parts, the first of which clarifies how "music in action" can be understood "as a medium through which social relations are forged" (19) and serves as foundation of the second part, in which DeNora presents her "demonstration," as an example of how "music actually works as an active ingredient, a structuring medium of social life" (20).

---

[*] All references to this article are included in text in this chapter.

Music into action: its "gestural" character

In fact, common sense tells us that "music into action" is music itself. Music is not the score, even though musicians have to study music in this form before they can play it, and the score is the daily bread of musicologists; music is what is produced as sounds by human voices and instruments, and this is the only way that it can have a meaning, whether social or musical. Ignoring this simple short-cut, DeNora soars in the rarefied air of theory, which seems to prevent her from exploring interesting musical and social aspects of the old and new worlds. She brings in several abstract concepts, of which the only one that she needs later is that of "music's gestural character" (24). Performed music exhibits both "sonic gestures" and "visual gestures." The former group includes "allegorical and gestural" sound devices (patterns), which were frequently built into a musical structure. DeNora writes that such sound devices were popular in the Baroque period, and identifies some in Bach's works (24); she could have advanced an even more illustrative example: the *stile rappresentativo*, known since the sixteenth century madrigalists and in later early Baroque opera, which invented such note-patterns that directly imitated, in singing, the speech when expressing emotions.[3]

The second kind of musical gestures are the visual ones—those displayed by the interpreter while performing. According to DeNora, "the gestures of musical display involved in the production of sound are not ancillary to music but part of music's configuration as event. These gestures may also serve as framing devices and contextualization cues for making sense of music as event" (25). This interesting point would have benefitted from discussion in the concrete (perhaps from both pro- and con- perspectives) but DeNora offers only one real-world hint—"think of Jacqueline Dupre's physicality when performing Elgar" (26).

One could, for example, object to the weight that DeNora assigns to visual gestures in defining the "meaning" of music, for the very simple reason that the most common way of enjoying music, whether classical or pop, "in action" is listening to recordings. Does listening to Elgar cello concerto (DeNora's example) convey a different "meaning" as compared to watching the video? On the other hand, one can argue that a live rendition adds something imponderable to the music, probably born from the feeling of a subconscious communication with the listeners, which makes it indeed a "social" event … and which does not happen when listening at home or when jogging with headphones. In this sense, music is, indeed "social," as DeNora claims (25), and it is a pity that, lost in her academic abstractions, she did not touch on this aspect. McClary is, when she does not give in to feminist ire, a very keen analyst of "music into action."

An overview of DeNora's thesis

In a nutshell, DeNora's demonstration of how "music into action" played a role in defining "gender" in the nineteenth century is three-step process. In the first step, she "genders" Beethoven as an expression of musical "masculinity." In the second, she genders the piano, separating the female and male performers by their playing (the males) or not playing (the females) Beethoven's music. In the third step, with women excluded from playing Beethoven's works,

> as this social relation was repeated over time, music following the

> Beethovenian "model" came to be associated with a masculine musical sphere. (30)

Also, as in a positive feed-back loop,

> Beethoven came to be associated with masculinity because the event of his music was increasingly appropriate by men [...] as a gesture of strength and heroism. (31)

This process is also illustrated by the composer's iconography, which shows him "increasingly masculinized in the pictorial representations," as Alexandra Comini has shown (31).[*] In DeNora's final verdict, Beethoven's music was not merely reflective of but helped constitute gender formation during the nineteenth century.

However, DeNora takes a less feminist stance: in her view, the links between musical sounds and their social significances were not present in Beethoven's music at the onset of the long process; they were rather forged in and through practice and repeated practice—through the circumstances of Beethoven's performance and through commentary upon his performance (31). Therefore, she claims that "it is less interesting, sociologically to make assumptions of a homological relationship between Beethoven's compositional processes and masculine or misogynist culture and more interesting to tell a story that emphasizes the mutual shaping of Beethoven's music and the ideas and images with which it is associated" (32).

The idea that such "gendering" of the act of performance might have a social impact cannot be rejected outright as outlandish because it is unprovable. DeNora never establishes a causal link in the alleged process, except "learning by repetition." It is really strange that she ignores the work of Marshall McLuhan, a cornerstone of so-called "media theory," which is actually part of the field of sociology. Some fifty years ago, McLuhan published his seminal book *The Medium Is the Message*, in which he showed, simply by analyzing the history of human society, how the changing "medium" of communicating, from oral to written, then to printed communication, and finally to the audio-visual environment of the twentieth century, has impacted the human mind, changing its ways of perceiving and scrutinizing the world. To McLuhan, the media are extensions of human bodies, senses and minds, and DeNora's "music into action" is just such a form of media. It is normal for it to have participated in the changing of the human mind.

Whether it happened in the ways that DeNora proposes is a different matter. I will show presently that her theory is undermined by major flaws in each of its steps.

An incongruent view of the gender concept of the nineteenth century

DeNora adopts the definitions of nineteenth century masculinity and femininity from Thomas Laquer's book *Making Sex*, a history of sexuality: the masculine meant active, stable and strong; the feminine meant passive, unstable

---

[*] In her book *The Changing Image of Beethoven. A Study in Mythmaking* (Rizzoli, New York, 1987).

and constitutionally delicate (27). One notices first that the definitions are based on opposing irreconcilables (active-passive, stable-unstable, strong-feeble). In fact, definitions have long been based on complementarity rather than irreconcilable halves, about which the sciences have added more and more insight, up to and including differences between the brains of the two sexes. For millennia at least, active-passive pairs referred to sexual selection, in which the male was supposed to choose (although popular wisdom was wondering); the stable-unstable pair had meant the reason and the emotions, the latter being indeed a stronger center in the female brain; finally, the constitutionally delicate had been nuanced far more accurately with the term "gracefulness" or even "beauty." This view had been prevalent in the Western world at least since Renaissance, so one also wonders why the nineteenth century needed a new definition of masculine and feminine.

In fact, according to DeNora's very source, Laquer, her definition of the genders was the product of the eighteenth century, when the concept of a "two-sexed" world rose to prominence (27). The concepts were already in place when Beethoven arrived, therefore there was no need for his contribution to enforce them, let alone shape their development.

Gendering Beethoven: A misconstrued argument

The first step in DeNora's demonstration is to enforce the idea that Beethoven was the prototypical "masculine" composer. She displays some strange "dialectics" in her take on the issue, because she is playing on McClary's field, elaborating the latter's thesis of Beethoven's "hegemonic masculinity" that would have been "associated with the rise of 'two-sexed' world during the eighteenth century." On the other hand, DeNora objects that "to locate homological relationship between music and, in this case, gender is to treat the latter—or any other social category—as if it were some type of solid block that is devoid of any internal diversity" (27). This objection is irrelevant because, while gender is certainly not a "solid block" today, it was so at the time of Beethoven. DeNora acknowledges further that "the idea that 'Beethoven is masculine' does indeed have an historical basis" in the Enlightenment concept of "Genius" and the "Sublime," which are both "masculine." She also quotes McClary's quoting Schumann's writing about Beethoven's "virile power," in contrast with Schubert's more sensitive, "feminine charm" (27). She finally accepts that "the lineaments of masculinity that could be 'found' in Beethoven's music [...] outlined a preferred mode of masculinity within 19th century culture," but then claims that "this issue, which is often so abstract as to be untenable, can be grounded by considering musical practices" (28). As one can see, she agrees with McClary's thesis and "genders" Beethoven, but for a different reason: in order to force him into her "music into action" mechanism that would prove her thesis.

In fact, the whole idea of Beethoven's "masculinity" must be taken with several grains of salt. Female contemporaries of Beethoven did not perceive his music as male-antagonistic. As Romain Rolland noted long ago, he "met with affectionate understanding on the part of the women of the aristocracy, many of whom were gifted musically and were remarkable interpreters of his music.⁴ In fact, women were Beethoven's best interpreters, as he himself testified.* As I described in chapter 10, be was particularly enthralled by Marie Bigot's performances, and asked her to sight-read his just-completed *Appassionata*.⁵ Baroness Dorothea Ertmann was his "Dorothea-Caecilia" (i.e., the patron saint of music) who promoted his music in private concerts even before he gave up playing in public, as Schindler testifies.⁶ Later, Beethoven wrote Marie Pachler-Koschak "I have never yet found anybody who plays my compositions as well as you do [...] You are the true guardian of my intellectual offspring".⁷ These women understood Beethoven's music, including both the "feminine" and "masculine" sides. He might have actually embodied their dream concept of masculinity—forceful and tender at the same time, giving a woman protection against the world, which is so often hurtful.

Beethoven's gendering the piano: Another misrepresentation

That the piano had gradually become a "province of women" (28, quoting Rosen) during the eighteen century has been known for a long time. The explanation has been around just as long—the "piano physicality" conformed to what DeNora calls "bodily decorum." Playing the piano did not require a position that would have been considered "immodest," like holding the cello between the legs (which would have also been hard because of the fashion in clothes of the time) or bodily contortions that are inevitable when playing the violin. We may call that a form of discrimination that has been only gradually been eliminated, but it did not imply any "gendering" at the time, as long as men were playing the piano, too. Actually, many (possibly even most) of the composers of the Classical era were piano virtuosos, too. However, DeNora introduces a new element—the gendering of the piano, which would have begun with Beethoven (28-29):

> Circa 1796, piano performance in Vienna was not gender specific. Women performed as well as, and with the frequency of men. [...] It is with the introduction of Beethoven's piano works that the first signs of gender segregation at the piano can be found. Not only was this segregation remarked upon by his contemporaries ("some new things in them which the ladies do not wish to play because they are incomprehensible and too difficult") but, at a time when he was the most frequently performed composer for the piano in Vienna, the data on the repertory suggests that women did not perform Beethoven's concertos—despite performing those by other composers (see Table 1).

---

* I am resuming here, shortened, my rebuttal of McClary's allegations in chapter 10 (page 208-209).

Table 1
Most frequently performed composers for the fortepiano (all piano genres) in Vienna 1787–1810

Beethoven	33 (21% by female pianists)
Mozart	26 (74% by female pianists)
Eberl	11 (72% by female pianists)
Steibelt	9 (39% by female pianists)

Source: Morrow (1989), public and private concert calendars. Beethoven's works were not performed in Vienna until after his arrival in that city at the end of 1792.

This table is actually very dubious proof. Statistics work by definition with large numbers. The author does not indicate how many cases she took into account, but it was very few, because the total number of pieces played by various performers is only 79. Moreover, the entities in the table are vague: we can assume that the number 33 in Beethoven's line represents the number of his pieces, and that only 7 of them (21%) were played by women; but were these pieces concertos, as DeNora's quote specifies ("women did not perform Beethoven's *concertos*"), and how many were these women pianists? It is "statistically" meaningful if there were two or twenty performers. DeNora does not give even a hint about this, but there must have been very few established concert pianists besides the already mentioned Marie Bigot and Dorothea Ertmann. (Marie Pachler-Koschak debuted only in 1811) I know only three female pianists active in Vienna at the time: Josepha Auernhammer (1758-1820), a pupil of Mozart (who dedicated several piano & violin sonatas to her);[8] Marianna Auenbrugger (1759-1882), who died too young to make it on to DeNora table; and Henriette von Pereira-Arnstein (1780-1859), who was active mostly in salons. They may have played Beethoven music on occasion, but that is not enough to constitute a "statistical proof" of DeNora's claim.

Statistics are not the only flaw in DeNora's argument. Her explanation of the alleged "gender segregation" of the piano repertoire is also misconstrued. The main cause, besides Beethoven's work being "incomprehensible and too difficult," would have been the "somatic habits that broke with prevailing conventions of a gentle, delicate, and graceful performance style:" (29). Beethoven's "physicality of the piano" involved

> Chords rather than "pearly" passage work, leaps from one range to another, double octave statements of themes, extreme dynamic contrasts, legato articulations, abrupt changes of mood or tempo, startling rhythmic figures and broken phrases, Beethoven's music called upon a pianist to engage in often abrupt, changeable and disconnected physical activities that entailed and routinised suddenness of movement and surprise which were the very antithesis of aristocratic corporeality and pianistic femininity [… therefore] to be a woman and play Beethoven was to risk one's decorum as a feminine being. To play Beethoven was to break with existing notions of feminine decorum, notions that stretched across Europe

and back at least a century. (30)*

This statement is, at best, a gross exaggeration. One cannot see how the "legato articulations" would have required a break of the prescribed "feminine decorum." Neither would have the "extreme dynamic contrasts" and the "abrupt changes of mood or tempo"; in fact, they were quite appropriate with the "feminine" concept of the age, which referenced the "unstable," as DeNora herself claims (27). Finally, the so-called "disconnected physical activities" were not typical for Beethoven's piano-playing; if he was indeed "hard on piano" and often "caused strings to break," as DeNora correctly mentions (29), this was because the fortepiano of the time was a "weak" instrument. The "disconnected physical activities" were actually the mark of the next generations of virtuosos, who benefitted of the first versions of the modern (Érard or Broadwood) pianos. Schindler testified that Beethoven showed "vigorous opposition to all bodily motion at the piano."[9] Could Schindler, who has since been exposed for bias and even falsifying evidence, have lied about that? Czerny, who had been Beethoven's pupil between 1801 and 1804 and had plenty of opportunity to see him playing, concurred: "His bearing while playing was masterfully quiet, noble and beautiful, without the slightest grimace."[10]

DeNora could have made a better case by quoting another of Schindler's statements: "throughout his life the master [Beethoven] maintained his "vigorous masculine piano style,"[11] which might suggest a masculine-feminine opposition in line with today's feminist stance. To her credit, DeNora does not do it, because it would have meant truncating the quote, in which Schindler states that this was the style of all "comparable" virtuosos of his time, among which he also mentions a woman that I have mentioned before, "Frau Auernhammer." The opposition that Schindler had in mind was that between the virtuoso and the amateur piano player.

In fact, the alleged gendering of the piano conflicts with all the known facts in Beethoven literature: *women played* his piano music, both during his life and after. I have already showed that he hailed three women as his best interpreters. He was not alone to say so: Reichardt listened to Dorothea Ertmann playing in 1808, and wrote: "As she performed a great Beethoven sonata I was surprised as almost never before. I have never seen such power and innermost tenderness combined even in the greatest virtuosi."[12] Of course, most "amateur" woman pianists were achieving less, but they also played Beethoven's music, and there is plenty evidence for that, too.

Let us return to Table 1 and notice that it applies to the period 1787† to 1810 and only in Vienna. Are we to believe that a process allegedly defining the concept of masculinity and femininity of the nineteenth century through repeated reinforcements was decided during its first twenty years in one European city?

---

* DeNora also conflates the "physicality" of the piano with another hardly credible speculation: during Beethoven's time "genius was masculine in [philosophical] conception," and Beethoven's music was hailed as possessing 'an earnest, manly style'" (30), therefore it was not appropriate for a woman to play it.

† In fact, it should begin in 1793, because Beethoven arrived in Vienna at the end of 1792.

This does not make any sense. Seemingly aware of this weakness, DeNora also invoked the research of Katharine Ellis,[13] a musicologist and professor specialized in music history, particularly about the nineteenth-century Paris. Ellis would have proven that "increasingly during the 19th century, women were edged out of performing the most fiery works in the repertory and, in Vienna and elsewhere, came to function as conservators of musical taste" (30). Actually, the examination of Eliss's work proves the opposite. Like DeNora, she claims that the typical "repertory that was gendered feminine [was] the keyboard music of Beethoven's predecessors," and even that "in France, most of Beethoven's orchestral music had been implicitly gendered male by 1840."[14] However, between these two statements, one can read:

> The reception of nineteenth-century female pianists was complicated still further by their active and successful participation in a second male-gendered repertory: the Beethovenian sonata, concerto, and chamber tradition.[15]

"Reception" consisted in the (presumably biased) opinion of the male music critics, but it is clear that it did not prevent female pianists from playing Beethoven to great acclaim. In fact, Ellis brings forward the name of several women pianists that "declare themselves priestesses of the cult that the artistic world dedicates to Beethoven": Marie Playel (1811-1875), with a "repertory reaching back only as far as Beethoven"; Louise Mattmann (1826-1861), "renowned for her performances of Beethoven"; Louise-Aglad Massart (1827-1887), another "renowned interpreter of Beethoven," whose *Appassionata* she rendered to "perfection," according to the most acerbic of male critics, Berlioz; Therese Wartel (1814-1865), "renowned as an interpreter of Beethoven and as a chamber pianist" and even "author of a book on Beethoven interpretation" published in 1865.[16] One can add to the list some internationally acclaimed female interpreters of Beethoven: Maria Szymanowska (1789-1831), one of the first pianist virtuosos of the century, who had a large repertoire from Bach to (early) Chopin and including Beethoven, whom, according to a legend, she would have met as a child prodigy.[17] We must also include the famous Clara Schumann (1819-1896), who played Beethoven's piano concertos and piano sonatas and variation sets in her touring recitals all over Europe; there are contemporary references to her "magnificent" rendering of his *Fifth Piano Concerto* and an "electrifying" one of the *Appassionata*.[18]

The second side of DeNora's "gendering" equation, the one involving the male pianists, also requires a closer examination. We must keep in mind a fact that actually limited their availability for playing Beethoven's music: unlike today, when there is a clear separation between composer and interpreter, at the time the musician was typically both. As a pianist was a virtuoso *and* a composer, he tended to play his own works primarily, recurring to other people's music only when he was in a creative dry spell or when it allowed him to display exceptional virtuoso prodigality. This was particularly true for the male pianists and they did not make an exception for Beethoven's sake. Three of his contemporaries illustrate this situation well. Johann Nepomuk Hummel (1778-1837), was raised in the Mozartean school and adapted its pianism to the first versions of the modern piano introduced in the 1820s. He was a virtuoso competitor of Beethoven,* but appreciated Beethoven's music nevertheless, even conducting his symphonic pieces during his life and after his death. He also arranged seven of his symphonies as well as some of his chamber works for piano. However, there is no record of him playing any piano work of Beethoven with a single exception: an 1823 performance of the *Choral Fantasy* Op. 80.[19] Carl Czerny (1791-1857) was Beethoven's pupil when a child prodigy and passed his instructions to his own students, even writing a book *On the Proper Performance of All Beethoven's Works for the Piano*.

His most famous pupil, Franz Liszt, left the testimony that "In the twenties [1820s], when a great portion of Beethoven's creations was a kind of sphinx, Czerny was playing Beethoven *exclusively* [...] It is only a pity that, by a superabundant productive-ness, he has necessarily weakened himself, and has not gone further on the road."[20] Indeed, Schindler complained later that Czerny did not continue playing his former teacher's music in public later because "his own prodigious output as a composer for many years kept him from the music of Beethoven [after the latter's death]."[21] It would be reasonable to assume that Beethoven's pupil and friend Ferdinand Ries (1784-1838), who had received his master's advice about how to interpret many of his works, played them during his successful virtuoso career, especially in London, where he settled—however, it did not seem to happen. Ries's ambition was to be, like his master, a composer: he wrote seven symphonies, nine piano concertos, three operas, piano pieces and chamber music. It is symptomatic that, of the thirty-odd letters that Beethoven wrote to Ries after the latter left Vienna for good, not one mentions an event where Ries played his teacher's music.

We have reached now a point where another flaw of DeNora's thesis becomes obvious.

The mistaken belief in Beethoven's piano music ubiquity

DeNora's thesis relies on a basic premise—that Beethoven's piano music was widely performed all throughout the nineteenth century. Only by this repeated enforcement could the "music into action" mechanism that she advances have succeeded in imprinting concepts of masculinity and femininity embodied in the sex of the interpreters on public mentality. In fact, Beethoven's piano music was very rarely performed during the first half of the century. He had been quickly "canonized" by the first Romanticist generation, but based essentially on his symphonies that were at the time dominating the public concert stage. His sonatas and even his piano concertos had fallen into oblivion. In his 1840 biography of Beethoven, Schindler wrote: "

A foreign visitor might find it strange not to find any opportunity in Vienna to hear a Beethoven sonata."[22] And in a second edition, printed twenty years

---

* There are also allegations that they competed also in the love field, where Hummel won – he married in 1812 the singer Elisabeth Röckel, who would have been also the object of Beethoven's affection (Schindler 1996, p. 167).

later, he commented, "had it not been for Frau von Ertmann, Beethoven's piano music would have disappeared even sooner from the repertoire in Vienna," which was at the time embracing "the emerging new direction in compositions and piano playing introduced by Hummel and his disciples."[23] We find plenty of evidence to confirm that this happened in every European country in which classical music was a significant social trend: in Paris, which had become the intellectual capital of the world; in England, with London a thriving music hub; and also in all German-speaking countries, notably in Leipzig, Berlin and Dresden, all cities with a long musical tradition.

As specific examples, in France, by *circa* 1850, "to present a Beethoven piano sonata was considered out-of-place." Even his piano concertos were "out-of-place"—among the hundreds of times that Beethoven's symphonic works were given by Paris *Société des Concerts* between 1828 and 1870, his piano concertos figured only fifteen times.[24] It is also worth noting that one of the first performances of a Beethoven piano concertos was given by a woman, Louise Mattmann, who played the first movement of Beethoven's *Third* on 11 February 1844.[25] The situation was similar in England. When Charles Hallé (1819-1895), a German-born pianist who used to play other music than his own, settled in London in 1848, he found that "the Beethoven solo pianoforte sonatas were still regarded as 'abstruse'"; they became gradually more "acceptable," but "only a small specialized public would appreciate his [Hallé's] Beethoven cycle" in 1863.[26] But why worry about Paris and London? Germany was even slower to responds than England and France; when Hans von Bülow decided to play Beethoven's last five piano sonatas in Berlin in 1878, he entertained no illusions about the success of his plan and, after he played, he wrote to a friend, "Berlin must have sunk very low."[27] Beethoven's great *Fourth Piano Concerto* was never listened to in Europe between its premiere in 1808 and its rediscovery in 1832.[28] No less pianistic talents than the great Franz Liszt and his dedication were needed to force Beethoven's piano music into the Canon—a process that did not gain momentum until around 1850.[29]

Beethoven's paradoxical "canonization," combining fame and oblivion, was a typical product of the musical life at the time, which is thoroughly different from our modern one. Nowadays, musicians are interpreters who play primarily the standard repertoire; back then, the musicians (most of them pianists), were composers who interpreted their own works and, only occasionally, those of other composers. Beethoven's piano music was forgotten the same way as Bach's had been in the previous century. At the same time, his symphonies were the basis of the repertoire; it took almost half a century for the Romantic generation to produce symphonies that could measure up to Beethoven's example. The foregoing analysis has shown the falsity of DeNora premises on which her thesis about the social impact of Beethoven's piano music "into action" during the nineteenth century is based. Beethoven cannot be "gendered" as typically masculine; he had a strong "feminine" side that women (piano virtuosos and others) could feel and attach to.

The nineteenth-century piano cannot be "Beethoven gendered," either: women pianists shared the Beethoven repertoire with their male counterparts. The timing of the alleged process is equally marred by flaws: for half of the century and possibly longer, Beethoven's piano music was not frequent enough in public concerts to facilitate the impact that DeNora attributes to its performance.

This being said, I will not claim that DeNora thesis is completely wrong. I gladly accept her idea that "music into action" must have played a significant, if subliminal, role in shaping the human mind (and body for that matter). What has been happening during the last hundred years forces this idea upon us, whether we like or not what has happened—basically the replacement of the Classical with pop genres. It is how DeNora puts this simple idea into action, involving Beethoven and "gendering," that fails.

14
Hollywood Beethoven

Given the recent evolution of Hollywood, now firmly devoted to the "me too" movement in which it was both a perpetrator and a prosecutor, it is unsurprising that the studios emerged as an actor in the post-modernist siege of Beethoven. It came out, in 2006, with *Copying Beethoven*, a rather paradoxical work: not made in the Los Angeles studios but in Europe and yet a truly post-modernist-feminist manifesto in the spirit of the new Hollywood ethos. It also fits well a long international tradition of portraying Beethoven in the film industry by falsifying his life.

Beethoven's predicament on screen

Paradoxically, Beethoven has never inspired a movie worth of his Fate, the worst that can afflict a musician. This is probably because his tragedy was essentially a psychological struggle for which cinematography seems not very well equipped, therefore it had to rely principally on his love life, which has been little known and long debated ... but not debatable enough to stir the imagination. The imagination of the producers of the handful of "Beethoven features" since the time of the silent movies[1] has distorted either his personality or the biographical truth, and usually both. Most, if not all, of them have observed a kind of traditional scheme in the presentation of the composer's love life, putting at its center his short-lived infatuation with his aristocratic pupil Giulietta Guicciardi, because it gives one the opportunity to shoot a very cinematographic moment with him playing, in a romantic setting, the *Moonlight Sonata* that he dedicated to her.

None of these early or later movies about Beethoven achieved the excellence of *Amadeus* (1984), which benefitted from a brilliant distortion of truth about Mozart provided by Peter Shaffer in his play that he turned into a script handsomely fulfilled cinematographically by Miloš Forman. As Alexandre Dumas *père*, the father of historical fiction, put it: "It is acceptable to violate history, on the condition of giving her beautiful children."[*] It happened with Mozart, but it did not happen with Beethoven, for better or worse. And things went much further with post-modernism.

The 1992 family comedy *Beethoven* was perversely a herald of post-modernism. This family comedy irreverently bearing the composer's name, still

---

[*] A disclaimer needed in the age of me-too: I ask my female readers to forgive my invoking this metaphor (I also avoided the usage of the infamous "r" word). This often quoted statement is actually the adaptation of an anecdote told by Dumas in his *Memoires*, in which he answered the accusation of having "violated history" with this sentence, "If I violated history, I gave her beautiful children."

popular twenty-five years later, has nothing to do with Beethoven: it is about a dog that received the composer's name because it barked when hearing the beginning of the *Fifth Symphony*; the sagging jaws of the Saint-Bernard recalling the bitter expression in many of the composer's pictorial representation are also tongue-in-the-cheek nods. Giving a dog the name of a cultural icon still revered by a certain elite is an iconoclastic act in line with post-modernist attacks on Beethoven. In some German-speaking countries, one thought it wiser to distribute the movie under the title *Ein Hund namens Beethoven* [A dog named Beethoven]. The movie received negative to lukewarm reviews from critics (on review aggregator Rotten Tomatoes, it shows an approval rating of 33%, based on reviews from 27 critics, with an average score of 4.7/10). Nevertheless, audiences world-wide liked it (granting it an A grade, according to CinemaScore),[2] which stimulated the production of no less than five sequels and three standalone movies, spreading over two decades. My guess is that the name Beethoven is the main explanation for this unusual success with the public; it is quite possible that the millennials got to know that such a composer existed from this movie—which the reader may consider, depending on his or her inclination, saddening or touching.

In 1994, Bernard Rose, a British young and upcoming director, proposed his own solution of the tantalizing Beethovenian mystery of the *Immortal Beloved* in the eponymous movie. The movie was not devoid of some positive qualities—inspired cinematography, Gary Oldman as an unexpectedly convincing Beethoven, seconded by a good female trio—Roger Ebert (of Siskel-and-Ebert fame) gave the movie a qualified thumbs-up at the time, granting it 3½ stars (of four).[3] However, Ebert considered it simply as a "fiction" about a certain character who only incidentally resembled Beethoven. In fact, although written and directed by a Brit, the movie is no less typical for the LA studios, always ready to sacrifice truth to sensationalism. It would be hard indeed to find a more sensational Immortal Beloved than Beethoven's sister-in-law Johanna, the woman with whom he in reality fought a ferocious six-year-long war in the Austrian courts over the custody of her son after his brother's death in 1815. And Rose was not aware of his "violating" truth—he was convinced that he had solved the mystery and he promised to "defy any of them [Beethoven scholars] to prove me wrong."[4] The few music scholars who condescended to consider the movie dismissed it as a "travesty,"[5] but without much ado and Rose was never forced to defend his theory. This is not the place to rebut Rose's theory, because, to his credit, at least it does not demean Beethoven in the name of modern-day feminism.[*]

Nevertheless, I think it necessary to point out that all forms of fiction, including movies, should refrain from distorting beyond recognition the major events in the lives of cultural icons whom they try to portray, as *Immortal Beloved* does. Nowadays, when so much of the pseudo-educational baggage of a person comes from fiction, especially movies, rather than from research, such abuses have a noxious cultural effect. The millennials will certainly know that

---

[*] The reader may find my rebuttal in my book *The Immortal Beloved Controversy*, chapter 9 (subchapter "The Hollywood Candidate").

285

Beethoven was not a dog, but many of them might think that he was a bastard who screwed his brother's wife and gave her a child (publically acknowledged as a nephew in this particular narrative). One may perhaps carefully distort any biographical fact in fiction, but only when it can make a good point, as does the 2003 made-for-television BBC/Opus Arte film *Eroica*. The movie dramatizes the 1804 private premiere of Beethoven's symphony at the palace of Prince Lobkowitz. It portrays Haydn as showing up late during the performance (he did not—had it happened, it would certainly have been recorded by the witnesses) to utter a synthesis of the moment and of Beethoven's place in the history of music. Haydn feels uneasy with this new, "revolutionary" music, but accepts that "it is quite, quite new. The artist as hero. Quite new. Everything is different from today." The *Eroica* movie is also worth a mention as a negation of the new feminist account of Beethoven's masculinity that I have discussed in the previous chapters: we see here the female audience receiving Beethoven's music warmly, while several male characters reject it. This is the nineteenth century feminism, so different from our modern one.

Copying Beethoven, a feminist travesty

Modern-day feminism is the subtext, pretext, and sometimes even "text" of the 2006 *Copying Beethoven* movie, directed by well-known Polish director Agnieska Holland (b. 1948). The movie supposedly dramatizes the composer's last years, beginning 1824, purportedly as viewed through the eyes of a woman. The story is entirely fictional: a young female student at the Vienna Conservatory (Anna Holz) would have been sent to him to copy the score of Beethoven's *Ninth* Symphony, which he was finishing at the time, and would remain close to him, evolving from copyist into music consultant, helper, confidant, muse and finally care-giver of the dying composer. The story goes against all known facts in Beethoven's life, except the most basic ones—he finished his *Ninth, D minor Symphony* which was premiered in Vienna in 1824, and died a few years later, after having composed his last string quartets. However, that was not the movie's only flaw. The critics unusually almost reached a consensus in their negative reviews. (It has only a 28% approval rate on the Tomatometer.) An overall report ran as "a disappointingly conventional biopic [...] altogether lacking the grandeur and insight of *Amadeus*," a "cliché portrait" of Beethoven, a "blatantly fictitious [story that] will likely offend the aficionado's sense of history," a "revisionist script." Most critics also noticed the "contemporaneous feminist streak [that] rings false," and the phrase "feminist fantasy" is ubiquitous.[6]

As I stated earlier, I have nothing against feminism per se and I am ready to give *Copying Beethoven* the benefit of my doubt. And I am also ready to accept distortion of biographical truth if it helps to achieve that already-mentioned goal of "giving history beautiful children." Let us pretend that the scholarly world missed the young Anna Holz whom Beethoven employed during his last three years. Let us also stipulate that this woman, as a student at the 1817 established Vienna Conservatory (*Universität für Musik und darstellende Kunst Wien* in the original German), was well-versed in composition—although this institution had only taught singing for several years, before adding courses in orchestral instruments. (No precise date is available for the introduction of composition classes.) It is well documented that Beethoven did not conduct his symphony at its first performance and only stayed next to the conductor, giving his the tempo beat at the beginning of each movement[7] ... nonetheless, let us accept that he did so guided by this woman's gestures visible in a place in the orchestra during the long scene of the performance of his symphony. Let us even accept that she continued to be Beethoven's helper and muse and was with him in his last illness and death, although no witness noticed her.

In fact, let us stipulate all this "fiction." Given that, what are the "children" that this movie gives us? Anne Holz (Diane Kruger, a model turned actress) is gorgeous—the kind for whom Beethoven used to fall for—but insipid and incredible, a sort of musical "superwoman" of the time, who can give Beethoven lessons in composition. In certain scenes, one expects the two protagonists starting to sing "Anything you can do I can do better" (Irving Berlin's 1946 song from his musical *Annie Get Your Gun*). No surprise that Diane Kruger could not breathe any life into this incredible (in the literal sense of the word) character, as critics have noticed.

As for Beethoven, everything about his movie persona is false, beginning with his physicality. He was in life a slim, short man not taller than the average woman (about 5' 4" or 1.64 m), while Ed Harris, who incarnated him on film, is a stout almost six-foot-tall man. The movie's Beethoven is a bear in constant confrontation with his female copyist, while the real Beethoven was a teddy bear when it came to women. The very idea of Beethoven mooning a woman ... and one as pretty as Diane Kruger for that matter! The scene is plainly ridiculous: the two are in his music room, where she does her copying work; after a confrontation stemming from his troubled relationship with his nephew Karl, Beethoven tells her, "go back to work," and she puts her glasses on and resumes copying; he begins to undress, taking off his collar scarf and his shirt and remaining with his torso naked, while she watches his behavior slyly while tension suggests violent sexuality. However, he only pours water on his head several times (actually, a well-documented habit of his—but when he was sweaty after a long summer walk in the woods, not when working), while leaning over a big pot and uttering bearish grunts. "Did you study my piano sonatas at the conservatory?" he asks her and when she answers "Yes, maestro," he continues, "And which is your favorite?—the *Waldstein*, the *Appassionata*, or ... er ... er ... the *Moonlight*." And he turns his back to her and, as he is only dressed in a sort of flannelled trousers, he lowers them down, laughing. The script simply throws a pun to the English-speaking audience, committing a triple misrepresentation: not only is the act of "mooning" thoroughly out of character; but Beethoven never referred to his sonata as *Moonlight*—a (quite inappropriate) name it received from a stranger after the composer's death; and the slang usage of "mooning" was invented much later in America, and has no such meaning in German. The episode may look like a parody of the previously mentioned tradition of centering Beethoven's love life on his infatuation with Giulietta Guicciardi, to whom he dedicated the sonata. The Beethoven scholar also knows that this sonata became so popular during his life that he came to dislike it because it cast shade on others of his works that he considered superior. However, how many in the audience in the movie theatre would realize any of this? 99.9 percent of the audience could only see a rude, stupid Beethoven, completely different from the real one. Historical Beethoven had flashes of rudeness in his relationships with his male friends, but he was delicate and courteous with women. This episode is purely bad taste—artistically and otherwise.

A second huge incongruity with Beethoven's known character pertains to his relationship with God. "God and I are like two bears in one cage," he tells Anna in a later scene. This is a total misrepresentation. Beethoven was not a church-goer, because he did not like institutionalized religion and any dogma, but he believed in the divine order.[8] He frequently prayed to God for advice, help and forgiveness and, although God did not always grant his desires (the most ardent of which he scribbled on a sheet of paper sometime between 1807 and 1810, reading, "O God, let me—let me finally find the one—who will strengthen me in virtue—who will lawfully be mine,"[9]) he never doubted the divine Wisdom. "With regard to T. there is nothing else but to leave it to God [...] leave this totally to Him, to Him alone, the all-knowing God!"[10] he wrote in his diary about one of his many mysterious references to women. And, on another occasion, he conceded that "it was often a good thing that man could not always have his wishes fulfilled."[11] Even in his *Heiligenstadt Testament*, the testimony of his fight against his unforgiving Fate, deafness, he does not ask God "Why? Why me?" but prays "Divine One, thou seest my inmost soul, thou knowest that therein dwells the love of mankind and the desire to do good."[12]

A third incongruity is Beethoven's assumed "sexism." When the heroine tells him that she studied composition at the Conservatory, and adds, for his knowledge, that "there have been many women composers" (a clear misrepresentation), he derides them commenting "like a dog walking on their hind legs." There is no evidence of such a trait of Beethoven's personality—on the contrary. Granted, he had a very low opinion of both his sisters-in-law, but he had good reasons to consider them "bad women." However, his warm relationships with women like Therese Brunsvik (who called him "our noble Beethoven,")[13] her sister Josephine (who was his most ardent known love), Antonie Brentano (who described him in a letter as "this great, excellent person [... who] is as a human being greater than as an artist [... and is] natural, simple, and wise, with pure intentions")[14] and other women are well documented. And I have documented in previous chapters his statements about how much he appreciated the female pianists who played his music. Another proof of Beethoven's alleged "sexism" in the movie: when Anna shows him some of her own compositions, he disparages them. False again! We have the testimony of Bettina Brentano, a young woman who showed up unannounced in 1810, and found him very open and ready for friendship—and, possibly, more. Bettina showed him some songs she had composed and she wrote in a letter to a friend that "Beethoven has seen them and said many pretty things about them, such as that if I had devoted myself to this lovely art I might cherish great hopes."[15] The long scene of Beethoven and Anna conducting his *Ninth* together, although beautifully filmed and benefitting from the sublime music, is not only a biographical fallacy, it is an artistic parody. In a 2006 interview given after the release of the movie, Holland claimed that she had filmed the scene as a suggestion that the two "were making love with one another over the vibrations of sound."[16] In reality, watching Anna's mechanical gesticulation with a facial expression miles away from "living" the music is more pathetic than erotic.

Copying Beethoven indeed portrays a modern feminist view of Beethoven. One wonders how Holland could have made such a work after several well-received movies—among them, *Europa Europa* (1990) and *The Secret Garden* (1993)—and after stating, in a 1998 interview, that feminism was not a central theme of her films, even though women were important in them.[17] In her quoted 2006 interview, she claimed that she felt close to the movie's heroine because she had been, when young, "in a similar relationship with someone [the great Polish director Andrej Vajda] where all my art was this kind of vague admiration and jealousy." The same interview, however, reveals Holland's long-time attachment to Beethoven's music, especially his "late" period, so she must have had a well-rounded portrait of the real Beethoven in her mind. How could she accept promotion of Beethoven as this despicable sexist? How did she "evolve" to re-cast herself in the new Hollywood mold?

One gets a plausible answer from the same 2006 interview. When asked about the "dynamic between Beethoven and Anna Holtz," she tersely stated, "It wasn't me, it was the writers." Indeed, this movie was a novelty in Holland's filmography: she had always written her own scripts—this time the story belonged to Stephen Rivele and Christopher Wilkinson, who also produced the movie for Metro-Goldwyn-Mayer. Holland also stated in her 2006 interview that it was hard "to make the money come together" and the movie "was mostly guided and co-financed by American producers." This apparently made a European work (director and cast, filming mostly so) into a typical Hollywood movie. As one knows, unlike in Europe, where the director is the author of the film, in the American "dream factory" the producers dictate. Wilkinson and Rivele, a team that had authored several well-received scripts before (notably 1995's *Nixon*, nominated for an Oscar for best original screen-play, and 2001's *Ali*) had to bow to the latest Hollywood politics. This might have cost Mr. Rivele some hard time, because his blogs reveal him as musically knowledgeable—and he is not quite so "politically correct" a person, daring to object to PC Talk as late as October 30, 2017. (I could not find enough to characterize Mr. Wilkinson.)

I think the best summing-up of Beethoven's career in Hollywood was given by Richard Roeper of the Ebert-and-Roeper team: "for now the best movie about any Beethoven I've ever seen stars a Saint Bernard."[18] Roeper also expressed his hope that "Someday someone will make a great movie about an immortal composer," but the perspective looks grim even now, with Beethoven's 250th anniversary getting near. And this is a great shame, because there exists the real but largely ignored story of *A Girl that Loved Beethoven* waiting to be movie-scripted.

The missed opportunity

We have already met that girl: Fanny Giannatasio, the young woman on whose diary so much of what we know about Beethoven's life between 1816 and 1820 relies. She saw and lived both sides of Beethoven that a Hollywood movie script requires: "the modesty and heartiness of his disposition," his "goodness of heart" that made her fall in love with him, although she felt that wish was impossible; and, later, his dark side—one of his paranoid attacks of distrust directed at her, in a murky episode that was obviously related to his obsession with his nephew and, possibly, with the boy's mother. She never dared to open up to him and he treated her only as a young friend whom he could teach a lot about life and music. He was, in fact, attracted by Fanny's younger and spectacularly beautiful sister, who was engaged and soon to be married—and, of course, he would compose a wedding-song for her, that he would sing, leading an amateur choir.

In this story, Fanny would never see Beethoven again, although she would from time to time get news about him through the housekeeper that they had recommended to him. He would refuse to receive her and her sister during his last illness, wanting to spare them the heartrending sight of his agony. She would get a last glimpse of his dead face in the casket, from the middle of the huge crowd of tens-of-thousands of people witnessing his funeral procession.

I wrote half of this script myself, but had no connection in the movie industry. After several unsuccessful attempts to develop some connection, I thought that Stephen Rivele, who co-authored the script of *Copying Beethoven*, and whose blogs reveal as a musically knowledgeable person, might be interested into redeeming himself by making "the real Beethoven movie." I managed to contact, in 2018, Mr. Rivele's agent (Gersh Agency), who promised to pass him my proposal, with my assurance that I am ready to help him to the fullest without expecting anything more than the satisfaction of seeing a wrong [i.e., *Copying Beethoven*] righted. I am still waiting for an answer ...

15
Skimming the Pandemic

All the theories that I have debunked in this book, with the exception of the one in chapter 7, are "Made in America." Like in all cultural developments of the Western World during the last one hundred years, America has been the innovator in Beethoven scholarship, with Europe joining after a few years' delay. I cannot claim to be as familiar with European Beethoven scholarship, but my "skimming" of it suggests that, after a relatively long "incubation" period, "Beethoven's masculinity" has become an international scholarly pandemic. It made a strong bridgehead at the heart of the field, Beethoven's Germany. The 2001 International Congress of Musicology in Berlin had a section dedicated to *The 'Masculine' and the 'Feminine' Beethoven,* the contributions of which were published two years later by no other than Beethoven-Haus Publishing House.[1] The 480-page volume was too much for my high-school German to digest (automated German translators are to date truly pathetic) but its table of contents (whose first section, of major interest, is presented in the box) clearly displays the traces of the American "new musicology."

First section of the Contents of the volume
The "Masculine" and the "Feminine" Beethoven
I. Thought patterns and projections

Helmut Rösing, "In search of symbols of masculinity—Beethoven and the (principal movement) sonata form"

Sanna Pederson' "Beethoven and the masculinity in the context of the 1848/49 Revolution"

Elmar Budde, "Music and Times—Beethoven and Schubert"

Christian Thorau, "Beethoven's masculine *Ars poetica*—contributions to the analysis / Analysis of contributions"

Ingeborg Pfingsten, "'Masculine'/'feminine:' not only a matter of speaking for Adolf Bernhard Marx"

Annegret Huber, "What mothers naturally produce—Anton Reicha's '*idée mère*' [mother idea] and other product specifications"

Albrecht Riethmüller, "Still an ideal [sic!]: Beethoven as a chauvinist"

The very first essay smacks heavily of McClary's theory of the sexist sonata form. The second one is certainly an elaboration of one of Sanna Pederson's theses that I debunked in chapter 12. The title of Ingeborg Pfingsten's essay intimates that the epithets "masculine" and "feminine" that A. B. Marx, the nineteenth century music critic, attached to the first and second theme in the sonata form were not simple figures of speech, but had a deeply sexist meaning. I also suspect that Albrecht Riethmüller's discovery of Beethoven's alleged "chauvinism" hints to the composer's "masculinity," too.

It is also remarkable that, judging by the titles of the essays (see the remaining sections of the volume in the next box on the following page), Beethoven's "feminine" side is conspicuously absent; it might be addressed *en passant* in some essays, but seems not to be a major feature, as the title of the collection promises.

The Contents of the volume *The "Masculine" and ...*, continuation
II. Childhood pattern specimen and family roles
Dagmar Hoffmann-Axthelm, "Conjectures about Adam and Eve, along with those about Beethoven and the far-away beloved"
Klaus Martin Kopitz, "Beethoven's nature—reflections on a 'Borderline personality'"
Dieter Schnebel, "Mother–father: musical and psychoanalytical considerations about Beethoven"
III. A feminine network
Freia Hoffmann, "A matter of perception: Beethoven and the women"
William Kinderman, "The 'Priestess' and the savior: On the roles of the genders in Beethoven's life and art"
Christian Lambour, "Nannette Streicher—not only a piano builder"
IV. Written for
Ernst Herttrich, "The policies of Beethoven's dedications"
Margret Jestremski, "Biographical references in Beethoven's songs: Dedication—affection?"
V. Berlin—an early Beethoven biotope
Renate Moering, "Bettine von Arnim's literary implementation of her Beethoven experience"
Thomas Schmidt-Beste, ""Written through" or "left-to-fill"? Felix Mendelssohn Bartholdy and the piano sonata after Beethoven"
Cornelia Bartsch, "Farewell [Sonata?]—Fanny Hensel's debate about Beethoven's late works"
Martina Sichardt, "Beethoven's spirit from Marx' hands. The female composer Emilie Mayer (1812-1883)"
VI. About priestesses and servants
Dörte Schmidt, "'Floating in quadruple-wrapped brotherly embrace.' Beethoven and the String Quartet as an aesthetical, political and social idea in the contemporary media"
Beatrix Borchard, "Quartet playing and the cultural politics in Berlin during the Imperial Age. The Joachim-Quartet"
Inka Prante, "Why shouldn't women also be able to excel in the art of music? Joachim's students in string quartet playing."
Philipp Albrecht, "A group of Amazons with an aesthetic program"
Beate Angelika Kraus, "Elly Ney und Thérèse Wartel: Beethoven interpretation by pianists—a matter of self-evidence?"
Martella Gutiérrez-Denhoff, "With Beethoven to music. Ways of teaching Beethoven to the youth".

A few years later, German scholarship revisited Beethoven's masculinity in another collection of essays dealing, in a larger scope, with Art, Sex, Politics, subtitled "Constructs of masculinity and art during the German Empire and Weimar Republic."[2] Among the various facets of masculinity in arts—visual arts, architecture, etc.—the musical one was, as one might expect, Beethoven. Professor Beatrix Borchard, a respected German musicologist known for her works on nineteenth century musical life, with a special emphasis on female musicians, signed the essay "Beethoven: Constructs of masculinity in the realm of music."[3] She builds therein, with apparently cold objectivity, a gradual argument based on quoting previous scholarly works: she first finds Beethoven guilty of having been a favorite of the Nazi regime: if "the Nazi musical icon par excellence was heroic Beethoven" (78),[*] his masculine heroism was clearly in the wrong; his "chauvinism"—quoted from the already mentioned essay of Riethmüller—could, of course, only make things worse (78). In the central sub-chapter, sensationally titled "Beethoven the pornographer," Dr. Borchard gives the floor to Professor McClary who, by virtue of her own perception of the *Ninth Symphony* and of her theory of the sexist sonata form, "declares Beethoven a composer who, through his music, calls for violence against women" (81). Finally, Borchard calls another surprise witness for the prosecution—Alex, the evil hero of Anthony Burgess' book *A Clockwork Orange* later brought on the screen in Stanley Kubrik's homonymous movie. Alex, a psychopathic murderous teenager, "loves Beethoven, whose music he associates with sexual violence" (82). Borchard's scholarly "objectivity" is, in this case, unfortunately a pretense. Objectivity requires at least a commonsensical look beyond assertions.

Since I have not read Riethmüller's essay and the issue of Beethoven's "chauvinism" is somewhat confusing to me (or, at least, counterintuitive), I will not discuss it, but I can at least introduce some common sense about the "Nazi issue." It was crucial for the Nazi ideology to appropriate Beethoven: he was a national icon, therefore very important in the manipulation of the nation. He was equally important to the other totalitarian ideology of the century, communism, to the same purpose but for an anti-symmetrical reason: he was a "revolutionary" as well as a visionary of the golden Communist future of the whole world. It may seem strange that, as I showed at the end of chapter 10, the Maoist version of communism banned Beethoven, but they had their own special reason, which was anti-symmetrical to both Soviet communism and Nazi ideology:[†] Beethoven was the product of the pre-WWII westernization of China, and therefore anti-national by definition.

The "Clockwork Orange evidence" is very different—a case of individual rather than ideological pathology. It shares one feature with the "Kreutzer case" discussed in chapter 11: Tolstoy hated Beethoven's music (together with almost all of the classical) and Burgess detested his *Ninth*, which he called a "damnable hybrid."[4] As a musicologist, Dr. Borchard was in a much better position than myself to understand the case of "Alex." Burgess (1917-1993), known today as a

---

[*] All references to Borchard's essay (my translation) are given within the text in this chapter.
[†] The complex "anti-symmetries" between the three totalitarian regimes are generally ignored, and not only in music literature. They are all offshoots of socialism: Nazi is a form of nationalist socialism (the name stands for "Nazional Sozialismus") with economic private entrepreneurship; Soviet communism was a state-property "internationalist" doctrine; Maoism, born as Chinese Soviet-type, moved quickly after the death of its founder towards the Chinese Nazi-type that we witness nowadays.

writer, wanted to be a musician also. He composed some 200 pieces, including three symphonies, the last of which he heard performed in a symphony hall, which he deemed to be "the truly great artistic moment" of his life,[5] but he never "made it" to the history of music treatises (like Taruskin's latest one). He must have felt terribly frustrated to see his work thrown to the canon's dustbin, while that "damnable hybrid" of Beethoven continues to be a myth of humankind and, moreover, comes always at the top of the classical music fans preferences. *A Clockwork Orange* was his vendetta against the monster and he half-succeeded— he did not manage to kill his enemy, but became a celebrity, and his book entered the *literary* canon. Needless to say, this does not make the book evidence for the toxic masculinity of Beethoven's music.

Borchard also introduces her personal contribution to the issue—her discovering that another woman, a certain Johanna Kinkel, had perceived the "war of the sexes" in the sonata form almost two hundred years before McClary (81-82). Johanna Kinkel (1810-1858) was an active member of the German artistic milieu of the first half of the nineteenth century, which included remarkable women like Bettina von Arnim and Fanny Mendelssohn-Hensel, whose friend Kinkel was. A talented musician, composer and pedagogue, she left an original instructional guide for her young students (1852) in which she wrote:

> In a great piece of music, the keys [tonalities] seem to rise to the light in their struggle with one another, like some developing forces of nature, finally embodying characters in their piece of the world history. But we also enjoy the trivial humorous intrigue performed in the most ordinary sonata by the family of the keys, in an ever-changing scene. There comes in the beginning the triad of the tonic, like the master of the house, fully conscientious of his dignity, who begins a conversation with his "dominant" wife and admonishes his "subdominant" son and the two "mediants," his fair daughters, for the good of them all.[6]

Borchard sees in Kinkel's "humorous play"—Borchard's own description— a foreboding of McClary's "serious identification of the functionality of Beethoven's music, as intended by the composer in a certain context" (82). This is typical of feminist tactics—seeing what one wants to see, not what is really there to be seen. Kinkel never used the term "war of the sexes" in either the general description of "a great piece of music," in which tonalities struggle with each other, or that of a "most ordinary sonata," where the husband and wife only pursue a "conversation." Even when the father "admonishes" his daughters, he does it "for the good of them all," not in order to "subjugate" them, as in McClary's thesis.

When I saw that Beethoven's masculinity epidemics had so expanded, I thought that it was the right time for the truth about its prophetess to be made known to German scholarship. In 2014, I submitted to the prestigious *Bonner Beethoven-Studien* journal an article about McClary's theories, which forms the core of chapter 10 of the present book. Professor Bernhard Appel, the editor-in-chief of the publication, was also the head of the Beethoven-Haus publisher that had issued *The Masculine and the Feminine Beethoven* volume: "I do not know the article or the book of Mrs. McClary," Dr. Appel answered, to my bemusement. He also rejected my submission advising that, "If your abstract gives its [McClary's theories'] contents in its whole truth, it must be a great humbug. Serious research should not waste time for refuting such kind of texts. Besides that, each replication would give the article an importance, which it should not have." Perfect logic, perhaps, but we do not live in a perfect world and Beethoven scholarship is no exception.

15½
Feminist Beethoven

To wrap up my rebuttal of the portrayal of Beethoven's music by several influential representatives of "new musicology" feminism, I re-state: their arguments are flagrant misrepresentations that go far beyond "acceptable" scholarly (or un-scholarly) mistakes. They involve non-existent "demonstrations", fabricate and distort statements, willfully omit well-known relevant facts if they prove contrary to their proffered theses, as well as defiantly disregard elementary logic. The attack of this "latter-day" feminism on Beethoven is a professional and intellectual sham.

However, my rebuttal should not be mistaken as an attack on feminism. On the contrary, it is intended to restore "true" feminism, the one that had always, before the advent of this "latter day" version, found solace, reassurance and inspiration in Beethoven's music. I have already mentioned several such feminist stands in the previous chapters. Here is another example, the most emotion-loaded one—that of Hellen Keller. Keller (1880-1968) was struck blind and deaf before she was two years old but, with proper care and help, developed into a person of extraordinary accomplishments. She became a world-famous speaker and author, an advocate for people with disabilities, a fighter for women's right to vote and a pacifist. When she learned that Beethoven turned deaf later in his life, she wrote, "I am 'wedded to silence,' like the great master." However, in 1924 she experienced his *Ninth Symphony*—McClary's great nemesis—in her own way: by putting her fingers on the sensitive diaphragm of the loudspeaker of the radio-set broadcasting the performance. "What was my amazement," she wrote, "to discover that I could feel not only the vibration, but also the impassioned rhythm, the throb and the urge of the music!" And she went on to tell how she could distinguish the various instruments and the entrances of the voices, "ecstatic, upcurving swift and flame-like"; how "the tones and harmonies conveyed to me moods of great beauty and majesty." She concluded:

> I marveled at the power of his [Beethoven's] quenchless spirit by which out of great pain he wrought such joy for others—and there I sat, feeling with my hand the magnificent symphony, which broke like a sea upon the silent shores of his soul and mine.[1]

One cannot help wondering who was truly the deaf one—the old or the new feminist?

How can we explain this general perception of Beethoven's music by women in previous generations? "Explaining music" is very subjective, and I have pledged to submit not my opinions but facts; I offer here the explanation advanced by a more authoritative voice than mine, that of the distinguished pianist and Professor Russell Sherman:

> Throughout his [Beethoven's] music one always hears the voice of Man, but one also hears the voices of men and women. Such that whatever the feminine may be, there has been no scribe more faithful to its careful and caring description than Beethoven. Not simply Woman idealized, but the characters of women who nourish, who dream, who endure are present and tangible in his music. This profound tenderness—in him, in them, in his blessing and insight—is unique and offers the most priceless lesson. Moreover, his *feminism* exceeded gender, and his humanity embraced all lifestyles of the living, the dead, and the nonhuman.[2] (my emphasis)

As one can see, Sherman does not hesitate to call Beethoven "feminist." I will also add that Beethoven developed in time an "advanced" view totally opposed to patriarchal ideology and held in common with modern-day feminism. We have the telling testimony of Fanny Giannatasio, the young woman who knew him and left a trove of evidence, whom I have already quoted many times in several chapters. She transcribed in her own words a particular conversation that she and her sister had with Beethoven on June 15, 1817, when he expressed a rather (at the time) unorthodox view on love and marriage:

> He declares that he does not like the idea of any indissoluble bond being *forced* between people in their personal relations to each other [...] that man or woman's liberty of action ought not to be limited. He would much rather a woman gave him her love, and with her love the highest part of her nature, without, as he means, being bound to him in the relation of wife and husband. He believes that the liberty of the woman is limited and circumscribed.[3] (emphasis in original)

It is high time that feminism got itself rid of the extremist deviances and stopped throwing baby Beethoven—and his like—out with the dirty patriarchal bathwater.

2020 Epilogue

This book was completed by the beginning of 2020; when the Covid-19 Pandemic erupted onto the world scene, the only contribution was some color added to the title of chapter 15. While the book lingered in the limbo of the publishing world, America was set aflame by the unintentional but thoughtless and abhorrent killing of a black man at the hands of a white police officer, and the resulting "woke" population surging in the streets proceeded, with the help of the political left, to "cancel" the country's "white culture." While the anger is perfectly rational, and the protests easy to understand, wholesale revisionism of history is harder to accept. I discovered after some delay that canceling Beethoven was part of that lunacy.

This was not the first injection of race into the Beethoven literature. The claim that Beethoven was one-sixteenth Black was launched long ago and has re-ignited in the social media over the past few years. I did not discuss this idea in my book because it was irrelevant to my topic. Besides, the suggestion was not born in the scholarly world. However, "Cancel Beethoven" is different: it is the product of Nate Sloan, a *musicology* professor at the Thornton School of Music of the University of Southern California, and bears the stamp of the postmodern theories that I debunk throughout my work. Therefore, it must be addressed.

Professor Sloan presented his "cancel" argument in the last two episodes of the *Switched on Pop* podcast "The 5th," which he produced with Charlie Harding, a songwriter and a music producer who also plays the part of the musicologist's diligent student. The two had already published in 2019 the book *Switched on Pop: How Popular Music Works, and Why It Matters*, which was praised for "covering pop music from a musicological perspective." I have not read the book, but if it fulfills the goal enounced in its title, I think I can almost fully agree with its thesis: whether we like it or not, pop defines the reality around us; therefore, it matters aplenty. From this perspective, I can easily accept that Beethoven does not belong to our world any longer, even though a tiny minority of us feel that he still fulfills a certain inner need.

But this is not Dr. Sloan's angle. He begins his argument (in the first two series of his podcast) with a very orthodox presentation of Beethoven's *Fifth*: a drama of struggle and victory, a monument of resilience and determination, plus an obsession about "a composer who wanted to break all the rules" of music. The latter is, of course, a gross exaggeration. If Beethoven had broken "all the rules," what would have remained for Wagner and other Romantics to break, not to mention Arnold Schönberg? If he broke *some* rules – well, what innovator *doesn't* re-write the rulebook? There is nothing in this "exposé," musically illustrated though it is with a fine rendition by the New York Philharmonics, to justify what follows in the third series of the podcast, Dr. Sloan's case for "canceling Beethoven." In a nutshell, Dr. Sloan blames Beethoven's music, particularly his Fifth Symphony, for having nurtured an "elitist classist culture" that promotes the oppressive rule of white males and suppresses the voices of women, blacks and the LGBTQ community.

I am not aware of any reaction of Beethoven scholarship to Sloan's thesis, but two public voices rose to the defense of the composer. Jonathan Tobin, a respected journalist, signed in the September 17 issue of *New York Post* an "opinion" that "Canceling Beethoven is the latest woke madness for the classical-music world," rejecting it on the grounds of both musical and common-sense (available online at https://nypost.com/2020/09/17/canceling-beethoven-is-the-latest-woke-madness-for-the-classical-music-world/). So too did Daniel Lelchuk, a distinguished cellist with Louisiana Philharmonic Orchestra, in his own allegedly viral podcast and on Facebook. I could not find a single comment on social media that did not agree with their stance. To this common-sensical approach I will add here the irrefutable facts proving that Dr. Sloan's argumentation is a scholarly fallacy, the progeny of the marriage between agenda and ignorance.

The legacy of Beethoven's *Fifth*, Sloan argues, has two sides: it is "a symbol of overcoming and resilience and inspiration," but it was also "used to create a narrative that turns classical music in a culture of exclusivity and elitism." More exactly, "it has become the soundtrack for a new class of self-made white men, the marker of their belonging and their individuality [...who] use this music as a way to police who belongs to this caste and who doesn't. They create a culture that divides and excludes."[*]

Here is Sloan's detailed argument: Beethoven's symphony initiated an evil trend in classical music – the requirement to listen to it quietly, in reverence, as if it were a sacred testimony. This is not how the classical music was enjoyed in society before Beethoven, Sloan claims, quoting from a letter Mozart wrote to his father telling him how his new symphony (the K297) was received by a Paris audience, which was "sent into raptures [and] big applaudissement" by a passage in the middle of the first Allegro and again when it was repeated towards the end of the movement, when "shouts of *Da capo*" erupted.[1]

Beethoven's music stifled this free, unrestrained participation by the audience with the music: listeners were assumed, actually normatively obligated, to sit quietly and to wait for the end of the piece to applaud, an imposition that was passed through the ages to the present. At this point, Sloan brings forward an 1845 entry in a diary of an American who had listened to Beethoven's symphony and exalted this experience, but who also proposed to have the women entering

---

[*] I am quoting as literally as I can from the podcast, episode 3.

the concert hall gagged, and even to suggest that the police be called to watch over them and "shoot the first female that opens her mouth." Unwilling to understand that it was the female chattering and not their being "sent into raptures" that the memorialist had in mind, and unable to appreciate the sarcasm, Sloan triumphantly concludes: "the idea that we should be quiet expresses the need to shut up the people who we don't want to be part of this world." And he does not forget to remind us that "The Symphony [hall] has been segregated during Jim Crow era and black audiences continue to be excluded today, often in the name of written etiquette and unwritten cultural norms" – an obvious lie (nobody and nothing prevents a black person from entering the Symphony Hall). The inevitable corollary of this logic is a rhetorical question – "In 2020, are we still going to celebrate this composer?" – followed by the expectedly negative answers collected by Dr. Sloan, which I will skip to go directly to the core of the matter.

The core of the matter is that the case that Nate Sloan makes against Beethoven is a scholarly fallacy analogous to the ones I have exposed in this book. Beethoven was no more guilty than Mozart of creating the alleged exclusivist, elitist "narrative" of the symphony hall. He also witnessed with pride and gratitude that some of his passages sent the audience "into raptures [and] big applaudissement." At the premiere of his Seventh Symphony, the public burst into applause after the second movement, the "Marcia funebre" shaped Allegretto, and asked for *Da capo*[2]; the same thing happened at the next concert, inaugurating a tradition that continued all through Beethoven's life, as reported by Fanny Giannattasio in her diary.[3] At the first performance of his Ninth Symphony, the second movement was "completely interrupted by applause" at the startling entry of the timpani and "there was a demand for a repetition."[4]

As for the incriminated Fifth Symphony, we possess a testimony about the passionate reaction of the Paris audience that dwarfs the one reported by Mozart. When it was introduced in France by the Orchestra of the Paris Conservatoire in 1828, the *Fifth* stirred an emotional response of the audience that would amaze the most devoted Beethoven buff of today. Here it is, as narrated by Berlioz, who witnessed it:

> «There has never been a performance of this symphony, since it was first played in France, when the entire audience did not jump to their feet like one man at bar 4 of the finale [the end of the crescendo leading to the finale], covering with their shrieks the thundering voice of the orchestra. Often, many instrumentalists, paralyzed with emotion, could not go on with their playing, dropping their bows. In the first row of the boxes, many young beautiful faces would hide to muffle their convulsive sobs; some youth would roar with laughter, some others would pull at their hair and make all kinds of grotesque contortions.»[5]

That the symphony hall (and the opera house, for that matter) is now a place of "elitism" is indeed a truism. However, if anyone were guilty of having created what Dr. Sloan calls "the culture of focused reverential listening [that] often turned the concert hall into a space of belonging and exclusion that permeates classical music today," that was clearly not Beethoven nor especially his *Fifth*. When and how this happened is certainly an issue worth exploring, but based on facts, not on politically correct sloganeering of the Orwellian four-legs-good-two-legs-bad kind.

Selected Bibliography
1. Besiegers
Shrinks

Newman, Ernest, *The Unconscious Beethoven. An Essay in Musical Psychology* (Alfred A Knopf, New York, 1927).

Solomon, Maynard, *Beethoven* (Schirmer Books, 1977).

Solomon, Maynard, *Beethoven Essays*, (Harvard University Press, Cambridge, Massachusetts, 1988)

Solomon, Maynard, *Beethoven*, Second revised edition (Schirmer Book, New York, 1998)

Steinberg, Michael P., *Listening to Reason: Culture, Subjectivity, and Nineteenth-Century Music* (Princeton University Press, New Jersey, 2004)

Sterba, Editha and Sterba, Richard, *Beethoven and His Nephew. A Psychoanalytical Study of Their Relationship* (Schocken Books, New York, 1971)

Physicians

Davies, Peter J., *Beethoven in Person: His Deafness, Illnesses and Death*, (Greenwood Press, Westport, Connecticut, 2001)

Davies, Peter J., *The Character of a Genius: Beethoven in Perspective* (Greenwood Press, Westport, Connecticut, 2002)

Lorenz, Michael, "Commentary on Wawruch's Report", *The Beethoven Journal*, 22/2 (Winter 2007)

Mai, François M., *Diagnosing Genius—The Life and Death of Beethoven*, (Mc Gill-Queen's University Press, 2007)

Wawruch, Andreas Ignatz, "Medical Review on the Final Stage of L. van Beethoven's Life," translated by Michael Lorenz, in *Beethoven Journal*, Winter 2007, Volume 22, Number 2, pp. 87-91

Socio-musicologists

"Miscellanea", in *The Beethoven Journal*, Fall 1996, Vol. 11, Number 2

"Miscellanea", in *The Beethoven Journal*, Spring 1997, Vol. 12, No. 1

DeNora, Tia, *Beethoven and the Construction of Genius, Musical Politics in Vienna, 1792-1803* (University of California Press, Berkeley, Los Angeles, 1985)

Goldschmidt, Harry, *Die Erscheinung Beethoven* (VEB Deutsche Verlag für Musik, Leipzig, 1974)

Feminists

DeNora, Tia,"Music into action: performing gender on the Viennese concert stage, 1790-1810," (*Poetics 30 (2002)*)

Kramer, Lawrence, *After the Lovedeath: Sexual violence and the Making of Culture* (University of California Press, 1997)

Kramer, Lawrence, C*ritical musicology and the responsibility of response:*

selected essays (Ashgate, 2006)

McClary, Susan, "Terminal Prestige: The Case of Avant-Garde Music Composition," (in *Cultural Critique* No. 12 (Spring 1989): 57-81)

McClary, Susan, "Getting Down Off the Beanstalk," (*Minnesota Composers Forum Newsletter*, January 1987)

McClary, Susan, *Feminine Endings: Music, Gender, and Sexuality*, (University of Minnesota Press, Minneapolis, 1991)

McClary, Susan, "Construction of Subjectivity in Schubert's Music" (*Queering the Pitch/The New Gay and Lesbian Musicology*, Routledge Press, 1994, pp. 205-233)

McClary, Susan, *Conventional Wisdom: The Content of Musical Forms* (University of California Press, Berkley-Los Angeles-London, 2001)

Pederson, Sanna, "Beethoven and Masculinity," in *Beethoven and his World*, Scott Burnham and Michael P. Steinberg, editors (Princeton University Press, 2000)

Thornton, Clara Rose, "Q&A: Agnieszka Holland, director of *Copying Beethoven*," Friday, November 10, 2006," Online at http://www.stopsmilingonline.com/story_detail.php?id=695.

Others

Tolstoy, Leo, *The Kreutzer Sonata and Other Stories* (Oxford University Press, 1998)

Tolstoy, Leo, *What is Art*, transl. From the original manuscript by Aylmer Maude (New York, Funk and Wagnalls, 1904)

2. Beethoven references
Documents

The Letters of Beethoven, Collected, translated and edited by Emily Anderson, Vol. 1-3 (W.W. Norton & Co, New York, London, 1961)

Ludwig van Beethoven: Briefwechsel Gesamtausgabe, Sieghard Brandenburg editor (G. Henle Verlag, 1996

Kalischer, Alfred C., *Beethovens sämtliche Briefe, Band V*, (Berlin & Leipzig, 1908)

Schmidt, Leopold, ed., *Beethoven-Briefe* (Hamburg Severus Verlag, 2014)

Beethoven—Letters, Journals and Conversations, Translated and edited by Michael Hamburger, (Anchor Books, Doubleday & Co Inc., Garden City, New York, 1960)

Letters to Beethoven and Other Correspondence, translated and edited by Theodore Albrecht, Vol. 3: 1824-1828, (Univ. of Nebraska Press, 1996)

Les Cahiers de conversation de Beethoven, Traduits et présentés par J.-G. Prod'homme (Editions Corrêa, Paris, 1946)

Ludwig van Beethovens Konversationhefte, Köhler, Karl-Heinz und Herre, Grita herausgegeben (Leipzig, VEB Deutscher Verlag fur Musik, 1968, vol. 1)

Schünemann, *Ludwig van Beethovens Konversationshefte, Band 2* (Max Hesse Verlag, Berlin 1941)

Testimonies

Des Bonner Bäckermeisters Gottfried Fischer: Aufzeichnungen über Beethovens Jugend, Schmidt-Gorg, Joseph, ed., (Beethovenhaus, Bonn, 1971)

Remembering Beethoven. The Biographical Notes of Franz Wegeler and Ferdinand Ries, transl. by Frederick Noonan (André Deutsch, 1987)

Beethoven, the man and the artist, as revealed in his own words, Compiled and annotated by Friederich Kerst, translated by Henry E. Krehbiel, (Dover Publications, New York, 1964)

Beethoven. Impressions by His Contemporaries, O. G. Sonneck edit (Dover Publications, New York, 1967)

Breuning, Gerhard von, *Memories of Beethoven—From the House of the Black-Robed Spaniards*, translated by Henry Mins and Maynard Solomon, (Cambridge University Press, 1992)

Nohl, Ludwig, *An Unrequited Love. An Episode in the Life of Beethoven: From the Diary of a Young Lady*, translated by Annie Wood, (Bentley & Son, London, 1876). More complete excerpts were published in volume 4 of the Thayer-Deiters-Riemann version of *Thayer's Life of Beethoven* (pages 513-541), but (for whatever reason) they were not included in the English Thayer-Forbes version.

Biographies

Thayer's Life of Beethoven, Revised and Edited by Elliot Forbes (Princeton University Press, 1969)

The Life of Ludwig van Beethoven By Alexander Wheelock Thayer, edited, revised and amended from the original English manuscript and the German editions of Hermann Deiters and Hugo Riemann, concluded, and all the documents newly translated By Henry Edward Krehbiel. (The Beethoven Association, New York, 1921)

Cooper, Barry, *Beethoven* (Oxford University Press, 2000)

Marek, George R., *Beethoven. Biography of a Genius* (Funk & Wagnalis, 1969)

Morris, Edmund, *Beethoven: The Universal Composer,* (Harper Collins Publishers, New York, 2005)

Schauffler, Robert H., *Beethoven, the Man who Freed Music*, (Doubleday, Doran & Co. Inc, Garden City, New York, 1937)

Schindler, Anton Felix, *Beethoven as I Knew Him,* Edited by Donald W. MacArdle, English translation by Constance S. Jolly (Dover Publications Inc., Mineola, New York, 1996)

Schindler, Anton, *Biographie von Ludwig van Beethove*, (Münster, Aschendorf, 1840)

Schindler, Anton, *Biographie von Ludwig van Beethoven*, Dritte, new verarbeite und vermehrte Auflage [third, revised and enriched edition] (Munster, 1860)

Encyclopedias and dictionaries

The Beethoven Encyclopedia, Nettl Paul, (London: P. Owen, 1957)

Clive, Peter, *Beethoven and His World: A Biographical Dictionary* (Oxford University Press, 2001)

della Corte, Andrea e Gatti, Guido M., *Dizionario di musica*, (G. B. Paravia, Padua, 1956)

Other studies

Wiener Zeitschrift fur Kunst, Literatur, Theater and Mode, 1837, October issues no. 120-123. Available online at https://books.google.com/books?id=tTNZAAAAcAAJ. (Oct 7, pp 956-7; Oct 10, pp 964-5; Oct 12, pp 972-3; Oct 14, pp 980-1)

Altman, Gail S., *Beethoven: A Man of His Word* (Anubian Press, Tallahassee, 1996).

Brandenburg, Sieghard, "Johanna van Beethoven's Embezzlement," (in *Haydn, Mozart & Beethoven: Studies in Music of the Classical Period. Essays in Honor of Alan Tyson* (Brandenburg ed., Oxford University Press, 1988) pp. 237-251)

Chenevez, Pierre-Jean, "Les tonalités dans les œuvres de Beethoven," (*Beethoven, la revue de l'ABF*, No. 9, 2008, pp. 72-78)

Comini Alessandra, *The Changing Image of Beethoven: A Study in Mythmaking*, (Rizzoli International Publications, Inc., 1987)

"Beethoven's Genius: An Exchange (DeNora-Rosen), in The New York Review of Books, April 10, 1997, pp. 66-67

Frimmel, Theodore von, "Beethovens Leiden und Ende," in the Viennese newspaper *Die Press*, September 8, 1880

Goldschmidt, Harry, *All About Beethoven's Immortal Beloved. A Stocktaking*, (CreatedSpace, an Amazon.com Company, 2014). This is John E. Klapproth's translation of the 1980 original *Um die Unsterbliche Geliebte. Eine Bestandaufnahme* (Munich, 1980)

Grove, George, *Beethoven and his Nine Symphonies* (Novello and Co., 1896)

Meredith, William, "The Eroica and Beethoven's Sexuality through a Feminist Lens: Susan McClary's Reading of Beethoven in *Queering the Pitch*," (*The Beethoven Newsletter*, Volume 8, No 3 & Volume 9 No 1 (Winter 1993-Spring 1994), pp. 107-109)

Morrow, Mary Sue, "Book Review: Tia DeNora, Beethoven and the Construction of Genius: Musical Politics in Vienna, 1792-1803" (*The Beethoven Journal*, Fall 1996, Volume 11, Number 2), pp.25-27

Nottebohm, Gustav, *Zweite Beethoviana* (Leipzig: C. F. Peters, 1887)

Rolland, Romain, *Beethoven the Creator. From Eroica to Appassionata*, translated by Ernest Newman (Dover Publications, New York, 1964)

Rosen, Charles, "Did Beethoven Have All the Luck?", The New York Review of Books, Vol. 43, Issue 18, 14 November 1996

Russell Martin, *Beethoven's Hair* (New York, Broadway, 2001)

Schmitz, Arnold, *Das Romantische Beethovenbild, Darstelleung und Kritik*, (Berlin und Bonn, 1927)

Tellenbach, Marie-Elisabeth, "Psychoanalysis and Historio-critical Method: On Maynard Solomon's Image of Beethoven, Part 1" in *The Beethoven Newsletter*, 1993-1994, Vol. 8, pp. 84-92.

Tellenbach, Marie-Elisabeth, *Beethoven and His "Immortal Beloved" Josephine Brunsvik*, translated by John Klapproth (CreatedSpace Independent Publishing Platform, 2014)

Van Aerde, Raymund, "A la recherche des ascendants de Beethoven," ("In Search of Beethoven's ancestors"), *Revue Belge d'Archéologie et d'Histoire de l'Art*, 1939, No. 2.

Vignal, Marc, *Beethoven et Vienne*, (Fayard, 2004)

Wagner, Richard, *Beethoven*, transl. by Edward Dannreuther (London: William Reeves, 1870)

Wallace, Robin, "Beethoven's Critics," in *The Critical Reception of Beethoven's Compositions by His German Contemporaries*, Vol. 2 (W. M. Senner, R. Wallace and W. Meredith, editors)

Wolf, Stefan, *Beethovens Neffenkonflikt*, (Munich, 1995)

3. General references
Biographies and documents

"Hellen Keller and Beethoven's Ninth," *The Beethoven Journal*, Vol. 28, No. 2, Winter 2013

The Bach Reader. A Life of Johann Sebastian Bach in Letters and Documents, revised edition, David, Hans T. and Mendel Arthur, eds. (W W Norton & co., New York, 1966)

Leaves from the Journal of Sir George Smart, published by H. Bertram and C. L. Fox, Longmans (Green & Co., London, 1907)

Blackburn, Bonnie J., *Masses on Popular Songs and Syllables*, (in *The Josquin Companion*, Richard Sherr, editor, Oxford University Press, 1999)

Bowers, Jane, "Women Composers of Italy, 1566-1700," (in *Women Making Music: The Western Art Tradition, 1150-1950*, Jane Bowers and Judith Tick editors, Urbana: University of Illinois Press, 1986)

Boyd, Malcolm, *Bach*, (Wintage Books, New York, 1987)

Corredor, J. Ma., *Conversations with Casals*, translated by André Mangeot, (Dutton & Co, Inc., New York, 1958)

Einstein, Alfred, *Mozart—His Character, His Work*, translated by Arthur Mendel and Nathan Broder, (Oxford University Press, New York, 1979)

Kroll, Mark, *Johann Nepomuk Hummel: A Musician's Life and World* (Scarecrow Press, 2007)

La Mara, *Letters of Franz Liszt*, translated by Constance Bache, Volume 1 (C. Scribner's sons, 1894)

Mozart Letters, Mozart's Life, Selected letters edited and newly translated by Robert Spaethling (W. W. Norton & Co, New York, London, 2000)

Oswald, Peter, *Schumann. The Inner Voices of a Musical Genius* (Northeastern University Press, Boston, 1985)

The Collected Correspondence and London Notebooks of Joseph Haydn, H. C. Robbins Landon, editor, (London 1959)

Walker, Alan, *Franz Liszt, Volume 1: The Virtuoso Years: 1811-1847*, revised edition (Cornell University Press, 1987)

Musicology

The Beethoven Journal, Vol. 10 no. 1, spring 1995, pp. 30-36 (letters to editor) and 37-42 (editor William Meredith's notes)

Neue Zeitschrift für Musik , Vol. 5, Juni 5, 1818, pp. 177-179. Online at http://www.anno. onb. ac.at/cgi-content/anno?aid=nzm&datum=18380605 &query=%22beethoven%22&ref=anno-search.

Broyles, Michael at https://currentmusicology.columbia.edu/article/review-of-tia-denora-1995-beethoven

Dahlhaus, Carl, *Nineteenth-Century Music*, translated by J. Bradford Robinson, (University of California Press, 1989

Dirst, Matthew, *Engaging Bach. The keyboard legacy from Marburg to Mendelssohn* (Cambridge University Press, 2012)

Hanslick, Eduard, *The Beautiful in Music: A Contribution to the Revisal of Musical Aesthetics*, 7th ed., translated by Gustav Cohen (Novello et Co., ltd, London, 1891)

Heriot, Angus, *The Castrati in Opera*, (Da Capo Books, London, 1956)

Kraus, Beate Angelika, "Komponieren in Schatten Beethovens: César Frank und das Pariser Musikleben seiner Zeit", [Composing in Beethoven's shadow: Cesar Franck and the Parisian musical life of his time], (in *César Franck. Werk und Rezepzion (Peter Jost Hrsg,* Steiner Verlag, 2004, pp. 22-33)

McVeigh, Simon, *Concert Life in London from Haydn to Mozart* (Cambridge University Press, 1993),

Ritterman, Janet and Weber, William, "Origins of the Piano Recital in England, 1830-1870," (in *The Piano in Nineteenth-Century British Culture. Instruments, Performers and Repertoire*, Therese Marie Ellsworth and Susan Wollenberg editors, (Ashgate 2007)

Schneider, Magnuss T., *Seeing the Empress Again: On Doubling in L'Incoronazione di Poppea*, (in *Cambridge Opera Journal*, Vol. 24, No. 3 (November 2012), pp. 249-291)

Schumann, Robert, *On Music and Musicians*, transl. by Paul Rosenfeld (University of California Press, Berkeley and Los Angeles, 1946), p. 117. This is a selection from the 1854 German collection book *Robert Schumann, Gesammelte Schriften über Musik und Musiker* (Complete Writings on Music and Musicians), which had been already published in English translation by Fanny Raymond Ritter in 1877.

Sherman, Russell, *Piano Pieces* (North Point Press, New York,, 1997)

Stravinsky, Igor, *Poetics of Music, in the Form of Six Lessons*, transl. by Arthur Knodel and Ingolf Dahl (Harvard University Press, 2003)

Wagner, Richard, *On Music & Drama*, translated by H. Ashton Ellis, edited by Albert Goldman & Evert Sprinchorn, (University of Nebraska Press, Lincoln & London, 1964)

Winemiller, John, "Recontextualizing Handel's Borrowing," (*The Journal of Musicology*, Vol. 15, No. 4, 1997, pp. 444-470).

Socio-historical background

The Musical Quarterly, Summer 97, Vol. 81 Issue 2

Marx Engels on Literature and Art, (Progress Publishers, Moscow, 1976). Available online at http://www.marxists.org/archive/marx/works/subject/art/index.htm.

Boulet, Daniel et Laporte, JeanPierre, "Les comportements de consommation de vin en France", *INRA, Sciences Sociales*, No 3, Juin 1997

Brion, Marcel, *La vie cotidienne à Vienne au temps de Mozart et de Schubert*, [Everyday's Life in Vienna During the Times of Mozart and Schubert] (Hachette, 1959)

Chang, Jung and Halliday, Jon, *Mao: The unknown Story*, (Jonathan Cape, London, 2005)

Chirot, Daniel, *Modern Tyrants: The Power and Prevalence of Evil in Our Age*, (Princeton University Press, 1996)

Doerner, Klaus, *Madmen and the Bourgeoisie: A Social History of Insanity and Psychiatry*, transl. by Joachim Neugroschel and Jean Steinberg, (Oxford: Basil Blackwell, 1981)

Foucault, Michel, *History of Sexuality, Vol. 1, An Introduction*, translated from French by Robert Hurley (New York, Vintage Books, 1980)

Hale, John, *The Civilization of Europe under Renaissance* (Touchstone, 1995)

Harari, Yuval Noah, *Sapiens. A Brief History of Humankind* (Vintage Books, London, 2011)

Crnković, Gordana & Holland, Agnieszka. "Interview with Agnieszka Holland", Quarterly Review of Film and Video, Vol. 52, No 2 (Winter, 1998-1999)

Lotman, Jurij, "The Origin of Plot in the light of Typology," translated by Julian Graffy, (in *Poetics Today* 1.1-2 (1979), pp. 161-184). Available online at http://www.zbi.ee/~kalevi/LotmanPlot.htm.

Lotman, Jurij, *Culture and Explosion*, edited by Marina Grishakova, translated by Wilma Clark, (Mouton de Gruyer, 2010)

MacFarquahr, Roderick and Schoenhals, Michael, *Mao's Last Revolution* (Harvard University Press, 2006)

Marcuse, Herbert, *The Aesthetic Dimension. Toward a Critique of Marxist Aesthetics*, (Beacon Press, Boston, 1979)

Maschietto, Francesco L., Vairo, Jan, Crochetiere, William, and Marshall, Catherine, *Elena Lucrezia Cornaro Piscopia (1646-1684): the first woman in the world to earn a university degree*, (Saint Joseph's University Press, Boston, 2007)

McLean, Hugh, *In Search of Tolstoy* (Boston, 2008)

Melvin, Sheila and Cai, Jindong, *Rhapsody in Red. How Western Classical Music Became Chinese* (Algora Publishing, New York, 2004)

Murphy, Daniel, *Comenius: A Critical Re-assessment of His Life and Work*, (Irish Academic Press, 1995)

Newman, Bruce, *San Jose Mercury News*, November 8, 2006

Pezzl, Johann, in H. C. Robbins Landon, *Mozart and Vienna—Including Selections from Johann Pezzl's Sketch of Vienna, 1786-90*, pp. 53-191 (Thames and Hudson, 1991)

Phillips, Roderick, *A Short History of Wine*, (Harper Collins Publishers, 2000)

Quétel, Claude, *History of Syphilis*, translated by Judith Braddock and Brian Pike (The Johns Hopkins University Press, Baltimore, 1990)

Russell, John, "Vienna: Chapter 5 of the 1828 Edition of John Russell's *Tour in Germany*. Facsimile," (*The Beethoven Journal*, Winter 2014, Volume 29 No. 2, pp. 66-83)

Schopenhauer, Arthur, *The World as Will and Representation,* volume I, Judith Norman, Alistair Welchman, and Christopher Janaway (eds.), (Cambridge Univ. Press, 2011)

Sullivan, Meg and Hutchinson, Reed, "Susan McClary, Musicologist," (*UCLA Spotlight*, May 1, 2002)

Watson, Hugh S., *Eastern Europe between the Wars: 1918-1941*, (Harper Torchbooks, New York, 1967)

Science, medicine and psychoanalysis

American Psychiatric Association: *Diagnostic and Statistical Manual of Mental Disorders* (American Psychiatric Association Press, Washington, D.C., 2020)

Benson, Frank and Ardilla, Alfredo, *Aphasia: A Clinical Perspective* (Oxford University Press, 1996)

Bunnell, Adam, *Before Infallibility: Liberal Catholicism in Biedermeier Vienna,* (Fairley Dickinson University Press, London & Toronto, 1990)

Cobb, Matthew, *The Egg & Sperm Race.* The Seventeenth-Century Scientists

Who Unraveled the Secrets of Sex, Life and Growth (Pocket Books, 2006)

Cross, Henry. A., Halcomb, Charles G. and Matter, Wlliam W. "Imprinting or exposure learning in rats given early auditory stimulation," (*Psychonomic Science, 7* (1967)., p. 233-234)

Edelson, Marshall, *Psychoanlysis—A Theory in crisis* (University of Chicago Press, 1988)

Eysenck, Hans J. and Eyesenck, Sybil B., *Psychoticism as a Dimension of Personality* (Crane, Russak & Co., 1976)

Freud, Siegmund, *Three Essays on the Theory of Sexuality*, translated and revised by James Strachey (Basic Books Inc., New York, 1975)

Freud, Sigmund, "Family Romances," in *The Standard Edition of the Complete Psychological Works of Sigmund Freud, Vol. IX (1906-1908)*, pp 235-242. Available online at http://www.arch.mcgill.ca/prof/bressani/arch653/winter2010/Freud_FamilyRomance.pdf.

Graziano, Amy B, Johnson, Julene K, "Music, neurology, and psychology in the nineteenth century," (Chapter 2 in Journal *Progress in Brain Research, 216*, 2015 pp. 33-47), p. 45.

Hall, Winfield S., *A Text-Book of Physiology, Normal and Pathological*, 2nd ed., (Les Brothers and Co., Philadelphia and New York, 1905)

Hallam Richard, Ashton Paul, Sherbourne Kateriana and Gailey Lorraine, "Acquired profound hearing loss: Mental health and other characteristics of a large sample", *International Journal of Audiology* 2006 vol. 45 (pp. 715-723)

Hobson, Allan J., *The Dreaming Brain*, (Basic Books, Harper Collins Publishers, 1988)

Johnson, Hugh, *The Story of Wine*, (Mitchell Beazley, 2004)

Keating, Korey, "Miscellanea," in *The Beethoven Journal*, Winter 2009, Vol. 25, No. 2, p.99

Keiser, Garret, *The Unwanted Sound of Everything We Want*: A Book About Noise, (Books Group, 2010)

Kramer, Lawrence, *Why Classical Music Still Matters* (University of California Press, 2007)

Larkin, Edward, "Beethoven's illness—a likely diagnosis," (*Proc R Soc Med*, 1971 May 64(5))

Lehrer, Jonah, *Proust was a Neuroscientist* (A Mariner Book. Houghton Miffin Company, 2008)

Levitin, Daniel J., *This is Your Brain on Music. The Science of a Human Obsession* (A Plume Book, 2006)

Levitin, Daniel J., *Your Brain on Music*, (A Plume Book, New York, London, 2006)

Lewis, Thomas, Amini, Fari, Richard Lannon, *A General Theory of Love* (Vintage Books, New York, 2000)

Littlewood, Rolland, *Religion, Agency, Restitution: The Wilde Lectures in Natural Religion, 1999*, (Oxford University Press, New York, 2001)

Lombroso, Cesare, *Man of Genius*, 2nd ed., (Scribner's Sons, New York, 1905)

Mackowiak, Philip A., *Post-Mortem. Solving History's Great Medical Mysteries*, (American College of Physicians, 2007)

Mahapatra, S. B., "Deafness and Mental Health: Psychiatric And Psychosomatic Illness In The Deaf," *Acta Psychiatrica Scandinava*, Vol. 50, No. 6, 1974

Mayr, Joseph Karl, *Wien im Zeitalter Napoleons, Staatsfinanzen, Lebensverhältnisse, Beamte und Militär*, (Wien 1940)

O'Shea, John, *Was Mozart Poisoned?—Medical Investigations into the Lives of the Great Composers*, (St. Martin's Press, New York, 1981)

Ober, Wilhelm, "Beethoven, a Medical Biography", *The Practitioner* 205 (1970)

Palferman Thomas G., "Classical notes: Beethoven's medical history," *J R Soc Med*, 1990

Powell, John, *How Music Works*, (Little, Brown & Co, New York, 2010)

Rauscher, Frances H., Robinson, K. Desix, and Jens, Jason J, "Improved maze learning through early music exposure in rats," *Neurological Research*, 20 (1998), 427- 432.

Robertson, Margaret, "Consequences Of Deafness For Late Deafened Adults," *Deafness Forum of Australia, National Deafness Sector Summit* 15-16 May, 2004

Rock, Andrea, *The Mind at Night—The New Science of How and Why We Dream* (Basic Books, 2004)

Sacks, Oliver, *Musicophilia. Tales of Music and the Brain* (Vintage Books, New York, 2007)

Sharma, Om P., "Beethoven's illness: Whipple's disease rather than sarcoidosis?" *JRSM*, 1994, pp. 283-285.

Sheryl, *Secrets of the Teenage Brain* (Corwin Press, Thousand Oaks, 2004)

Solms, Mark, "The Conscious Id,"in *Neuropsychoanalysis*, Vol. 15, No. 1, (2013)

Solms, Mark; Turnbull, Oliver, *The brain and the inner world: an introduction to the neuroscience of subjective experience* (Other Press, LLC, 2002)

Strasser, Helmut, Irle, Hartmut, and Scholz, Roland,"Physiological Cost of the Hearing after Exposures to White Noise, Industrial Noise, Heavy Metal, and Classical Music of 94db (A) for 1 hour," (in *Traditional Rating of Noise Versus Physiological Costs of Sound*, Volume 66, edited by Helmut Strasser, IOS Press, Amsterdam, 2005, pp 128-137)

Sulloway, Frank J. *Freud. Biologist of the Mind*, (Harvard University Press, 1992)

Torrey, E. Filler, *Freudian Fraud. The Malignant Effect of Freud's Theory on American Thought and Culture* (Harper Collins, 1992).

Tremble, Edward, "The deafness of Beethoven," *Can. Med. Ass. Journal*, 1932, 27

Walker, Robert S, Flinn, Mark V., and Hill, Kim R., "Evolutionary history of partible paternity in lowland South America," *Proceedings of the National Academy of Sciences*, 2010; 107 (45), November 9, 2010

Feminist studies

Burr, Vivien, *Gender and Social Psychology* (Routledge, London, 1998)

De Lauretis, Teresa, *Alice Doesn't—Feminism Semiotics* (Indian University Press, 1984)

De Lauretis, Teresa, *Freud's Drive: Psychoanalysis, Literature, and Film*, (Palgrave/Macmillan, U.K., 2008)

Ellis, Katherine, "Female pianists and their male critics in nineteenth-century Paris," (*Journal of the America Musicological Society* 50 (1997), pp. 353-385)

Head, Matthew, *Sovereign Feminine: Music and Gender in Eighteenth-Century Germany* (University of California Press, 2013)

Paglia, Camille, *Sex, Art, and American Culture* (Vintage Books, New York, 1992)

Pateman, Carole, *The Sexual Contract* (Stanford University Press, 1988)

Rich, Adrienne, *Diving into the Wreck* (W. W. Norton, 1973)

Ross, Sarah Gwyneth, *The Birth of Feminism: Woman as Intellect in Renaissance Italy and England*, (Harvard Univ. Press, 2009)

Sayrs, Elisabeth, "Deconstructing McClary: Narrative, Feminine Sexuality, and Feminism in Susan McClary's *Feminine Endings*," (*College Music Symposium 33/34* (1993/1994): 41-55)

Encyclopedias, dictionaries and treatises

Brittanica, available at https://www.britannica.com/biography/Carl-Ditters-von-Dittersdorf

The New Grove Dictionary of Music and Musicians, Macmillan Publishers 1980, (London, Washington, D.C, Vol. 12)

The Mozart Compendium, H.C. Robbins Landon editor, (Borders Press, 1990)

Norton/Grove Dictionary of Women Composers, J. A. Sadie and R. Samuel, eds., (New York, London: W. W. Norton & Company, 1995)

Choron, Alexandre Étienne et Fayllole, François Joseph M., *Dictionnaire historique des musiciens*, (Paris, Chez Valade et Lenormant, 1810)

Musique de fêtes et cérémonies de la révolution française: oeuvres de Gossec, Cherubini, Lesueur, Mehul, Catel, etc, [Music for Feasts and Ceremonies of the French Revolution], recueillies et transcrites par Constant Pierre (Paris, Imprimerie Nationale, 1899)

Hirsch, Rudolf, *Gallerie lebender Tondichter: Biographisch- kritischer Beitrag.* [The Gallery of Living Composers: Biographical and Critical Contribution],

(Güns by C. Reichards, 1836)

Kennedy, Michael and Bourne, Joyce, "Bastien und Bastienne." (The Concise Oxford Dictionary of Music. 1996)

Rushton, Julian, in *The Mozart Compendium*, edited by H. C. Robbins Landon (Borders Press, 1990)

Slonimsky, Nicolas, *Lexicon of Musical Invective. Critical Assaults on Composers since Beethoven's Time, 2nd edition* (University of Washington Press, 1990)

Slonimsky, Nicolas, *Webster's New World Dictionary of Music*, (Wiley Publishing Inc., 1998)

Taruskin, Richard, *Music from the Earliest Notation to the Sixteenth Century*, The Oxford History of Western Music, (Oxford University Press, 2010)

Taruskin, Richard, *Music in the Seventeenth and Eighteenth Centuries* (Oxford University Press, 2010)

Taruskin, Richard, *Music in the Nineteenth Century* (The Oxford History of Western Music, Oxford University Press, 2010)

Taruskin, Richard, *Music in the Early Twentieth Century* (Oxford University Press, 2010)

4. Online sources

Nunnelly, Andrew, https://www.thecrimson.com/article/2006/11/8/movie-review-copying-beethoven

Feld, Bruce, November 9, 2006, http://fj.webedia.us/copying-beethoven

https://www.rottentomatoes.com/m/copying_beethoven/reviews

www.rogerebert.com/reviews/immortal-beloved-1995

www.rottentomatoes.com/m/1038726_beethoven

French, Phillip, *The Guardian*, August 19, 2007

Levy, Emanuel, http://emanuellevy.com/review/copying-beethoven-6

Roeper, Richard, Nov. 13, 2006 (https://www.rottentomatoes.com/m/copying_beethoven)

Rothsteinjan, Edward, "Classical View: How Can a Movie So Right Be So Wrong?", The New York Times, Jan. 1, 1995. (Online at https://www.nytimes.com/1995/01/01/movies/classical-view-how-can-a-movie-so-right-be-so-wrong.html).

Tobin, Jonathan, https://nypost.com/2020/09/17/canceling-beethoven-is-the-latest-woke-madness-for-the-classical-music-world/

Notes

Chapter 1

[1] Siegmund Freud, *Three Essays on the Theory of Sexuality*, translated and revised by James Strachey (Basic Books Inc., New York, 1975), pp. 29-30.

[2] E. Fuller Torrey, M.D., *Freudian Fraud. The Malignant Effect of Freud's Theory on American Thought and Culture* (Harper Collins, 1992).

[3] Quoted from Frank J. Sulloway's *Freud. Biologist of the Mind*, (Harvard University Press, 1992), pp. 499 and 358. This monograph surveys the Freud's theory in the context of its times and ends up with a positive critical review, even though it accepts that some fundamental criticism is valid (pages XII-XIII).

[4] J. Allan Hobson, *The Dreaming Brain*, (Basic Books, Harper Collins Publishers, 1988), p. 13.

[5] Hobson 1988, p. 258.

[6] Andrea Rock, *The Mind at Night – The New Science of How and Why We Dream* (Basic Books, 2004), p.131-132.

[7] Sheryl Feinstein, *Secrets of the Teenage Brain* (Corwin Press, Thousand Oaks, 2004), pp. 2 and 54.

[8] Feinstein, p 13.

[9] Feinstein, p. 100-101

[10] Sulloway, p. 372.

[11] Sulloway, p. 373.

[12] Peter J. Bowler, *Darwin Deleted: Imagining a World Without Darwin* (University of Chicago Press, 2013), p. 21.

[13] Robert S. Walker, Mark V. Flinn, and Kim R. Hill, "Evolutionary history of partible paternity in lowland South America," *Proceedings of the National Academy of Sciences*, 2010; 107 (45), November 9, 2010. Online at https://doi.org/10.1073/pnas.1002598107. The scientific term is "partible paternity."

[14] Yuval Noah Harari, *Sapiens. A Brief History of Humankind* (Vintage Books, London, 2011), p. 46

[15] Thomas Lewis, Fari Amini, Richard Lannon, *A General Theory of Love* (Vintage Books, New York, 2000), p. 9.

[16] Marshall Edelson, *Psychoanlysis – A Theory in crisis* (University of Chicago Press, 1988), p. 131.

[17] Mark Solms, "The Conscious Id," (in *Neuropsychoanalysis*, Vol. 15, No. 1, (2013), pp. 5-19), p. 5.

[18] Mark Solms; Oliver Turnbull, *The brain and the inner world: an introduction to the neuroscience of subjective experience* (Other Press, LLC, 2002), p. 207-208.

[19] Lewis, Amini & Lannon, p. 85.

Chapter 2

[1] *The Letters of Beethoven*, Collected, translated and edited by Emily Anderson, Vol. 1-3 (W.W. Norton & Co, New York, London, 1961), letter 16 (p. 22). Referred hereafter as *Anderson* with the letter number and, if needed, the page.

[2] *Thayer's Life of Beethoven*, Revised and Edited by Elliot Forbes (Princeton University Press, 1969), p. 624-5. Further referenced as Thayer-Forbes.

A second version of Thayer's book is

The Life of Ludwig van Beethoven By Alexander Wheelock Thayer, edited, revised and amended from the original English manuscript and the German editions of Hermann Deiters and Hugo Riemann, concluded, and all the documents newly translated By Henry Edward Krehbiel. (The Beethoven Association, New York, 1921). Hereafter referred as Thayer-Krehbiel.

[3] Letter to Frau Nanette Streicher (Anderson 904, vol. 2, p 770).

[4] Thayer-Forbes, p. 697.

[5] Newman, p. 13.

[6] Editha Sterba and Richard Sterba, *Beethoven and His Nephew. A Psychoanalytical Study of Their Relationship*, (Schocken Books, New York, 1971). Any further reference to this book will be indicated as Sterba & Sterba.

[7] Anderson 1.

[8] Thayer-Forbes, p. 625.

[9] Anderson 1397, p 1217.

[10] Letter to his lawyer, Johann Baptist Bach, August 1824 (Anderson, 1302, v3, p 1134).

[11] Ludwig Nohl, *An Unrequited Love. An Episode in the Life of Beethoven: From the Diary of a Young Lady*, translated by Annie Wood, (Bentley & Son, London, 1876). More excerpts were published in volume 4 of the Thayer-Deiters-Riemann version of *Thayer's Life of Beethoven* (pages 513-541), but (for whatever reason) they were not included in the English Thayer-Forbes version.

[12] Nohl, p. 165.

[13] Thayer-Forbes, p. 52.

[14] Nohl, p. 55.

[15] Thayer-Forbes, p. 293. Testimony of Dolezalek, a musician that knew Beethoven in his youth.

[16] Thayer-Forbes, p. 772.

[17] *Wiener Zeitschrift fur Kunst, Literatur, Theater and Mode*, 1837, October issues no. 120-123. Available online at
https://books.google.com/books?id=tTNZAAAAcAAJ. (Oct 7, pp 956-7; Oct 10, pp 964-5; Oct 12, pp 972-3; Oct 14, pp 980-1). At page 973: "[…] so scheint auch die Macht der Liebe ihn nie beherrscht zu haben."

[18] Anderson 389 and 390.

[19] Harry Goldschmidt, *All About Beethoven's Immortal Beloved. A Stocktaking*, (CreatedSpace, an Amazon.com Company, 2014), p. 231. Goldschmidt was the first to signal this fact; he discusses other examples of the same kind in his book. The quote reffers John E. Klapproth's translation of the 1980 original *Um die Unsterbliche Geliebte. Eine Bestandaufnahme* (Munich, 1980). All references to Goldschmidt's book pertain to this English translation.

[20] Feinstein, p. 4-6.

[21] *Beethoven, the man and the artist, as revealed in his own words,* Compiled and annotated by Friederich Kerst, translated by Henry E. Krehbiel, (Dover Publications, New York, 1964), pp. 43 and 45-46.

[22] *Remembering Beethoven. The Biographical Notes of Franz Wegeler and Ferdinand Ries,* transl. by Frederick Noonan (André Deutsch, 1987), p. 24. Hereafter referenced as Wegeler-Ries.

[23] Wegeler-Ries, p. 54. Anderson (9, p. 14-15) and Thayer-Forbes (p. 163) give a slightly different translation.

[24] Maynard Solomon, *Beethoven Essays*, (Harverd University Press, Cambridge, Massachusetts, 1988), p. 149.

[25] Solomon 1988, p. 334.

[26] *Les Cahiers de conversation de Beethoven*, Traduits et présentés par J.-G. Prod'homme (Editions Corrêa, Paris, 1946), p. 302.

[27] Thayer-Forbes, p. 911.

[28] Tellenbach 1993-4, p. 89.

[29] Anderson 1521, p. 1307.

[30] Thayer-Forbes, p. 697.

[31] Anderson 33 and 34, p. 35. The friend was, presumably, Ignaz von Gleichenstein.

[32] Anderson 1315 (p. 1146) and 1323 (p. 1153).

[33] Thayer-Forbes p. 624 and 625.

[34] Thayer-Forbes p. 710.

[35] Adam Bunnell, *Before Infallibility: Liberal Catholicism in Biedermeier Vienna,* (Fairley Dickinson University Press, London & Toronto, 1990), p. 34.

[36] Thayer-Forbes, pp. 634, 704 and 749; T-D-R, p 563. This version's error originated with its English translation of the original German ("Vergehen einer Veruntreuung gegen ihren Mann"); Anderson restored the right term in her edition of Beethoven's letters.

[37] Sieghard Brandenburg, "Johanna van Beethoven's Embezzlement," in *Haydn, Mozart & Beethoven: Studies in Music of the Classical Period. Essays in Honor of Alan Tyson* (Brandenburg ed., Oxford University Press, 1988) pp. 237-251. Although the original court files preserved in the Superior Provincial

Court in Vienna were destroyed in a fire in 1927, Brandenburg was able to reconstruct the essentials of the case based on copy excerpts kept by local Viennese historian Robert Franz Müller (now preserved in the Austrian National library).

[38] Brandenburg 1988, p. 242-243.
[39] Anderson Appendix C #15, p. 1390.
[40] Brandenburg 1988, p. 240.
[41] Thayer-Forbes, p. 457.
[42] Brandenburg 1988, p. 246.
[43] Brandenburg 1988, p. 246.
[44] Brandenburg 1988, p. 242-243.
[45] Brandenburg 1988, pp. 246-248.
[46] Anderson 611, p. 561-562.
[47] Johann Pezzl, in H. C. Robbins Landon, *Mozart and Vienna – Including Selections from Johann Pezzl's Sketch of Vienna, 1786-90*, pp. 53-191 (Thames and Hudson, 1991)
[48] John Russell, "Vienna: Chapter 5 of the 1828 Edition of John Russell's *Tour in Germany*. Facsimile," (in *The Beethoven Journal*, Winter 2014, Volume 29 No. 2, pp. 66-83), p. 74-75 (199-203 in the original book).
[49] Brandenburg 1988, p. 241.
[50] George Marek, *Beethoven. Biography of a Genius* (Funk & Wagnalis, 1969), p 497.
[51] Anderson, Appendix C, #9, p. 1389.
[52] Both quotes from Anderson, Appendix C, # 15, p. 1390.
[53] Brandenburg 1988, p. 248.
[54] Blöchlinger's entry in a June 1820 conversation book (Thayer-Forbes, p. 757).
[55] Quoted by Tellenbach 1993-4, p. 89 (source in endnote).
[56] Anderson, Appendix C, #9, pp 1391, 1389 and 1395.
[57] Quoted from Solomon 1988, p. 310 (its source, that I could not locate, is at note 15, page 470).
[58] Thayer-Forbes, p. 624-25.
[59] Thayer-Forbes, p. 550.
[60] Anderson, Appendix C, # 15, p. 1390.
[61] Thayer-Forbes, pp 624-625.
[62] Thayer-Forbes p. 624 and 625.
[63] Anderson, Appendix C, # 15, p. 1376.
[64] Letter to Gajetan Giannatasio del Rio (Anderson 611, vol. 2, p. 561-2)
[65] Anderson, Appendix C, #4, p. 1363-1364 (my italics).

[66] Anderson 603, p 555.
[67] Anderson Appendix C #4, p 1365.
[68] Anderson 611, p 561 (original emphasys).
[69] Solomon 1988. Numbers 117 (p. 182), 159 and 160 (p. 192) in his English edition of the *Tagebuch*.
[70] June 18, 1818, letter to Frau Nanette Streicher (Anderson 904, p. 770).
[71] Thayer-Forbes, p. 752.
[72] Brandenburg 1988, p. 237.
[73] Brandenburg 1988, p. 246.
[74] Thayer-Forbes p. 751. Quoting the more explicit report that the *Appellate Court* demanded from the *Magistrat*.
[75] Brandenburg 1988, p. 245.
[76] Brandenburg 1988, p. 238.
[77] Thayer-Forbes, p. 751.
[78] Anderson, Appendix C, # 7 p 1368.
[79] Thayer-Forbes, p. 711.
[80] Thayer-Forbes, p. 710.
[81] Thayer-Forbes, p. 712, quoting an entry in an 1820 Conversions book. In *Konversationshefte* (p. 164) the "M" is completed as Magistrate (the judicial court of commoners).
[82] Brandenburg 1988, p. 237, note 1.
[83] Thayer-Forbes, p. 752.
[84] Anderson, Appendix C, # 15, p. 1397 & 1400.
[85] Thayer-Forbes, p. 726.
[86] Nohl, p. 122, 70 and 156.
[87] Nohl, p. 95.
[88] Anderson, Appendix C #15, p. 1395.
[89] Anderson, Appendix C, #9, p. 1377.
[90] Thayer-Forbes, pp. 756, 757, 882.
[91] All from Thayer-Forbes, pp. 756, 991, 993, 995. I have not included page 994 ("[the] usual suspicion of the company he kept and of his desire to gamble"), because originating from Schindler.
[92] Thayer-Forbes p. 708-709.
[93] Prod'homme, pp. 60, 120, 128, 148 (my translations).
[94] Anderson 956, p. 824.
[95] Thayer-Forbes, p. 882.
[96] Stefan Wolf, *Beethovens Neffenkonflikt*, (Munich, 1995). The "puberty conflict" is tackled at pages 149-163. Wolf's work revisited the issue tackled

by the Sterbas also from a psychoanalytical standpoint. Unfortunately, my high school German is not good enough for digesting a three-hundred pages book, therefore I cannot undertake an analysis of it. However, I can appreciate Wolf's insight in re-discovering what popular wisdom has known for ages.

[97] Cooper 2000, p. 321.

[98] Feinstein p. 6.

[99] Goldschmidt 2014, p. 355-356.

[100] Thayer-Forbes, p. 999.

[101] Feinstein, p. 117-118.

[102] Thayer-Forbes, p. 757

[103] Quoted from Schünemann, *Ludwig van Beethovens Konversationshefte, Band 2* (Max Hesse Verlag, Berlin 1941), p. 286.

[104] Anderson 1374 (p. 1198) and 1470 (p. 1277).

[105] Thayer-Forbes, p. 917, quoting an 1824 conversation book.

[106] Quoted by Nohl, p. 87, a recollection of Dr. Karl Bursy, who visited Beethoven in 1816 (omitted in Thayer-Forbes narration of the visit).

[107] Thayer-Forbes, p. 922.

[108] Thayer-Forbes, p. 993.

[109] Thayer-Forbes, p. 995.

[110] Thayer-Forbes, p. 994-5.

[111] Thayer-Forbes, p. 1015.

[112] Blöchlinger's entry in June 1820 conversation book (Schünemann, *Konversationhefte*, Band 2, p. 153).

[113] Anderson 1256 (p. 1101), 1259 (p. 1103) and 1257 (p. 1101-1102), the last to Johanna.

[114] Quoting Schünemann, II, p. 122.

[115] Quoting Schünemann, II, p. 116. The entry mentions that Hofbauer claimed that "with the child had already cost him 30,000 florins" (a huge, incredible sum). Tellenbach (1993-4, p. 89) quotes this entry as proof that Hofbauer was not the father, but paid alimony.

[116] Thayer-Forbes, p. 950.

[117] Anton Felix Schindler, *Beethoven as I Knew Him,* Edited by Donald W. MacArdle, English translation by Constance S. Jolly (Dover Publications Inc., Mineola, New York, 1996), p. 385.

[118] Thayer-Forbes, p. 917.

[119] Anderson 1489, p. 1289.

[120] Thayer-Forbes p. 995.

[121] Feinstein, p. 126.

[122] Thayer-Forbes p. 999.

[123] Cooper 2000, p. 343.
[124] Prod'homme pp. 415 and 418. These quotes are not included in Thayer-Forbes.
[125] Thayer-Forbes, p. 1103.
[126] Prod'homme, pp. 414 and 415. These quotes are not included in Thayer-Forbes.
[127] Thayer-Forbes p. 1000.
[128] Schindler 1996, p. 315.
[129] Thayer-Forbes, p 1001, quoting from an August 1826 conversation Book.
[130] Thayer-Forbes, pp. 1013, 1015.
[131] Thayer-Forbes, p. 1016.
[132] Schindler 1996, p. 318.
[133] Thayer-Forbes, p. 1016-17.
[134] Thayer-Forbes, p. 115-16.
[135] Anderson 1541, p. 1320.
[136] Thayer-Forbes, p. 1028.
[137] Andreas Ignatz Wawruch, "Medical Review on the Final Stage of L. van Beethoven's Life," translated by Michael Lorenz, (*Beethoven Journal*, Winter 2007, Volume 22, Number 2, pp. 87-91), p. 89.
[138] Lewis et al, p. 204.
[139] Thayer-Forbes, p. 57.
[140] Letter to Dr. Joseph Wilhelm von Schaden (Anderson 1, vol. 1, p. 3).
[141] Wegeler-Ries, p. 109-110.
[142] Anderson 612, p 562; 654, p. 597.
[143] Letter to Cajetan Giannatasio (Anderson 644, p.589).
[144] Anderson, Appendix C #9, p. 1379.
[145] Goldschmidt 2014, p. 355-356.

Chapter 3

[1] Maynard Solomon, *Beethoven*, Second revised Edition (Schirmer Book, New York, 1998). All further references to it in this chaper are included directly in the text as (page …).
[2] Sigmund Freud, "Family Romances," in *The Standard Edition of the Complete Psychological Works of Sigmund Freud, Vol. IX (1906-1908)* , pp 235-242. Online at http://www.arch.mcgill.ca/prof/bressani/arch653/winter2010/Freud_FamilyRomance.pdf.
[3] Freud 1906, p. 237. He calls it "neurotic family romance," but the first word got lost in the English-speaking world.

[4] Alexandre Étienne Choron, François Joseph M. Fayllole, *Dictionnaire historique des musiciens*, (Paris, Chez Valade et Lenormant, 1810). The composer's entry (p. 60) begins, "Beethoven (Louis-van), que l'on a dit fils naturel de Frédéric Guillaume II, roi de Prusse, est né à Bonn en 1772." The *Dictionnaire*'s entry is very shallow: it doesn't mention Beethoven's symphonies (he had six under his belt in 1810), his concertos and *Fidelio*.

[5] Karl-Heinz Köhler & al., eds, *Ludwig van Beethovens Konversationshefte*, Vol, 1 (Leipzig, VEB Deutscher Verlag fur Musik, 1968, vol. 1), p. 179. Se also p. 247. Further quoted as *Konversationshefte*.

[6] Wegeler-Ries, p. 48-49. Letter to Wegeler from December 6, 1826; his friend rebutted the gossip only in 1838, in this book he co-authored with Ries, by writing that "the nonsense [...] needs no refutation." (p. 10).

[7] My translation of the first two stanzas, which is more literal than Solomon's. I have omitted the next stanzas, where God is invoked as the ultimate "Giver." The original runs: "Noch weisst du nicht, wes Kind du bist ,/ Wer dir die Windeln schenket. / Wer um dich wacht and wer sie ist / Die dich erwärmt and trinket. / Geneuss indes mit frommem Sinn. / Geneuss! Nah wenig Jahern / wird sich in deiner Pflegerin / Die Mutter offenbaren. / So hegt und pflegt verborg'ne Weise / Ein Geber – Dank sein ihm dafür! – / Mit Gütern, Trank and Speise. / Zwar fast ihn nicht mein dunkler Sinn, / Allein nach Wenig Jahren / Wird, wenn ich from und gläubig bin, / Er mir sich offernbaren."

[8] Tellenbach, 1993-4, p. 87. Her inability to see the full scope of Solomon's theory is hard to understand: Solomon's biography of Beethoven had been translated into German in 1978.

[9] Thayer-Forbes: "He liked to speak of his grandfather with the friends of his youth and his pious mother [...], whom he loved much more than he did his father, who was only severe, was obliged to tell him much of his grandfather The picture of him [...] is the only one that he moved from Bonn to Vienna and which gave him much pleasure until his death" (p. 54); "a portrait of Beethoven's grandfather for whom, as is known, he had a child-like reverence [...] was the sole ornament" of his room." (p. 849, testimony of Louis Schlösser, a visiting musician)

[10] Thayer-Forbes p. 66; one assumes that the score, a cantata by Emmanuel Bach, was introduced to him by his teacher Neefe, who arrived in Bonn in 1779 (Thayer-Forbes, p. 64.)

[11] Wegeler-Ries, p. 109-110.

[12] Nohl, p. 68.

[13] Tellenbach 1993-4, p. 87. See quote in Thayer-Krehbiel, vol. 2, p. 69.

[14] Wegeler-Ries, p. 41. Solomon quotes the sentence in a different context (149), without realizing its implication for the nobility pretense issue..

[15] *Letters to Beethoven and Other Correspondence*, translated and edited by Theodore Albrecht, Vol. 3: 1824-1828, (Univ. of Nebraska Press, 1996). Beethoven's letter 439 (p. 144), not included in Anderson's collection; Schlesinger's letter 443 (p. 151-152).

[16] Nohl, p. 53.

[17] *Konversationhefte*, p. 115. Entry not included in Thayer-Forbes.

[18] Anderson 1008, p. 875.
[19] Anderson, Appendix C # 15, Vol. 3, p. 1400. The memorandum was probably not submitted, since it was not found in the Court's archives.
[20] Thayer-Forbes, p. 752.
[21] Anderson, Appendix C, # 15, p. 1375-6.
[22] Sterba, p. 231.
[23] Schindler 1996, p. 52.
[24] Schindler 1996, p. 121.
[25] *Beethoven. Impressions by His Contemporaries,* O. G. Sonneck edit., p. 20-21.
[26] Thayer-Forbes, p. 403. The evidence, originating from several sources, is not fully consistent. In October 1806, Beethoven was the guest of his patron and (almost) friend Prince Lichnowsky at his residence in Silesia (now around the tri-country border of Czechia, Poland and Germany). Lichnowsky had also some French officers visiting him and they were eager to hear Beethoven playing, but the latter refused to play for them. When the Prince tried to coerce him (one account says that the Prince even threatened to have the composer arrested), Beethoven protested furiously and left abruptly and broke up with the Prince. At the time, France was at war with the "Fourth Coalition" of European powers. The Habsburg Empire did not join the coalition, but had been part of the previous one and was defeated and dismembered and reduced to Austria (with the Emperor Franz II demoted to King Franz I). Prince Lichnowsky invited the French officers, who were passing through Silesia on their way to join the army, out of an old tradition of military "esprit de corps." For Beethoven, the French were the enemy.
[27] Wegeler-Ries, p. 98. Ries mentions that the Prince took care to right the wrong by having Beethoven sit at his table next to him at the supper following the musical soirée that he gave.
[28] H. C. Robbins Landon, *Mozart and Vienna,* including selections from Johan Pezzl's "Sketch of Vienna (1786-1790)" (Thames and Hudson, 1991), Pezzl's book at pp. 54-200.
[29] Pezzl, p. 70 and 72.
[30] Pezzl, p. 81. He enumerates the corresponding female scale at the beginning: Frau, Frau von, etc.
[31] Thayer-Forbes, p. 149.
[32] Albrecht 1996, p. 397 and 400. Beethoven never kept the letters he received. Schindler saved some of them during the years when he acted like his secretary, but we have no similar letters from his early years in Vienna.
[33] Albrecht 1996, p 341. The "Geselschaft" addressed the same way their letter to Beethoven's friend Carl Bernard, the author of the oratorio's libretto; had they believed that Beethoven was noble, they would have addressed him differently from Bernard, a commoner.
[34] Online at *Heraldik-Wiki.*
[35] Schindler 1996, p. 112 and 245. This testimony of his has never disputed.
[36] In his later book *Beethoven Essays* (1988, p. 45.

[37] Peter Clive, *Beethoven and His World: A Biographical Dictionary* (Oxford University Press, 2001), p. 386.
[38] Quoting *Konversationshefte*, vol. 1, p. 219. The original includes an odd deletion: "Da es erfuhr dass mein Brud[er] nicht von *adel* sey. Es ist auffallend, soviel ist gewiss, dass hier eine Lücke herrscht, die nicht sollte ausgefüllt werden, den[n] ich gehöre nicht gemäss meiner Beschaffenheit unter diese *plebs* M" (original emphasis). A more accurate translation reads: "So it was found out that my brother would not be of nobility. It is striking, so much is certain that there is a gap here that should not be filled out, because according to my nature I do not belong to these plebeian M." *M* was the commoners' court, called Magistrat.
[39] Thayer-Forbes, p. 711.
[40] Thayer-Forbes, p. 254.
[41] Tellenbach 1993-4, p. 86-87.
[42] Anderson 1194. Beethoven included in his letter to Schindler his response to the applicant stating, "A capable fellow requires no other recommendations than those from some respectable houses to others" (Anderson 1193).
[43] Letters to Countess Erdödy (Anderson 633) and to Antonie Brentano (Anderson 660).
[44] "Letter to the Editor," in The Beethoven Journal 12/1 (1997): 48-49.
[45] Solomon 1998, p. 244. The ellipsis marks a display of erudition that does not fail to quote Mircea Eliade, the well-known historian of religions.
[45] Altman, p. 204-205.

Chapter 4

[1] Thayer-Forbes, p. 53-54.
[2] Thayer-Forbes, p. 57.
[3] Thayer-Forbes p. 69.
[4] Thayer-Forbes, p. 54.
[5] Thayer-Forbes, p. 66. Thayer does not indicate in what publication the notice was printed.
[6] Solomon quotes Theodor Frimmel (*Beethoven-Forschung* I (1911), p. 27). Müller continues telling how he provided Beethoven a copy of his baptismal certificate, which the composer accepted as the truth. Thayer missed this evidence, although he quoted (pp. 56, 57 and 72) from W. C. Müller's article published in *Allgemeine Musikalische Zeitung* in May 1827, reporting some reminiscences of Franz Ries (the father of Ferdinand Ries) and Nikolas Simrock, who had known Beethoven in his childhood.
[7] Theodore Albrecht and Elaine Schwensen, "More Than Just Peanuts: Evidence for December 16 as Beethoven's Birthday," (*The Beethoven Newsletter, Vol. 3 No. 3 (Winter 1988)*, pp. 49, 60-63), p. 49, 60-63), p. 60.
[8] Solomon quotes Theodor Frimmel (*Beethoven-Forschung* I (1911), p. 27).
[9] My translation of the original: "Du wirst mir eine freundschaftliche Bitte nicht abschlagen, wenn ich Dich ersuche, mir meinen Taufschein zu besorgen. [...]

Etwas is unterdessen in Acht zu nehmen; nämlich: das noch ein Bruder <u>früherer Geburt von mir war</u>, der ebenfalls Ludwig hies, nur mit dem Zusatze: <u>Maria</u>, aber gestorben ist. Um mein gewisses Alter zu bestimmen, muss man also diesen erst finden, da ich ohnedies [ohne dies] schon Weiss, das durch Andere hierin ein Irrthum enstanded, da man mich älter angegeben, als ich war. — Leider habe ich eine Zeitlang gelebt, ohne selbst zu wissen, wie alt ich bin. — Eine Familienbuch hatte ich, aber es hat sich verloren, der Himmel Weiss {weisst}, wie. — Also, lass Dich's nicht verdriessen, wenn ich Dir diese Sache sehr warm empfehle, den <u>Ludwig Maria</u> und den jetzigen nach ihm gekommenen <u>Ludwig</u> ausfindig zu Machen." (from *Biographische Notizen über Ludwig van Beethoven* von Dr. F. G. Wegeler und Ferdinand Ries (Coblenz, bei K. Bädeker, 1838), p. 46-47). It is very similar to Anderson's version (256, p. 270-71), but more accurate about the tenses.

[10] Thayer-Forbes, p. 52.

[11] Wegeler-Ries, p. 120-121. It is in the notes to this letter that we find the whole story.

[12] Wegeler-Ries, p 152 (Wegeler's 1845 Supplement).

[13] Thayer-Forbes, p. 54.

[14] Thayer-Forbes, p. 54.

[15] Arthur Helps and Elizabeth Jane Howard, *Bettina. A Portrait*, (Chatto & Windus, London, 1957), p 116.

[16] Solomon quotes from Wegeler's *Supplement*, p. 7. In my sources, Wegeler-Ries, p. 146 (slightly differently worded). In original: "Beethoven galt hin und wieder für einen Adligen."

[17] Thayer-Forbes, p. 712. Unfortunately, Thayer was apparently not able to get that "knowledge" either, through his interviews with aristocrats who had known Beethoven later in his life. Therefore, he could only offer another unsupported statement: "It is scarcely conceivable that Beethoven should have cherished the thought that he was of noble birth or that he seriously encouraged such a belief among his exalted friends."

[18] Anderson 953 (original emphasis). The original reads, "ich hatte stolz genug zu erklären, daß ich mich <u>nie um meinen Adel</u> bekümmert."

[19] Rudolf Hirsch. *Gallerie lebender Tondichter: Biographisch- kritischer Beitrag.* (The Gallery of Living Composers: Biographical and Critical Contribution), Güns by C. Reichards, 1836, p. 146-7.

[20] Brittanica, available at https://www.britannica.com/biography/Carl-Ditters-von-Dittersdorf.

[21] Thayer-Forbes, p. 135, quoting from the surviving notes of Beethoven's expenses mentioning "Andreas Lindner, dancing-master."

[22] Russell 2001, p. 76/204.

[23] Thayer-Forbes, p. 711.

[24] Thayer-Forbes, p. 712.

[25] Thayer-Forbes p. 624 and 625. The shortening used by Thayer, "R. I. L." stands for the "Royal Imperial Landrecht," (in German K.K.L, "Könighlich Keiserlich Landrecht," which designed the Nobility Court.

[26] Thayer-Forbes, p. 626.

²⁷ Thayer-Forbes, p. 399.
²⁸ Thayer-Forbes, p. 552.
²⁹ Evidence in Beethoven's letters to his lawyer J. N. Kanka referring to *Landrechte*, the German name of the nobility courts (e.g. Anderson 520 and 522 p 490).
³⁰ Thayer-Forbes, p. 398.
³¹ *The Collected Correspondence and London Notebooks of Joseph Haydn,* H. C. Robbins Landon, editor, (London 1959), p. XXIII. Solomon buries this information in a note (17 at page 311).
³² Joseph Schmidt-Gorg, ed., *Des Bonner Bäckermeisters Gottfried Fischer: Aufzeichnungen über Beethovens Jugend*, (Beethovenhaus, Bonn, 1971), p. 33-34. Solomon, who quotes the Fischer testimony, thinks that "Herr" must be translated as "Lord" (1998, p. 28), but it is unlikely that the little boy jumped that high in his day-dreaming.
³³ Raymund Van Aerde, "A la recherche des ascendants de Beethoven," ("In Search of Beethoven's ancestors"), *Revue Belge d'Archéologie et d'Histoire de l'Art*, 1939, No. 2.
³⁴ *Konversationshefte*, p. 56. "Sie könnten es einleiten als ob Sie bloss den ältern Adel Ihrer Familie renovi[e]ren liessen."
³⁵ *Konversationshefte*, p. 16. "*Van* verzeichnet den Adel und das Patriciat nur wenn es zwischen zwei Eigen Nahmen in der Mitte steht z. B. Bentink van Dieperheim, Hooft van Vreeland etc etc. Bey Niederländer würde man die beste Aufkunft über diese Unbedeutende Bedeutenhait erhalten."
³⁶ Thayer-Forbes, p. 399.
³⁷ Tellenbach 1993-4, p. 85.
³⁸ Tellenbach 1993-4, p. 85.
³⁹ Solomon uses Anderson's translation (No. 978, vol. 2, p. 849-850), with slight modifications, but also gives the original German in note 12. He dismisses an interesting phrase, "Dream, alone" ("Traum, allein") which explicitly connects the final dream sentence to the next one. A literal translation runs: "Dream, alone, in my waking hours too I think of Y. I. H."
⁴⁰ Russell 2001, pp 66-83, p. 76 (206-207 of facsimile).
⁴¹ Prod'homme, p. 89.
⁴² Solomon 1998, p. 361.
⁴³ Anderson 1518, p. 1304. Some more complicated German grammar is involved in the sentence: "könnte" is the German *subjunctive mode II* that is commonly used to indicate politeness (like in "I would like" instead of "I want") or an unlikely conditional ("If I had ... I could"). None of them clarifies the meaning here.
⁴⁴ Alfred C. Kalischer, *Beethovens sämtliche Briefe, Band V*, (Berlin & Leipzig, 1908), p. 254. If this reading is correct, the dating of the letter must be reconsidered; although Holz's birth year is a matter of controversy (1798; according to the German Wikipedia, 1799 in the English Wikipedia and Peter Clive (p. 168), 1801 in Nettle's *Beethoven Encyclopedia*), the day is not –

March 3. Peter Clive B and His World: A Biographical Dictionary, Oxford Univ. Press, 2001.

[45] Marie-Elisabeth Tellenbach, *Beethoven and His "Immortal Beloved" Josephine Brunsvik*, translated by John Klapproth (CreatedSpace Independent Publishing Platform, 2014), p. 71, quoting a (draft) letter of Josephine to Beethoven.

[46] Michael P. Steinberg, *Listening to Reason: Culture, Subjectivity, and Nineteenth-Century Music* (Princeton University Press, New Jersey, 2004), p. 70.

Chapter 5

[1] Peter J. Davies: *The Character of a Genius: Beethoven in Perspective* (Greenwood Press, Westport, Connecticut, 2002). The issue is dealt with in pages 97-104.

[2] François Martin Mai, *Diagnosing Genius – The Life and Death of Beethoven*, (Mc Gill-Queen's University Press, 2007). He deals with the issue on pages 141-151.

[3] Michael Lorenz, "Commentary on Wawruch's Report", *The Beethoven Journal*, 22/2 (Winter 2007): 92-98. The quote from page 98.

[4] Thayer-Forbes, p. 1021.

[5] Wilhelm Ober, "Beethoven, a Medical Biography", *The Practitioner* 205 (1970), p. 824.

[6] Theodore von Frimmel, "Beethovens Leiden und Ende," in the Viennese newspaper *Die Press*, September 8, 1880. Frimmel was one of the early Beethoven scholars.

[7] John O'Shea, *Was Mozart Poisoned? – Medical Investigations into the Lives of the Great Composers*, (St. Martin's Press, New York, 1981); a second edition appeared in 1991. The chapter on Beethoven (pp. 39-65) is the most substantial, but the present topic occupies only part of the pages 43-44.

[8] Phillips, *A Short History of Wine*, (Harper Collins Publishers, 2000), p. 24.

[9] Hugh Johnson, *The Story of Wine*, (Mitchell Beazley, 2004), p. 12.

[10] Johnson, p. 26. The word "symposium" means "drinking together."

[11] Johnson, p. 55-56.

[12] Phillips, p. 81.

[13] Phillips, p. 105.

[14] Johnson, p. 12.

[15] Phillips, p. 149.

[16] Phillips, p. 194-195.

[17] Phillips, p. 225.

[18] Phillips, p. 231.

[19] Phillips, p. 105

[20] Johnson, p. 12.

[21] Johnson, p. 208.

[22] Phillips, p. 132.

[23] Lorenz 2007: 97. On December 7, 1826 Beethoven's nephew Karl entered a note about "one Mass [quarter] of the white Austrian [wine] that would also be for the servants."

[24] Pezzl, p. 55.

[25] Joseph Karl Mayr, *Wien im Zeitalter Napoleons, Staatsfinanzen, Lebensverhältnisse, Beamte und Militär,* Wien 1940, p. 134. The consumption is given in kegs (700000 and 600000) and converted to liters: 174 and 148, respectively (one liter is about 1.1 quarts). Davies (p 97) quotes statistics given by Pezzl for the end of the eighteenth century (494000 and 400000 respectively for 270000 people), resulting in about 100 liter wine and 80 liter beer. Mayr records a continuous increase of consumption: 500000 kegs of wine in 1802 and 600000 in 1808, and a decrease of population to 230000.

[26] D. Boulet et J.-P. Laporte, "Les comportements de consommation de vin en France", *INRA, Sciences Sociales,* No 3, Juin 1997. Over a quarter (27.8%) of French adult population are "comsommateurs réguliers"; the vast majority of them (over 75%) are men over 45, and represent more than 40% of the French adult male population. These statistics were recorded after several decades of steady decrease of wine consumption in France.

[27] Theyer-Forbes, 943-4.

[28] Wegeler_Ries, p. 151.

[29] Davies 2002, p. 101. He quotes the German version of Thayer's biography (Alexander Wheelock Thayer, *Ludwig van Beethovens Leben,* continued by Hermann Deiters, completed by Hugo Riemann, Hildesheim, 1970-72, Vol. 4, p. 581). In Thayer-Forbes (p. 842), we can only find that Spohrchil proposed an opera libretto to Beethoven, who never used it.

[30] Andreas Ignaz Wawruch, "Medical Review on the Final Stage of L. van Beethoven's Life," translated by Michael Lorenz, *The Beethoven Journal,* 22/2 (Winter 2007): 87-91, p. 88. This article was published after the death of its author in 1842.

[31] Wegeler-Ries, p.151. Titus Livius (59BC-AD17) was one of the foremost historians of Roman antiquity.

[32] Davies 2002, p. 98. He quotes from Bankl and Jesserer, *Die Krankenheiten Ludwig van Beethovens* (Vienna: W. Maudrich, 1987), p. 79.

[33] Lorenz 2007, p. 92. All references to his article are given in the text as (L page) in this sub-chapter. I have abridged and reduced to its essence the author's long laudatory paragraph.

[34] All references to Wawruch's account are given in the text (W page) in this subchapter.

[35] Quoting from Brandenburg, vol. 6, 394.

[36] Breuning, p. 93.

[37] Maynard Solomon, in Breuning (1992), "Editor's introduction" p. 6 and 8, respectively.

[38] Schindler 1996, p. 457.

[39] Marek, p. 312. In 1831, Bertolini, afraid of dying during a cholera epidemics, had his Beethoven file burned; he survived.

[40] Pezzl, p. 56 and 165, respectively.

[41] Anderson 92.
[42] Thayer-Forbes, p. 300.
[43] Wawruch, p. 88. The original reads: "Nie gewohnt, an einen ärtzlichen Rath zu denken,fing er an, geistige Getränke zu lieben, um die abnehmende Esslust zu wecken, *und* der Schwäche der Wagens durch starken Punsch und Gefrorenes im Übermass genossen, durch lange ermüdende Excursionen zu Fusse einigermassen aufzuhelfen" (my emphasis). The sentence is long and somewhat confusing because of the typical German syntax with the verb at the end. Lorenz rightly decided to split this long sentence to make it more palatable, but chose the wrong splitting point – not at the italicized conjunction *und* (and, which juxtaposes two sentences of the same level) but immediately after the first verb group, resulting in: "[...] he began to enjoy alcoholic beverages. In order to stimulate his declining appetite and remedy the weakness of his stomach – that had been caused by the consumption of strong punch and too much ice cream – he began taking long and strenuous walks" (W 88). This allowed him to intimate that the strong punch and ice cream had decreased Beethoven's appetite, while it was intended to stimulate it.
[44] Anderson 258, p. 273.
[45] Thayer-Forbes, p. 62.
[46] Thayer-Forbes, p. 776-77. Literature records no major illness in 1820; Brandenburg re-assigned to 1823 the letter to Joseph Lind mentioning "the sensitive condition of my abdomen," dated by Anderson (1041) to March 1820 and quoted by Mai (table 3.1, page 105).
[47] Anderson 1054, p. 920.
[48] Schindler 1840, p. 180 and 182, respectively.
[49] Quoting from Brandenburg, vol. 6, 394.
[50] Testimonies of Johann Baptist Junger, who visited the composer in December and January and of Ferdinand Hiller, who visited him with Moscheles on March 13, 1827 (Thayer-Forbes, p. 1025 and 1046).
[51] Cf. March letter to Pasqualatti (Anderson 1569).
[52] Russell Martin, *Beethoven's Hair* (New York, Broadway, 2001), p. 202. Did his physicians recommend them, but Beethoven turned them down? There is no trace of such a debate in the existing evidence.
[53] Davies 2002 includes more such episodes, but Mai's way of presenting his data in tables rather than in narratives has a stronger psychological impact on the reader.
[54] Wegeler-Ries, p. 151.
[55] Anderson 92.
[56] Mai quotes the German edition version of Thayer's biography, *Beethovens Leben* (vol. 3, p. 33).
[57] Anderson 296, vol. 1, p. 313.
[58] *Konversationshefte*, p. 355.
[59] Theyer-Forbes, 943-4. Karl Holz joined the circle of Beethoven friends in the spring of 1825 and aroused Schindler's jealousy, because he won Beethoven's trust and "usurped" the function of private un-paid secretary that Schidler had held.

⁶⁰ Prod'homme, p. 346.
⁶¹ Thayer-Forbes, p. 958.
⁶² Thayer-Forbes, p. 965.
⁶³ Prod'homme, p. 234.
⁶⁴ Thayer-Forbes, p. 494.
⁶⁵ Thayer-Forbes, p. 618. His old friend Amenda sent him a libretto titled *Bacchus*.
⁶⁶ *Beethoven – Letters, Journals and Conversations*, Translated and edited by Michael Hamburger, (Anchor Books, Doubleday & Co Inc., Garden City, New York, 1960), p. 161.
⁶⁷ Thayer-Forbes, p. 943.
⁶⁸ Johnson, p. 189.
⁶⁹ American Psychiatric Association: *Diagnostic and Statistical Manual of Mental Disorders*, pp. 181-183. A new version (DSM-V) is in effect now, but since we are discussing Davies and Mai's *circa* 2000 diagnosis in this book, we will follow it to the letter of the DSM-IV. DSM-V collapses the two forms of the alcohol-related disorders (dependence and abuse) in one – alcohol use disorder – but keeps the current criteria. Therefore, it would not change substantially Mai's perspective on the issue; he would claim that Beethoven had an alcohol use disorder.
⁷⁰ National Institute of Health, Press Release, December 5, 2007.
⁷¹ Thayer-Forbes, p. 94-95.
⁷² Thayer-Forbes, p. 777-8. An episode in 1821 or 1822, related to Thayer by a certain Professor Höfel in 1860.
⁷³ S. B. Mahapatra, "Deafness And Mental Health: Psychiatric And Psychosomatic Illness In The Deaf," *Acta Psychiatrica Scandinava*, Vol. 50, No. 6, 1974; Margaret Robertson, "Consequences Of Deafness For Late Deafened Adults," *Deafness Forum of Australia, National Deafness Sector Summit* 15-16 May, 2004.
⁷⁴ Gerhard von Breuning, *Memories of Beethoven – From the House of the Black-Robed Spaniards*, translated by Henry Mins and Maynard Solomon, (Cambridge University Press, 1992), p. 43-44.
⁷⁵ Thayer-Forbes, p. 963.
⁷⁶ Thayer-Forbes, p. 943.
⁷⁷ Schindler 1996, p. 304.
⁷⁸ Thayer-Forbes, p. 943.
⁷⁹ Theyer-Forbes, p. 304.
⁸⁰ Beethoven's height is also a bit of a mystery. He described himself in one of his letters as "the smallest [kleinste] of all persons" in a note to Amalia Sebald (Anderson. 382); Schindler's indication that he was 5 feet 5 inches tall (5 feet 4 inches, Vienna Measure, according to *The Life of Beethoven*, edited by Ignace Moscheles [the English version of Schindler's first edition of the biography of the composer], Henry Colburn Publishers, 1841, Vol. 2, p. 191) fits Breuning's description of "medium height" (Breuning, p. 19). This was the male average height in the eighteenth century Habsburg Empire (John Komlos, **Nutrition and economic development in the eighteenth-century Habsburg monarchy: an anthropometric history**, Princeton University Press,

1989), but it was computed from measurements of the military conscripts, mostly peasants whose food was primarily vegetarian; the male Viennese, who consumed plenty of meat (cf. statistics in Pezzl, p. 68) was certainly taller. Beethoven must have indeed appeared rather short to the world he lived in.

[81] Thayer-Forbes, p. 962.

[82] The old popular wisdom has been scientifically proved: a delay in alcohol absorption is noted when alcohol is ingested along with most foods, especially fatty or heavy, solid, proteinaceous meals, which are known to retard the gastric emptying rate. (Stephen Holt, "Observations on the relation between alcohol absorption and the rate of gastric emptying," *Can. Med. Ass. Journal*, February 1 1981, vol. 124 (3, 267-277): 270.

[83] Edward Tremble, "The deafness of Beethoven," *Can. Med. Ass. Journal*, 1932, 27, 456-9.

[84] Edward Larkin, "Beethoven's illness – a likely diagnosis," *Proc R Soc Med*, 1971 May 64(5), 493:496 (systemic Lupus erythematosus); Palferman T.G., "Classical notes: Beethoven's medical history," *J R Soc Med*, 1990; 83; 640-645 (sarcoidosis); Om P. Sharma, "Beethoven's illness: Whipple's disease rather than sarcoidosis?" *J R Soc Med*, 1994, 87; 283-285.

[85] Davies, p. 186. Syphilis had been advanced a long time ago, but it was deemed very unlikely recently (Davies, p. 121-131). The analysis of Beethoven's hair revealed no trace of mercury (Martin, p. 226-7), which was the standard (completely inefficient and highly toxic) treatment of the illness at the time; it is hard to believe that Beethoven, who consulted so many physicians, would not have been diagnosed with the disease and not treated if they had thought that he had it. A misdiagnose cannot be excluded, however.

[86] Martin 2001, p. 234.

[87] Phillips, p. 49-50; Johnson, p. 156.

[88] Phillips, p. 194.

[89] Schindler 1996, p. 387.

[90] Philip A. Mackowiak, *Post-Mortem. Solving History's Great Medical Mysteries*, (American College of Physicians, 2007), p. 217.

[91] Edmund Morris, *Beethoven: The Universal Composer,* (Harper Collins Publishers, New York, 2005), p. 225.

[92] Schindler 1996, p. 387. Lorenz claims that this was a Schindler fabrication intended to hide Beethoven's love of wine (p. 95).

[93] Pezzl, p. 56.

[94] *Leaves from the Journal of Sir George Smart*, published by H. Bertram and C. L. Fox, Longmans (Green & Co., London, 1907).

Chapter 6

[1] Thayer-Forbes, p. 232.

[2] Thayer-Forbes, p. 738.

[3] Schindler 1996, p. 386.

[4] Thayer-Forbes, p. 1007.

[5] Thayer-Forbes, p. 967.

[6] Wegeler-Ries, p. 34-35 and 83-84, respectively.
[7] Peter J. Davies, *The Character of a Genius. Beethoven in Perspective* (Greenwood Press, 2002).
[8] Davies/2, p. 135, quoting American Psychiatric Association, *Diagnostic and Statistical Manual of Mental Disorders*, 3rd edition, 1987, pp. 337-339.
[9] Davies/2. The whole volume is dedicated to Beethoven's medical condition.
[10] The terms paranoia and paranoid disorder were introduced much later (1893) by the German physician and founder of psychiatry Emil Kraepelin in his book *Lehrbuch der Psychiatrie* (Manual of Psychiatry).
[11] Anderson 669 and 650. The recommendation letters constituted a servant's "file" at the time and followed him from one employer to the other.
[12] Thayer-Forbes, p. 648.
[13] Anderson 53 (vol. 1, p. 65).
[14] Thayer-Forbes, p. 259. The testimony of Beethoven's friend Dolezalek.
[15] Anderson 88.
[16] Marc Vignal, *Beethoven et Vienne* (Fayard, 2004), p. 81-82. Vignal endeavored an in-depth survey of Beethoven's musical career in Vienna.
[17] Vignal, p. 87.
[18] Vignal, p. 90. Davies could have have found at least a hint about this story in Thayer-Forbes, which quotes (p. 300) a letter written by Beethoven's brother Carl to Breitkopf and Härtel publishers, complaining about Braun's attitude.
[19] Wegeler-Ries, p. 74.
[20] Thayer-Forbes, p. 259. Account of Beethoven's friend Dolezalek (1780-1848).
[21] Thayer-Forbes, p. 272-273.
[22] One can read it in *Grove*'s Kraus' entry (vol. 10, p. 242). German by birth, Kraus chose to live in Sweden, where he was hailed as "The Swedish Mozart."
[23] Vignal, p. 28-29.
[24] Breuning, pp. 98-99.
[25] Thayer-Forbes, p. 403.
[26] Letter to Breitkopf & Hartel (Anderson 108, vol. 1, p. 129).
[27] Wegeler-Ries, pp. 89-90.
[28] Cf. Beethoven's 1795 letter to Eleonore von Breuning, in Wegeler-Ries, p. 54.
[29] Anderson 110 (vol. 1, p. 130): "there was nothing which he [Lichnosky] desired more than the formation of such an association between you and me..."
[30] Anderson 125, vol. 1, p. 142.
[31] He may have done so later. According to some testomonies, he would have send Lichnowsky a note saying, "Prince, what you are you are by accident of birth; what I am I am through myself. There have been and will still be thousands of princes; there is only one Beethoven." (Thayer-Forbes, p. 403 note 10).
[32] Anderson 895.
[33] From 4000 to 3400 florins, as Davies acknowledges (page 149).
[34] Thayer-Forbes, p. 318. Among other things, in 1804 Carl sent the publisher André two early piano sonatas (now known as No. 19 and 20, Opus 49) that

Beethoven deemed not good enough to be included among his Opus numbered pieces.
[35] Breuning, p. 53.
[36] Thayer-Forbes, p. 1014.
[37] Anderson 1315.
[38] Thayer-Forbes, p. 1007, quoting Johann's entry in an 1824 conversation book.
[39] Thayer-Forbes, p. 999.
[40] Schindler 1996, p. 315.
[41] Wawruch, p. 89.
[42] Wegeler-Ries, p 57.
[43] Nohl, p. 171-172.
[44] Thayer-Forbes, p. 625. Davies calls it an autopsy, but it seems to have been something lest than that.
[45] Anderson 1397, vol. 3, p. 1217.
[46] Anderson 1404 (vol. 3, p. 1224). Beethoven's own emphasis.
[47] Sterba, p. 80-81.
[48] Davies/1, p. 269. We only skipped the irrelevant names.
[49] Wegeler-Ries, p. 83.
[50] Desk Reference to the Diagnostic Criteria from DSM-IV-TR, 2000, p. 289.
[51] Anderson 1.
[52] Thayer-Forbes, p. 315. Since she was born in 1780 (Thayer-Forbes, p. 63), her memories must pertain to Beethoven's last years in Bonn.
[53] Thayer-Forbes, p. 104-105.
[54] Wegeler-Ries, p. 15-16.
[55] Wegeler-Ries, p. 39.
[56] Wegeler-Ries, p. 34-35. Wegeler quotes from a Beethoven letter: "I come to you and throw myself into your arms, asking for my lost friend back." Ries also acknowlwdges that "Beethoven was extremely good natured, but he was also easily irritated or quick to be suspicious" (Wegeler-Ries, p. 83).
[57] S. B. Mahapatra, "Deafness and Mental Health: Psychiatric And Psychosomatic Illness In The Deaf," *Acta Psychiatrica Scandinava*, Vol. 50, No. 6, 1974; Margaret Robertson, "Consequences Of Deafness For Late Deafened Adults," *Deafness Forum of Australia, National Deafness Sector Summit* 15-16 May, 2004.)
[58] He also quoutes (page 169) the opinion of musicologist Joseph Kerman that Beethoven's "paranoid tendencies really passed the bounds that can be ascribed, conventionally, to deafness." Kerman's statement is just an opinion, not supported by a serious argument. In fact, this is not a novel results of medical research; as early
[59] Thayer-Forbes, p. 370.
[60] Thayer-Forbes, p. 280.
[61] Wegeler-Ries, p. 149.
[62] Frank Benson, Alfredo Ardilla, *Aphasia: A Clinical Perspective* (Oxford University Press, 1996), p. 335. See also Zimbardo, P. G., Andersen, S. M., &

Kabat, L. G. (1981). Induced hearing deficit generates experimental paranoia. Science, 212 (1981), pp. 1529 – 1531.

[63] Solomon 1998, p. 201. Barry Cooper shares the opinion in his biography (*Beethoven*, p. 178).

[64] Hallam R., Ashton P., Sherbourne K., Gailey L., "Acquired profound hearing loss: Mental health and other characteristics of a large sample", *International Journal of Audiology* 2006 vol. 45 (pp. 715-723).

[65] Anderson, 651.

[66] Anderson 94, p. 114.

[67] Wegeler-Ries, p. 106.

[68] Wegeler-Ries, p. 96.

[69] Anderson 68.

[70] Baronetcy was just a little bit higher than the status of the commoner ("freiherr" in Herman). There were many, perhaps thousands of barons in the Hapsburg Empire.

[71] Anderson 34. Note 5 explains: Beethoven begins, "Dear little Natzerl of my heart" and Natzerl is a diminutive of Ignatz, hence the possibility that the two notes have been for Ignatz von Gleichenstein.

[72] Mai first utters cautious terms like *may* and *likely,* but then reaches the unequivocal affirmation.

[73] Schindler 1996, pp. 101, 104.

[74] Survey of this author. See also Pierre-Jean Chenevez, "Les tonalités dans les œuvres de Beethoven," (*Beethoven, la revue de l'ABF*, No. 9, 2008, pp. 72-78), p. 73. His survey shows slightly different results; it seems to miss some important works; for example, E minor (Op. 59 No. 2 and Op. 90) shows only one case in his table (p. 73).

[75] DSM-IV guide, p. 168 and 169.

[76] Wegeler-Ries, p. 39.

[77] Thayer-Forbes p. 496.

[78] The correlation between them is negative (Thorson J. A., Powell F. C., "Depression and sense of humor," *Psychological Reports*. 1994 Dec; vol. 75(3, Part 2): 1473-4).

[79] Thayer-Forbes, p. 304.

[80] Wegeler-Ries, pp. 16 and 34.

[81] DSM-IV guide, p. 296-297.

[82] Hans J. Eysenck and Sybil B. Eyesenck, *Psychoticism as a Dimension of Personality* (Crane, Russak & Co., 1976), p. 1-2.

Chapter 7

[1] Harry Goldschmidt, *Die Erscheinung Beethoven* (VEB Deutsche Verlag für Musik, Leipzig, 1974). The topic is presented in the first essay „Beethoven and Progress" (pp. 11-25).

[2] https://de.wikipedia.org/wiki/Harry_Goldschmidt.

[3] Richard Taruskin, *Music in the Early Twentieth Century* (Oxford University Press, 2010), p. 777.

⁴ Nicolas Slonimsky, *Lexicon of Musical Invective. Critical Assaults on Composers since Beethoven's Time*, 2nd edition (University of Washington Press, 1990), p. 3.

⁵ *The Bach Reader. A Life of Johann Sebastian Bach in Letters and Documents*, revised edition, Hans T. David and Arthur Mendel eds. (W W Norton & co., New York, 1966), p. 238. Letter quoted by Johann Adolph Scheibe (1708-1776), a musician, and a prominent critic and theorist of his times,

⁶ Wikipedia quotes an opinion that "Sibelius was the first great composer since Beethoven whose mind thinks naturally in terms of symphonic form."

⁷ Amy B Graziano, Julene K Johnson, "Music, neurology, and psychology in the nineteenth century," (Chapter 2 in Journal *Progress in Brain Research, 216*, 2015 pp. 33-47), p. 45. Online at https://escholarship.org/content/qt47x082v7/qt47x082v7.pdf. The Wallaschek reference at p. 45. This essay is a good introduction to the topic of music and science.

⁸ Cross, H. A., Halcomb, C. G., & Matter, W. W. (1967). "Imprinting or exposure learning in rats given early auditory stimulation," *Psychonomic Science, 7*(7), p. 233-234.

⁹ Rauscher, F.H., Robinson, K.D., & Jens, J. "Improved maze learning through early music exposure in rats," *Neurological Research*, 20 (1998), 427- 432. The team convincingly defended their results when other scholars criticized the experiment, because rats have a very different hearing range from humans so they perceived only one third of the frequencies involved. Unfortunately, no similar experiment has been, to my knowledge, carried out with "Schönberg rats."

¹⁰ Daniel J. Levitin, *This is Your Brain on Music. The Science of a Human Obsession* (A Plume Book, 2006).
Oliver Sacks, *Musicophilia. Tales of Music and the Brain* (Vintage Books, New York, 2008).

¹¹ Levitin, p. 72. He touches expectation in some thirty pages spread all over his book.

¹² Levitin, p. 114. Here he also pays special attention to the role of expectation with children's listening to music.

¹³ Wikipedia article on Jonah Lehrer.

¹⁴ Jonah Lehrer, *Proust was a Neuroscientist* (A Mariner Book. Houghton Miffin Company, 2008). Chapter 6 is dedicated to the musical topic here discussed.

¹⁵ Lehrer, p. 125. I reversed the order of the two statements to make the point clearer.

¹⁶ Lehrer, p. 130, 132 and 133, respectively. His elaboration, "when we listen to music, we are moved by an abstraction," because "we feel, but we don't know why" (p. 134) does not add poise to his thesis.

¹⁷ Lehrer, p. 135, 138 and 139, respectively.

¹⁸ Lehrer, p. 140.

¹⁹ Korey Keating, "Miscellanea," in *The Beethoven Journal*, Winter 2009, Vol. 25, No. 2, p.99.

20 Lawrence Kramer, *Why Classical Music Still Matters* (University of California Press, 2007), pp. 55ff.
21 Kramer, p. 69.
22 Igor Stravinsky *Poetics of Music, in the Form of Six Lessons*, transl. by Arthur Knodel and Ingolf Dahl (Harvard University Press, 2003), p. 39. This 2003 edition is the 16th print of 1942 copyright. He compared Beethoven with Bellini: "Beethoven bequeathed to the world riches partly attributable to the recalcitrance of the [his] melodic gift. […] Bellini inherited melody without having seen even so much as asked for it, as if Heaven had said to him, "I shall give you the one thing Beethoven lacks." Stravinsky wrote this book during his so-called "neo-classical period," and acknowledged therein that, after having been a staunch member of the Avant-Garde, "I am beginning to think, in full agreement with the general public, that melody must keep its place at the summit of the hierarchy of elements that make up music" (p. 40). Nevertheless, he converted back to the Avant-Garde later, succumbing to Schoenberg's serial ism.
23 Richard Wagner, *Beethoven*, transl. by Albert R. Parsons, (Boston: Lee & Shepard, 1872), p. 99. Quote: "melody has now regained the natural simplicity."
24 Jacques Chailley, *40,000 years of Music* (Farrar, Straus & Giroux, New York, 1964), p. 133. He quotes experiments presented in Robert Francès 1958 book, *La perception de la musique* (pp. 140-144).
25 Richard Taruskin, *Music in the Early Twentieth Century* (Oxford University Press, 2010), p. 195.
26 Solomon 1988, p. 272 (# 79). Solomon's book includes the only English translation of Beethoven's *Tagebuch* (diary).

Chapter 8

[1] Tia DeNora, *Beethoven and the Construction of Genius, Musical Politics in Vienna*, 1792-1803, (University of California Press, Berkeley, Los Angeles, London, 1985).
[2] Michael Broyles, at https://currentmusicology.columbia.edu/article/review-of-tia-denora-1995-beethoven.
[3] Charles Rosen, "Did Beethoven Have All the Luck?", The New York Review of Books, Vol. 43, Issue 18, 14 November 1996.
[4] Mary Sue Morrow, "Book Review: Tia DeNora, Beethoven and the Construction of Genius: Musical Politics in Vienna, 1792-1803" (*The Beethoven Journal*, Fall 1996, Volume 11, Number 2), pp.25-27.
[5] "Beethoven's Genius: An Exchange (DeNora-Rosen), in The New York Review of Books, April 10, 1997, pp. 66-67.
[6] "Beethoven's Genius: An Exchange," p. 66.
[7] Thayer-Forbes, p. 155.
[8] Marcel Brion, *La vie cotidienne à Vienne au temps de Mozart et de Schubert*, [Everyday's Life in Vienna During the Times of Mozart and Schubert] (Hachette, 1959), p 87 ff (my translation).

[9] Julian Rushton, in *The Mozart Compendium*, edited by H. C. Robbins Landon (Borders Press, 1990), p. 91.
[10] Wegeler-Ries, p. 80.
[11] Thayer-Forbes, p. 171.
[12] Thayer-Forbes, p. 206.
[13] Thayer-Forbes, p. 120.
[14] Thayer-Forbes, p. 119. The Cantata was never sung until 1884 and was first published in 1888 as WoO 87.
[15] Thayer-Forbes, p. 115.
[16] Broyles, p. 140.
[17] Wegeler-Ries, p. 74.
[18] Thayer-Forbes, p. 259. Account of Beethoven's friend Dolezalek (1780-1848). DeNora quotes this evidence in a different context, when writing about the negative criticism of Beethoven (159). She fails to realize the inconsistency with her statement at page 110-111.
[19] One can read it in *New Grove*'s Kraus' entry (vol. 10, p. 242). German by birth, Kraus chose to live in Sweden, where he was hailed as "The Swedish Mozart." He was "rediscovered" recently, as part of the post-modernist campaign for the rehabilitation of the "little guy."
[20] Thayer-Forbes, p. 272-273.
[21] Thayer-Krehbiel vol. 2, p 69.
[22] Thayer-Forbes, p. 242.
[23] Thayer-Forbes, p. 207.
[24] Wegeler-Ries, p. 87.
[25] Thayer-Forbes, p. 337. The non plus ultra description was used by Wilibrord Joseph Mähler, who lived until 1860 and talked with Thayer (p. 185).
[26] Thayer-Forbes, pp. 61 and 82. He had lessons in 1779-80 with Franz Rovantini, a distant relative of the family; and later with Franz Ries, the father of his later pupil and friend Ferdinand Ries. The pieces were his 1785 three Piano Quartets WoO 36 (published posthumously) and his Variations for Piano and Violin on Mozart's "Se vuol ballare" air (WoO 40), published in 1793.
[27] Thayer-Forbes, p. 264.
[28] Richard Taruskin, *Music in the Nineteenth Century* (The Oxford History of Western Music, Oxford University Press, 2010), p. 65.
[29] Taruskin, p. 65.
[30] Thayer-Forbes, p. 694.
[31] Simon McVeigh, *Concert Life in London from Haydn to Mozart* (Cambridge University Press, 1993), p 53.
[32] McVeigh, p. 69.
[33] Thayer-Forbes, p. 155.
[34] Malcolm Boyd, *Bach*, (Wintage Books, New York, 1987), p. 218.
[35] Matthew Dirst, *Engaging Bach. The keyboard legacy from Marburg to Mendelssohn* (Cambridge University Press, 2012), p. 90.
[36] Anton Schindler, *Biographie von Ludwig van Beethoven*, (Münster, Aschendorf, 1840), p. 112 (my translation).
[37] Schindler 1860, p. 210-11, confirmed at p. 408.

Chapter 9

[1] "Miscellanea", in *The Beethoven Journal,* Fall 1996, Vol. 11, Number 2, p.46.

[2] "Miscellanea", in *The Beethoven Journal,* Spring 1997, Vol. 12, No. 1, p. 51.

[3] Nimbus 5175 CD, featuring several pieces by eighteenth and nineteenth century French composers, including also Berlioz's *Grande symphonie funèbre et triomphale.*

[4] Robert Haven Schauffler, *Beethoven, the Man who Freed Music*, (Doubleday, Doran & Co. Inc, Garden City, New York, 1937), pp. 219-220. He indicates Haydn's Sonata No. 3, according to an older catalogue. Hoboken records it as XVI 49.

[5] Reproduced after Arnold Schmitz, *Das Romantische Beethovenbild, Darstelleung und Kritik*, (Berlin und Bonn, 1927), p. 167.

[6] Bonnie J. Blackburn, *Masses on Popular Songs and Syllables*, (in *The Josquin Companion*, Richard Sherr, editor, Oxford University Press, 1999), p. 53-54 and note 9.

[7] John Winemiller, "Recontextualizing Handel's Borrowing," (*The Journal of Musicology*, Vol. 15, No. 4, 1997, pp. 444-470). Available online at http://www.jstor.org/stable/764003.

[8] Nicolas Slonimsky, *Webster's New World Dictionary of Music*, (Wiley Publishing Inc., 1998), p. 385.

[9] Winemiller, p. 448.

[10] *Musique de fêtes et cérémonies de la révolution française: oeuvres de Gossec, Cherubini, Lesueur, Mehul, Catel, etc*, [Music for Feasts and Ceremonies of the French Revolution], recueillies et transcrites par Constant Pierre (Paris, Imprimerie Nationale, 1899), p. 278. Available online in piano transcription at https://www.partitions-anciennes.com/en/12517-lefevre-xavier-hymne-a-l-agriculture-chant-piano-1796.html.

[11] Gustav Nottebohm, Zweite Beethoviana (Leipzig: C. F. Peters, 1887). p. 531.

[12] George Grove, Beethoven and his Nine Symphonies (Novello and Co., 1896), p. 60.

[13] A play with songs, a very popular genre in the German-speaking countries during the eighteenth century, whose best "high" implementation is Mozart's later opera *The Abduction from the Serail. Bastien* was later considered by musicologists the seed from which both the German opera, as well as its lighter counterpart, the "operetta," were born (Alfred Einstein, *Mozart – His Character, His Work*, translated by Arthur Mendel and Nathan Broder, (Oxford University Press, New York, 1979), p. 449). By an ironic twist, this "seed" from which the German opera opera grew was a remake of the French opera buffa *Le Devin du village* [The village fortune teller] by Jean-Jacques Rousseau.

[14] *The Mozart Compendium,* H.C. Robbins Landon editor, (Borders Press, 1990), p.242.

[15] Michael Kennedy and Joyce Bourne, "Bastien und Bastienne." (The Concise Oxford Dictionary of Music. 1996). Available online at *Encyclopedia.com.* 23 Sep. 2013 http://www.encyclopedia.com>.

[16] Thayer-Forbes, pp. 80, 97-98.
[17] Romain Rolland, *Beethoven the Ceator. From Eroica to Appassionata*, translated by Ernest Newman (Dover Publications, New York, 1964), Note 125, p. 318.
[18] Nägel quoted after Rolland 1964, Note 174, p. 334-335.
[19] *The New Grove Dictionary of Music and Musicians,* Macmillan Publishers 1980, (London, Washington, D.C, Vol. 12), p. 727.
[20] *The Mozart Compendium,* p. 186.
[21] Sacks, p. 207-208.
[22] Lewis et al, p. 138ff.

Chapter 10

[1] Susan McClary, "Getting Down Off the Beanstalk," (*Minnesota Composers Forum Newsletter,* January 1987), p. 5. McClary's statement was actually an *avant-la-lettre* "me too" proclamation. In 1973, Adrienne Rich, an American poet and radical feminist, had issued an almost similar accusation in her poem "The Ninth Symphony of Beethoven Understood at Last as a Sexual Message" (in her volume *Diving into the Wreck* (W. W. Norton, 1973), p. 205-6). The symphony would be the work of "a man in terror of impotence / or infertility, not knowing the difference / a man trying to tell something / howling from the climacteric / music of the entirely / isolated soul / yelling at Joy from the tunnel of the ego." The poem continues, "music without the ghost / of another person in it, music / trying to tell something the man / does not want out, would keep if he could / gagged and bound and flogged with chords of Joy / where everything is silence and the / beating of a bloody hand upon / a splintered table." Rich's charge seems to have been ignored at the time and re-emerged only in hindsight of McClary's new diatribe, and only in the music's scholarly world, which had to cope with a startling new situation – a Beethoven detractor towards the end of the Twentieth Century.
[2] Susan McClary, *Feminine Endings*: *Music, Gender, and Sexuality* (University of Minnesota Press, Minneapolis, 1991).
[3] Elisabeth Sayrs, "Deconstructing McClary: Narrative, Feminine Sexuality, and Feminism in Susan McClary's *Feminine Endings,*" (*College Music Symposium 33/34* (1993/1994): 41-55), p. 42.
[4] Meg Sullivan and Reed Hutchinson, "Susan McClary, Musicologist," (*UCLA Spotlight*, May 1, 2002)
[5] John Powell, *How Music Works*, (Little, Brown & Co, New York, 2010), p. 95; also Levitin, p. 71. A sound 10 decibels higher than another sound is twice as loud.
[6] Garret Keiser, *The Unwanted Sound of Everything We Want: A Book About Noise,* (Books Group, 2010), note p. 29. The author gives no loudness for a classical music concert in his list of everyday noises (at page 275), but the loudest rock concerts shows at 135 db.
[7] H. Strasser, H. Irle and R. Scholz, "Physiological Cost of the Hearing after Exposures to White Noise, Industrial Noise, Heavy Metal, and Classical Music

338

of 94db (A) for 1 hour," (in *Traditional Rating of Noise Versus Physiological Costs of Sound ...*, Volume 66, edited by Helmut Strasser, IOS Press, Amsterdam, 2005 (pp 128-137)). The physiological cost was measured by the "temporary threshold shift" (TTS), which measures how quick the hearing is restored to normal level after being exposed to sound; the lower the TTS, the quicker the recovery. Quote from the paper's abstract (p. 128): "Classical music was associated with the least severe TTS, which disappeared much more quickly [than with noise or heavy metal]."

[8] Susan McClary, "Construction of Subjectivity in Schubert's Music," (in *Queering the Pitch/The New Gay and Lesbian Musicology*, Routledge Press, 1994, pp. 205-233).

[9] William Meredith, "The Eroica and Beethoven's Sexuality through a Feminist Lens: Susan McClary's Reading of Beethoven in *Queering the Pitch*," (*The Beethoven Newsletter*, Volume 8, No 3 & Volume 9 No 1 (Winter 1993-Spring 1994), pp. 107-109).

[10] Angus Heriot, *The Castrati in Opera*, (Da Capo Books, London, 1956), p. 31 ff.

[11] Magnuss T. Schneider, *Seeing the Empress Again: On Doubling in L'Incoronazione di Poppea*, (in *Cambridge Opera Journal*, Vol. 24, No. 3 (November 2012), pp. 249-291), pp. 259ff.

[12] Jane Bowers, "Women Composers of Italy, 1566-1700," (in *Women Making Music: The Western Art Tradition, 1150-1950*, Jane Bowers and Judith Tick editors, Urbana: University of Illinois Press, 1986), p. 140.

[13] Andrea della Corte, Guido M. Gatti, *Dizionario di musica*, (G. B. Paravia, Padua, 1956).

[14] *Norton/Grove Dictionary of Women Composers*, J. A. Sadie and R. Samuel, eds., (New York, London: W. W. Norton & Company, 1995), pp. 74 and 136.

[15] Reinier de Graff (1641-1673), quoted in Matthew Cobb, *The Egg & Sperm Race. The Seventeenth-Century Scientists Who Unraveled the Secrets of Sex, Life and Growth* (Pocket Books, 2006), p. 117.

[16] Francesco Ludovico Maschietto, Jan Vairo, William Crochetiere, Catherine Marshall, *Elena Lucrezia Cornaro Piscopia (1646-1684): the first woman in the world to earn a university degree*, (Saint Joseph's University Press, Boston, 2007), p.79.

[17] Maschietto et al, 2007, p. 252.

[18] Daniel Murphy, *Comenius: A Critical Re-assessment of His Life and Work*, (Irish Academic Press, 1995), p. 90ff.

[19] Sarah Gwyneth Ross, *The Birth of Feminism: Woman as Intellect in Renaissance Italy and England*, (Harvard Univ. Press, 2009), p 1.

[20] Thayer-Forbes, p. 407.

[21] Thayer-Forbes, p. 526. The musician Reichardt, who witnessed the Baroness playing wrote, "As she performed a great Beethoven sonata I was surprised as almost never before. I have never seen such power and innermost tenderness combined even in the greatest virtuosi." (Thayer-Forbes, p. 412)

[22] Anderson 815.

[23] I owe this quote to Alessandra Comini (*The Changing Image of Beethoven: A Study in Mythmaking*, (Rizzoli International Publications, Inc., 1987), p. 114-115); I only added a few more elisions to shorten it.

[24] Thayer-Forbes, p. 1057.

[25] Teresa De Lauretis, an Italian-born turned-American author and professor at several U.S. universities, is a feminist scholar particularly dedicated to the art of film but with a broader area of interests, including semiotics, psychoanalysis, literary theory and lesbian and queer studies. Her book, *Alice Doesn't – Feminism Semiotics* (Indian University Press, 1984) is further referred here in the text as *AD* page.

[26] Jurij Lotman, "The Origin of Plot in the light of Typology," translated by Julian Graffy, (in *Poetics Today* 1.1-2 (1979), pp. 161-184). Also http://www.zbi.ee/~kalevi/LotmanPlot.htm.

[27] The enumeration is morphologically inconsistent, using both definite and indefinite and zero articles. This inconsistency is the translator's attempt to make the text more palatable in English. The Russian language has no articles and the original said, literally, "пещера", "могила", "дом", "женщина" (cave, grave, house, woman); both an *a* and a *the* can be applied to all the enumeration items. The original (*Stat'i po tipologii kul'tury*, 2, Tartu, 1973, pp. 9-41) by courtesy of Prof. Julian Graffy, who translated it for the 1979 article; the quoted line appears at page 20.

[28] De Lauretis, *Freud's Drive: Psychoanalysis, Literature, and Film*, (Palgrave Macmillan, U. K., 2008).

[29] Jurij Lotman, *Culture and Explosion*, edited by Marina Grishakova, translated by Wilma Clark, (Mouton de Gruyer, 2010), p. 165.

[30] McClary 1987, p. 3-4.

[31] Michel Foucault, *History of Sexuality, Vol. 1, An Introduction*, translated from French by Robert Hurley (New York, Vintage Books, 1980), p. 12. Available online at http://suplaney.files.wordpress.com/2010/09/foucault-the-history-of-sexuality-volume-1.pdf.

[32] Foucault never mentions singing, because he deals only with language communication. "Sing" is McClary's own contribution to the "demonstration."

[33] Foucault, p. 17. He goes on elaborating: "Calling sex by its name thereafter became more difficult and more costly. As if in order to gain mastery over it in reality, it had first been necessary to subjugate it at the level of language, control its free circulation in speech, expunge it from the things that were said, and extinguish the words that rendered it too visibly present. And even these prohibitions, it seems, were afraid to name it. Without even having to produce the word, modern prudishness was able to ensure that one did not speak of sex, merely through the interplay of prohibitions that referred back to one another: instances of muteness which, by dint of saying nothing, imposed silence. Censorship." One recognizes the pleasure of the philosopher to utter a hundred words when one would have sufficed.

[34] Foucault, p. 17-18.

[35] Foucault, p. 24.

[36] Foucault, p. 27.
[37] Claude Quétel, *History of Syphilis*, translated by Judith Braddock and Brian Pike (The Johns Hopkins University Press, Baltimore, 1990), p. 73.
[38] McClary also decries the purely musical flaws of the dominant male side of tonality: it is "deceptively simplistic, sadistic, inductive of an artificial need (the tonic), a banal cliché, an agent of death" (*FE* 125-129) – but I promised not to venture upon this side of the issue.
[39] This view of the Russian mystic philosopher is best expressed in his 1924 book *The End of Our Time* [aka *The New Middle Ages*].
[40] Available online at http://www.janikavandervelde.com/catalog.html.
[41] John Hale, The Civilization of Europe under Renaissance (Touchstone, 1995), p. 94
[42] Vivien Burr, *Gender and Social Psychology* (Routledge, London, 1998), p. 46-47.
[43] Winfield S. Hall, *A Text-Book of Physiology, Normal and Pathological*, 2nd ed., (Les Brothers and Co., Philadelphia and New York, 1905), pp. 695 ff.
[44] Levitin, pp 184, 226-227, 263.
[45] Susan McClary, *Conventional Wisdom: The Content of Musical Forms* (University of California Press, Berkley-Los Angeles-London, 2001). Further referred in the text as *CW* with page number.
[46] Richard Taruskin, *Music from the Earliest Notation to the Sixteenth Century*, The Oxford History of Western Music, (Oxford University Press, 2010), p. 252.
[47] Richard Wagner, *On Music & Drama*, translated by H. Ashton Ellis, edited by Albert Goldman & Evert Sprinchorn, (University of Nebraska Press, Lincoln & London, 1964), p 154. He defines folk as "the epitome of all those men *who feel a common and collective want.*" (Wagner's italics, p. 85).
[48] McClary refers only to the French and Italian dances (Courante, Minuet, Gavotte, Bourrée, Loure), because they are the ones most represented in Bach's suites. However, we can also safely include those originating in other European countries (Spain, Germany or the British Islands) or even in Colonial Spain (the *Saraland*). All the dance names were formalized in French, the lingua franca of the eighteenth century; the Italian *Corrente* became *Courante*, the British *Jig – Gigue*, etc.; the *Allemande* was a Renaissance dance so named because a favorite of the German courts.
[49] Granted, some of these European dances (such as the *La Volta*) were deemed "obscene" and were even banned at the time, but the obscenity consisted in the man's touching the woman's body in a manner that was athletic rather than sexual, basically to lift her, in what would later become a standard ballet figure.
[50] Such decorum was not the result of a Christian imposition. In the Balkans – Greece, Bulgaria, Romania, territories of former Yugoslavia – where one can track the roots of the folk music back to the pre-Christian times, the traditional dances observe the same etiquette; in all these countries, the most common group (circle) dance stems from the ancient Greek dance of the chorus (χορός)

in the tragedies and has names derived from it (*horo* in Bulgaria, *oro* in Macedonia, *hora* in Romania, etc.).

[51] "[...] under the conditions that would have existed throughout most of our evolutionary history in which music and dance were completely intertwined, musicianship/danceship would have been a sign of sexual fitness [...] anyone who could sing and dance was advertising to potential mates his stamina and overall good health, physical and mental." (Levitin, p. 252).

[52] An example of such dramatic contradictions: in February 1785, the captured leaders of a revolt of the peasant serfs in Transylvania (at the time a province of the Habsburg Empire) were executed on the St. Catherine wheel (Hugh Seton Watson, *Eastern Europe between the Wars: 1918-1941*, (Harper Torchbooks, New York, 1967), p. 59). The same month, Mozart was composing his D minor *Piano Concerto*.

[53] There are so many questions that apparently defy such explanations. Why, for example, has the eighteenth century produced two outstanding music styles, the high Baroque and the Classical Age, but much less valuable visual arts and architecture?

[54] It is strange that McClary consistently avoids passing an explicitly negative judgment on twentieth-century music in *Feminine Ending* and *Conventional Wisdom*. She had dared to do that in a 1989 article deploring the avant-garde's "withdrawal from the public" in order to be free to write "difficult music" that the audience would reject as unintelligible ("Terminal Prestige: The Case of Avant-Garde Music Composition," in *Cultural Critique* No. 12 (Spring 1989): 57-81). However, she toned her critique down later and even paid a vague tribute to "the accomplishments of the high serialists" (*CW* 137).

[55] Klaus Doerner, *Madmen and the Bourgeoisie: A Social History of Insanity and Psychiatry*, transl. by Joachim Neugroschel and Jean Steinberg, (Oxford: Basil Blackwell, 1981), p. 195.

[56] It is a summary of Doerner's attempt to clarify the development of psychiatry in Germany as a response to the facts (the existence of the "unreason," as he calls it) and the social perception of them within a "belated nation," that is one that developed a national self-awareness later (during the early nineteenth century) and had known no real Enlightenment age (the whole analysis is on pages 175-180 of his book).

[57] Doerner states this objective from the very beginning (page 1): "The reflection that the bourgeoisie established psychiatry specifically for the *poor* insane leads to the awareness that these thematic processes were one aspect of the class struggle."

[58] Doerner, p. 186.

[59] Arthur Schopenhauer, *The World as Will and Representation*, volume I, Judith Norman, Alistair Welchman, and Christopher Janaway (eds.), (Cambridge Univ. Press, 2011), p. 211.

[60] James and Maudsley's quotes from Rolland Littlewood: *Religion, Agency, Restitution: The Wilde Lectures in Natural Religion, 1999*, (Oxford University Press, New York, 2001), p. 12. John Dryden (1631-1700): "Great wits are

sure to madness near allied, and thin partitions do their bounds divide." (Absalom and Achitophel, 1681, part 1, line 163-4)

[61] Cesare Lombroso, *Man of Genius*, 2nd ed., (Scribner's Sons, New York, 1905), pp.333 and 359 respectively. Lombroso's book *L'uomo di genio in rapporto alla psichiatria* (1888) was published in English under this title.

[62] Richard Taruskin, *Music in the Nineteenth Century. The Oxford History of Western Music*, (Oxford University Press, New York, 2010), p. 422.

[63] Susan McClary, "Terminal Prestige: The Case of Avant-Garde Music Composition," in *Cultural Critique* No. 12 (Spring 1989): 57-81.

[64] Taruskin 2010, p. 685. The letter was privately circulated all around Germany for sign-ups, but was leaked to the press and published with only four signatures: Brahms (who held Wagner in high esteem, but not his disciples), Joseph Joachim, Julius Grimm and Bernhard Scholz.

[65] Charles Ives entry in *New Grove Dictionary of Music and Musicians*, Stanley Sadie, ed., Macmillan Publishers Ltd., London, 1980, Volume 9, pp. 415-417.

[66] Like other musicologists (for example Grout in his older history of music and Taruskin in his recent one), McClary avoids the use of the term "formalism," a term preferred by the now defunct Soviet musicology.

[67] Robin Wallace, "Beethoven's Critics," in *The Critical Reception of Beethoven's Compositions by His German Contemporaries,* Vol. 2 (W. M. Senner, R. Wallace and W. Meredith, editors), p. 9.

[68] Quoted in Taruskin 2010, p 293; the author endorses Pederson's conclusion.

[69] Eduard Hanslick, *The Beautiful in Music: A Contribution to the Revisal of Musical Aesthetics*, 7th ed., translated by Gustav Cohen (Novello et Co., ltd, London, 1891), p. 26.

[70] The original German term is stronger than "representing;" the title of the chapter 2 in Hanslick's book is "Emotions are not the Content [Inhalt] of Music."

[71] Taruskin 2010, p. XXI, 251.

[72] The interaction between the light and serious genres has never received the attention it deserves in the treatises of the history of classical music.

[73] Taruskin 2010, p. 292.

[74] J. Ma. Corredor, *Conversations with Casals*, translated by André Mangeot, (Dutton & Co, Inc., New York, 1958), pp. 62, 63.

[75] Carl Dahlhaus, *Nineteenth-Century Music*, translated by J. Bradford Robinson, (University of California Press, 1989), pp. 313-314.

[76] Engels' letter to W. Borgius, January 25, 1894, in *Marx Engels On Literature and Art*, (Progress Publishers, Moscow, 1976). Available online at http://www.marxists.org/archive/marx/works/subject/art/index.htm.

[77] Herbert Marcuse, *The Aesthetic Dimension. Toward a Critique of Marxist Aesthetics*, (Beacon Press, Boston, 1979), p. IX. He adds: "although this essay speaks of 'art' in general, my discussion is essentially focused on literature, primarily the literature of the eighteenth and nineteenth centuries. I do not feel qualified to talk about music and the visual arts, though I believe that what holds true for literature, mutatis mutandis, may also apply to these arts."

[78] McClary is essentially interested in music, but she touches other arts en passant; for instance, she describes Ancient Greece architecture as defined by "phallic" columns (*FE* 130).

[79] There is yet no official figure of the number of the victims of the *Cultural Revolution*. Roderick MacFarquahr and Michael Schoenhals (*Mao's Last Revolution*, (Harvard University Press, 2006)) give a count between 750,000 and 1.5 million dead in rural China alone (p. 262). Jung Chang and Jon Halliday (*Mao: The unknown Story*, (Jonathan Cape, London, 2005)) advance a figure of 3 million (p. 569); Daniel Chirot (*Modern Tyrants: The Power and Prevalence of Evil in Our Age*, (Princeton University Press, 1996)) has a wide estimate between 1 and 20 millions (p. 198).

[80] Sheila Melvin and Jindong Cai, *Rhapsody in Red. How Western Classical Music Became Chinese* (Algora Publishing, New York, 2004), p. 278.

Chapter 11

[1] Lawrence Kramer, *After the Lovedeath: Sexual violence and the Making of Culture* (University of California Press, 1997).

[2] At pages 216, 238 (note 32) and 241.

[3] Carole Pateman, *The Sexual Contract* (Stanford University Press, 1988), p. 2.

[4] *Neue Zeitschrift für Musik* , Vol. 5, Juni 5, 1818, pp. 177-179. Online at http://www.anno.onb. ac.at/
cgi-
content/anno?aid=nzm&datum=18380605&query=%22beethoven%22&ref=anno-search.

[5] Robert Schumann, *On Music and Musicians*, transl. by Paul Rosenfeld (University of California Press, Berkeley and Los Angeles, 1946), p. 117. This is a selection from the 1854 German collection book *Robert Schumann, Gesammelte Schriften über Musik und Musiker* (Complete Writings on Music and Musicians), which had been already published in English translation by Fanny Raymond Ritter in 1877.

[6] Thayer-Forbes, p. 536. In German "Zusammergefasst."

[7] Schumann, p. 121. Translation again deficient: the original (in *Neue Zeitschrift für Musik* , Vol. 4, No 52, 26 December 1836 issue, p. 208) reads, "leidend," (suffering, not passive) for the B Flat major Trio.

[8] Schumann, p. 115.

[9] Camille Paglia, *Sex, Art, and American Culture* (Vintage Books, New York, 1992), p. 27-28, 49-74.

[10] Tolstoy, Leo, *The Kreutzer Sonata and Other Stories* (Oxford University Press, 1998), p. 125.

[11] Tolstoy, p. 119.

[12] Tolstoy, p. 119 and 129 respectively.

[13] Tolstoy, p. 144 and 145, respectively. The 1996 edition of the work, replaces the word "terrible" of the old translation of Louise and Aylmer Maude with "terrifying." The change is discussed in the text (see page 195).

[14] Pozdnyshev holds a long tirade about female seductiveness (Tolstoy, pp. 100-103).

[15] Tolstoy, p. 131.
[16] Tolstoy, p. 118.
[17] Pateman, p. 2. Kramer, too, claims in passing that "social order is geared to serve male genital interests in women" (p. 186).
[18] Tolstoy, p. 114.
[19] Tolstoy, p. 163.
[20] Tolstoy, p. 131.
[21] Lawrence Kramer, C*ritical musicology and the responsibility of response: selected essays* (Ashgate, 2006). He reprinted it as chapter 19 (pp. 429-450) of his book "Song Acts: Writing on Words and Music," in *Words and Music Studies*, Vol. 16 (Brill/Rodopi, 2017).
[22] Tolstoy, p. 125 and 131, respectively.
[23] Tolstoy, p. 107-108.
[24] Tolstoy, p. 131.
[25] Tolstoy, p. 119.
[26] Tolstoy, p. 129.
[27] Tolstoy, p. 139.
[28] Tolstoy, p. 144-45.
[29] Tolstoy, p. 144-146. I discuss later the terms "terrible," which in this edition is substituted by "terrifying."
[30] Tolstoy, p. 147.
[31] All references from Tolstoy, p. 144-146.
[32] Tolstoy, p. XXXI (Notes on the text).
[33] Tolstoy, p. 137.
[34] Hugh McLean, *In Search of Tolstoy* (Boston, 2008), p. 211.
[35] Leo Tolstoy, *What is Art*, transl. From the original ms. by Aylmer Maude (New York, Funk and Wagnalls, 1904). The English translation was published before the Russian original, which was delayed by the censure.
[36] Tolstoy 1904, p. 122.
[37] McLean, p. 159.
[38] Tolstoy 1904, p. 172.
[39] Tolstoy 1904, p. 169.
[40] Tolstoy 1904, p. 170 and 172, respectively.
[41] Tolstoy 1904, p. 173-174.
[42] Thayer-Forbes, p. 340-341.

Chapter 12

[1] Sanna Pederson, "Beethoven and Masculinity," in *Beethoven and his World*, Scott Burnham and Michael P. Steinberg, editors (Princeton University Press, 2000), pp. 313-331. In 2001, Pederson presented some of her theses at the 2001 *International Congress of* Musicology in Berlin, in a paper titled "Beethoven and masculinity in the context of the 1848 Revolutions." It was published in *Der "männliche" und der "weibliche" Beethoven. Bericht über den Internationalen musikwissenschaftlichen Kongress vom 31. Oktober bis 4. November 2001 an der Universität der Künste Berlin*, Cornelia Bartsch,

Beatrix Borchard, Rainer Cadenbach Hg. [*The "Masculine" and "Feminine" Beethoven. Proceedings of the 2001, at the Berlin Art University*, Cornelia Bartsch, Beatrix Borchard, Rainer Cadenbach, eds.] (Verlag Beethoven-Haus., Bonn, 2003), pp. 21-31.

[2] Rolland, p. 3.

[3] Ross, p. 276 and passim.

[4] A survey of the topic can be found in Matthew Head, *Sovereign Feminine: Music and Gender in Eighteenth-Century Germany* (University of California Press, 2013).

[5] Wegeler-Ries, p. 42.

[6] Tellenbach 2014, p. 71, quoting a (draft) letter of Josephine to Beethoven.

[7] Marek, p. 58. Thayer mentions Schneider only about his role in promoting Beethoven's "Cantata on the death of Emperor Joseph II," whose libretto is infused with Enlightenment ideas (Thayer-Forbes, p. 119).

[8] In a letter to his friend Zmeskal (Anderson 30).

[9] Leopold Schmidt, ed., *Beethoven-Briefe* (Hamburg Severus Verlag, 2014), p. 11. The text reads, "Kraft is die Moral der Menschen, die sich von anderen auchzeichnen, und sie is auch die meine [...]"

[10] Wagner, *Beethoven*, p. 63.

[11] Sanna Pederson, "A. B. Marx, Berlin Concert Life and German National Identity," (in 19th-Century Music, 18 (1994): 87-107), p. 96.

[12] Anderson 296. Note 1 identifies the replay in Schiller's *Jungfrau von Orleans* (The Maid of Orleans), Act. 5, Scene 2.

[13] Thayer-Forbes, p. 619.

[14] Anderson 563. Her translation of the original German is slightly different from the one given by Pedersen.

Chapter 13

[1] Tia DeNora, "Music into action: performing gender on the Viennese concert stage, 1790-1810," (*Poetics 30 (2002)*, pp. 19-33),

[2] DeNora 1985, p. 126-127.

[3] Richard Taruskin, *Music in the Seventeenth and Eighteenth Centuries* (Oxford University Press, 2010), p 643.

[4] Rolland, p. 261.

[5] Thayer-Forbes, p. 407.

[6] Thayer-Forbes, p. 526.

[7] Anderson 815.

[8] *The Norton/Grove Dictionary of Women Composers*, J. A. Sadie and R. Samuel, ed. (W W Norton & Co., 1995), p. 27.

[9] Schindler 1996, p. 415.

[10] Thayer-Forbes, p. 368.

[11] Schindler 1996, p. 413.

[12] Thayer-Forbes, p. 412.

[13] Katherine Ellis, "Female pianists and their male critics in nineteenth-century Paris," (*Journal of the American Musicological Society* 50 (1997), pp. 353-385).
[14] Ellis, p. 362 and 363 respectively.
[15] Ellis, p. 362.
[16] Ellis, p. 355, 359, 359 and 360 respectively.
[17] Norton/Grove, p. 450.
[18] Peter Oswald, *Schumann. The Inner Voices of a Musical Genius* (Northeastern University Press, Boston, 1985), p. 127 and 135 respectively.
[19] Mark Kroll, *Johann Nepomuk Hummel: A Musician's Life and World* (Scarecrow Press, 2007), p. 64.
[20] La Mara, *Letters of Franz Liszt*, translated by Constance Bache, Vol. 1, (C Scribner's Son, 1894), p. 266. 1856 letter to Dionys Bruckner.
[21] Anton Schindler, *Biographie von Ludwig van Beethoven*, Dritte, new verarbeite und vermehrte Auflage [third, revised and enriched edition] (Munster, 1860), p. 408 (my translation). Czerny's output outdoes even Bach's: over a thousand opuses.
[22] Schindler 1840, p. 112 (my translation).
[23] Schindler 1860, p. 210-11, confirmed at p. 408.
[24] Kraus, p. 28. My translation of the original: "Etwa eine klaviersonate Beethovens vorzutragen, wäre deplaziert gewesen."
[25] Ellis, p. 359.
[26] Ritterman & Weber, p. 186 and 188 respectively.
[27] Alan Walker, *Hans von Bülow: A Life and Times* (Oxford University Press, 2010), p. 258. The quote from note 23.
[28] Kraus, p. 28. Other sources indicate the year 1836. Beethoven's *Violin Concerto*, had also to be re-discovered by the great virtuoso Joseph Joachim in 1844 to become a main staple of the repertoire.
[29] Alan Walker, *Franz Liszt, Volume 1: The Virtuoso Years: 1811-1847*, revised edition (Cornell University Press, 1987), p. 85-86.

Chapter 14

[1] The list includes: the 1927 Austrian silent movie *Das Leben des Beethoven* [Beethoven's life]; *Un grand amour de Beethoven* [translated somewhat inaccurately as The Life and Loves of …], the first of the "Beethoven talkies," (1936-7) made by Abel Gance, one of the outstanding directors of the time; the Austrian *Eroica* (1949) – not to be confused with the 1958 Polish film (originally titled *Heroism*), which is not about Beethoven, or with the later 2003 movie with the same title; the 1962 Disney *Magnificent Rebel*, ; and the 1976 *Beethoven – Days in a Life*, produced by the studios in the now deceased East Germany and politicized according to the tenets of the communist ideology.
[2] www.rottentomatoes.com/m/1038726_beethoven
[3] www.rogerebert.com/reviews/immortal-beloved-1995.
[4] Edward Rothsteinjan, "Classical View: How Can a Movie So Right Be So Wrong?", The New York Times, Jan. 1, 1995. (Online at https://www.nytimes.com/1995/01/01/movies/

classical-view-how-can-a-movie-so-right-be-so-wrong.html). Rothsteinjan values the movie as cinematography ("so right") but rejects the story ("so wrong").

[5] See *The Beethoven Journal*, Vol. 10 no. 1, spring 1995, pp. 30-36 (letters to editor) and 37-42 (editor William Meredith's notes); see also *The Musical Quarterly,* Summer 97, Vol. 81, Issue 2, p. 190.

[6] Bruce Newman, *San Jose Mercury News*, November 8, 2006. The previous potpourri opinions from: Phillip French (*The Guardian*, August 19, 2007); Emanuel Levy (http://emanuellevy.com/review/copying-beethoven-6); Andrew Nunnelly (https://www.thecrimson.com/article/2006/11/8/movie-review-copying-beethoven); Bruce Feld (November 9, 2006, http://www.filmjournal.com/copying-beethoven).

[7] Thayer-Forbes, p. 909.

[8] Schindler 1996, p. 365.

[9] Brandenburg 1996, un-numbered letter, vol. 1, p 320. (Beethoven's emphasis)

[10] Solomon 1988, p. 279. Solomon's translation of the *Tagebuch,* item 104, dated 1816.

[11] Nohl, p. 166, quoting from Fanny Giannatasio's diary (1816 entry).

[12] Thayer-Forbes, p. 305.

[13] Thayer-Forbes, p. 504.

[14] Solomon 1998, p. 238. The author claims this statement as proof that Antonie was the Immortal Beloved, a theory I rebut in ny *Immortal Beloved Controversy* book (on this website).

[15] Thayer-Forbes, p. 497. Her friend was the great poet Goethe.

[16] Clara Rose Thornton, "Q&A: Agnieszka Holland, director of *Copying Beethoven,*" Friday, November 10, 2006," (http://www.stopsmilingonline.com/story_detail.php?id=695).

[17] Crnković, Gordana & Holland, Agnieszka. "Interview with Agnieszka Holland", Quarterly Review of Film and Video, Vol. 52, No 2 (Winter, 1998-1999)

[18] Richard Roeper, Nov. 13, 2006 (https://www.rottentomatoes.com/m/copying_beethoven).

Chapter 15

[1] *Der "männliche" und der "weibliche" Beethoven. Bericht über den Internationalen musikwissenschaftlichen Kongress vom 31. Oktober bis 4. November 2001 an der Universität der Künste Berlin*, Cornelia Bartsch, Beatrix Borchard, Rainer Cadenbach Hg. [*The "Masculine" and "Feminine" Beethoven. Proceedings of the 2001 International Congress of Musicology, at the Berlin Art University*, Cornelia Bartsch, Beatrix Borchard, Rainer Cadenbach, eds.] (Verlag Beethoven-Haus., Bonn, 2003).

[2] *Kunst, Geschlecht, Politik. Männlichtkeitskonstruktionen und Kunst im Kaiserreich und der Weimarer Republik*, Martina Kessel Hsg. (Campus Verlag Frankfurt, 2005).

³ Beatrix Borchard, "Beethoven: Männlichtkeitskonstruktionen im Bereich der Musik" (p. 65-84).

⁴ Peter Höyng, "Ambiguities of Violence in Beethoven's Ninth through the Eyes of Stanley Kubrick's *A Clockwork Orange*," (*The German Quarterly*, Volume 84/2, Spring 2011, pp. 159-176), p. 159.

⁵ The International Anthony Burgess Foundation website (https://www.anthonyburgess.org/ blog-posts/manchester-international-festival-symphony-c/)

⁶ Borchard, p. 82, note 57, my translation. The original reads: "In einer grossartigen Tonstück scheinen die Tonarten in ihrem Kampfe mit einander gleich sich entwickelnden Naturkräftem zum Licht empor zu dringen, endlich Gestalten anzunehmen und ihr Stück Weltgeschichte mit zu erleben. Doch ergötzt uns auch schon im Kleinem die humoristische Intrigue, die in der gewöhnlichsten Sonate von der Familie der Tonarten in immer wechselnder Scene aufgeführt wird. Da trit zum Eingange der Dreiklang der Tonics gleich dem Hausherrn in vollen Gefühl seiner Würde auf un beginnt ein Gespräch mit seine Hausfrau Dominante, und ermahnt den Sohn Subdominant und die beiden Medianten, seine holden Töchter, zu allem Guten."

Chapter 15½

¹ "Hellen Keller and Beethoven's Ninth," *The Beethoven Journal*, Vol. 28, No. 2, Winter 2013, p. 95.

² Russell Sherman, *Piano Pieces* (North Point Press, New York, 1997), p. 210.

³ Nohl, p. 165.

2020 Epilogue

¹ *Mozart Letters, Mozart's Life*, Selected letters edited and newly translated by Robert Spaethling (W. W. Norton & Co, New York, London, 2000), p. 160.

² Thayer-Forbes, p. 566.

³ Nohl, p. 143.

⁴ Thayer-Forbes, p. 909.

⁵ Berlioz' chronique in the Paris magazine *Le Rénovateur*, quotted in Adolphe Boschot, *Un propagateur de Beethoven, H. Berlioz*, (in "Revue Musicale," Paris, 1er April 1927).

Reflection Books, P.O. Box 1413
Citrus Heights, California 95611-1413
E-mail: info@reflectionbooks.com

www.reflectionbooks.com

www.ingramcontent.com/pod-product-compliance
Lightning Source LLC
Chambersburg PA
CBHW070823250426
43671CB00036B/1852